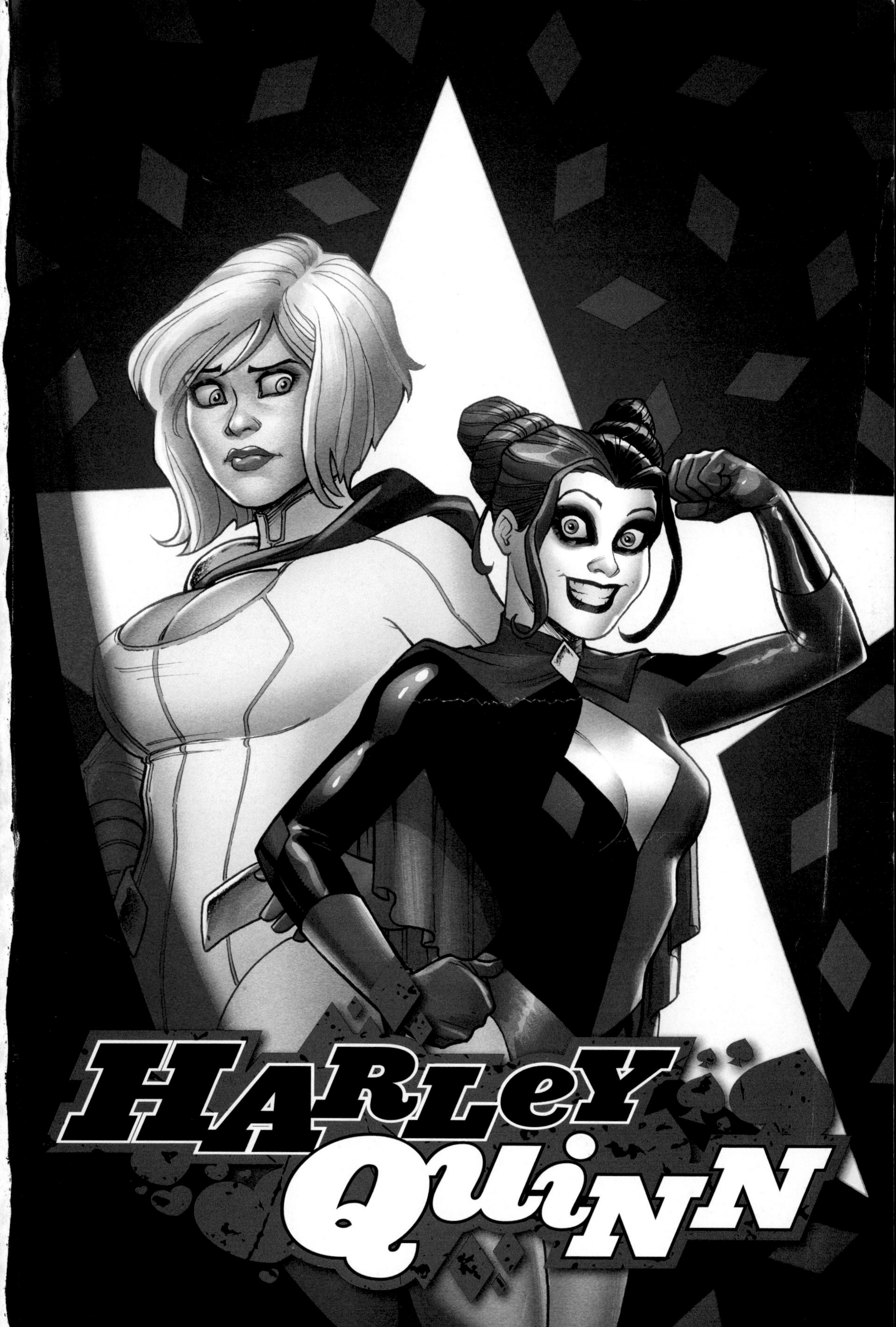
HARLEY QUINN

VOLUME 2 POWER OUTAGE

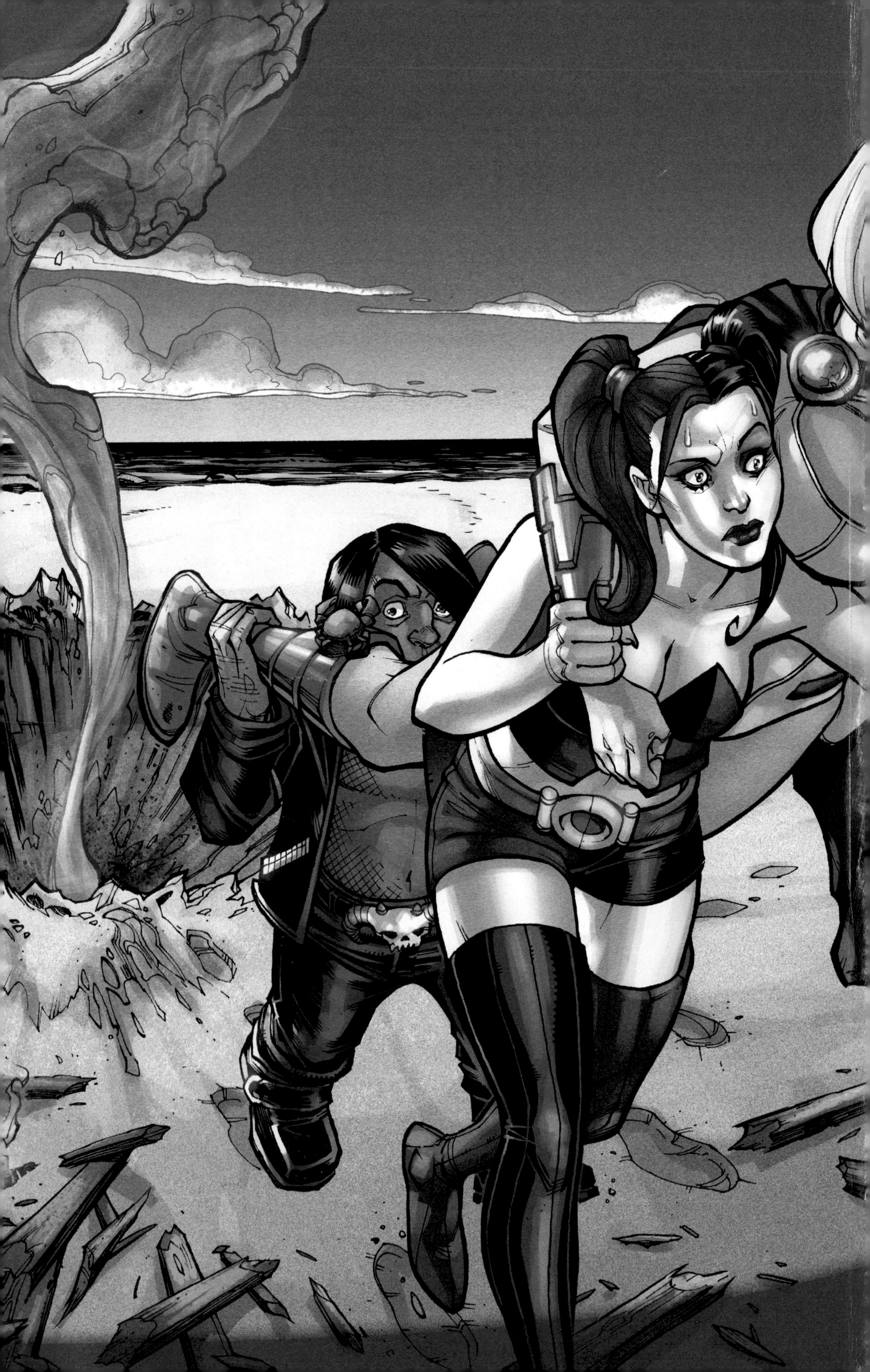

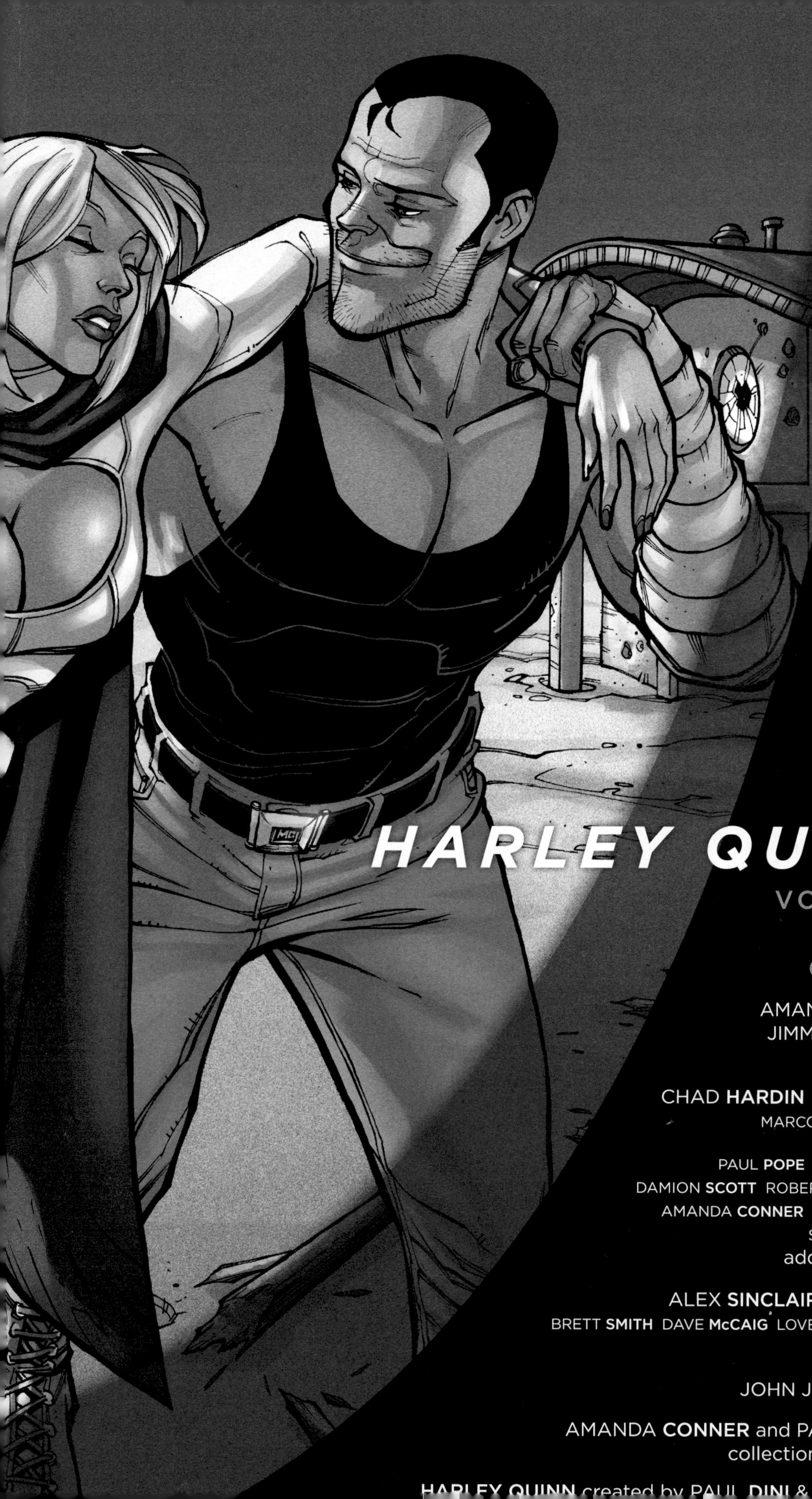

HARLEY QUINN

VOLUME 2
POWER OUTAGE

AMANDA **CONNER**
JIMMY **PALMIOTTI**
writers

CHAD **HARDIN** JOHN **TIMMS**
MARCO **FAILLA** artists

PAUL **POPE** JAVIER **GARRÓN**
DAMION **SCOTT** ROBERT **CAMPANELLA**
AMANDA **CONNER** DAVE **JOHNSON**
STÉPHANE **ROUX**
additional artists

ALEX **SINCLAIR** PAUL **MOUNTS**
BRETT **SMITH** DAVE **McCAIG** LOVERN **KINDZIERSK**
colorists

JOHN J. **HILL** letterer

AMANDA **CONNER** and PAUL **MOUNTS**
collection cover artists

HARLEY QUINN created by PAUL **DINI** & BRUCE **TIMM**

CHRIS CONROY KATIE KUBERT Editors – Original Series DAVE WIELGOSZ MATT HUMPHREYS Assistant Editors – Original Series
ROBIN WILDMAN Editor ROBBIN BROSTERMAN Design Director – Books ROBBIE BIEDERMAN Publication Design

BOB HARRAS Senior VP – Editor-in-Chief, DC Comics

DIANE NELSON President DAN DIDIO and JIM LEE Co-Publishers GEOFF JOHNS Chief Creative Officer
AMIT DESAI Senior VP – Marketing and Franchise Management
AMY GENKINS Senior VP – Business and Legal Affairs NAIRI GARDINER Senior VP – Finance
JEFF BOISON VP – Publishing Planning MARK CHIARELLO VP – Art Direction and Design
JOHN CUNNINGHAM VP – Marketing TERRI CUNNINGHAM VP – Editorial Administration
LARRY GANEM VP – Talent Relations and Services ALISON GILL Senior VP – Manufacturing and Operations
HANK KANALZ Senior VP – Vertigo and Integrated Publishing JAY KOGAN VP – Business and Legal Affairs, Publishing
JACK MAHAN VP – Business Affairs, Talent NICK NAPOLITANO VP – Manufacturing Administration SUE POHJA VP – Book Sales
FRED RUIZ VP – Manufacturing Operations COURTNEY SIMMONS Senior VP – Publicity BOB WAYNE Senior VP – Sales

HARLEY QUINN VOLUME 2: POWER OUTAGE

Published by DC Comics. Compilation Copyright © 2015 DC Comics. All Rights Reserved.

Originally published in single magazine form in HARLEY QUINN #9-13, HARLEY QUINN FUTURES END #1, HARLEY QUINN INVADES
COMIC-CON INTERNATIONAL SAN DIEGO #1 © 2014 DC Comics. All Rights Reserved. All characters, their distinctive likenesses and
related elements featured in this publication are trademarks of DC Comics. The stories, characters and incidents featured in this
publication are entirely fictional. DC Comics does not read or accept unsolicited ideas, stories or artwork.

DC Comics, 1700 Broadway, New York, NY 10019
A Warner Bros. Entertainment Company.
Printed by RR Donnelley, Salem, VA, USA. 3/06/15. First Printing.

ISBN: 978-1-4012-5478-0

Library of Congress Cataloging-in-Publication Data

Palmiotti, Jimmy, author.
Harley Quinn. Volume 2, Power outage / Jimmy Palmiotti, Amanda Conner.
pages cm. — (The New 52!)
ISBN 978-1-4012-5478-0 (hardback)
1. Graphic novels. I. Conner, Amanda, illustrator. II. Title. III. Title: Power Outage.

PN6728.H367P35 2014
741.5'973—dc23

2014034093

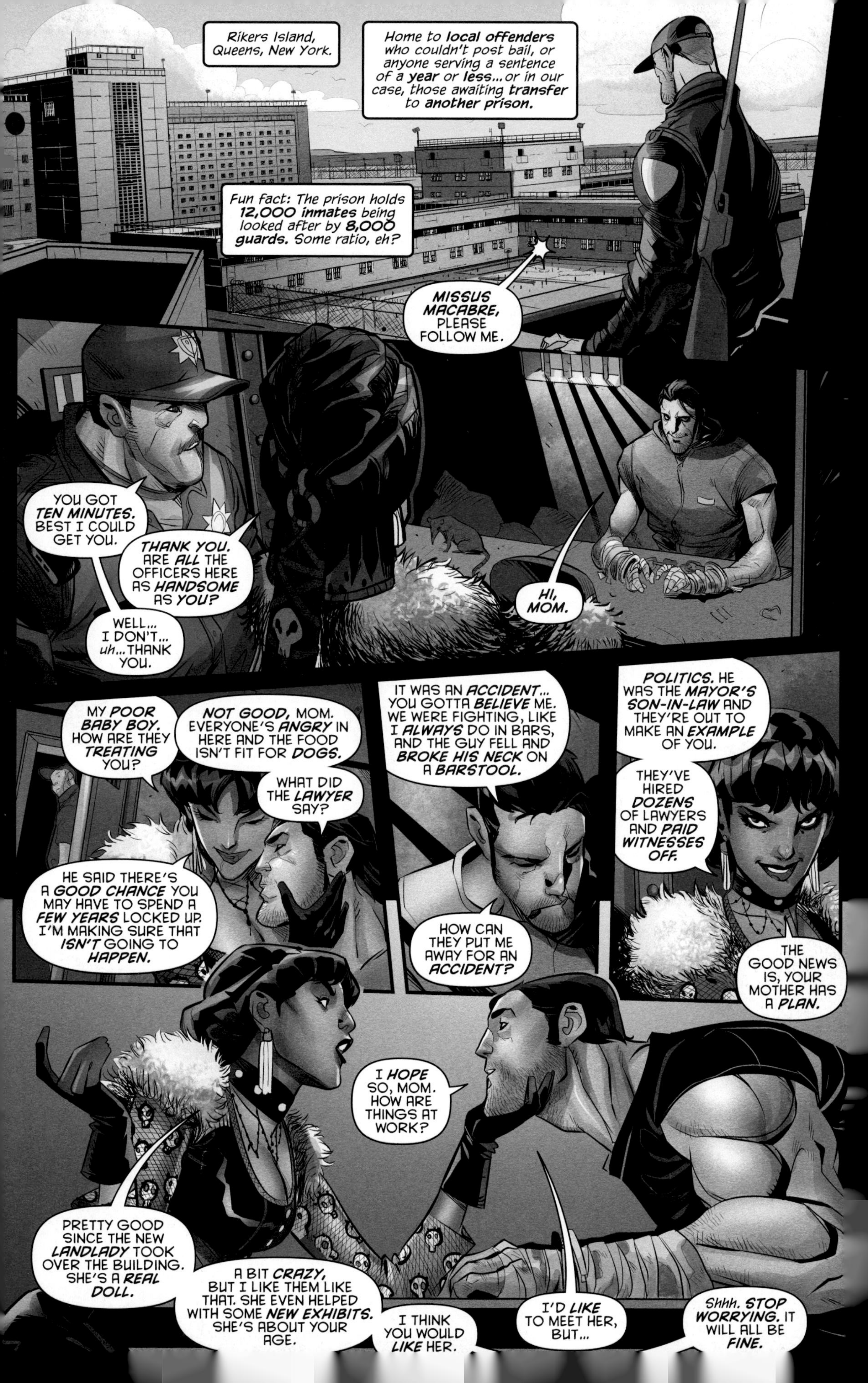
Rikers Island, Queens, New York.
Home to local offenders who couldn't post bail, or anyone serving a sentence of a year or less...or in our case, those awaiting transfer to another prison.
Fun fact: The prison holds 12,000 inmates being looked after by 8,000 guards. Some ratio, eh?
MISSUS MACABRE, PLEASE FOLLOW ME.
YOU GOT TEN MINUTES. BEST I COULD GET YOU.
THANK YOU. ARE ALL THE OFFICERS HERE AS HANDSOME AS YOU?
WELL... I DON'T... uh...THANK YOU.
HI, MOM.
MY POOR BABY BOY. HOW ARE THEY TREATING YOU?
NOT GOOD, MOM. EVERYONE'S ANGRY IN HERE AND THE FOOD ISN'T FIT FOR DOGS.
WHAT DID THE LAWYER SAY?
HE SAID THERE'S A GOOD CHANCE YOU MAY HAVE TO SPEND A FEW YEARS LOCKED UP. I'M MAKING SURE THAT ISN'T GOING TO HAPPEN.
IT WAS AN ACCIDENT... YOU GOTTA BELIEVE ME. WE WERE FIGHTING, LIKE I ALWAYS DO IN BARS, AND THE GUY FELL AND BROKE HIS NECK ON A BARSTOOL.
HOW CAN THEY PUT ME AWAY FOR AN ACCIDENT?
POLITICS. HE WAS THE MAYOR'S SON-IN-LAW AND THEY'RE OUT TO MAKE AN EXAMPLE OF YOU.
THEY'VE HIRED DOZENS OF LAWYERS AND PAID WITNESSES OFF.
THE GOOD NEWS IS, YOUR MOTHER HAS A PLAN.
I HOPE SO, MOM. HOW ARE THINGS AT WORK?
PRETTY GOOD SINCE THE NEW LANDLADY TOOK OVER THE BUILDING. SHE'S A REAL DOLL.
A BIT CRAZY, BUT I LIKE THEM LIKE THAT. SHE EVEN HELPED WITH SOME NEW EXHIBITS. SHE'S ABOUT YOUR AGE.
I THINK YOU WOULD LIKE HER.
I'D LIKE TO MEET HER, BUT...
Shhh. STOP WORRYING. IT WILL ALL BE FINE.

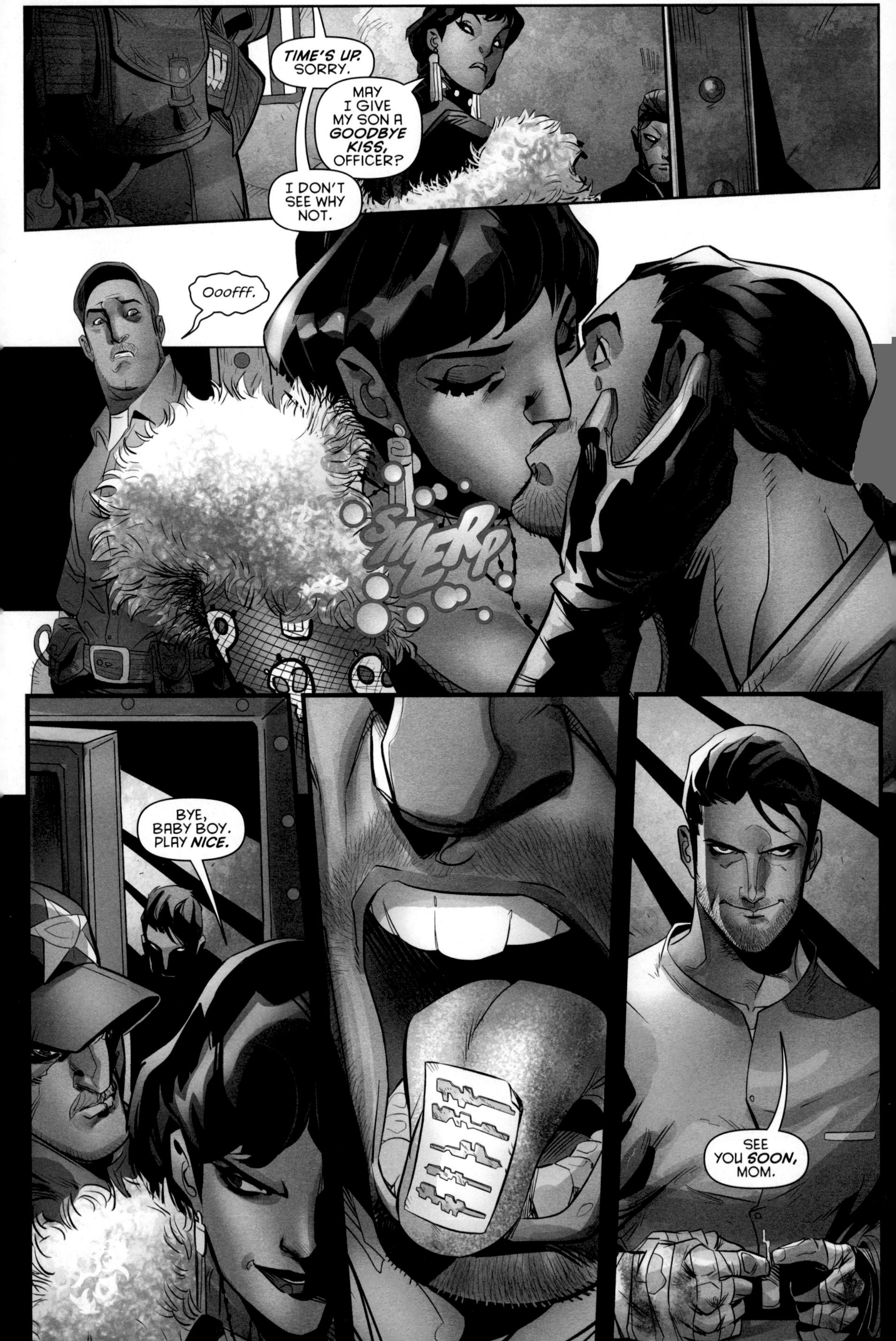

TIME'S UP. SORRY.
MAY I GIVE MY SON A GOODBYE KISS, OFFICER?
I DON'T SEE WHY NOT.
Ooofff.
SMERP
BYE, BABY BOY. PLAY NICE.
SEE YOU SOON, MOM.

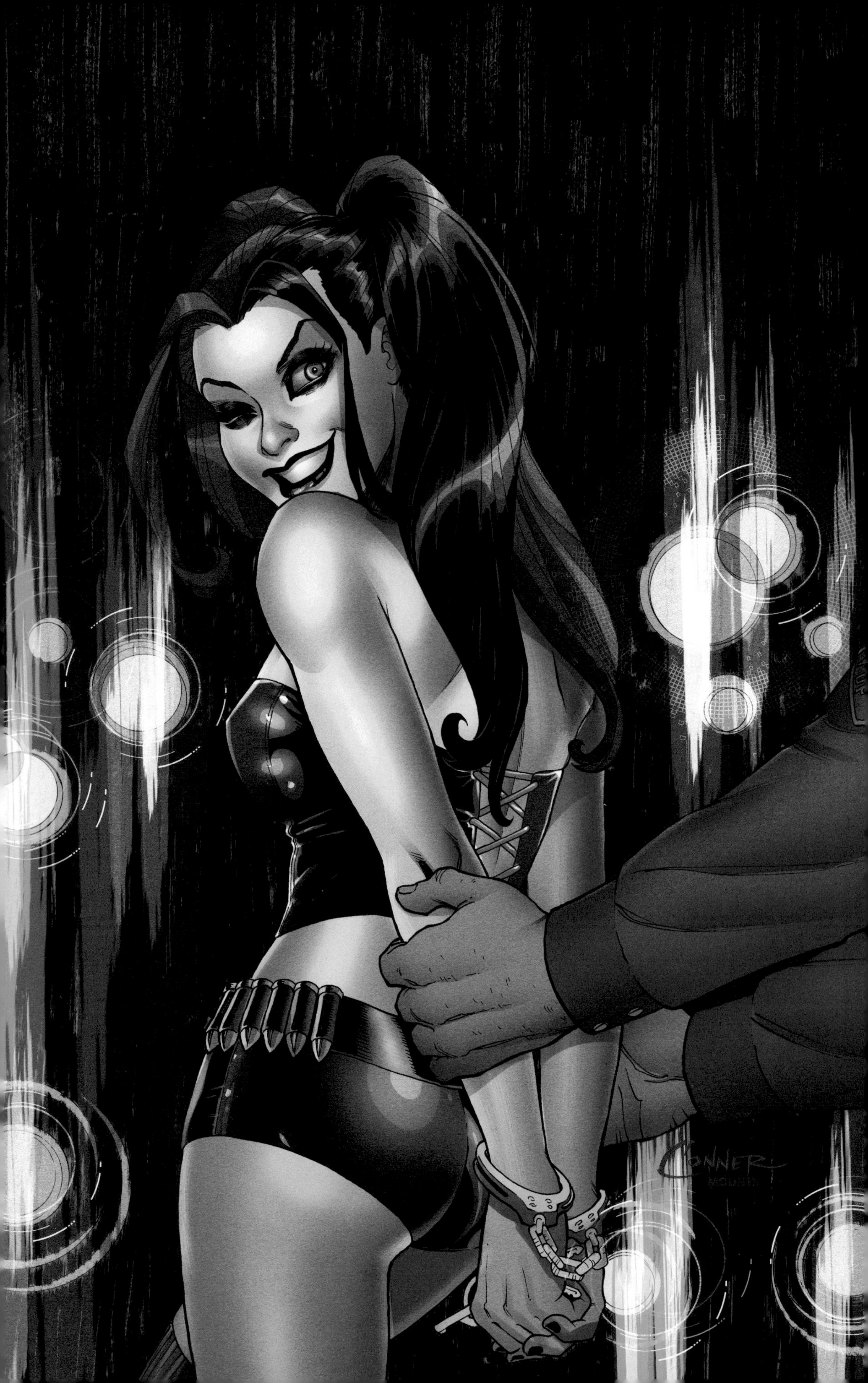
CONNER

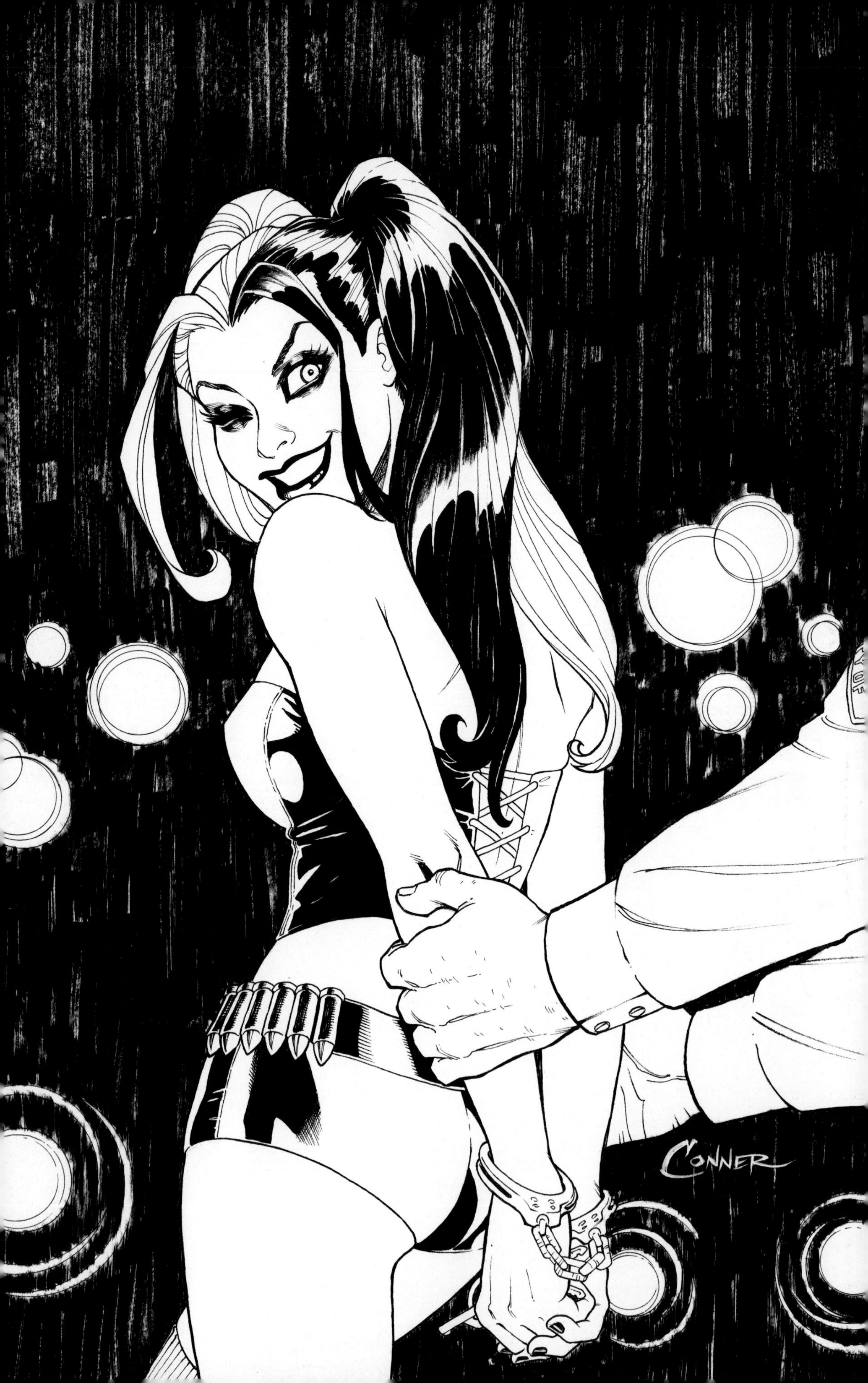
CONNER

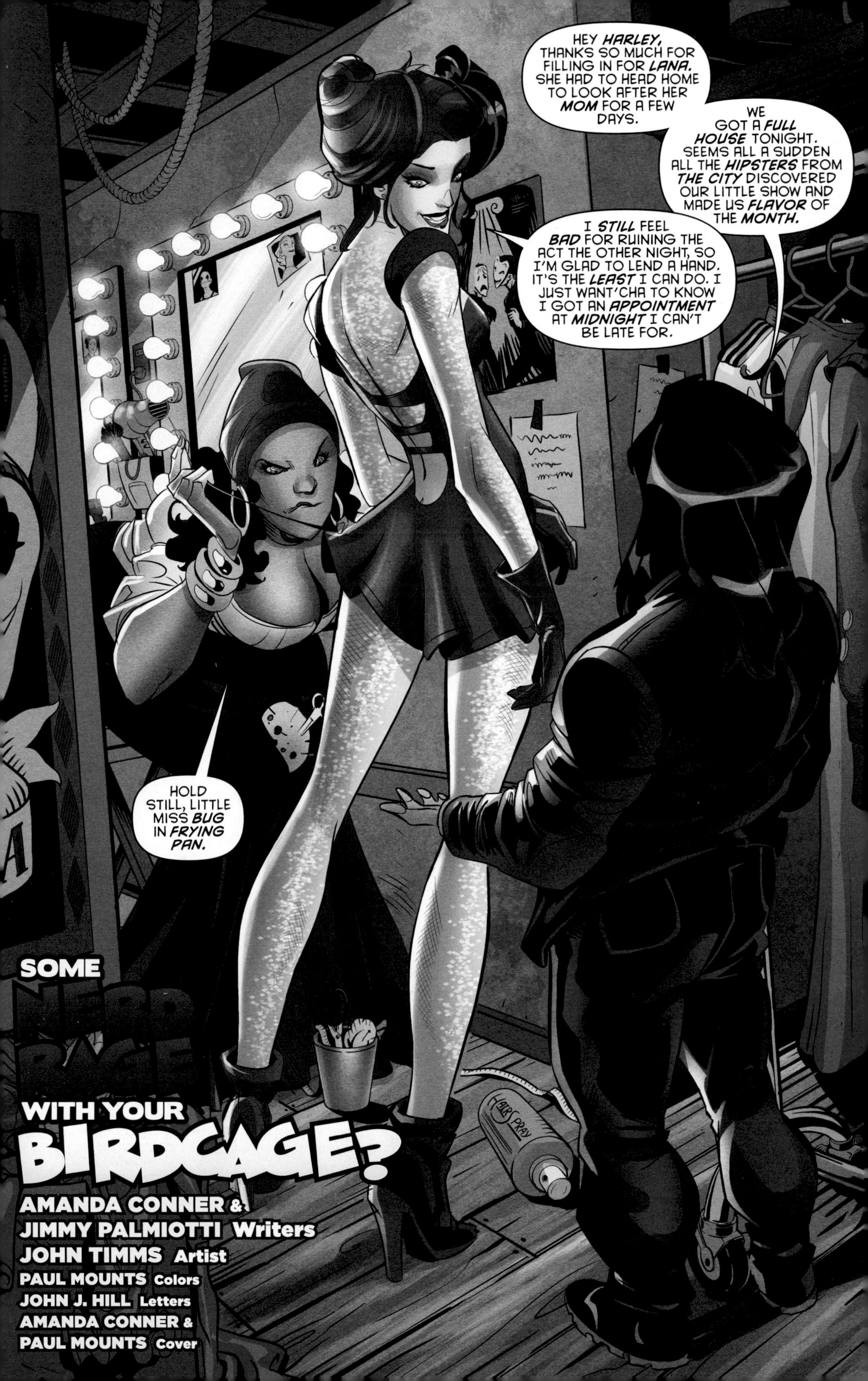
HEY HARLEY, THANKS SO MUCH FOR FILLING IN FOR LANA. SHE HAD TO HEAD HOME TO LOOK AFTER HER MOM FOR A FEW DAYS.
WE GOT A FULL HOUSE TONIGHT. SEEMS ALL A SUDDEN ALL THE HIPSTERS FROM THE CITY DISCOVERED OUR LITTLE SHOW AND MADE US FLAVOR OF THE MONTH.
I STILL FEEL BAD FOR RUINING THE ACT THE OTHER NIGHT, SO I'M GLAD TO LEND A HAND. IT'S THE LEAST I CAN DO. I JUST WANT'CHA TO KNOW I GOT AN APPOINTMENT AT MIDNIGHT I CAN'T BE LATE FOR.
HOLD STILL, LITTLE MISS BUG IN FRYING PAN.
HAIR SPRAY
SOME NERD RAGE WITH YOUR BIRDCAGE?
AMANDA CONNER & JIMMY PALMIOTTI Writers
JOHN TIMMS Artist
PAUL MOUNTS Colors
JOHN J. HILL Letters
AMANDA CONNER & PAUL MOUNTS Cover

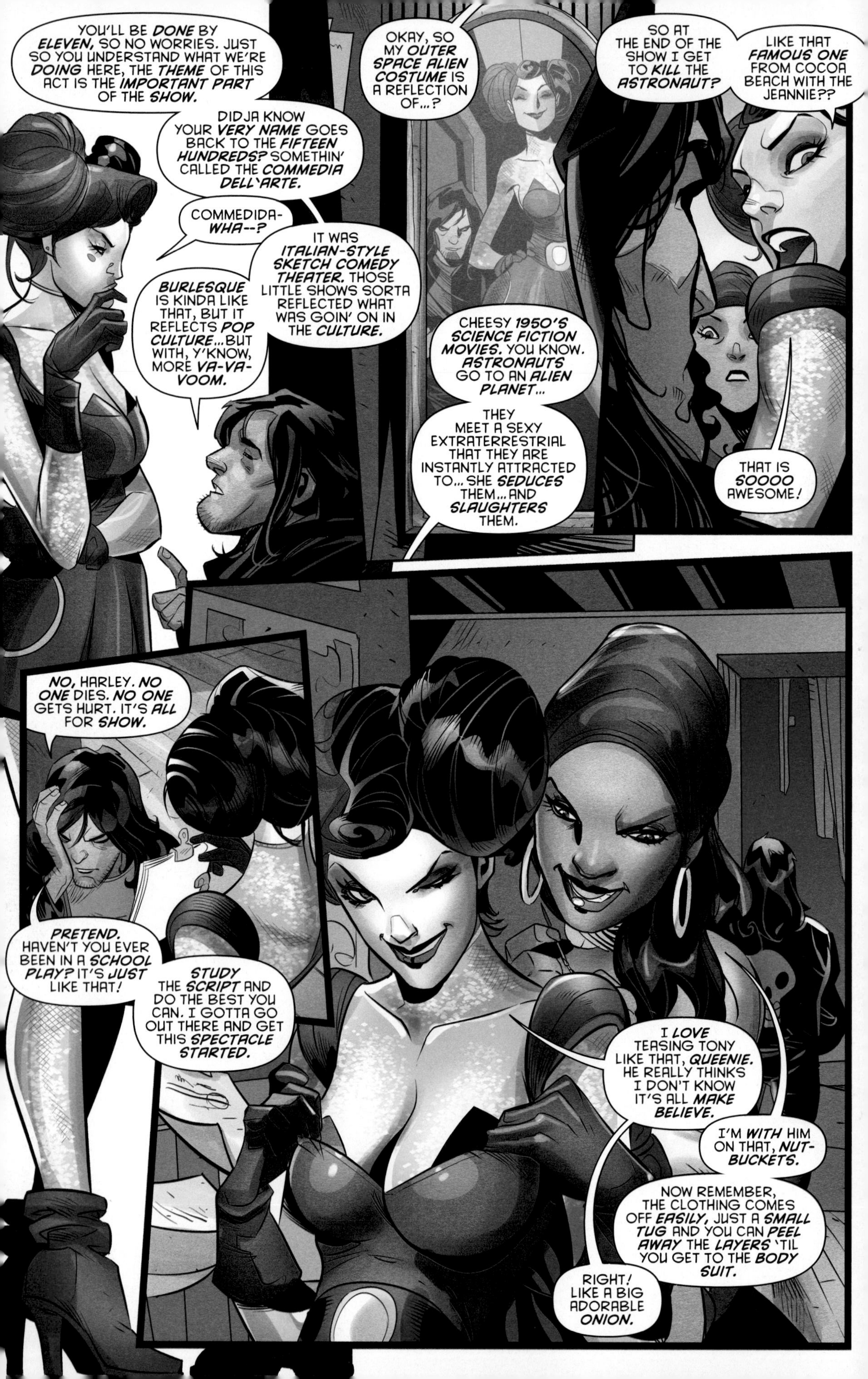

YOU'LL BE DONE BY ELEVEN, SO NO WORRIES. JUST SO YOU UNDERSTAND WHAT WE'RE DOING HERE, THE THEME OF THIS ACT IS THE IMPORTANT PART OF THE SHOW.
DIDJA KNOW YOUR VERY NAME GOES BACK TO THE FIFTEEN HUNDREDS? SOMETHIN' CALLED THE COMMEDIA DELL'ARTE.
COMMEDIDA-WHA--?
IT WAS ITALIAN-STYLE SKETCH COMEDY THEATER. THOSE LITTLE SHOWS SORTA REFLECTED WHAT WAS GOIN' ON IN THE CULTURE.
BURLESQUE IS KINDA LIKE THAT, BUT IT REFLECTS POP CULTURE...BUT WITH, Y'KNOW, MORE VA-VA-VOOM.
OKAY, SO MY OUTER SPACE ALIEN COSTUME IS A REFLECTION OF...?
CHEESY 1950'S SCIENCE FICTION MOVIES. YOU KNOW. ASTRONAUTS GO TO AN ALIEN PLANET...
THEY MEET A SEXY EXTRATERRESTRIAL THAT THEY ARE INSTANTLY ATTRACTED TO... SHE SEDUCES THEM... AND SLAUGHTERS THEM.
SO AT THE END OF THE SHOW I GET TO KILL THE ASTRONAUT?
LIKE THAT FAMOUS ONE FROM COCOA BEACH WITH THE JEANNIE??
THAT IS SOOOO AWESOME!
NO, HARLEY. NO ONE DIES. NO ONE GETS HURT. IT'S ALL FOR SHOW.
PRETEND. HAVEN'T YOU EVER BEEN IN A SCHOOL PLAY? IT'S JUST LIKE THAT!
STUDY THE SCRIPT AND DO THE BEST YOU CAN. I GOTTA GO OUT THERE AND GET THIS SPECTACLE STARTED.
I LOVE TEASING TONY LIKE THAT, QUEENIE. HE REALLY THINKS I DON'T KNOW IT'S ALL MAKE BELIEVE.
I'M WITH HIM ON THAT, NUT-BUCKETS.
NOW REMEMBER, THE CLOTHING COMES OFF EASILY, JUST A SMALL TUG AND YOU CAN PEEL AWAY THE LAYERS 'TIL YOU GET TO THE BODY SUIT.
RIGHT! LIKE A BIG ADORABLE ONION.

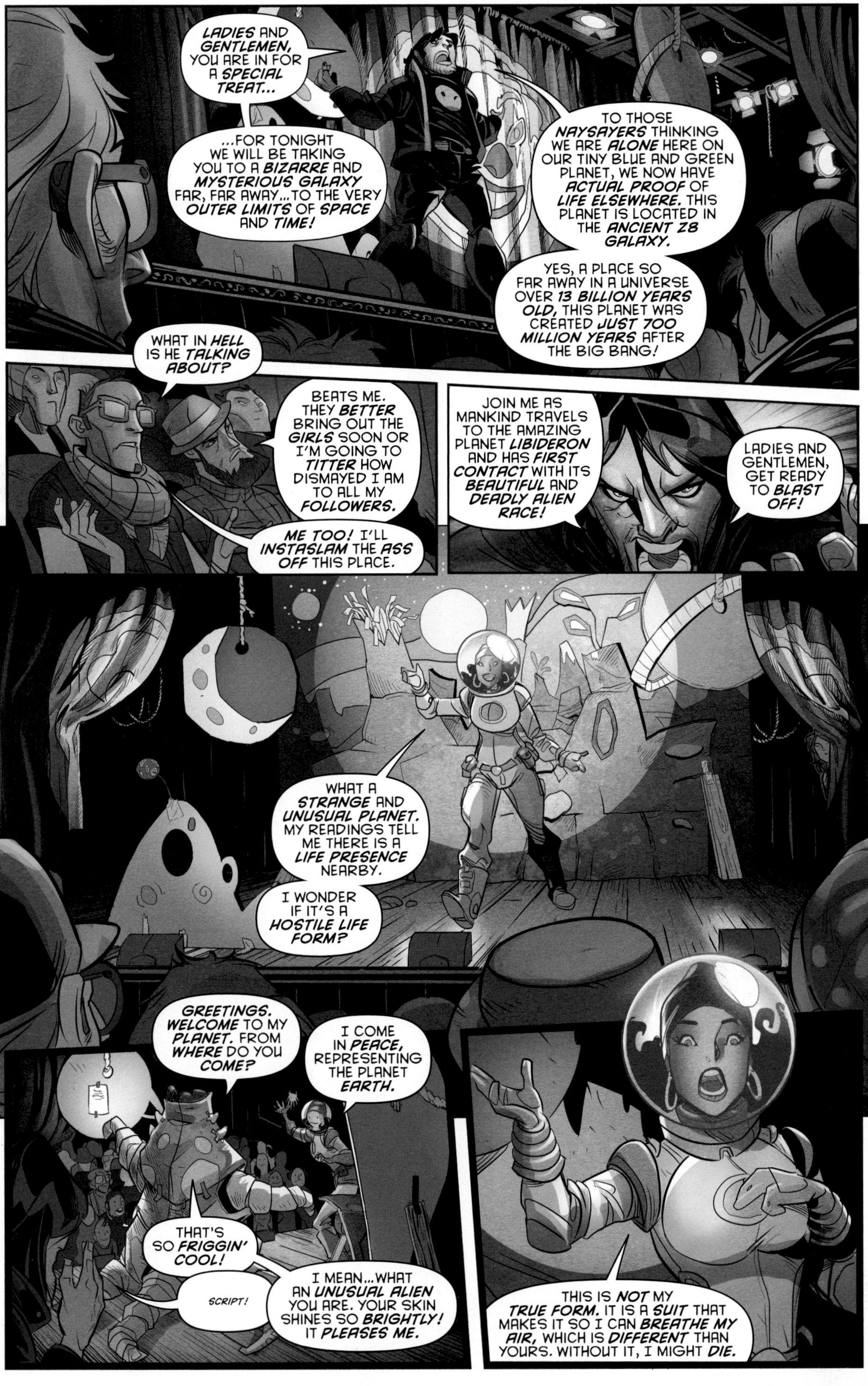
LADIES AND GENTLEMEN, YOU ARE IN FOR A SPECIAL TREAT...
...FOR TONIGHT WE WILL BE TAKING YOU TO A BIZARRE AND MYSTERIOUS GALAXY FAR, FAR AWAY...TO THE VERY OUTER LIMITS OF SPACE AND TIME!
TO THOSE NAYSAYERS THINKING WE ARE ALONE HERE ON OUR TINY BLUE AND GREEN PLANET, WE NOW HAVE ACTUAL PROOF OF LIFE ELSEWHERE. THIS PLANET IS LOCATED IN THE ANCIENT Z8 GALAXY.
YES, A PLACE SO FAR AWAY IN A UNIVERSE OVER 13 BILLION YEARS OLD, THIS PLANET WAS CREATED JUST 700 MILLION YEARS AFTER THE BIG BANG!
WHAT IN HELL IS HE TALKING ABOUT?
BEATS ME. THEY BETTER BRING OUT THE GIRLS SOON OR I'M GOING TO TITTER HOW DISMAYED I AM TO ALL MY FOLLOWERS.
ME TOO! I'LL INSTASLAM THE ASS OFF THIS PLACE.
JOIN ME AS MANKIND TRAVELS TO THE AMAZING PLANET LIBIDERON AND HAS FIRST CONTACT WITH ITS BEAUTIFUL AND DEADLY ALIEN RACE!
LADIES AND GENTLEMEN, GET READY TO BLAST OFF!
WHAT A STRANGE AND UNUSUAL PLANET. MY READINGS TELL ME THERE IS A LIFE PRESENCE NEARBY.
I WONDER IF IT'S A HOSTILE LIFE FORM?
GREETINGS. WELCOME TO MY PLANET. FROM WHERE DO YOU COME?
I COME IN PEACE, REPRESENTING THE PLANET EARTH.
THAT'S SO FRIGGIN' COOL!
SCRIPT!
I MEAN...WHAT AN UNUSUAL ALIEN YOU ARE. YOUR SKIN SHINES SO BRIGHTLY! IT PLEASES ME.
THIS IS NOT MY TRUE FORM. IT IS A SUIT THAT MAKES IT SO I CAN BREATHE MY AIR, WHICH IS DIFFERENT THAN YOURS. WITHOUT IT, I MIGHT DIE.

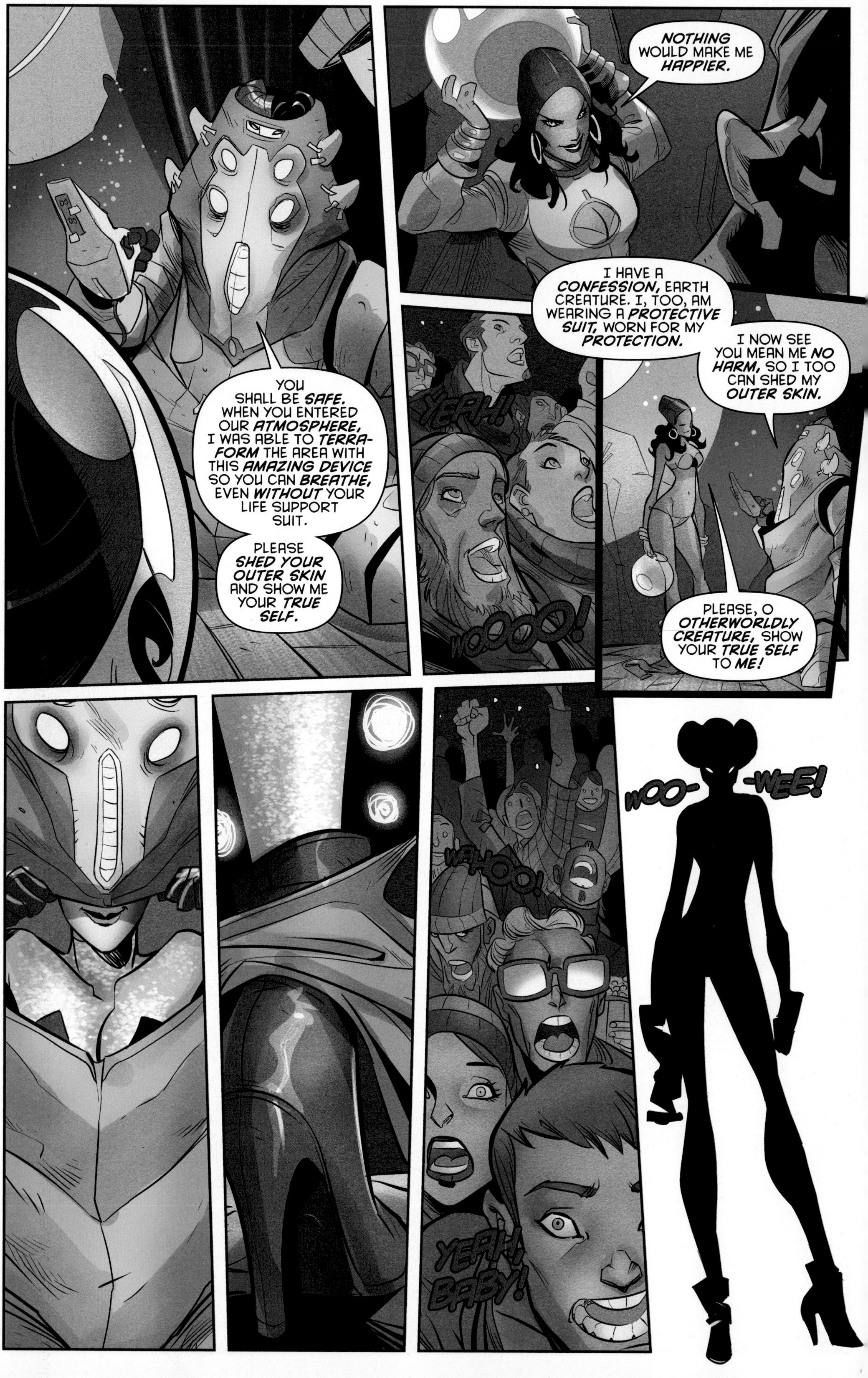
NOTHING WOULD MAKE ME HAPPIER.
YOU SHALL BE SAFE. WHEN YOU ENTERED OUR ATMOSPHERE, I WAS ABLE TO TERRAFORM THE AREA WITH THIS AMAZING DEVICE SO YOU CAN BREATHE, EVEN WITHOUT YOUR LIFE SUPPORT SUIT.
PLEASE SHED YOUR OUTER SKIN AND SHOW ME YOUR TRUE SELF.
I HAVE A CONFESSION, EARTH CREATURE. I, TOO, AM WEARING A PROTECTIVE SUIT, WORN FOR MY PROTECTION.
YEAH!
WOOOOO!
I NOW SEE YOU MEAN ME NO HARM, SO I TOO CAN SHED MY OUTER SKIN.
PLEASE, O OTHERWORLDLY CREATURE, SHOW YOUR TRUE SELF TO ME!
WAHOO!
YEAH! BABY!
WOO- -WEE!

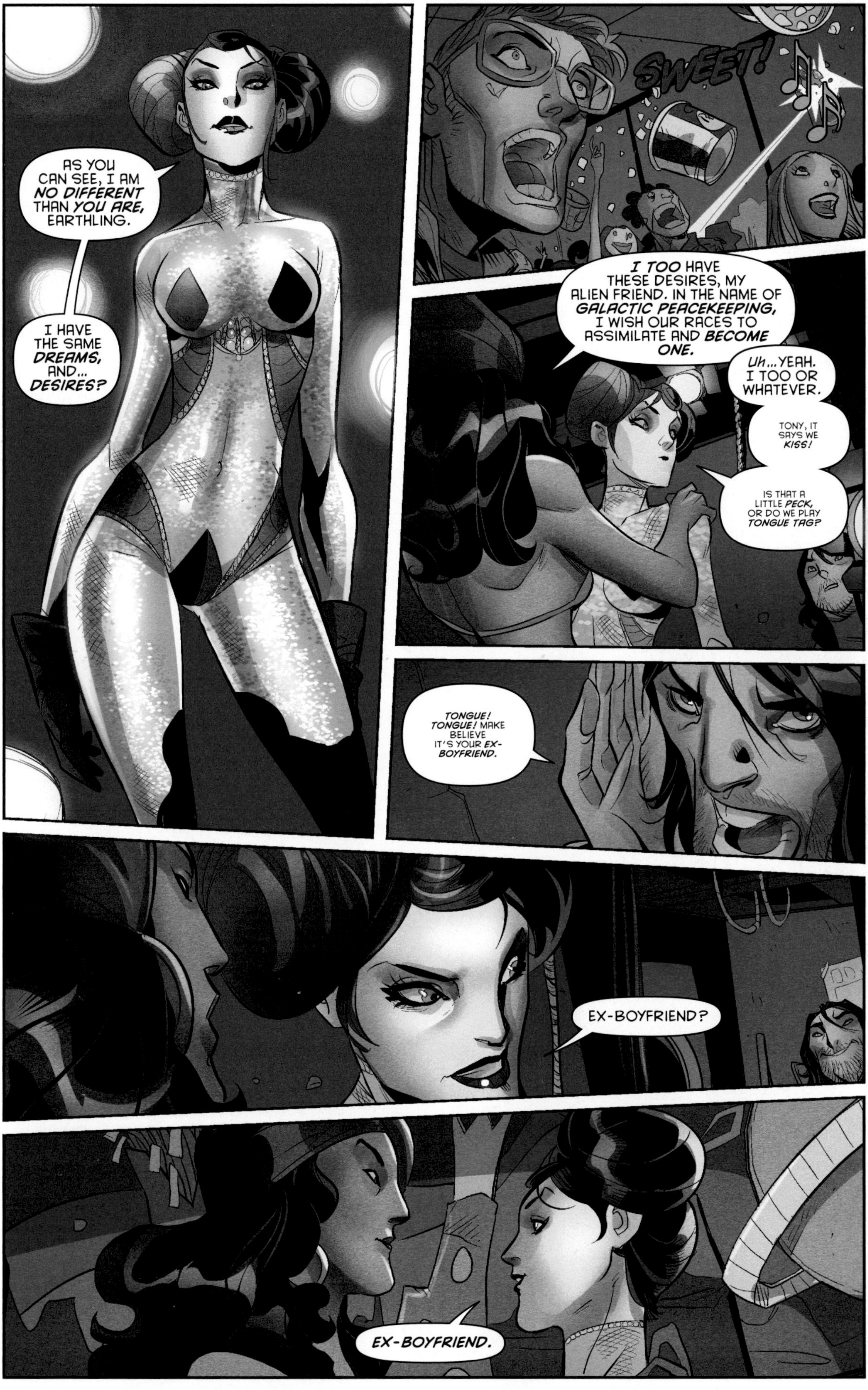
AS YOU CAN SEE, I AM NO DIFFERENT THAN YOU ARE, EARTHLING.
I HAVE THE SAME DREAMS, AND... DESIRES?
SWEET!
I TOO HAVE THESE DESIRES, MY ALIEN FRIEND. IN THE NAME OF GALACTIC PEACEKEEPING, I WISH OUR RACES TO ASSIMILATE AND BECOME ONE.
Uh...YEAH. I TOO OR WHATEVER.
TONY, IT SAYS WE KISS!
IS THAT A LITTLE PECK, OR DO WE PLAY TONGUE TAG?
TONGUE! TONGUE! MAKE BELIEVE IT'S YOUR EX-BOYFRIEND.
EX-BOYFRIEND?
EX-BOYFRIEND.

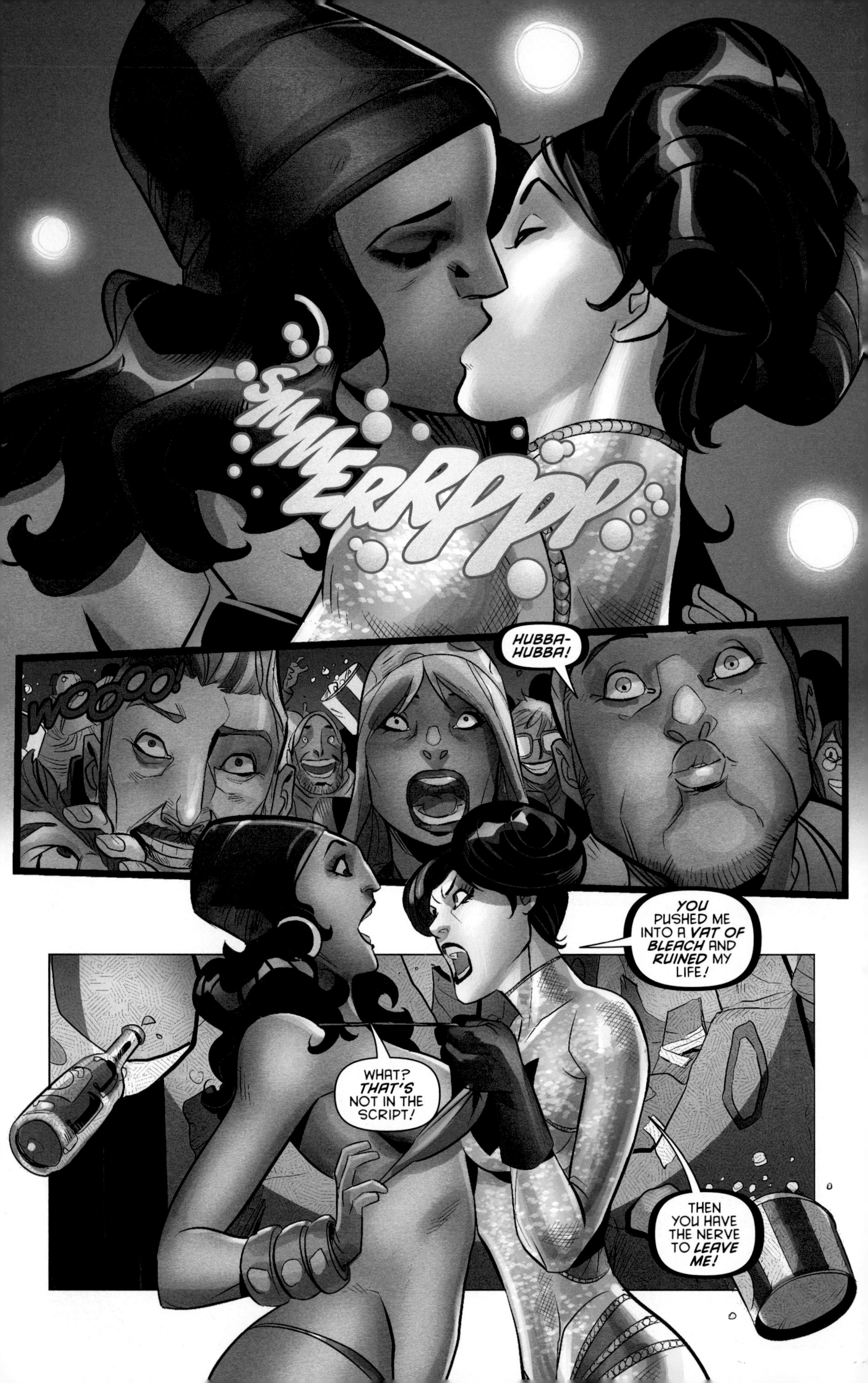

SMMERRPPP
WOOOO!
HUBBA-HUBBA!
YOU PUSHED ME INTO A VAT OF BLEACH AND RUINED MY LIFE!
WHAT? THAT'S NOT IN THE SCRIPT!
THEN YOU HAVE THE NERVE TO LEAVE ME!

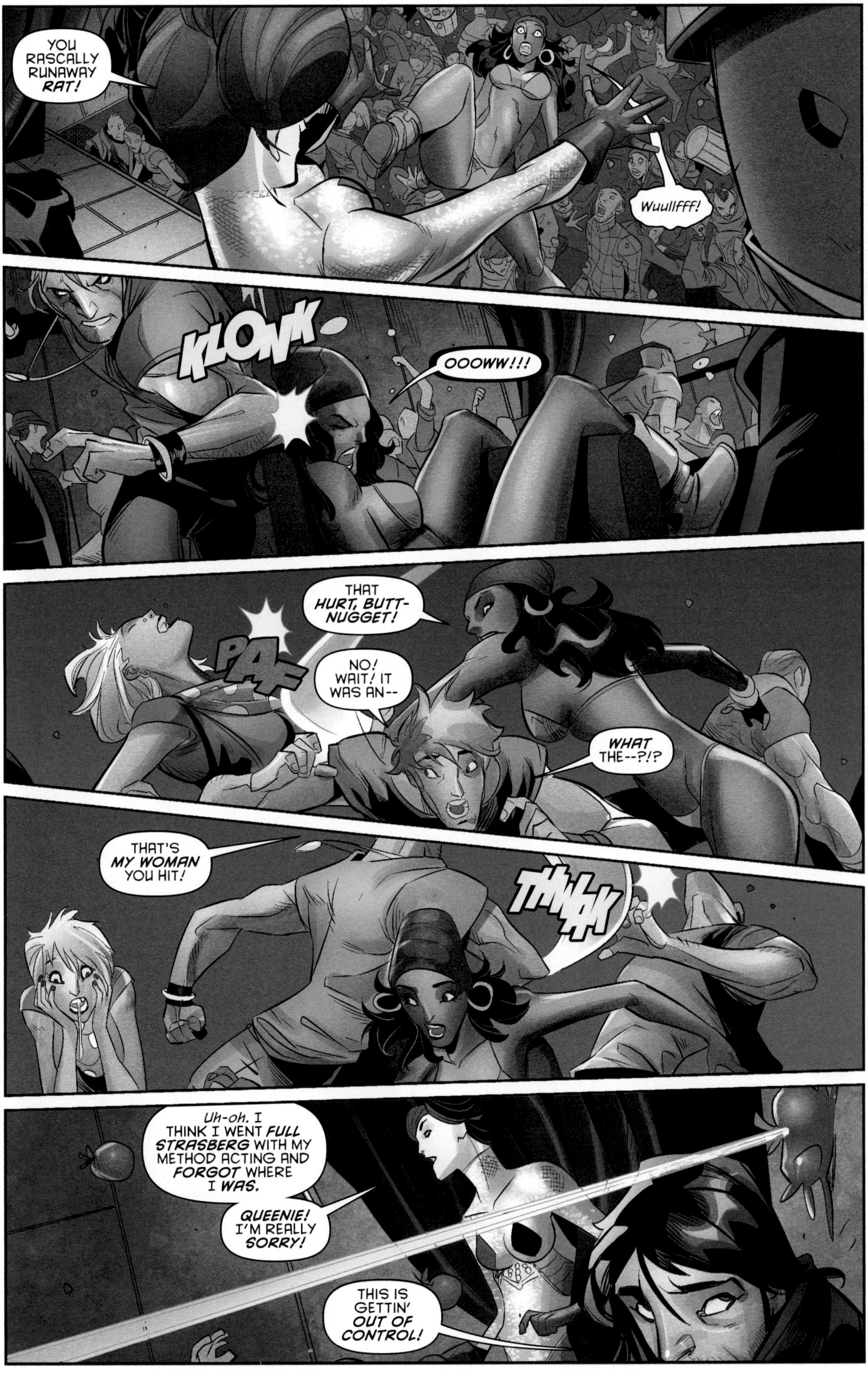
YOU RASCALLY RUNAWAY RAT!
Wuullfff!
KLONK
OOOWW!!!
THAT HURT, BUTT-NUGGET!
PAF
NO! WAIT! IT WAS AN--
WHAT THE--?!?
THAT'S MY WOMAN YOU HIT!
THWAK
Uh-oh. I THINK I WENT FULL STRASBERG WITH MY METHOD ACTING AND FORGOT WHERE I WAS.
QUEENIE! I'M REALLY SORRY!
THIS IS GETTIN' OUT OF CONTROL!

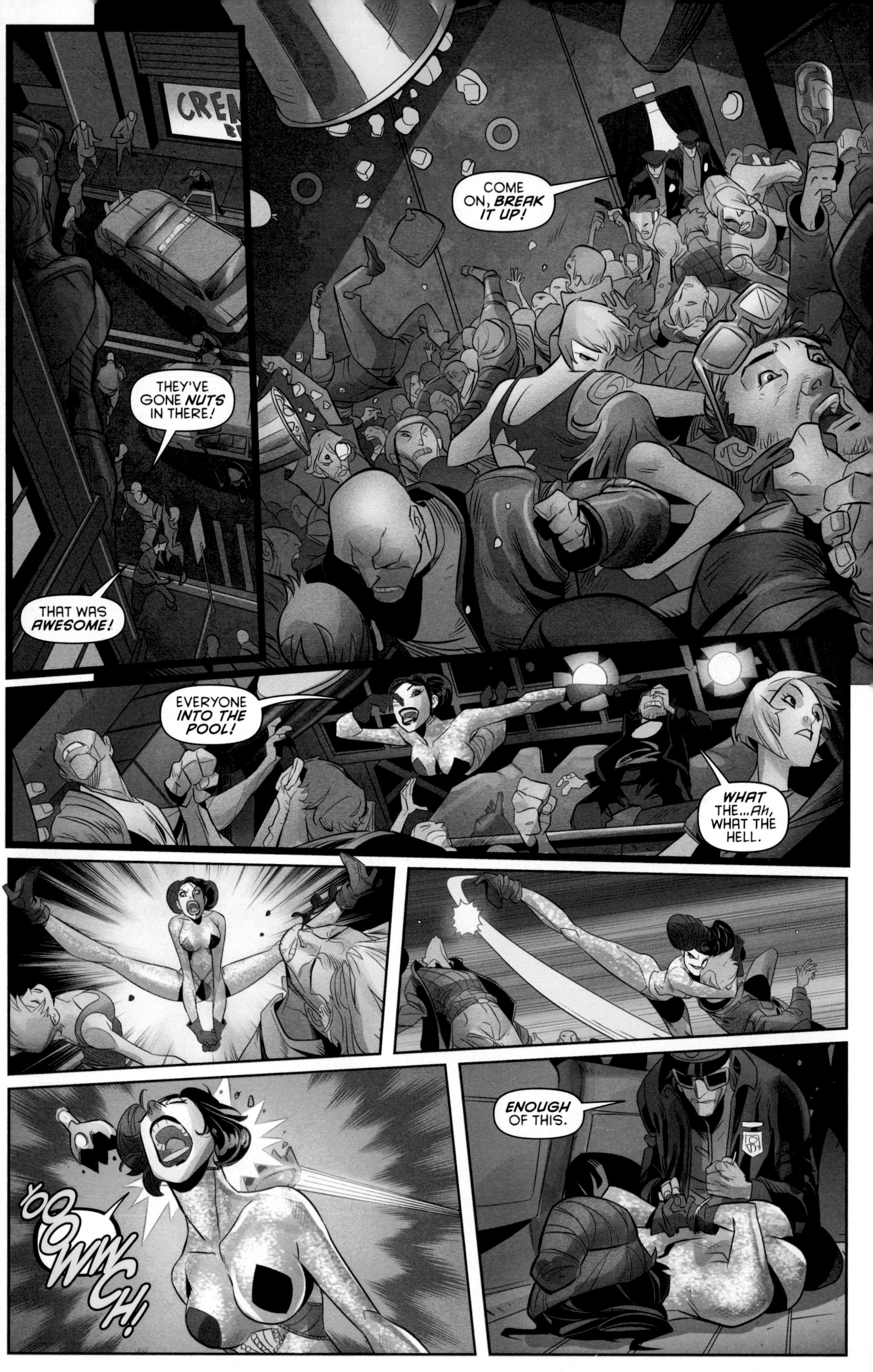
CREA
THEY'VE GONE NUTS IN THERE!
THAT WAS AWESOME!
COME ON, BREAK IT UP!
EVERYONE INTO THE POOL!
WHAT THE...Ah, WHAT THE HELL.
YOOOWWCH!
ENOUGH OF THIS.

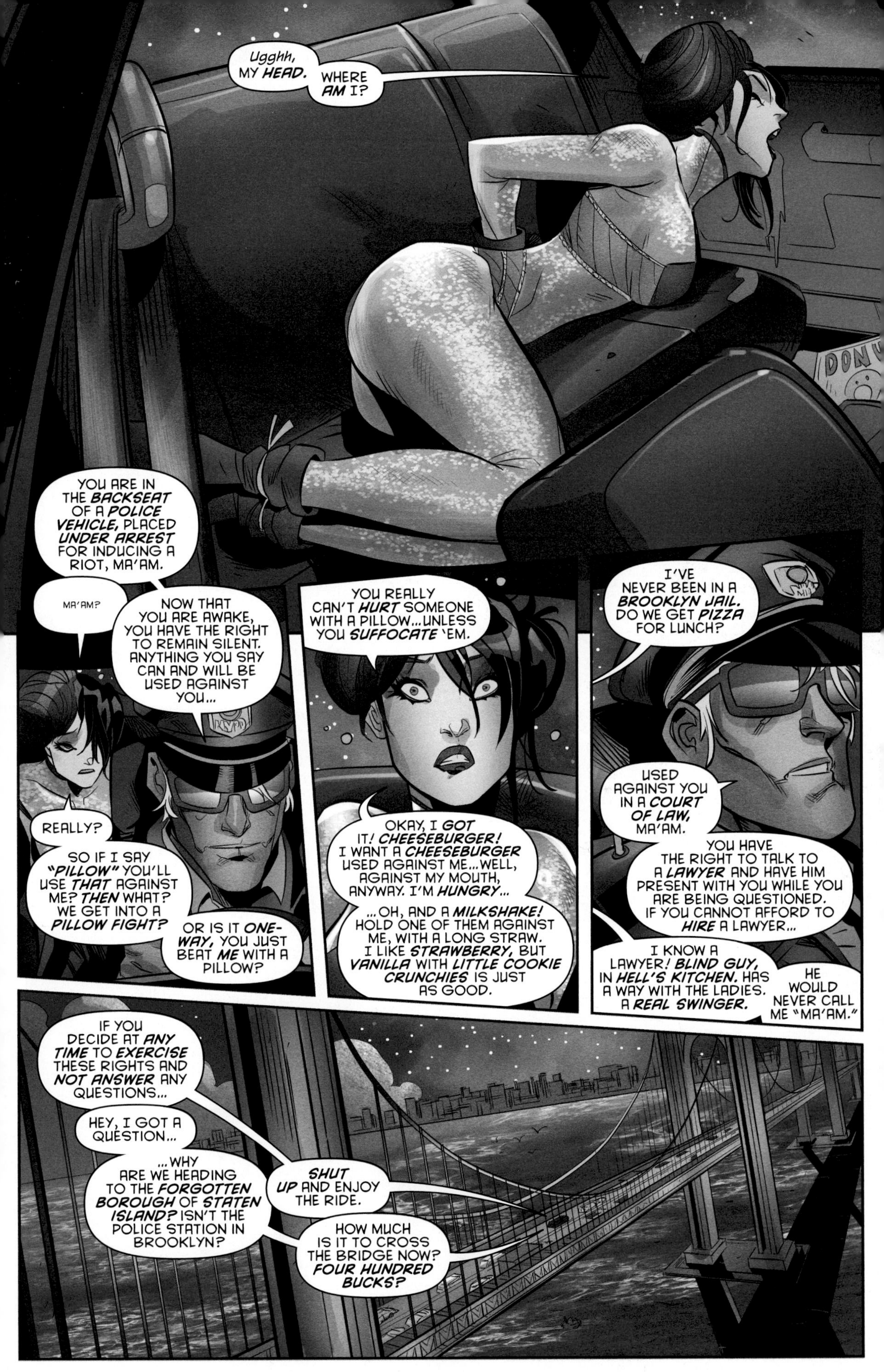

Ugghh, MY HEAD.
WHERE AM I?
DONU
YOU ARE IN THE BACKSEAT OF A POLICE VEHICLE, PLACED UNDER ARREST FOR INDUCING A RIOT, MA'AM.
MA'AM?
NOW THAT YOU ARE AWAKE, YOU HAVE THE RIGHT TO REMAIN SILENT. ANYTHING YOU SAY CAN AND WILL BE USED AGAINST YOU...
REALLY?
SO IF I SAY "PILLOW" YOU'LL USE THAT AGAINST ME? THEN WHAT? WE GET INTO A PILLOW FIGHT?
OR IS IT ONE-WAY, YOU JUST BEAT ME WITH A PILLOW?
YOU REALLY CAN'T HURT SOMEONE WITH A PILLOW...UNLESS YOU SUFFOCATE 'EM.
OKAY, I GOT IT! CHEESEBURGER! I WANT A CHEESEBURGER USED AGAINST ME...WELL, AGAINST MY MOUTH, ANYWAY. I'M HUNGRY...
...OH, AND A MILKSHAKE! HOLD ONE OF THEM AGAINST ME, WITH A LONG STRAW. I LIKE STRAWBERRY, BUT VANILLA WITH LITTLE COOKIE CRUNCHIES IS JUST AS GOOD.
I'VE NEVER BEEN IN A BROOKLYN JAIL. DO WE GET PIZZA FOR LUNCH?
USED AGAINST YOU IN A COURT OF LAW, MA'AM.
YOU HAVE THE RIGHT TO TALK TO A LAWYER AND HAVE HIM PRESENT WITH YOU WHILE YOU ARE BEING QUESTIONED. IF YOU CANNOT AFFORD TO HIRE A LAWYER...
I KNOW A LAWYER! BLIND GUY, IN HELL'S KITCHEN. HAS A WAY WITH THE LADIES. A REAL SWINGER.
HE WOULD NEVER CALL ME "MA'AM."
IF YOU DECIDE AT ANY TIME TO EXERCISE THESE RIGHTS AND NOT ANSWER ANY QUESTIONS...
HEY, I GOT A QUESTION...
...WHY ARE WE HEADING TO THE FORGOTTEN BOROUGH OF STATEN ISLAND? ISN'T THE POLICE STATION IN BROOKLYN?
SHUT UP AND ENJOY THE RIDE.
HOW MUCH IS IT TO CROSS THE BRIDGE NOW? FOUR HUNDRED BUCKS?

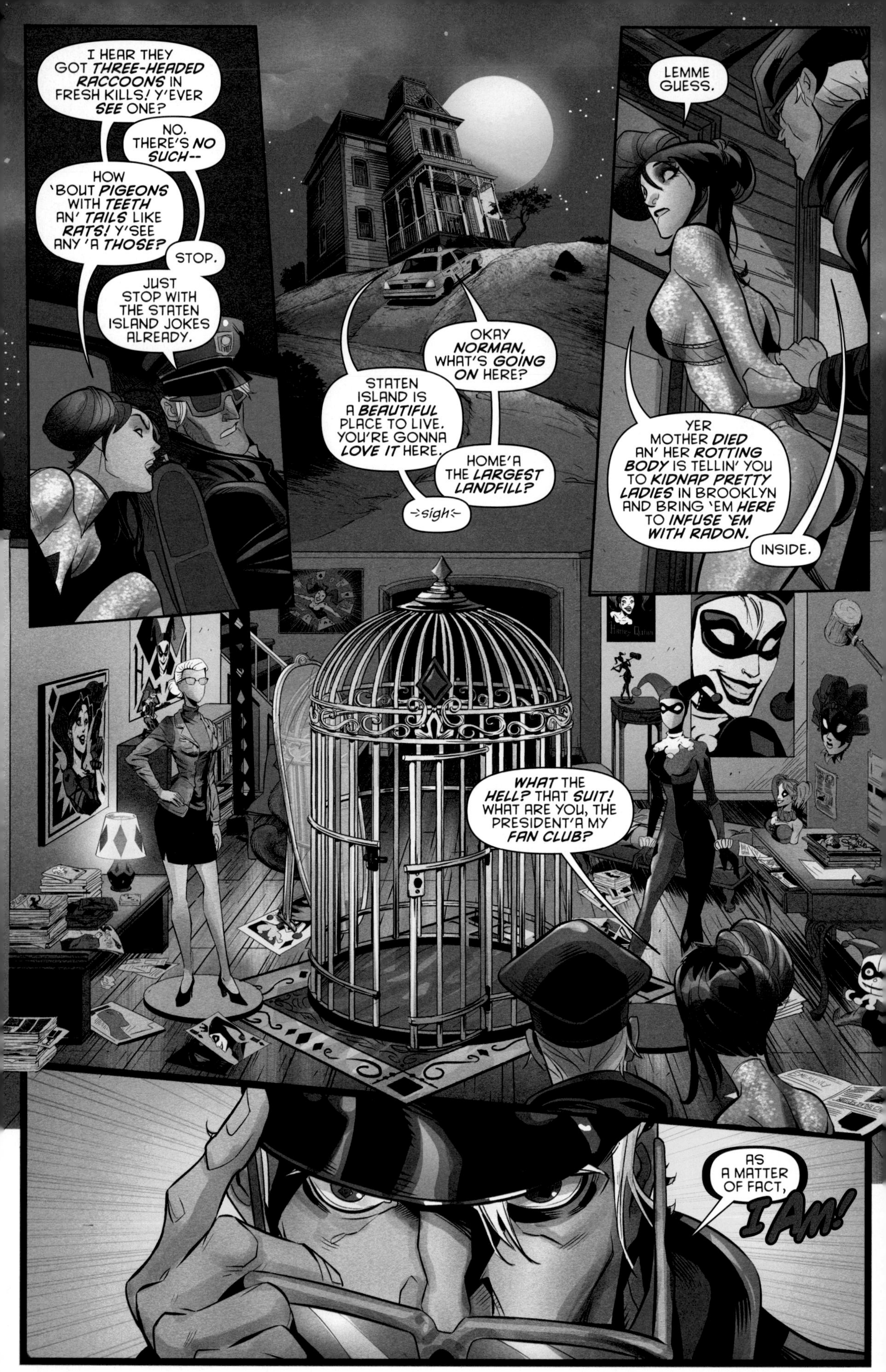

I HEAR THEY GOT THREE-HEADED RACCOONS IN FRESH KILLS! Y'EVER SEE ONE?
NO. THERE'S NO SUCH--
HOW 'BOUT PIGEONS WITH TEETH AN' TAILS LIKE RATS! Y'SEE ANY 'A THOSE?
STOP.
JUST STOP WITH THE STATEN ISLAND JOKES ALREADY.
OKAY NORMAN, WHAT'S GOING ON HERE?
STATEN ISLAND IS A BEAUTIFUL PLACE TO LIVE. YOU'RE GONNA LOVE IT HERE.
HOME'A THE LARGEST LANDFILL?
sigh
LEMME GUESS.
YER MOTHER DIED AN' HER ROTTING BODY IS TELLIN' YOU TO KIDNAP PRETTY LADIES IN BROOKLYN AND BRING 'EM HERE TO INFUSE 'EM WITH RADON.
INSIDE.
WHAT THE HELL? THAT SUIT! WHAT ARE YOU, THE PRESIDENT'A MY FAN CLUB?
AS A MATTER OF FACT, I AM!

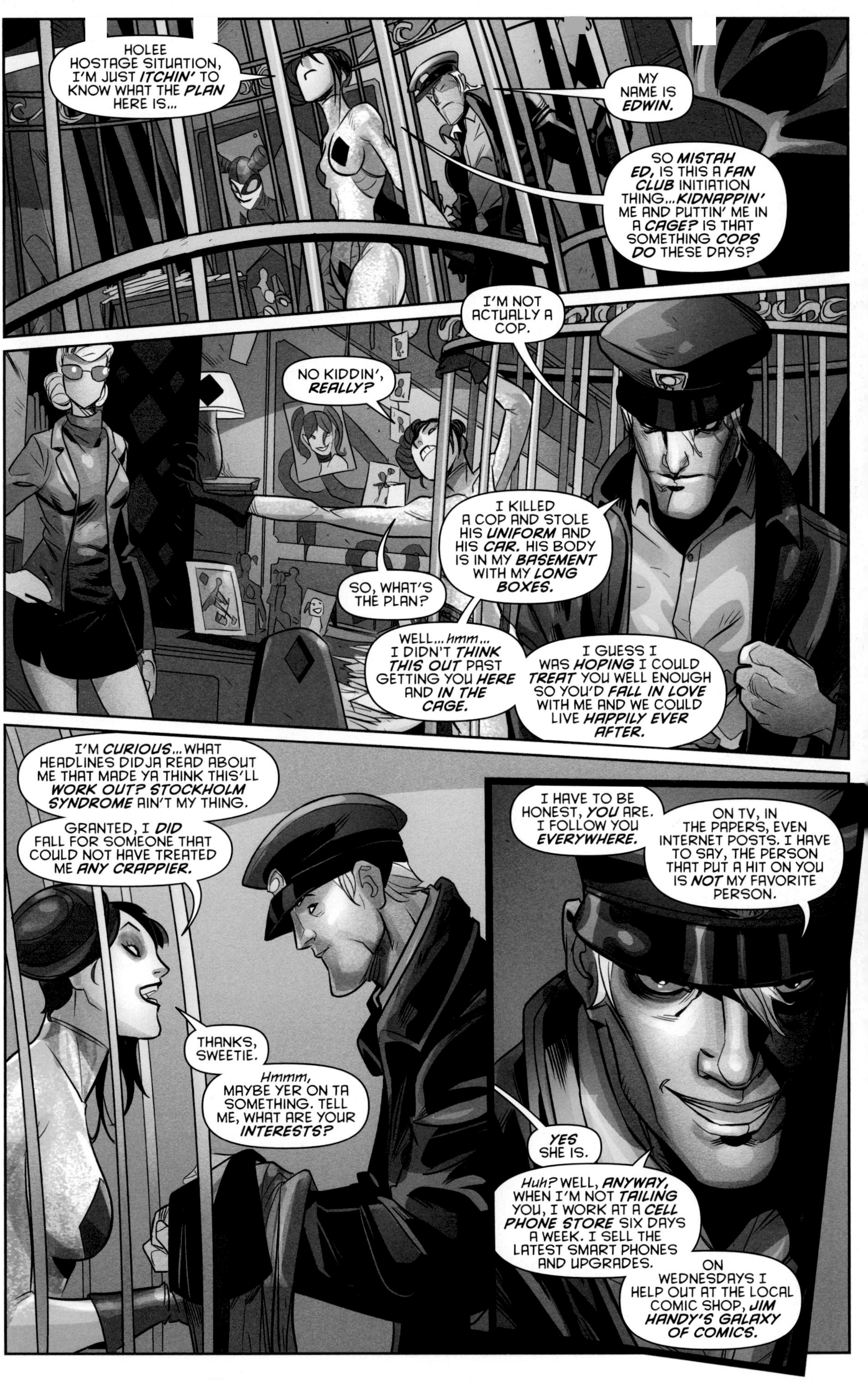
HOLEE HOSTAGE SITUATION, I'M JUST ITCHIN' TO KNOW WHAT THE PLAN HERE IS...
MY NAME IS EDWIN.
SO MISTAH ED, IS THIS A FAN CLUB INITIATION THING...KIDNAPPIN' ME AND PUTTIN' ME IN A CAGE? IS THAT SOMETHING COPS DO THESE DAYS?
I'M NOT ACTUALLY A COP.
NO KIDDIN', REALLY?
I KILLED A COP AND STOLE HIS UNIFORM AND HIS CAR. HIS BODY IS IN MY BASEMENT WITH MY LONG BOXES.
SO, WHAT'S THE PLAN?
WELL... hmm... I DIDN'T THINK THIS OUT PAST GETTING YOU HERE AND IN THE CAGE.
I GUESS I WAS HOPING I COULD TREAT YOU WELL ENOUGH SO YOU'D FALL IN LOVE WITH ME AND WE COULD LIVE HAPPILY EVER AFTER.
I'M CURIOUS... WHAT HEADLINES DIDJA READ ABOUT ME THAT MADE YA THINK THIS'LL WORK OUT? STOCKHOLM SYNDROME AIN'T MY THING.
GRANTED, I DID FALL FOR SOMEONE THAT COULD NOT HAVE TREATED ME ANY CRAPPIER.
I HAVE TO BE HONEST, YOU ARE. I FOLLOW YOU EVERYWHERE.
ON TV, IN THE PAPERS, EVEN INTERNET POSTS. I HAVE TO SAY, THE PERSON THAT PUT A HIT ON YOU IS NOT MY FAVORITE PERSON.
THANKS, SWEETIE.
Hmmm, MAYBE YER ON TA SOMETHING. TELL ME, WHAT ARE YOUR INTERESTS?
YES SHE IS.
Huh? WELL, ANYWAY, WHEN I'M NOT TAILING YOU, I WORK AT A CELL PHONE STORE SIX DAYS A WEEK. I SELL THE LATEST SMART PHONES AND UPGRADES.
ON WEDNESDAYS I HELP OUT AT THE LOCAL COMIC SHOP, JIM HANDY'S GALAXY OF COMICS.

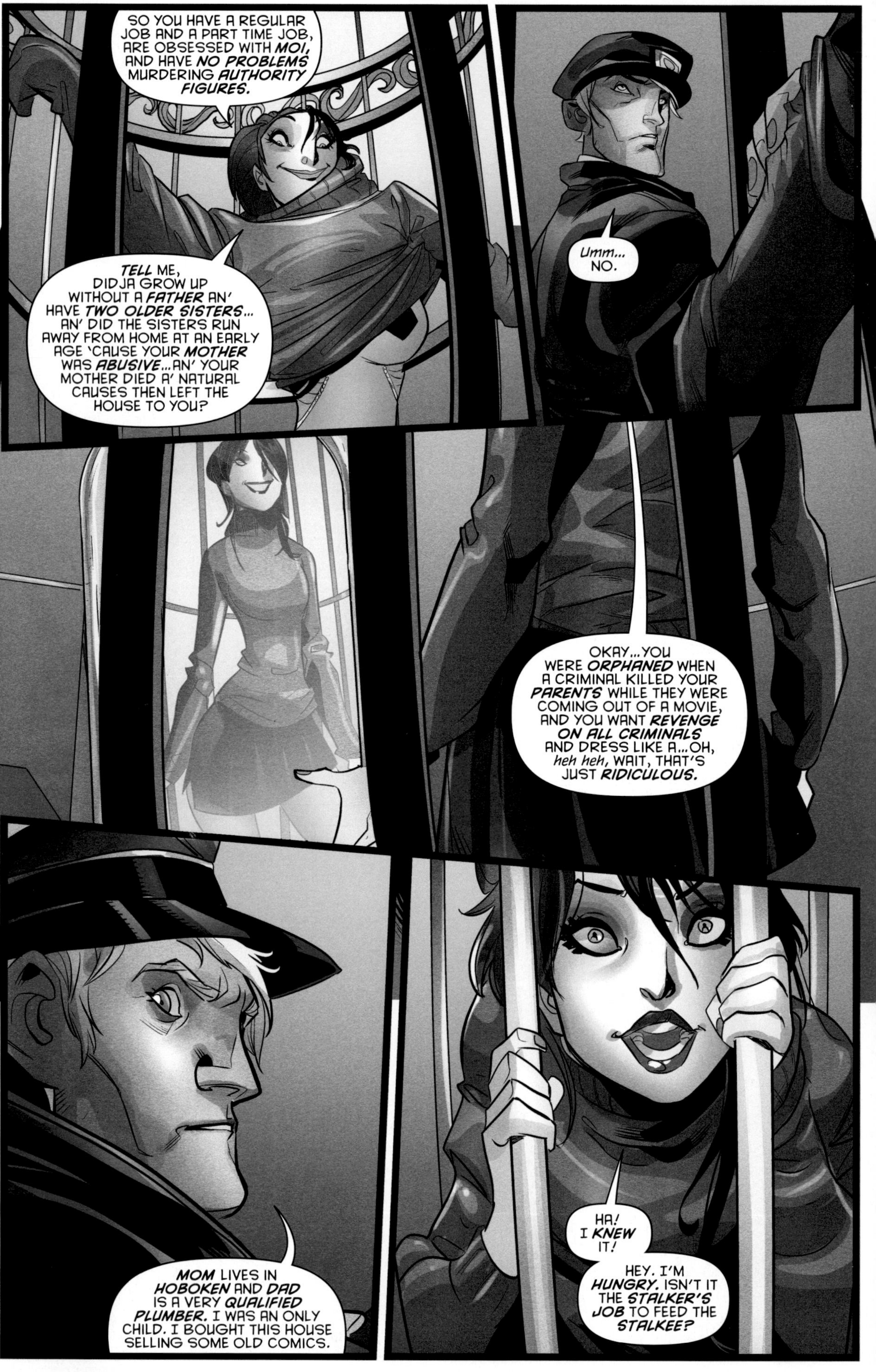
SO YOU HAVE A REGULAR JOB AND A PART TIME JOB, ARE OBSESSED WITH MOI, AND HAVE NO PROBLEMS MURDERING AUTHORITY FIGURES.
TELL ME, DIDJA GROW UP WITHOUT A FATHER AN' HAVE TWO OLDER SISTERS... AN' DID THE SISTERS RUN AWAY FROM HOME AT AN EARLY AGE 'CAUSE YOUR MOTHER WAS ABUSIVE...AN' YOUR MOTHER DIED A' NATURAL CAUSES THEN LEFT THE HOUSE TO YOU?
Umm... NO.
OKAY...YOU WERE ORPHANED WHEN A CRIMINAL KILLED YOUR PARENTS WHILE THEY WERE COMING OUT OF A MOVIE, AND YOU WANT REVENGE ON ALL CRIMINALS AND DRESS LIKE A...OH, heh heh, WAIT, THAT'S JUST RIDICULOUS.
MOM LIVES IN HOBOKEN AND DAD IS A VERY QUALIFIED PLUMBER. I WAS AN ONLY CHILD. I BOUGHT THIS HOUSE SELLING SOME OLD COMICS.
HA! I KNEW IT!
HEY. I'M HUNGRY. ISN'T IT THE STALKER'S JOB TO FEED THE STALKEE?

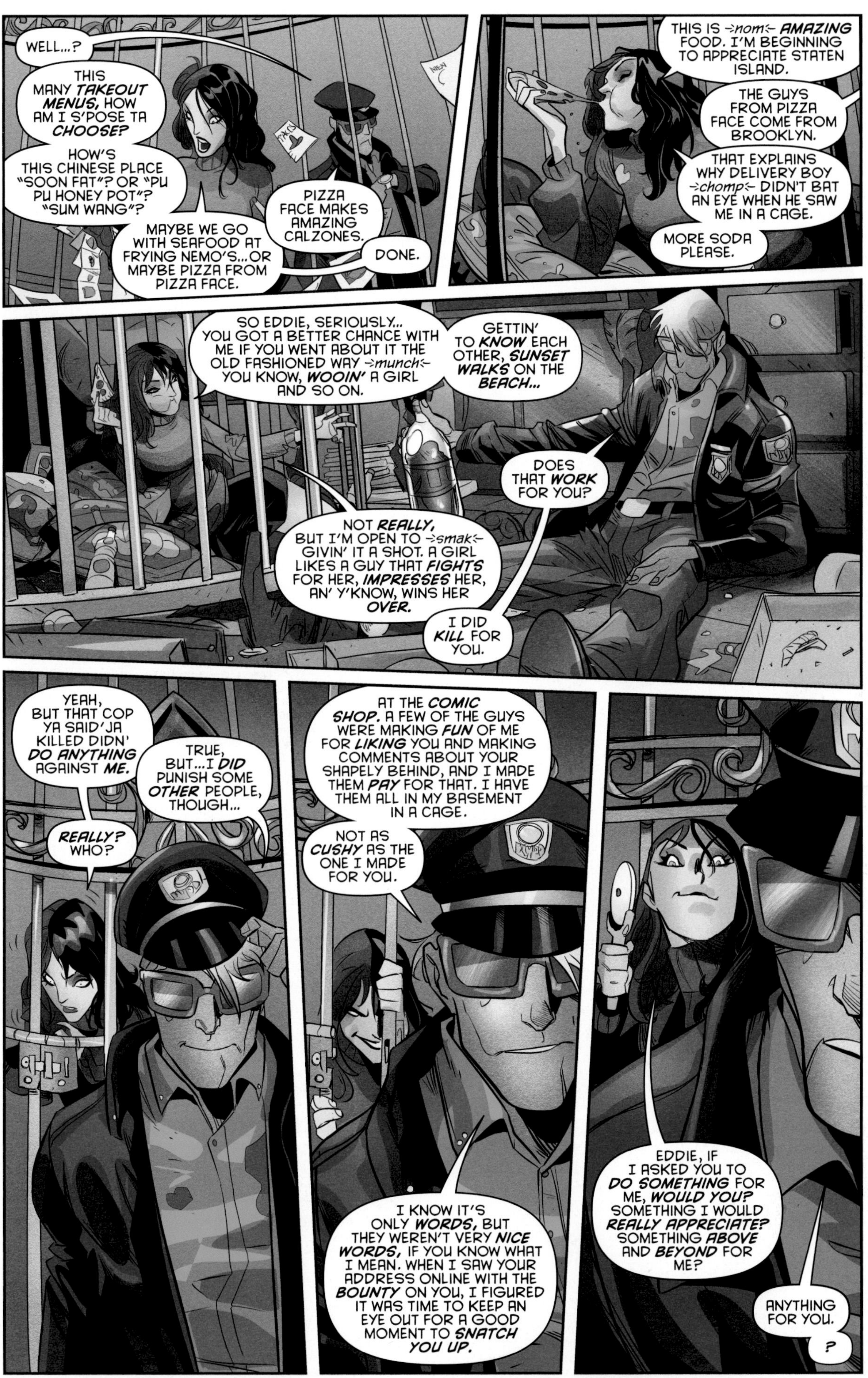
WELL...?
THIS MANY *TAKEOUT MENUS,* HOW AM I S'POSE TA *CHOOSE?*
HOW'S THIS CHINESE PLACE "SOON FAT"? OR "PU PU HONEY POT"? "SUM WANG"?
MAYBE WE GO WITH SEAFOOD AT FRYING NEMO'S...OR MAYBE PIZZA FROM PIZZA FACE.
PIZZA FACE MAKES AMAZING CALZONES.
DONE.
THIS IS ⁓nom⁓ *AMAZING* FOOD. I'M BEGINNING TO APPRECIATE STATEN ISLAND.
THE GUYS FROM PIZZA FACE COME FROM BROOKLYN.
THAT EXPLAINS WHY DELIVERY BOY ⁓chomp⁓ DIDN'T BAT AN EYE WHEN HE SAW ME IN A CAGE.
MORE SODA PLEASE.
SO EDDIE, SERIOUSLY... YOU GOT A BETTER CHANCE WITH ME IF YOU WENT ABOUT IT THE OLD FASHIONED WAY ⁓munch⁓ YOU KNOW, *WOOIN'* A GIRL AND SO ON.
GETTIN' TO *KNOW* EACH OTHER, *SUNSET WALKS* ON THE *BEACH...*
DOES THAT *WORK* FOR YOU?
NOT *REALLY,* BUT I'M OPEN TO ⁓smak⁓ GIVIN' IT A SHOT. A GIRL LIKES A GUY THAT *FIGHTS* FOR HER, *IMPRESSES* HER, AN' Y'KNOW, WINS HER *OVER.*
I DID *KILL* FOR YOU.
YEAH, BUT THAT COP YA SAID'JA KILLED DIDN' *DO ANYTHING* AGAINST *ME.*
TRUE, BUT...I *DID* PUNISH SOME *OTHER* PEOPLE, THOUGH...
REALLY? WHO?
AT THE *COMIC SHOP.* A FEW OF THE GUYS WERE MAKING *FUN* OF ME FOR *LIKING* YOU AND MAKING COMMENTS ABOUT YOUR SHAPELY BEHIND, AND I MADE THEM *PAY* FOR THAT. I HAVE THEM ALL IN MY BASEMENT IN A CAGE.
NOT AS *CUSHY* AS THE ONE I MADE FOR YOU.
I KNOW IT'S ONLY *WORDS,* BUT THEY WEREN'T VERY *NICE WORDS,* IF YOU KNOW WHAT I MEAN. WHEN I SAW YOUR ADDRESS ONLINE WITH THE *BOUNTY* ON YOU, I FIGURED IT WAS TIME TO KEEP AN EYE OUT FOR A GOOD MOMENT TO *SNATCH YOU UP.*
EDDIE, IF I ASKED YOU TO *DO SOMETHING* FOR ME, *WOULD YOU?* SOMETHING I WOULD *REALLY APPRECIATE?* SOMETHING *ABOVE* AND *BEYOND* FOR ME?
ANYTHING FOR YOU.
?

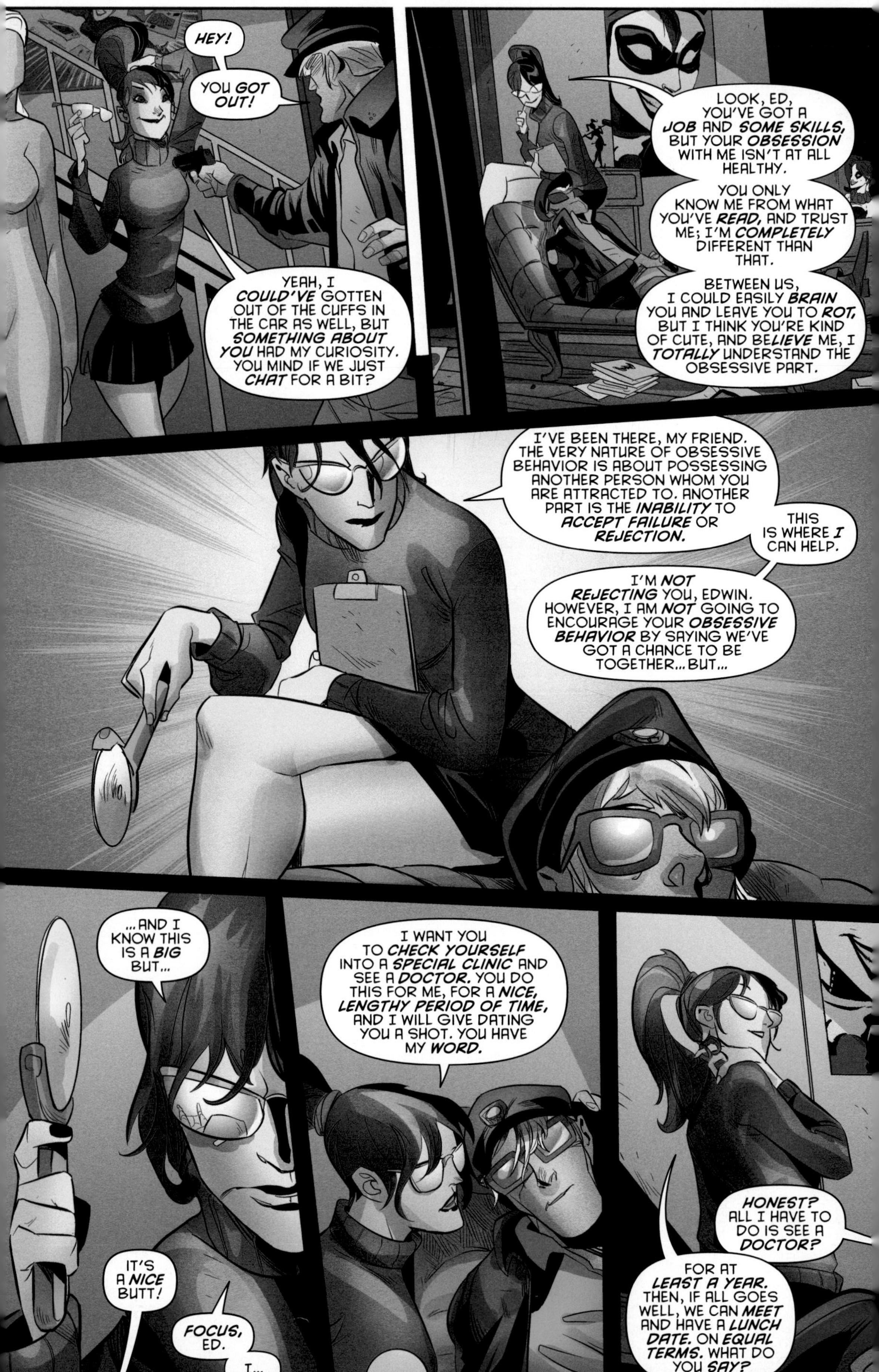
HEY!
YOU GOT OUT!
YEAH, I COULD'VE GOTTEN OUT OF THE CUFFS IN THE CAR AS WELL, BUT SOMETHING ABOUT YOU HAD MY CURIOSITY. YOU MIND IF WE JUST CHAT FOR A BIT?
LOOK, ED, YOU'VE GOT A JOB AND SOME SKILLS, BUT YOUR OBSESSION WITH ME ISN'T AT ALL HEALTHY.
YOU ONLY KNOW ME FROM WHAT YOU'VE READ, AND TRUST ME; I'M COMPLETELY DIFFERENT THAN THAT.
BETWEEN US, I COULD EASILY BRAIN YOU AND LEAVE YOU TO ROT, BUT I THINK YOU'RE KIND OF CUTE, AND BELIEVE ME, I TOTALLY UNDERSTAND THE OBSESSIVE PART.
I'VE BEEN THERE, MY FRIEND. THE VERY NATURE OF OBSESSIVE BEHAVIOR IS ABOUT POSSESSING ANOTHER PERSON WHOM YOU ARE ATTRACTED TO. ANOTHER PART IS THE INABILITY TO ACCEPT FAILURE OR REJECTION.
THIS IS WHERE I CAN HELP.
I'M NOT REJECTING YOU, EDWIN. HOWEVER, I AM NOT GOING TO ENCOURAGE YOUR OBSESSIVE BEHAVIOR BY SAYING WE'VE GOT A CHANCE TO BE TOGETHER... BUT...
...AND I KNOW THIS IS A BIG BUT...
IT'S A NICE BUTT!
FOCUS, ED.
I...
I WANT YOU TO CHECK YOURSELF INTO A SPECIAL CLINIC AND SEE A DOCTOR. YOU DO THIS FOR ME, FOR A NICE, LENGTHY PERIOD OF TIME, AND I WILL GIVE DATING YOU A SHOT. YOU HAVE MY WORD.
HONEST? ALL I HAVE TO DO IS SEE A DOCTOR?
FOR AT LEAST A YEAR. THEN, IF ALL GOES WELL, WE CAN MEET AND HAVE A LUNCH DATE. ON EQUAL TERMS. WHAT DO YOU SAY?

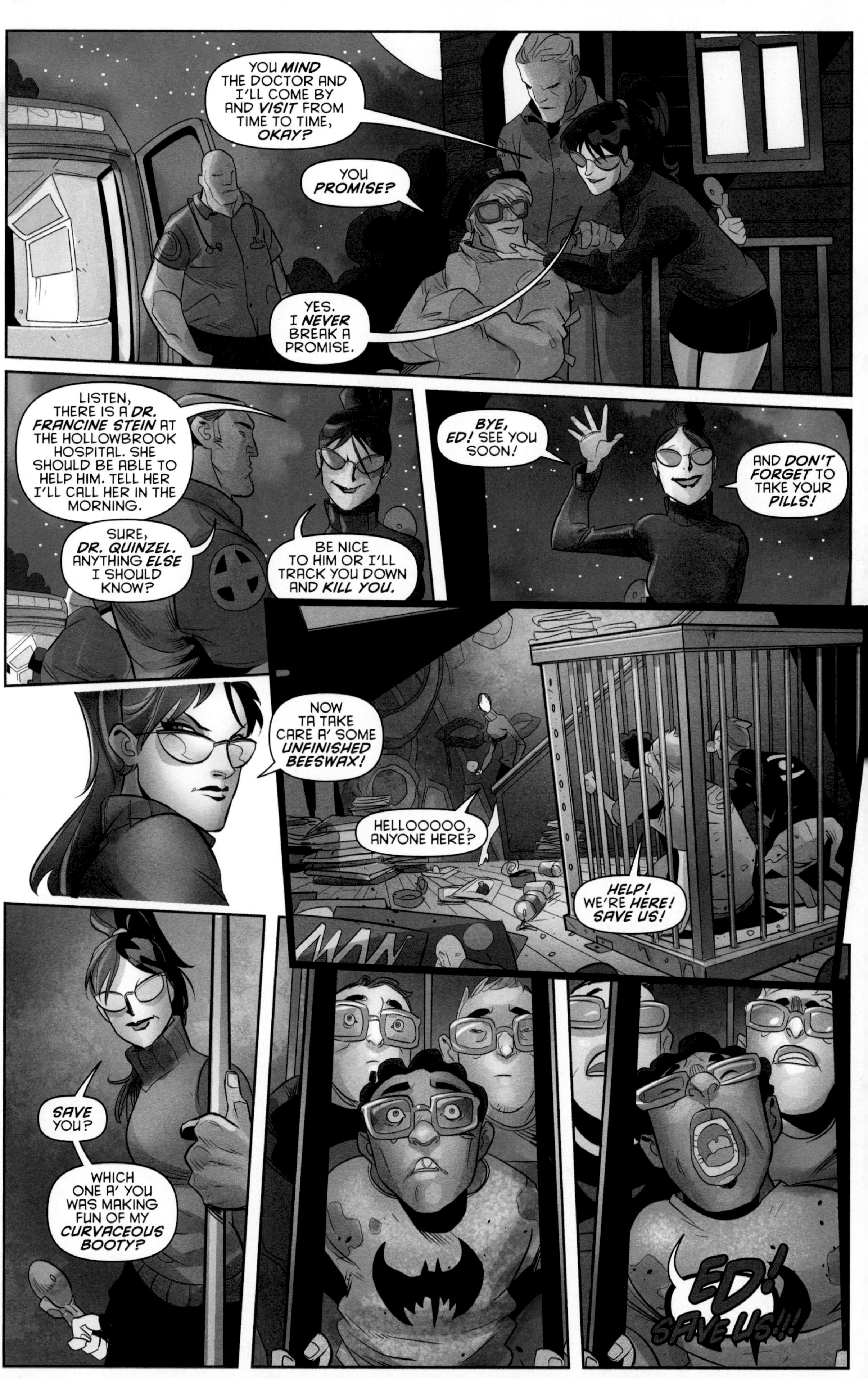

YOU MIND THE DOCTOR AND I'LL COME BY AND VISIT FROM TIME TO TIME, OKAY?
YOU PROMISE?
YES. I NEVER BREAK A PROMISE.
LISTEN, THERE IS A DR. FRANCINE STEIN AT THE HOLLOWBROOK HOSPITAL. SHE SHOULD BE ABLE TO HELP HIM. TELL HER I'LL CALL HER IN THE MORNING.
SURE, DR. QUINZEL. ANYTHING ELSE I SHOULD KNOW?
BE NICE TO HIM OR I'LL TRACK YOU DOWN AND KILL YOU.
BYE, ED! SEE YOU SOON!
AND DON'T FORGET TO TAKE YOUR PILLS!
NOW TA TAKE CARE A' SOME UNFINISHED BEESWAX!
HELLOOOOO, ANYONE HERE?
HELP! WE'RE HERE! SAVE US!
SAVE YOU?
WHICH ONE A' YOU WAS MAKING FUN OF MY CURVACEOUS BOOTY?
ED! SAVE US!!!

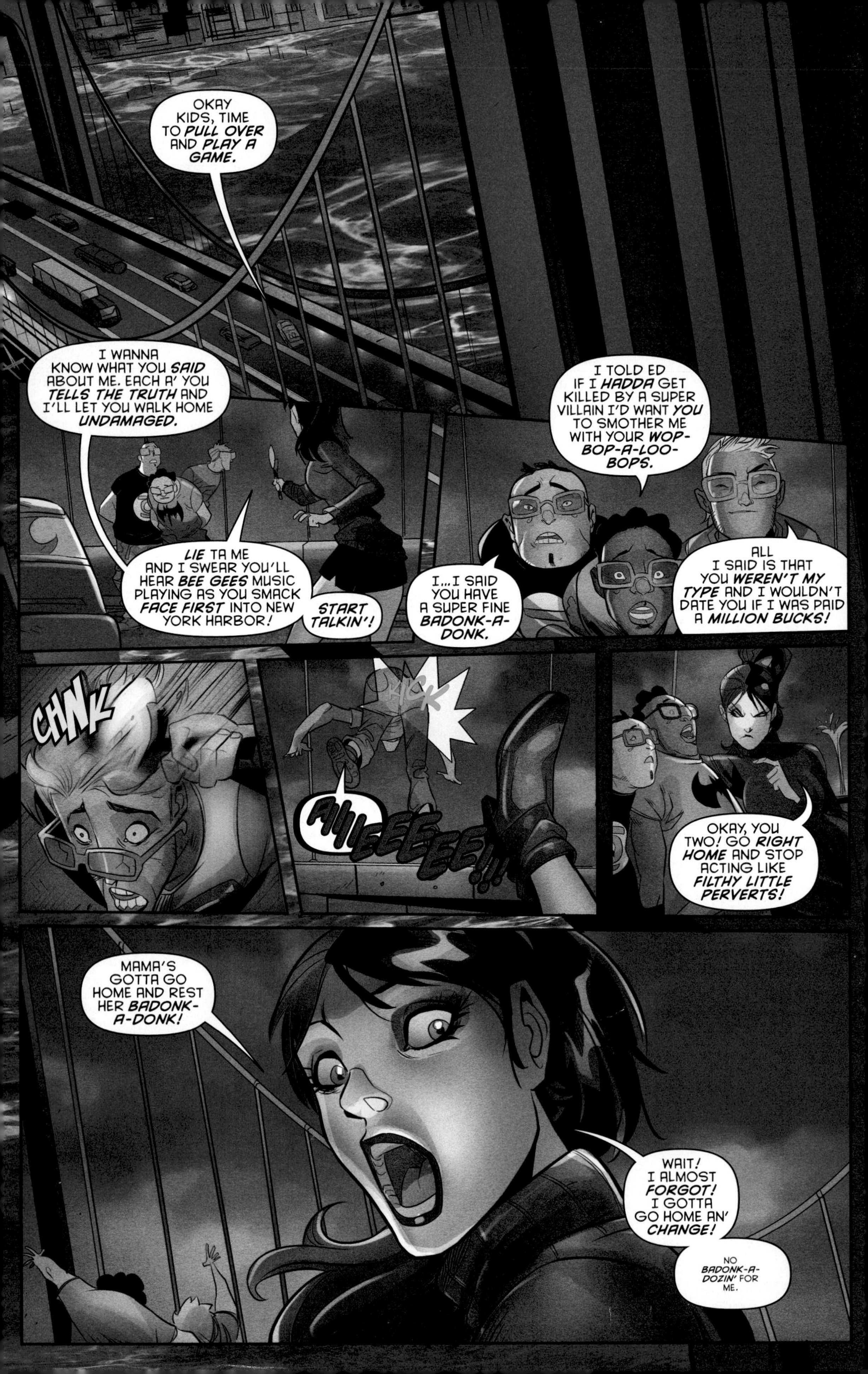

OKAY KIDS, TIME TO PULL OVER AND PLAY A GAME.
I WANNA KNOW WHAT YOU SAID ABOUT ME. EACH A' YOU TELLS THE TRUTH AND I'LL LET YOU WALK HOME UNDAMAGED.
LIE TA ME AND I SWEAR YOU'LL HEAR BEE GEES MUSIC PLAYING AS YOU SMACK FACE FIRST INTO NEW YORK HARBOR!
START TALKIN'!
I...I SAID YOU HAVE A SUPER FINE BADONK-A-DONK.
I TOLD ED IF I HADDA GET KILLED BY A SUPER VILLAIN I'D WANT YOU TO SMOTHER ME WITH YOUR WOP-BOP-A-LOO-BOPS.
ALL I SAID IS THAT YOU WEREN'T MY TYPE AND I WOULDN'T DATE YOU IF I WAS PAID A MILLION BUCKS!
CHNK
KICK
AIIIEEEEEE!!!
OKAY, YOU TWO! GO RIGHT HOME AND STOP ACTING LIKE FILTHY LITTLE PERVERTS!
MAMA'S GOTTA GO HOME AND REST HER BADONK-A-DONK!
WAIT! I ALMOST FORGOT! I GOTTA GO HOME AN' CHANGE!
NO BADONK-A-DOZIN' FOR ME.

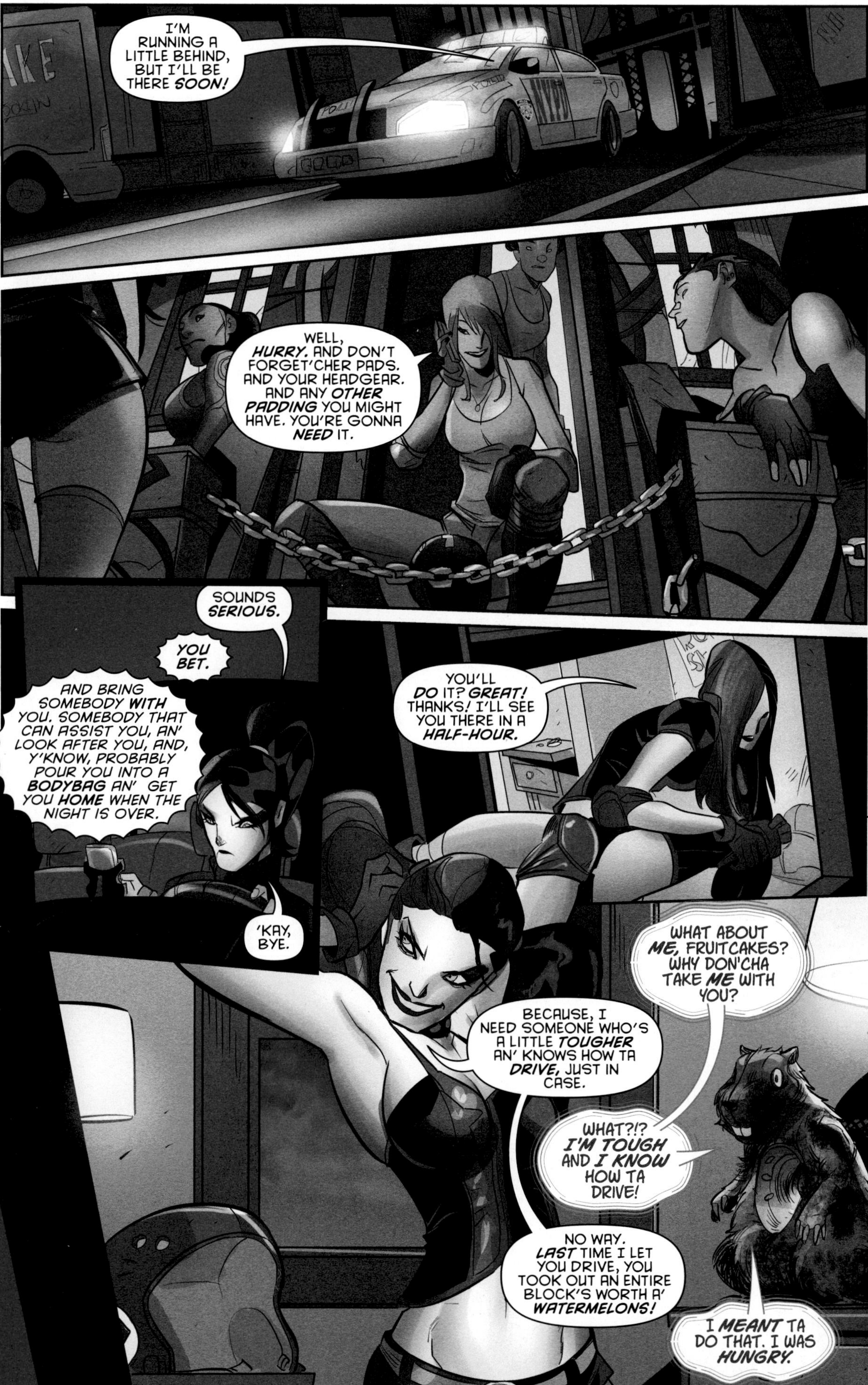
I'M RUNNING A LITTLE BEHIND, BUT I'LL BE THERE SOON!
WELL, HURRY. AND DON'T FORGET'CHER PADS. AND YOUR HEADGEAR. AND ANY OTHER PADDING YOU MIGHT HAVE. YOU'RE GONNA NEED IT.
SOUNDS SERIOUS.
YOU BET.
AND BRING SOMEBODY WITH YOU. SOMEBODY THAT CAN ASSIST YOU, AN' LOOK AFTER YOU, AND, Y'KNOW, PROBABLY POUR YOU INTO A BODYBAG AN' GET YOU HOME WHEN THE NIGHT IS OVER.
YOU'LL DO IT? GREAT! THANKS! I'LL SEE YOU THERE IN A HALF-HOUR.
'KAY, BYE.
WHAT ABOUT ME, FRUITCAKES? WHY DON'CHA TAKE ME WITH YOU?
BECAUSE, I NEED SOMEONE WHO'S A LITTLE TOUGHER AN' KNOWS HOW TA DRIVE, JUST IN CASE.
WHAT?!? I'M TOUGH AND I KNOW HOW TA DRIVE!
NO WAY. LAST TIME I LET YOU DRIVE, YOU TOOK OUT AN ENTIRE BLOCK'S WORTH A' WATERMELONS!
I MEANT TA DO THAT. I WAS HUNGRY.

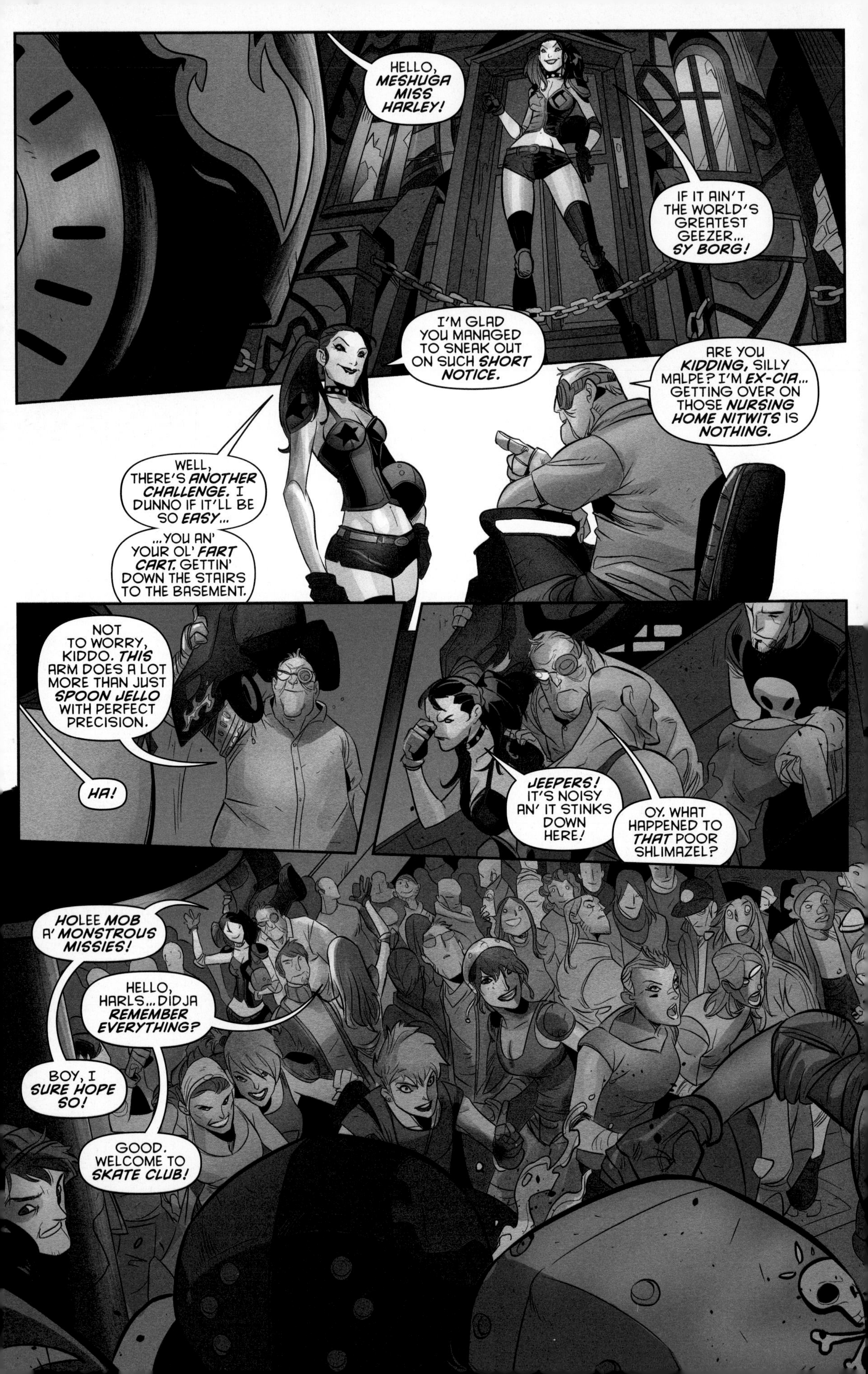
HELLO, MESHUGA MISS HARLEY!
IF IT AIN'T THE WORLD'S GREATEST GEEZER... SY BORG!
I'M GLAD YOU MANAGED TO SNEAK OUT ON SUCH SHORT NOTICE.
ARE YOU KIDDING, SILLY MALPE? I'M EX-CIA... GETTING OVER ON THOSE NURSING HOME NITWITS IS NOTHING.
WELL, THERE'S ANOTHER CHALLENGE. I DUNNO IF IT'LL BE SO EASY...
...YOU AN' YOUR OL' FART CART. GETTIN' DOWN THE STAIRS TO THE BASEMENT.
NOT TO WORRY, KIDDO. THIS ARM DOES A LOT MORE THAN JUST SPOON JELLO WITH PERFECT PRECISION.
HA!
JEEPERS! IT'S NOISY AN' IT STINKS DOWN HERE!
OY. WHAT HAPPENED TO THAT POOR SHLIMAZEL?
HOLEE MOB A' MONSTROUS MISSIES!
HELLO, HARLS... DIDJA REMEMBER EVERYTHING?
BOY, I SURE HOPE SO!
GOOD. WELCOME TO SKATE CLUB!

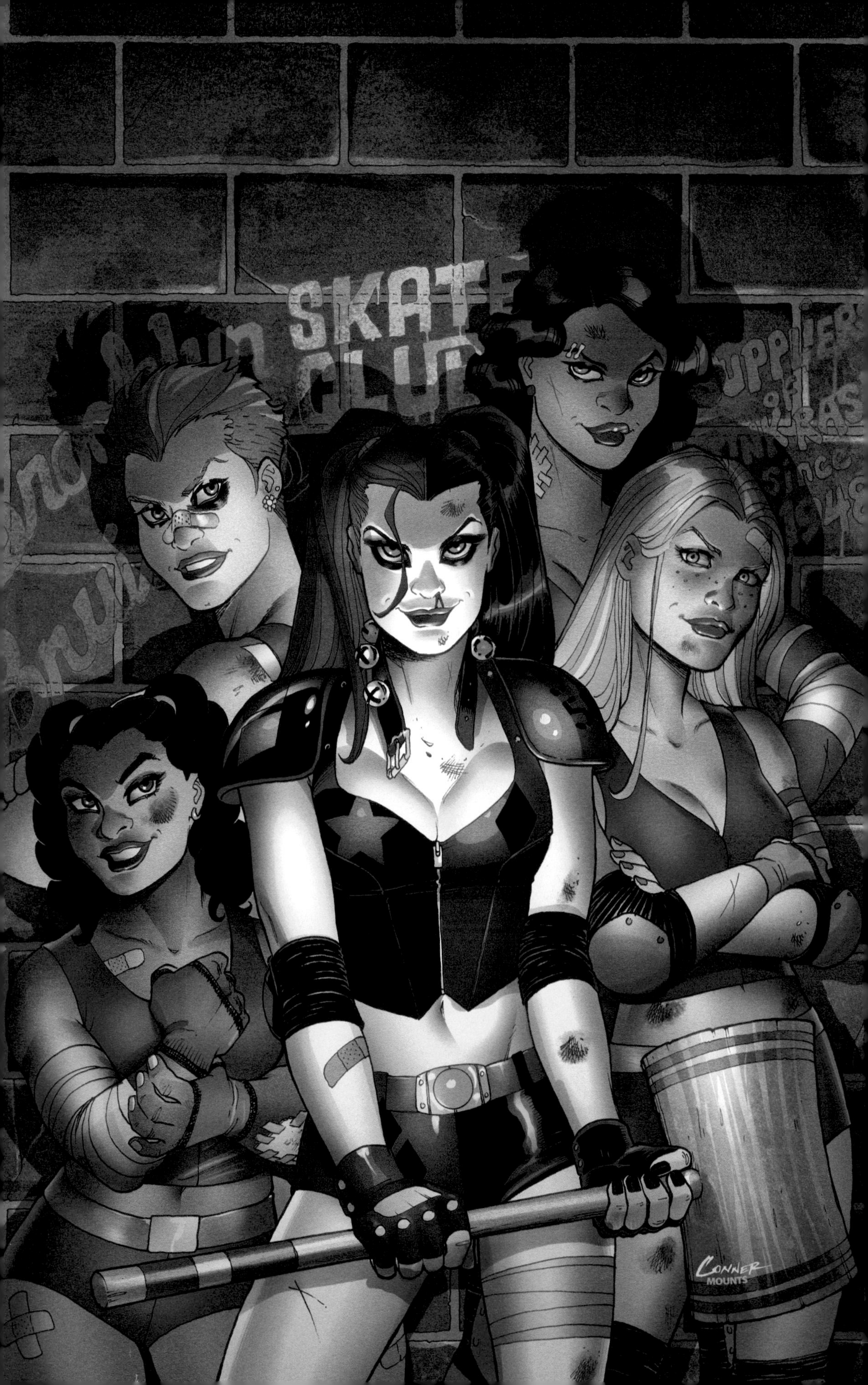
SKATE
CONNER
MOUNTS

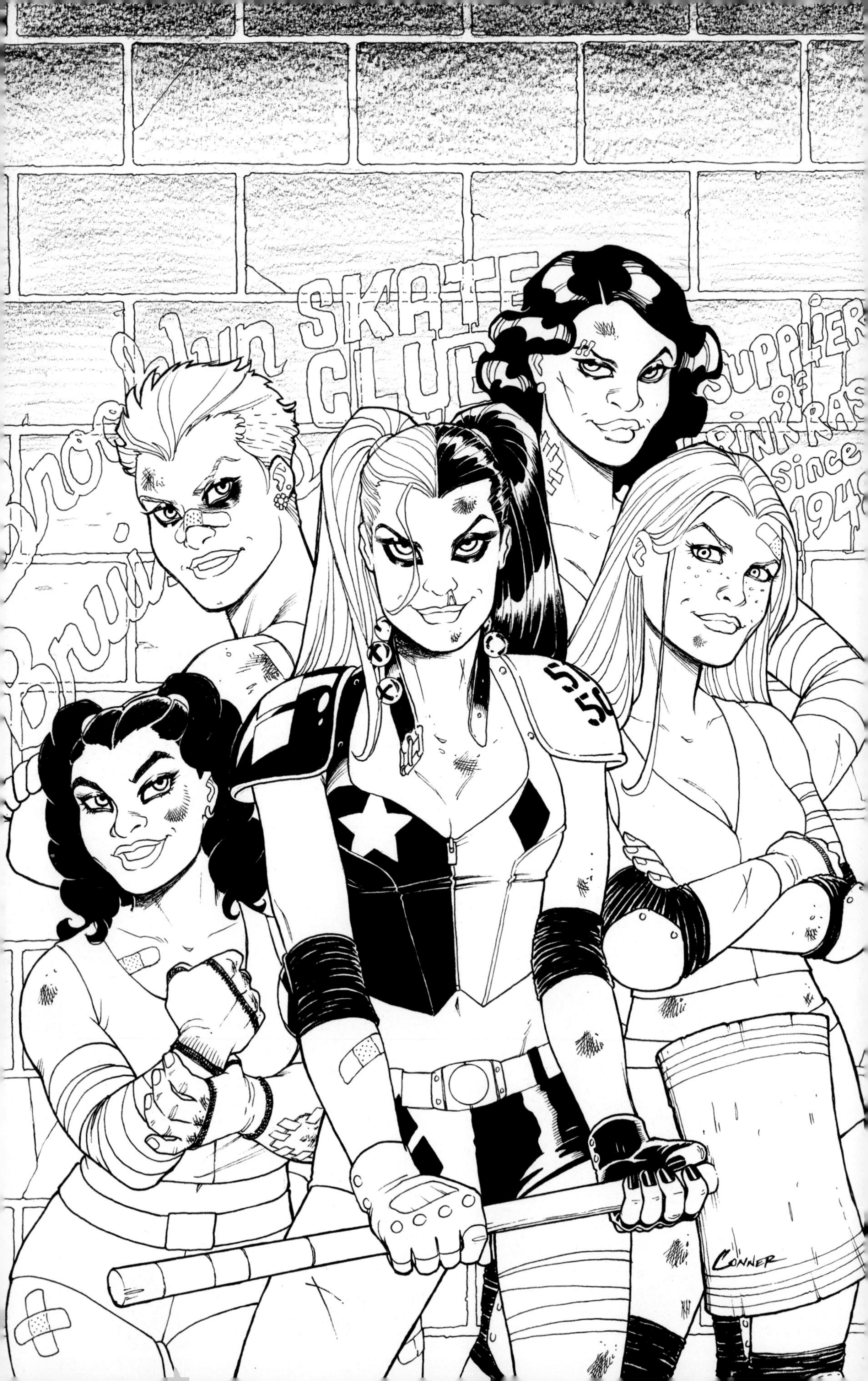
SKATE
since
CONNER

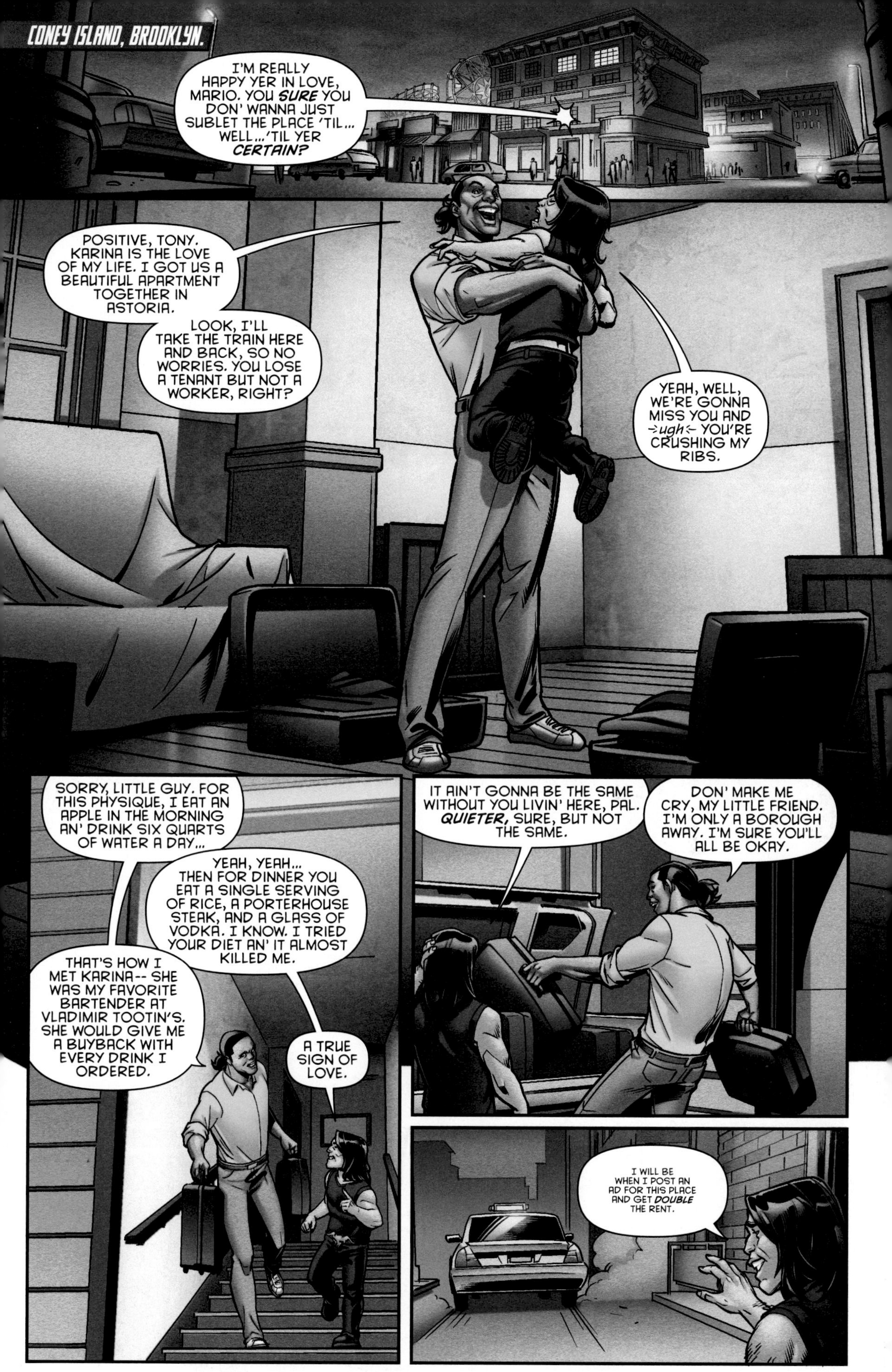
CONEY ISLAND, BROOKLYN.
I'M REALLY HAPPY YER IN LOVE, MARIO. YOU *SURE* YOU DON' WANNA JUST SUBLET THE PLACE 'TIL... WELL...'TIL YER *CERTAIN?*
POSITIVE, TONY. KARINA IS THE LOVE OF MY LIFE. I GOT US A BEAUTIFUL APARTMENT TOGETHER IN ASTORIA.
LOOK, I'LL TAKE THE TRAIN HERE AND BACK, SO NO WORRIES. YOU LOSE A TENANT BUT NOT A WORKER, RIGHT?
YEAH, WELL, WE'RE GONNA MISS YOU AND *ugh* YOU'RE CRUSHING MY RIBS.
SORRY, LITTLE GUY. FOR THIS PHYSIQUE, I EAT AN APPLE IN THE MORNING AN' DRINK SIX QUARTS OF WATER A DAY...
YEAH, YEAH... THEN FOR DINNER YOU EAT A SINGLE SERVING OF RICE, A PORTERHOUSE STEAK, AND A GLASS OF VODKA. I KNOW. I TRIED YOUR DIET AN' IT ALMOST KILLED ME.
THAT'S HOW I MET KARINA-- SHE WAS MY FAVORITE BARTENDER AT VLADIMIR TOOTIN'S. SHE WOULD GIVE ME A BUYBACK WITH EVERY DRINK I ORDERED.
A TRUE SIGN OF LOVE.
IT AIN'T GONNA BE THE SAME WITHOUT YOU LIVIN' HERE, PAL. *QUIETER,* SURE, BUT NOT THE SAME.
DON' MAKE ME CRY, MY LITTLE FRIEND. I'M ONLY A BOROUGH AWAY. I'M SURE YOU'LL ALL BE OKAY.
I WILL BE WHEN I POST AN AD FOR THIS PLACE AND GET *DOUBLE* THE RENT.

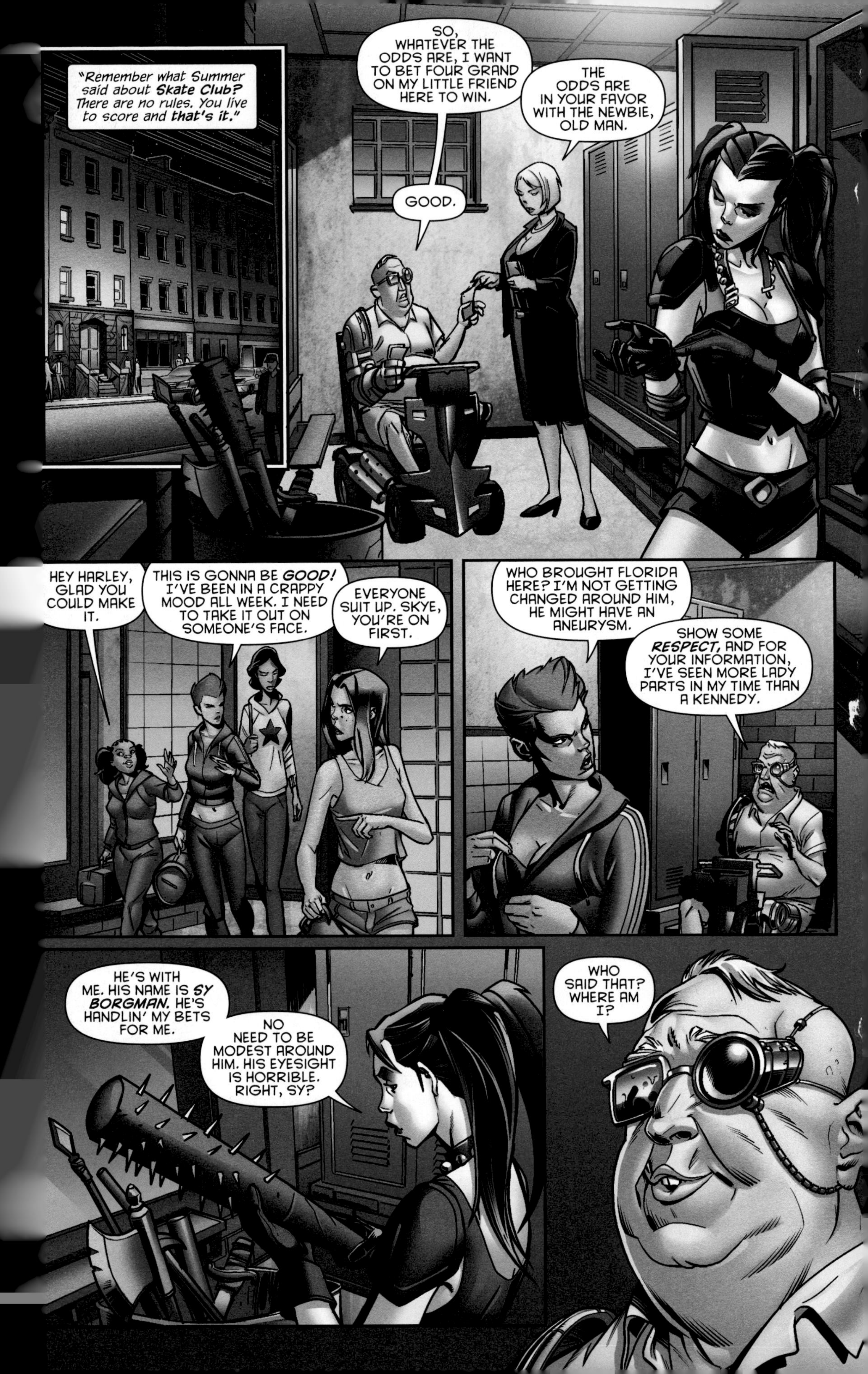
"Remember what Summer said about Skate Club? There are no rules. You live to score and that's it."
SO, WHATEVER THE ODDS ARE, I WANT TO BET FOUR GRAND ON MY LITTLE FRIEND HERE TO WIN.
THE ODDS ARE IN YOUR FAVOR WITH THE NEWBIE, OLD MAN.
GOOD.
HEY HARLEY, GLAD YOU COULD MAKE IT.
THIS IS GONNA BE GOOD! I'VE BEEN IN A CRAPPY MOOD ALL WEEK. I NEED TO TAKE IT OUT ON SOMEONE'S FACE.
EVERYONE SUIT UP. SKYE, YOU'RE ON FIRST.
WHO BROUGHT FLORIDA HERE? I'M NOT GETTING CHANGED AROUND HIM, HE MIGHT HAVE AN ANEURYSM.
SHOW SOME RESPECT, AND FOR YOUR INFORMATION, I'VE SEEN MORE LADY PARTS IN MY TIME THAN A KENNEDY.
HE'S WITH ME. HIS NAME IS SY BORGMAN. HE'S HANDLIN' MY BETS FOR ME.
NO NEED TO BE MODEST AROUND HIM. HIS EYESIGHT IS HORRIBLE. RIGHT, SY?
WHO SAID THAT? WHERE AM I?

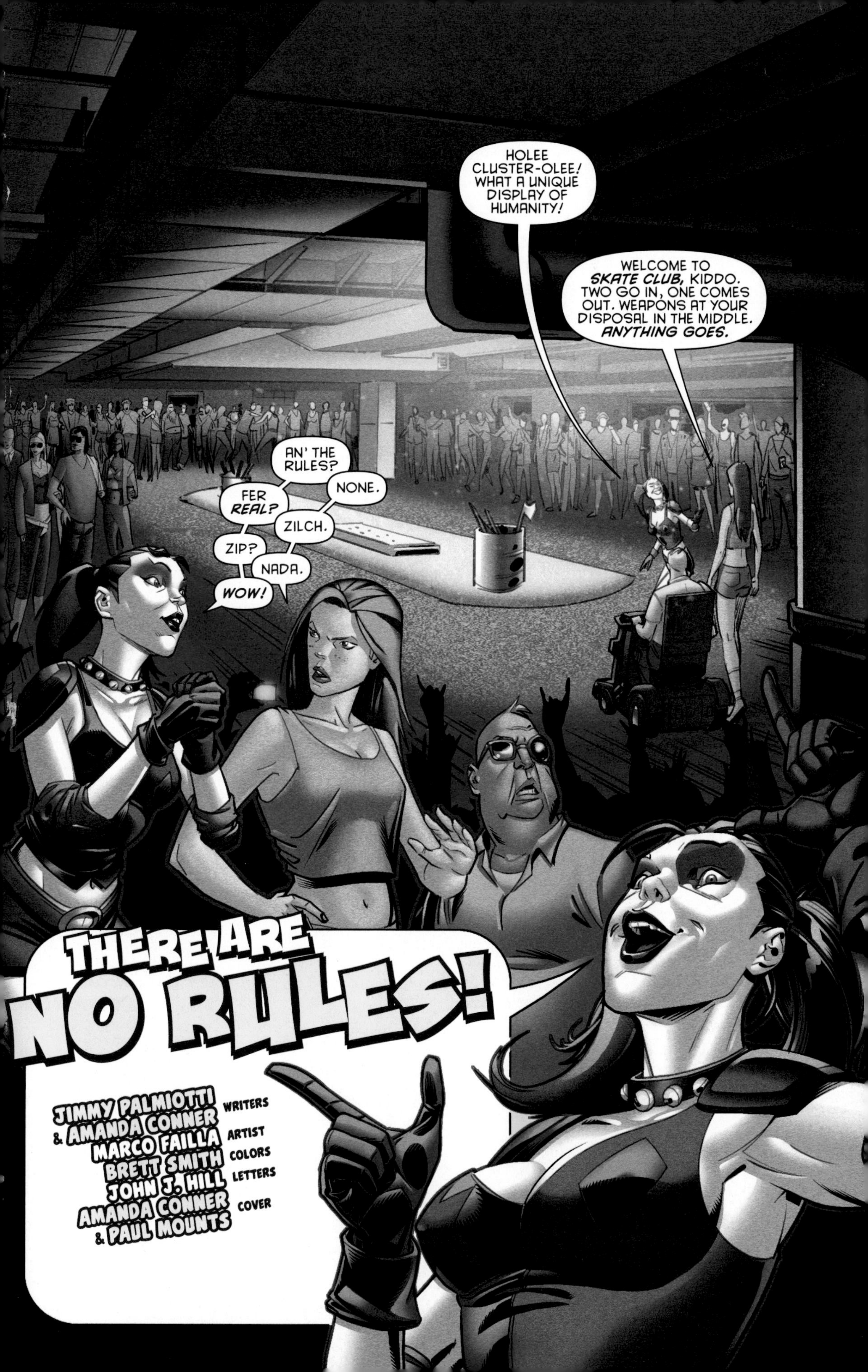

HOLEE CLUSTER-OLEE! WHAT A UNIQUE DISPLAY OF HUMANITY!
WELCOME TO SKATE CLUB, KIDDO. TWO GO IN, ONE COMES OUT. WEAPONS AT YOUR DISPOSAL IN THE MIDDLE. ANYTHING GOES.
AN' THE RULES?
NONE.
FER REAL?
ZILCH.
ZIP?
NADA.
WOW!
THERE ARE NO RULES!
JIMMY PALMIOTTI & AMANDA CONNER WRITERS
MARCO FAILLA ARTIST
BRETT SMITH COLORS
JOHN J. HILL LETTERS
AMANDA CONNER & PAUL MOUNTS COVER

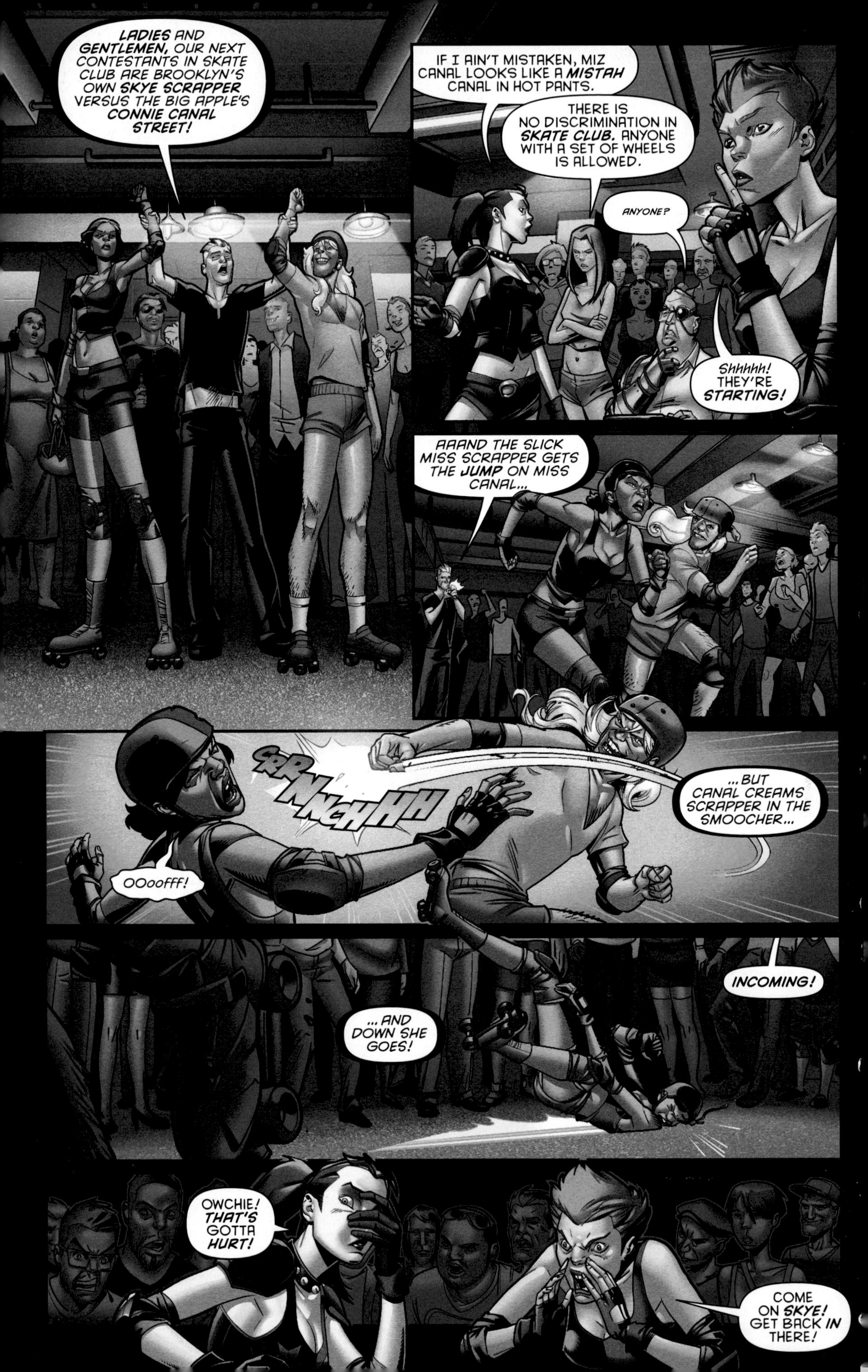
LADIES AND GENTLEMEN, OUR NEXT CONTESTANTS IN SKATE CLUB ARE BROOKLYN'S OWN SKYE SCRAPPER VERSUS THE BIG APPLE'S CONNIE CANAL STREET!
IF I AIN'T MISTAKEN, MIZ CANAL LOOKS LIKE A MISTAH CANAL IN HOT PANTS.
THERE IS NO DISCRIMINATION IN SKATE CLUB. ANYONE WITH A SET OF WHEELS IS ALLOWED.
ANYONE?
Shhhhh! THEY'RE STARTING!
AAAND THE SLICK MISS SCRAPPER GETS THE JUMP ON MISS CANAL...
CRRNNCHHHH
...BUT CANAL CREAMS SCRAPPER IN THE SMOOCHER...
OOoofff!
INCOMING!
...AND DOWN SHE GOES!
OWCHIE! THAT'S GOTTA HURT!
COME ON SKYE! GET BACK IN THERE!

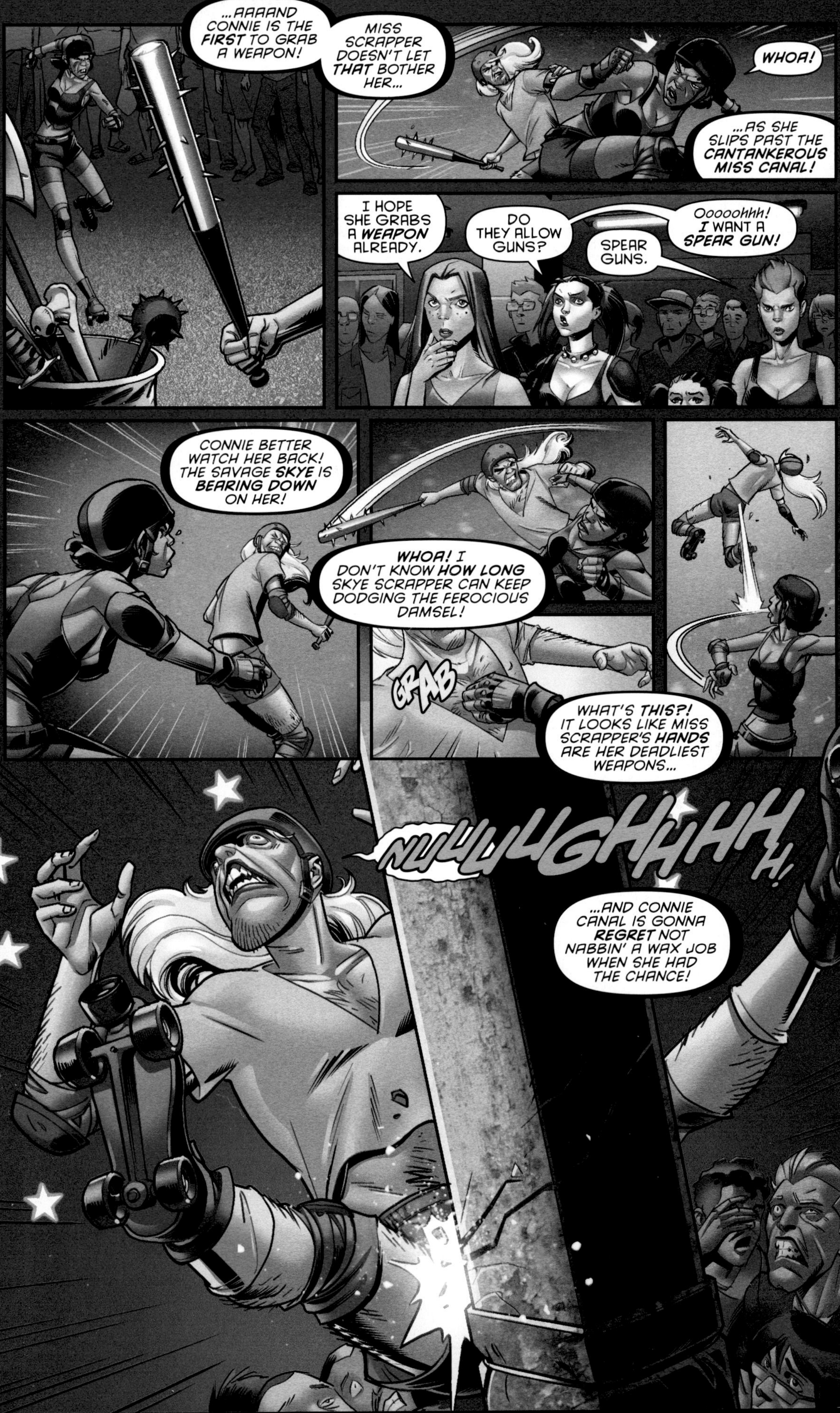
...AAAAND CONNIE IS THE FIRST TO GRAB A WEAPON!
MISS SCRAPPER DOESN'T LET THAT BOTHER HER...
WHOA!
...AS SHE SLIPS PAST THE CANTANKEROUS MISS CANAL!
I HOPE SHE GRABS A WEAPON ALREADY.
DO THEY ALLOW GUNS?
SPEAR GUNS.
Ooooohhh! I WANT A SPEAR GUN!
CONNIE BETTER WATCH HER BACK! THE SAVAGE SKYE IS BEARING DOWN ON HER!
WHOA! I DON'T KNOW HOW LONG SKYE SCRAPPER CAN KEEP DODGING THE FEROCIOUS DAMSEL!
GRAB
WHAT'S THIS?! IT LOOKS LIKE MISS SCRAPPER'S HANDS ARE HER DEADLIEST WEAPONS...
NUUUUGHHHHH!
...AND CONNIE CANAL IS GONNA REGRET NOT NABBIN' A WAX JOB WHEN SHE HAD THE CHANCE!

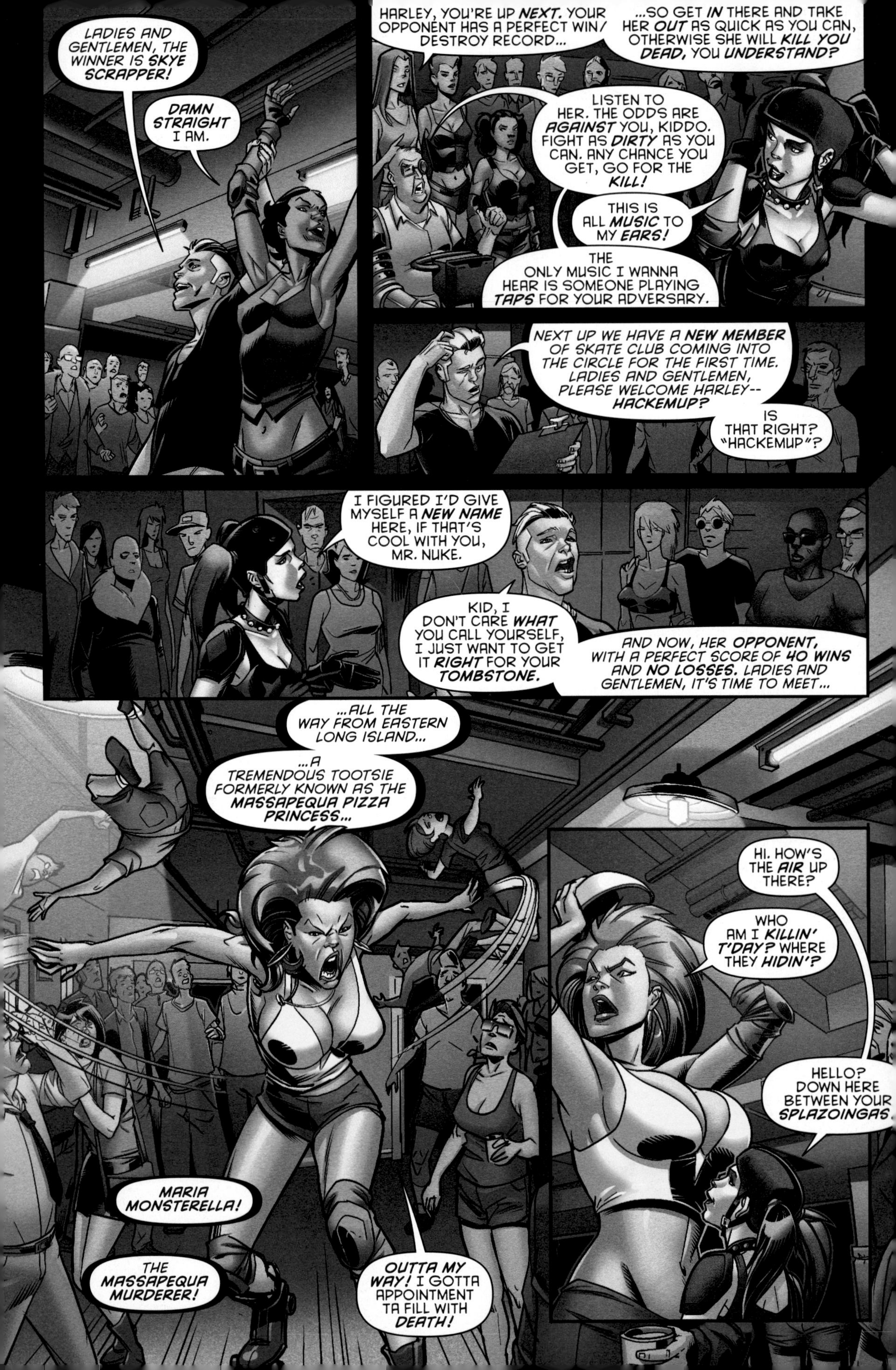

LADIES AND GENTLEMEN, THE WINNER IS SKYE SCRAPPER!
DAMN STRAIGHT I AM.
HARLEY, YOU'RE UP NEXT. YOUR OPPONENT HAS A PERFECT WIN/ DESTROY RECORD...
...SO GET IN THERE AND TAKE HER OUT AS QUICK AS YOU CAN, OTHERWISE SHE WILL KILL YOU DEAD, YOU UNDERSTAND?
LISTEN TO HER. THE ODDS ARE AGAINST YOU, KIDDO. FIGHT AS DIRTY AS YOU CAN. ANY CHANCE YOU GET, GO FOR THE KILL!
THIS IS ALL MUSIC TO MY EARS!
THE ONLY MUSIC I WANNA HEAR IS SOMEONE PLAYING TAPS FOR YOUR ADVERSARY.
NEXT UP WE HAVE A NEW MEMBER OF SKATE CLUB COMING INTO THE CIRCLE FOR THE FIRST TIME. LADIES AND GENTLEMEN, PLEASE WELCOME HARLEY--HACKEMUP?
IS THAT RIGHT? "HACKEMUP"?
I FIGURED I'D GIVE MYSELF A NEW NAME HERE, IF THAT'S COOL WITH YOU, MR. NUKE.
KID, I DON'T CARE WHAT YOU CALL YOURSELF, I JUST WANT TO GET IT RIGHT FOR YOUR TOMBSTONE.
AND NOW, HER OPPONENT, WITH A PERFECT SCORE OF 40 WINS AND NO LOSSES. LADIES AND GENTLEMEN, IT'S TIME TO MEET...
...ALL THE WAY FROM EASTERN LONG ISLAND...
...A TREMENDOUS TOOTSIE FORMERLY KNOWN AS THE MASSAPEQUA PIZZA PRINCESS...
MARIA MONSTERELLA!
THE MASSAPEQUA MURDERER!
OUTTA MY WAY! I GOTTA APPOINTMENT TA FILL WITH DEATH!
HI. HOW'S THE AIR UP THERE?
WHO AM I KILLIN' T'DAY? WHERE THEY HIDIN'?
HELLO? DOWN HERE BETWEEN YOUR SPLAZOINGAS.

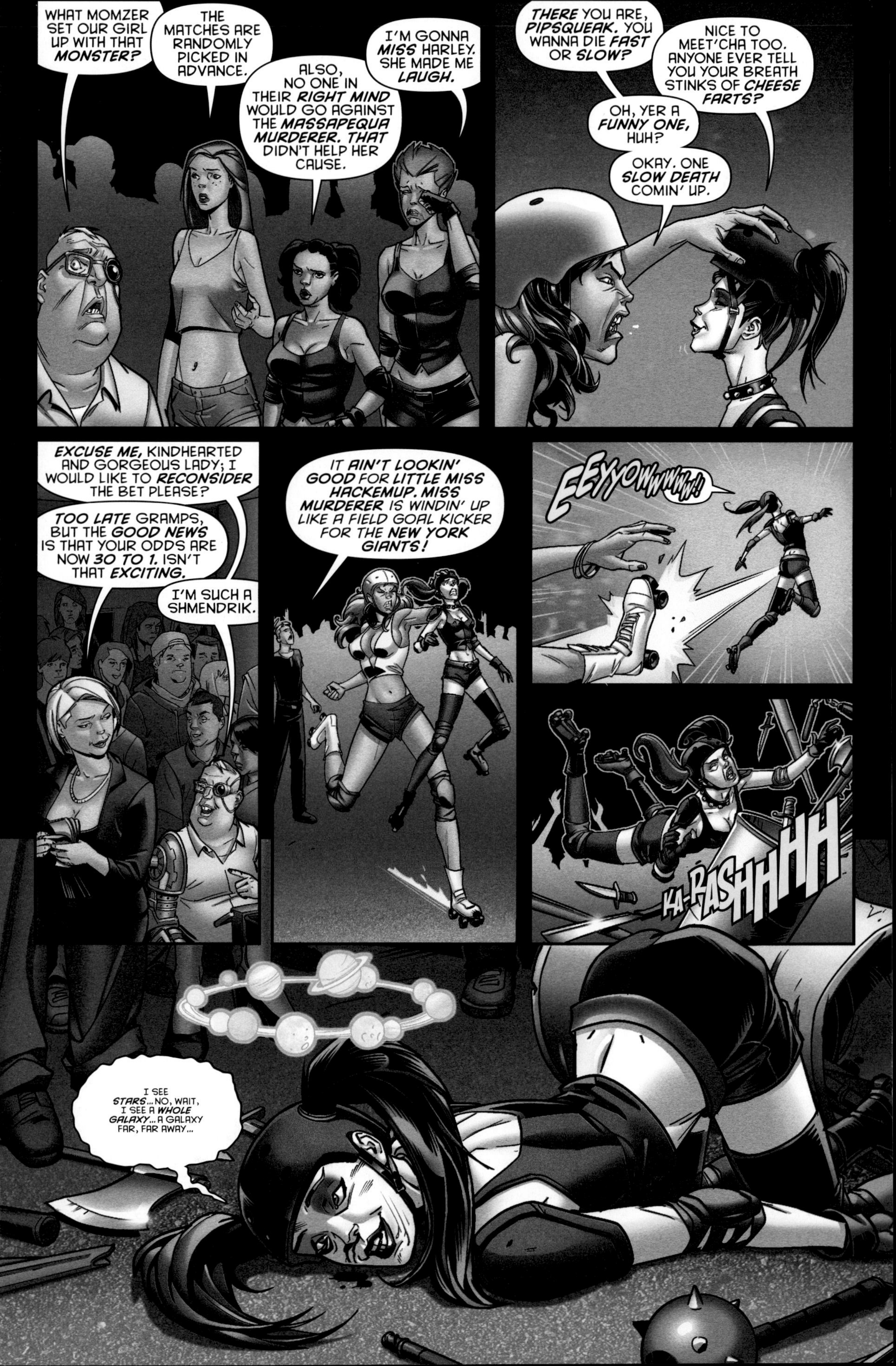
WHAT MOMZER SET OUR GIRL UP WITH THAT MONSTER?
THE MATCHES ARE RANDOMLY PICKED IN ADVANCE.
ALSO, NO ONE IN THEIR RIGHT MIND WOULD GO AGAINST THE MASSAPEQUA MURDERER. THAT DIDN'T HELP HER CAUSE.
I'M GONNA MISS HARLEY. SHE MADE ME LAUGH.
THERE YOU ARE, PIPSQUEAK. YOU WANNA DIE FAST OR SLOW?
NICE TO MEET'CHA TOO. ANYONE EVER TELL YOU YOUR BREATH STINKS OF CHEESE FARTS?
OH, YER A FUNNY ONE, HUH?
OKAY. ONE SLOW DEATH COMIN' UP.
EXCUSE ME, KINDHEARTED AND GORGEOUS LADY; I WOULD LIKE TO RECONSIDER THE BET PLEASE?
TOO LATE GRAMPS, BUT THE GOOD NEWS IS THAT YOUR ODDS ARE NOW 30 TO 1. ISN'T THAT EXCITING.
I'M SUCH A SHMENDRIK.
IT AIN'T LOOKIN' GOOD FOR LITTLE MISS HACKEMUP. MISS MURDERER IS WINDIN' UP LIKE A FIELD GOAL KICKER FOR THE NEW YORK GIANTS!
EEYYOWWWWW!
KA-RASHHHHH
I SEE STARS... NO, WAIT, I SEE A WHOLE GALAXY... A GALAXY FAR, FAR AWAY...

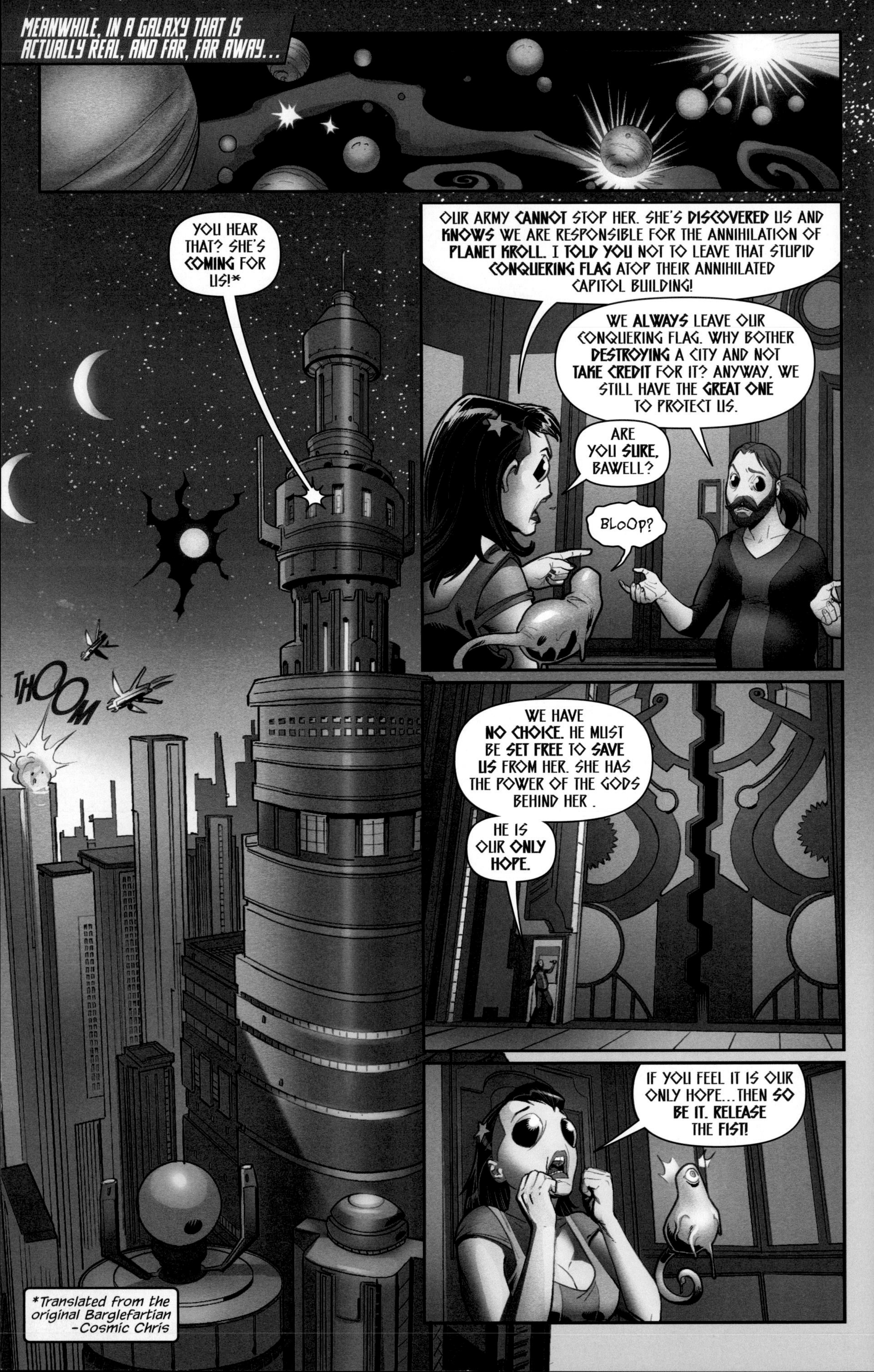
MEANWHILE, IN A GALAXY THAT IS ACTUALLY REAL, AND FAR, FAR AWAY...
YOU HEAR THAT? SHE'S COMING FOR US!*
THOOOM
OUR ARMY CANNOT STOP HER. SHE'S DISCOVERED US AND KNOWS WE ARE RESPONSIBLE FOR THE ANNIHILATION OF PLANET KROLL. I TOLD YOU NOT TO LEAVE THAT STUPID CONQUERING FLAG ATOP THEIR ANNIHILATED CAPITOL BUILDING!
WE ALWAYS LEAVE OUR CONQUERING FLAG. WHY BOTHER DESTROYING A CITY AND NOT TAKE CREDIT FOR IT? ANYWAY, WE STILL HAVE THE GREAT ONE TO PROTECT US.
ARE YOU SURE, BAWELL?
BLOOP?
WE HAVE NO CHOICE. HE MUST BE SET FREE TO SAVE US FROM HER. SHE HAS THE POWER OF THE GODS BEHIND HER .
HE IS OUR ONLY HOPE.
IF YOU FEEL IT IS OUR ONLY HOPE...THEN SO BE IT. RELEASE THE FIST!
*Translated from the original Barglefartian -Cosmic Chris

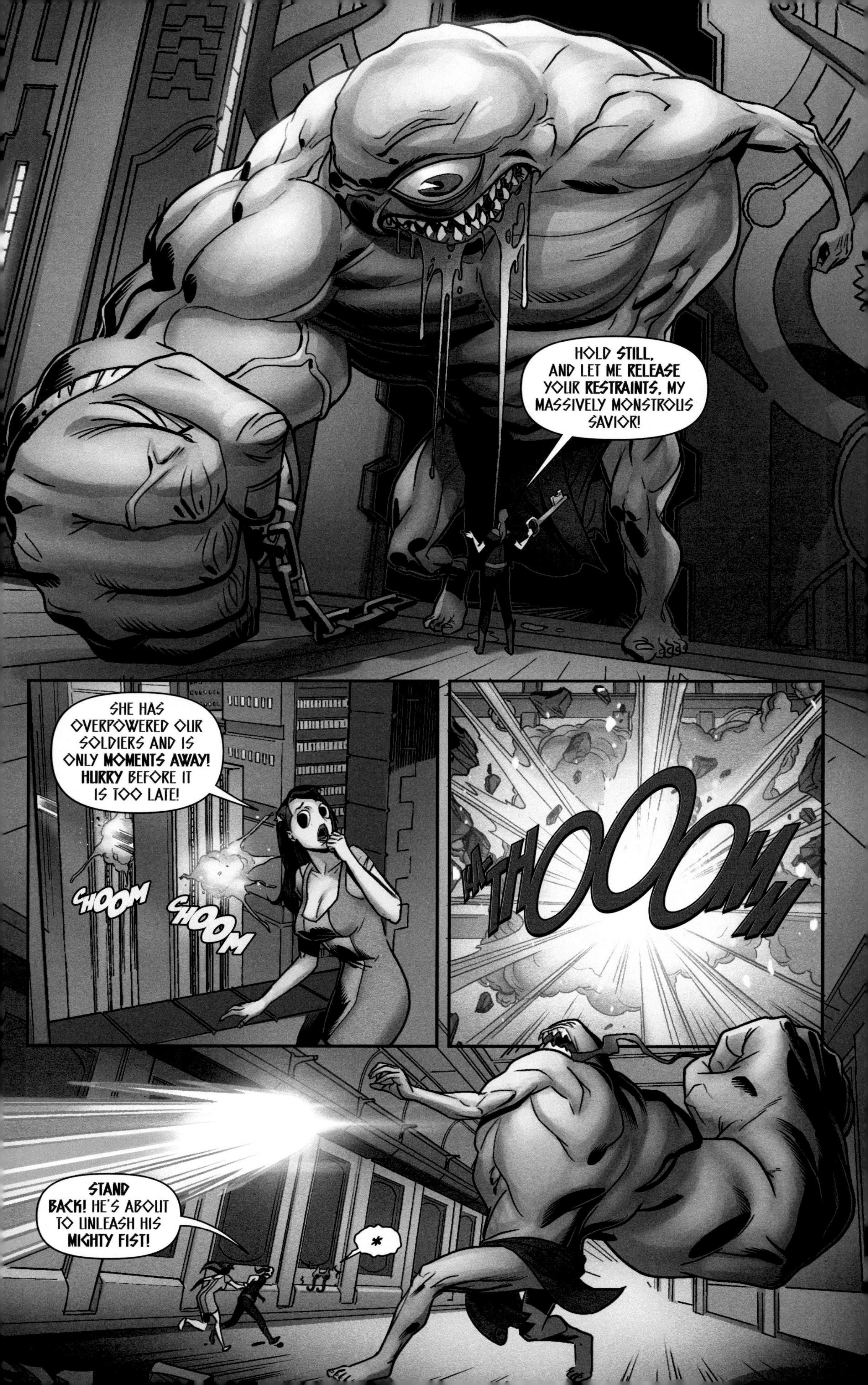
HOLD STILL, AND LET ME RELEASE YOUR RESTRAINTS, MY MASSIVELY MONSTROUS SAVIOR!
SHE HAS OVERPOWERED OUR SOLDIERS AND IS ONLY MOMENTS AWAY! HURRY BEFORE IT IS TOO LATE!
CHOOM
CHOOM
KA-THOOOOMM
STAND BACK! HE'S ABOUT TO UNLEASH HIS MIGHTY FIST!
*

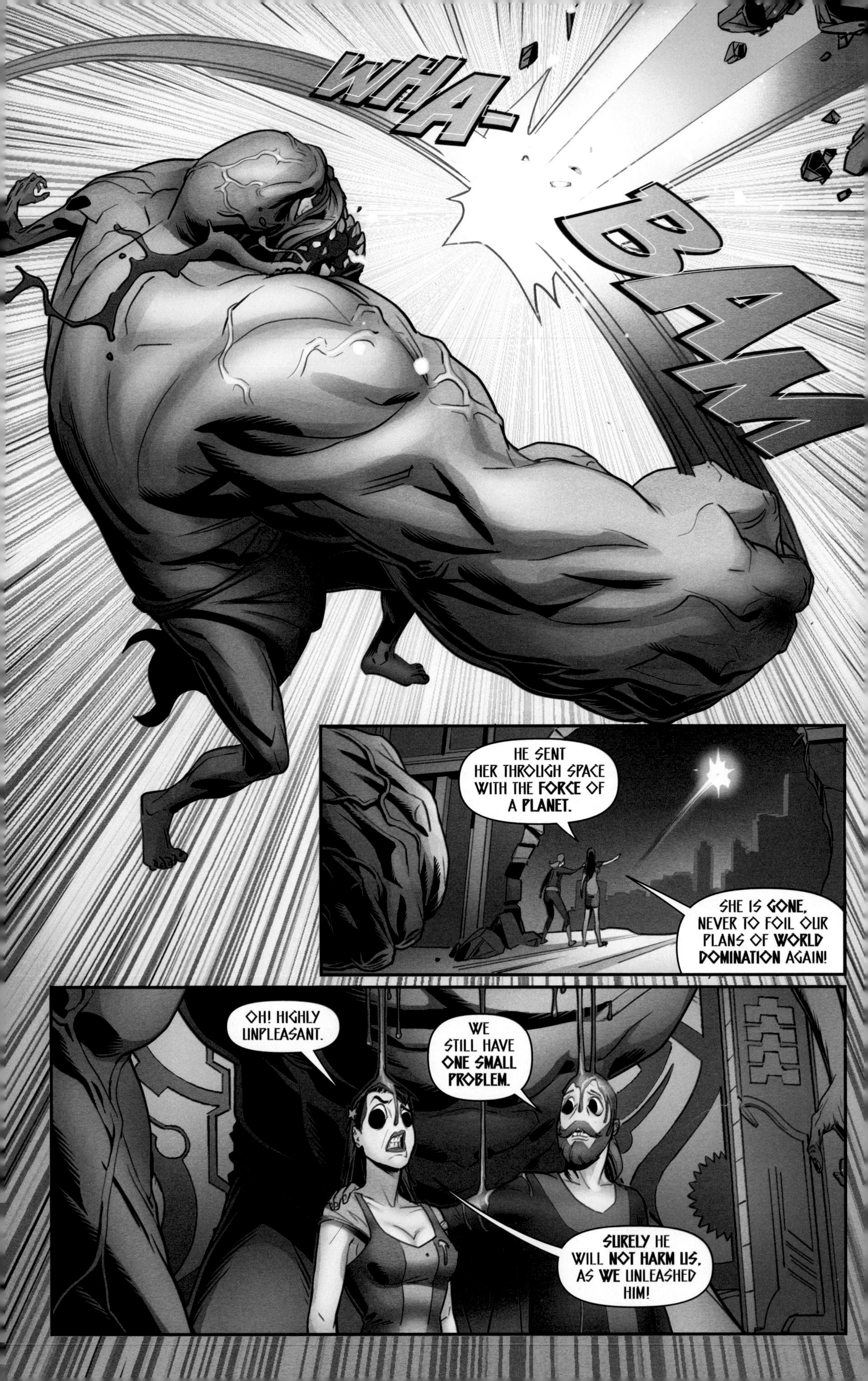
WHA-
BAM
HE SENT HER THROUGH SPACE WITH THE FORCE OF A PLANET.
SHE IS GONE, NEVER TO FOIL OUR PLANS OF WORLD DOMINATION AGAIN!
OH! HIGHLY UNPLEASANT.
WE STILL HAVE ONE SMALL PROBLEM.
SURELY HE WILL NOT HARM US, AS WE UNLEASHED HIM!

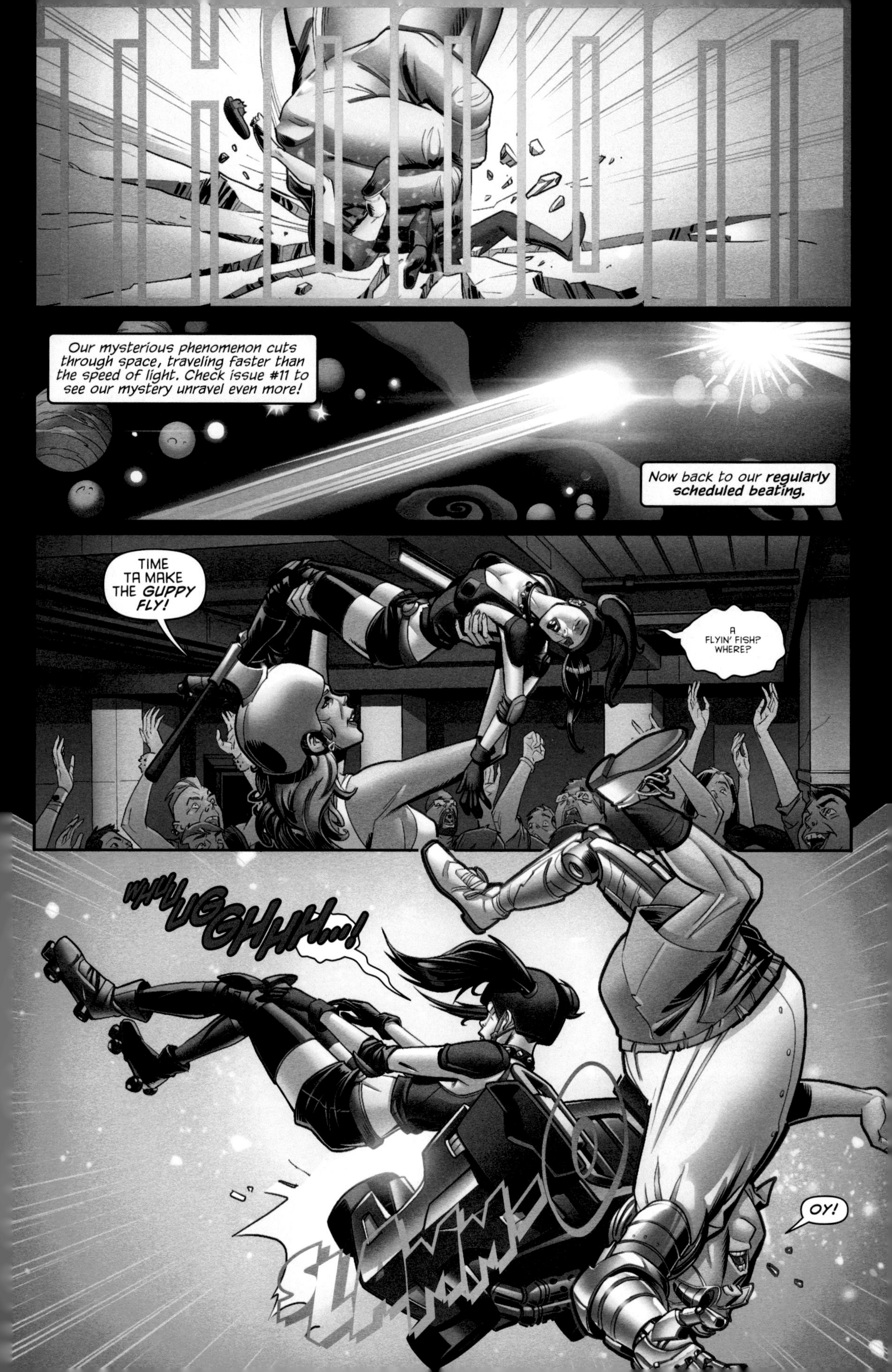
THOOOM
Our mysterious phenomenon cuts through space, traveling faster than the speed of light. Check issue #11 to see our mystery unravel even more!
Now back to our **regularly scheduled beating.**
TIME TA MAKE THE *GUPPY FLY!*
A FLYIN' FISH? WHERE?
WHUUUGHUUH...!
SLAM
OY!

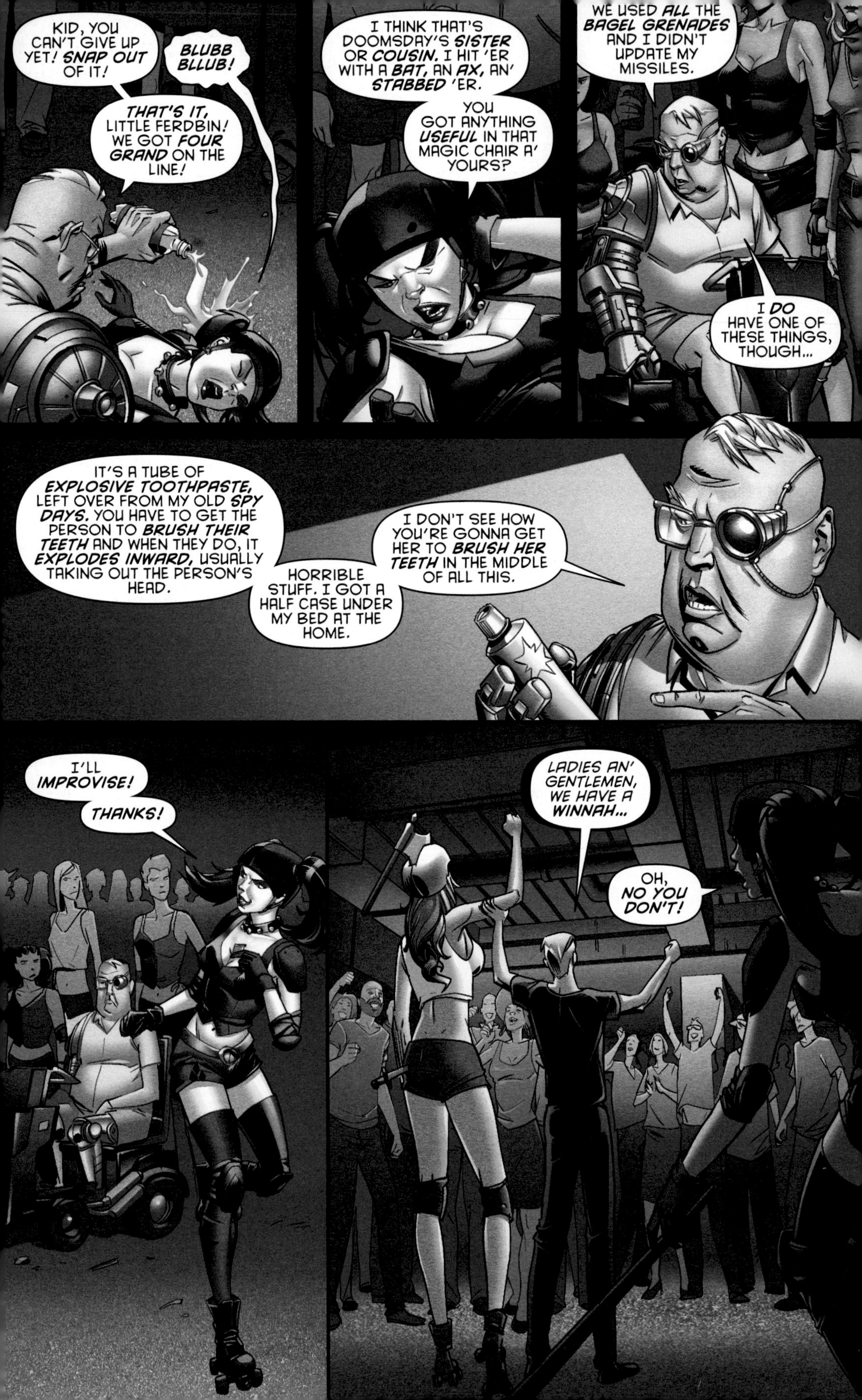
KID, YOU CAN'T GIVE UP YET! SNAP OUT OF IT!
BLUBB BLLUB!
THAT'S IT, LITTLE FERDBIN! WE GOT FOUR GRAND ON THE LINE!
I THINK THAT'S DOOMSDAY'S SISTER OR COUSIN. I HIT 'ER WITH A BAT, AN AX, AN' STABBED 'ER.
YOU GOT ANYTHING USEFUL IN THAT MAGIC CHAIR A' YOURS?
WE USED ALL THE BAGEL GRENADES AND I DIDN'T UPDATE MY MISSILES.
I DO HAVE ONE OF THESE THINGS, THOUGH...
IT'S A TUBE OF EXPLOSIVE TOOTHPASTE, LEFT OVER FROM MY OLD SPY DAYS. YOU HAVE TO GET THE PERSON TO BRUSH THEIR TEETH AND WHEN THEY DO, IT EXPLODES INWARD, USUALLY TAKING OUT THE PERSON'S HEAD.
HORRIBLE STUFF. I GOT A HALF CASE UNDER MY BED AT THE HOME.
I DON'T SEE HOW YOU'RE GONNA GET HER TO BRUSH HER TEETH IN THE MIDDLE OF ALL THIS.
I'LL IMPROVISE!
THANKS!
LADIES AN' GENTLEMEN, WE HAVE A WINNAH...
OH, NO YOU DON'T!

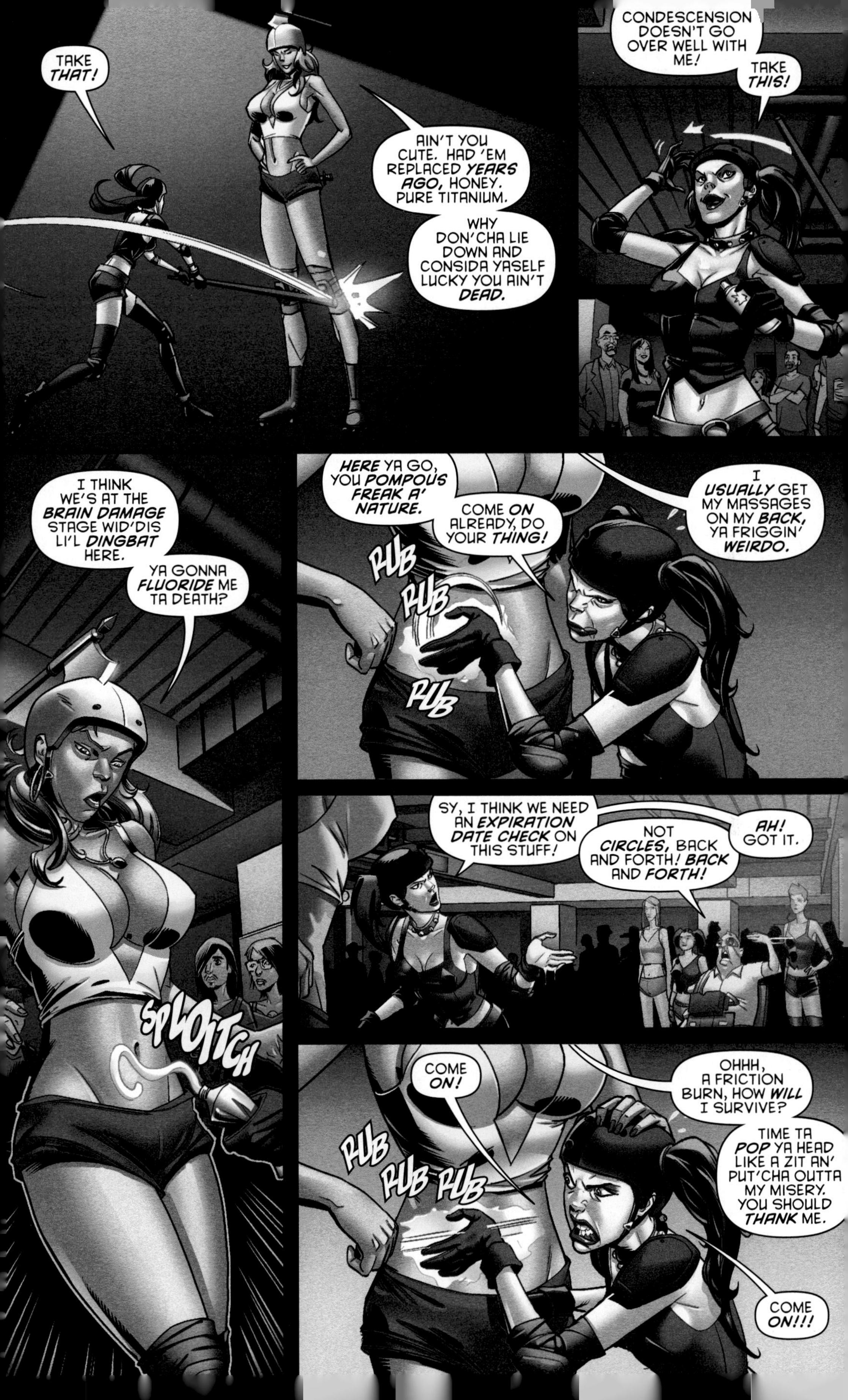
TAKE THAT!
AIN'T YOU CUTE. HAD 'EM REPLACED YEARS AGO, HONEY. PURE TITANIUM.
WHY DON'CHA LIE DOWN AND CONSIDA YASELF LUCKY YOU AIN'T DEAD.
CONDESCENSION DOESN'T GO OVER WELL WITH ME!
TAKE THIS!
I THINK WE'S AT THE BRAIN DAMAGE STAGE WID'DIS LI'L DINGBAT HERE.
YA GONNA FLUORIDE ME TA DEATH?
SPLOITCH
HERE YA GO, YOU POMPOUS FREAK A' NATURE.
COME ON ALREADY, DO YOUR THING!
I USUALLY GET MY MASSAGES ON MY BACK, YA FRIGGIN' WEIRDO.
RUB
RUB
RUB
SY, I THINK WE NEED AN EXPIRATION DATE CHECK ON THIS STUFF!
NOT CIRCLES, BACK AND FORTH! BACK AND FORTH!
AH! GOT IT.
COME ON!
OHHH, A FRICTION BURN, HOW WILL I SURVIVE?
TIME TA POP YA HEAD LIKE A ZIT AN' PUT'CHA OUTTA MY MISERY. YOU SHOULD THANK ME.
RUB
RUB
RUB
COME ON!!!

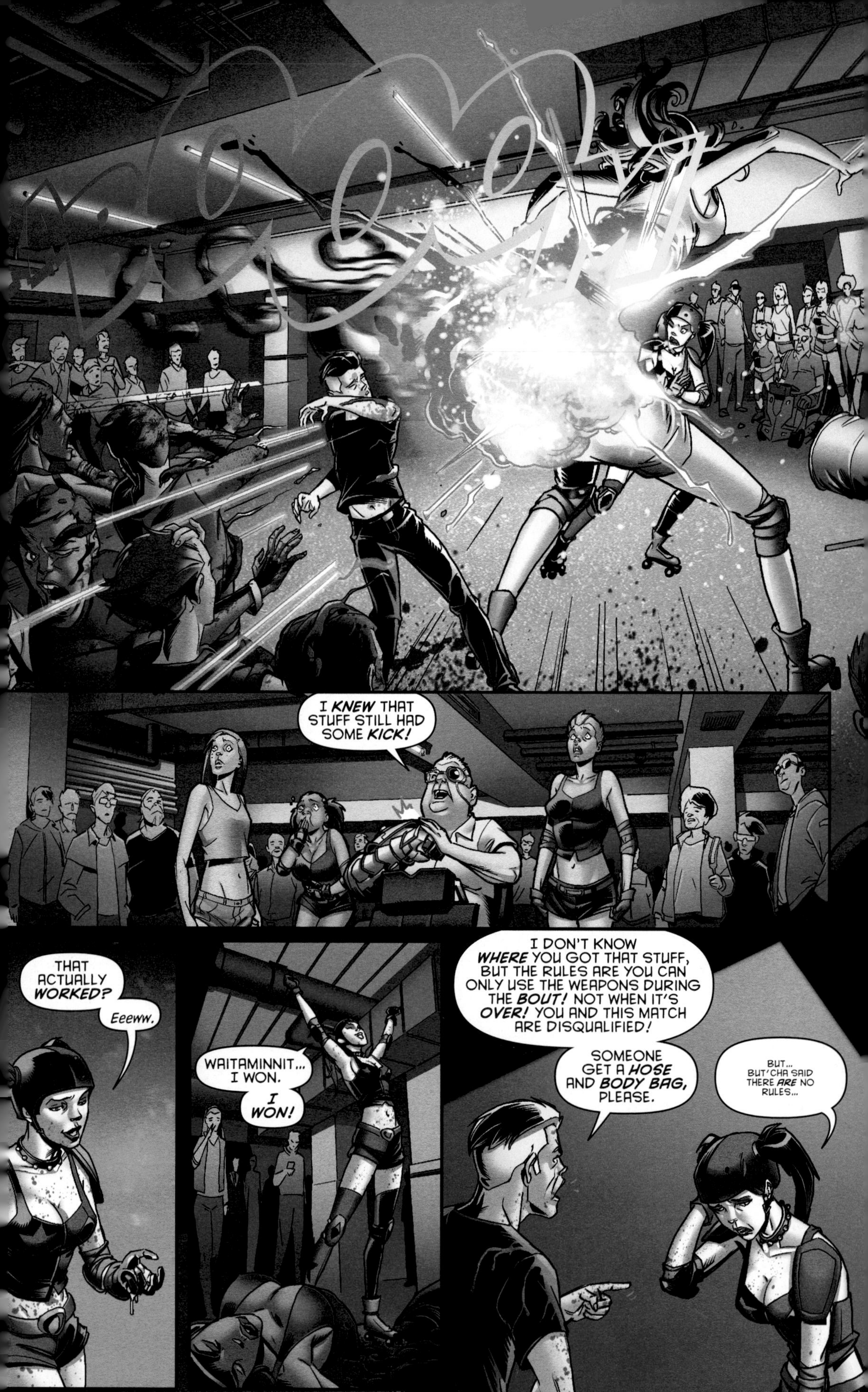
I KNEW THAT STUFF STILL HAD SOME KICK!
THAT ACTUALLY WORKED?
Eeeww.
WAITAMINNIT... I WON.
I WON!
I DON'T KNOW WHERE YOU GOT THAT STUFF, BUT THE RULES ARE YOU CAN ONLY USE THE WEAPONS DURING THE BOUT! NOT WHEN IT'S OVER! YOU AND THIS MATCH ARE DISQUALIFIED!
SOMEONE GET A HOSE AND BODY BAG, PLEASE.
BUT... BUT'CHA SAID THERE ARE NO RULES...

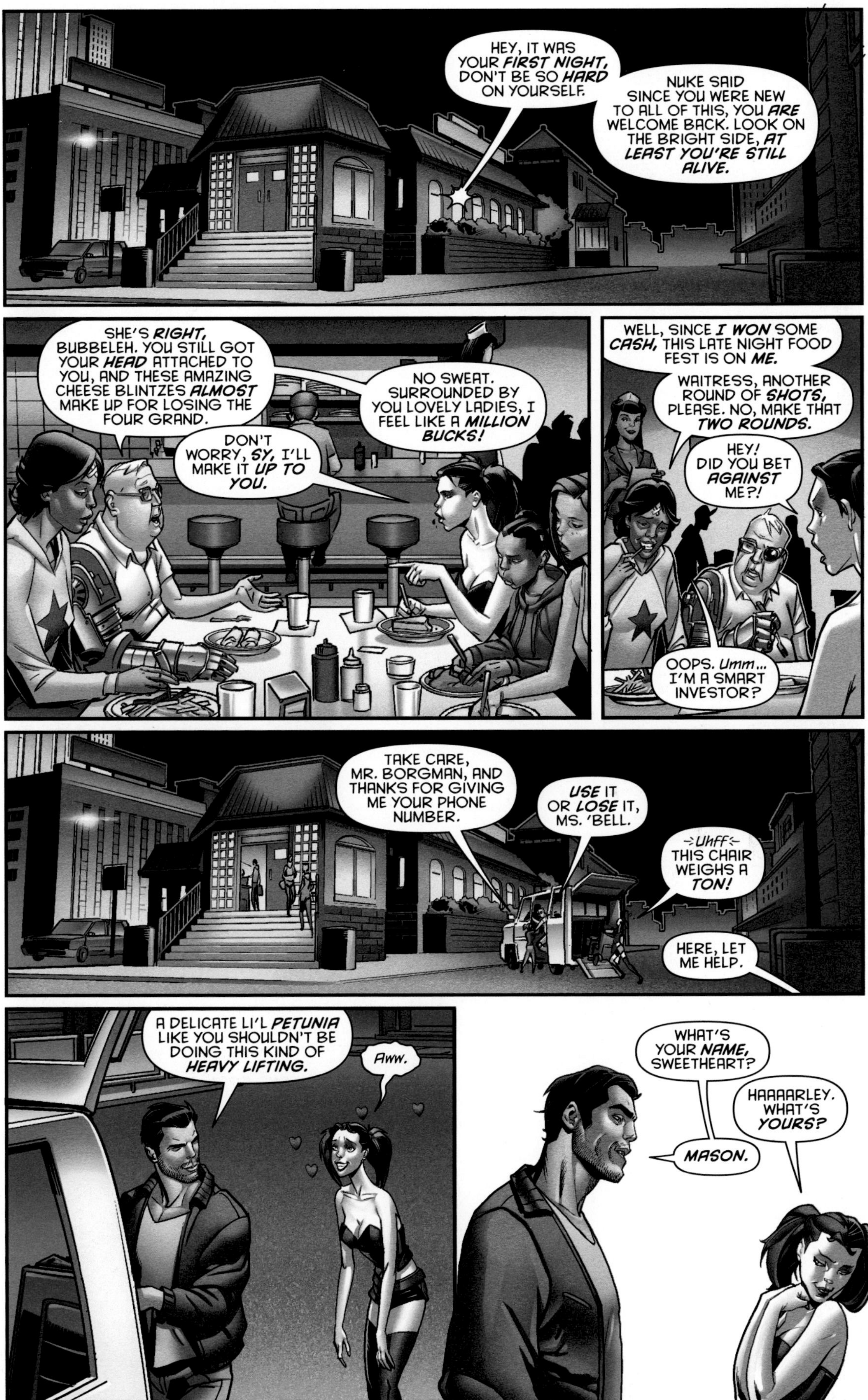
HEY, IT WAS YOUR FIRST NIGHT, DON'T BE SO HARD ON YOURSELF.
NUKE SAID SINCE YOU WERE NEW TO ALL OF THIS, YOU ARE WELCOME BACK. LOOK ON THE BRIGHT SIDE, AT LEAST YOU'RE STILL ALIVE.
SHE'S RIGHT, BUBBELEH. YOU STILL GOT YOUR HEAD ATTACHED TO YOU, AND THESE AMAZING CHEESE BLINTZES ALMOST MAKE UP FOR LOSING THE FOUR GRAND.
DON'T WORRY, SY, I'LL MAKE IT UP TO YOU.
NO SWEAT. SURROUNDED BY YOU LOVELY LADIES, I FEEL LIKE A MILLION BUCKS!
WELL, SINCE I WON SOME CASH, THIS LATE NIGHT FOOD FEST IS ON ME.
WAITRESS, ANOTHER ROUND OF SHOTS, PLEASE. NO, MAKE THAT TWO ROUNDS.
HEY! DID YOU BET AGAINST ME?!
OOPS. Umm... I'M A SMART INVESTOR?
TAKE CARE, MR. BORGMAN, AND THANKS FOR GIVING ME YOUR PHONE NUMBER.
USE IT OR LOSE IT, MS. 'BELL.
Uhff THIS CHAIR WEIGHS A TON!
HERE, LET ME HELP.
A DELICATE LI'L PETUNIA LIKE YOU SHOULDN'T BE DOING THIS KIND OF HEAVY LIFTING.
Aww.
WHAT'S YOUR NAME, SWEETHEART?
MASON.
HAAAARLEY. WHAT'S YOURS?

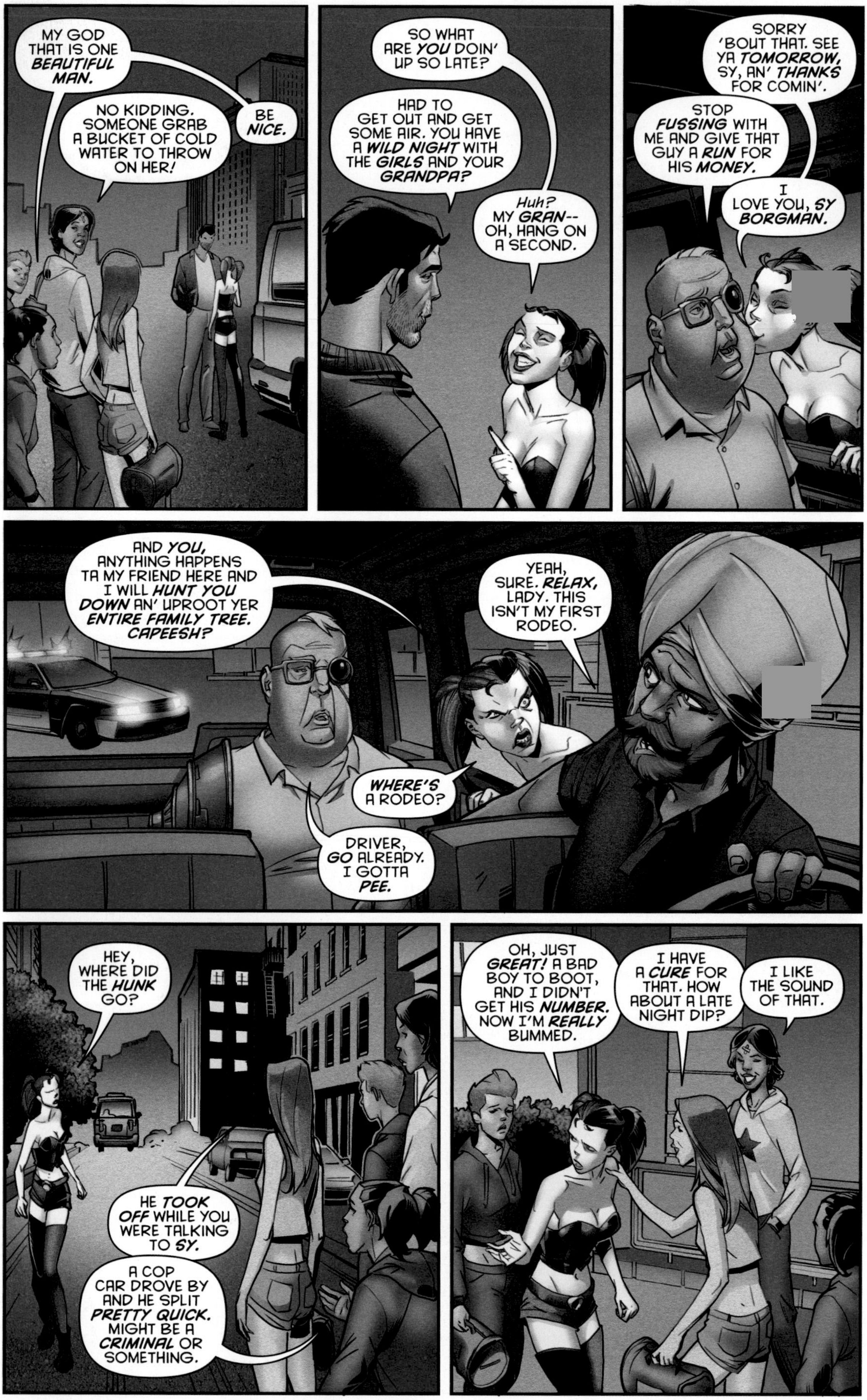
MY GOD THAT IS ONE BEAUTIFUL MAN.
NO KIDDING. SOMEONE GRAB A BUCKET OF COLD WATER TO THROW ON HER!
BE NICE.
SO WHAT ARE YOU DOIN' UP SO LATE?
HAD TO GET OUT AND GET SOME AIR. YOU HAVE A WILD NIGHT WITH THE GIRLS AND YOUR GRANDPA?
Huh? MY GRAN-- OH, HANG ON A SECOND.
SORRY 'BOUT THAT. SEE YA TOMORROW, SY, AN' THANKS FOR COMIN'.
STOP FUSSING WITH ME AND GIVE THAT GUY A RUN FOR HIS MONEY.
I LOVE YOU, SY BORGMAN.
AND YOU, ANYTHING HAPPENS TA MY FRIEND HERE AND I WILL HUNT YOU DOWN AN' UPROOT YER ENTIRE FAMILY TREE. CAPEESH?
YEAH, SURE. RELAX, LADY. THIS ISN'T MY FIRST RODEO.
WHERE'S A RODEO?
DRIVER, GO ALREADY. I GOTTA PEE.
HEY, WHERE DID THE HUNK GO?
HE TOOK OFF WHILE YOU WERE TALKING TO SY.
A COP CAR DROVE BY AND HE SPLIT PRETTY QUICK. MIGHT BE A CRIMINAL OR SOMETHING.
OH, JUST GREAT! A BAD BOY TO BOOT, AND I DIDN'T GET HIS NUMBER. NOW I'M REALLY BUMMED.
I HAVE A CURE FOR THAT. HOW ABOUT A LATE NIGHT DIP?
I LIKE THE SOUND OF THAT.

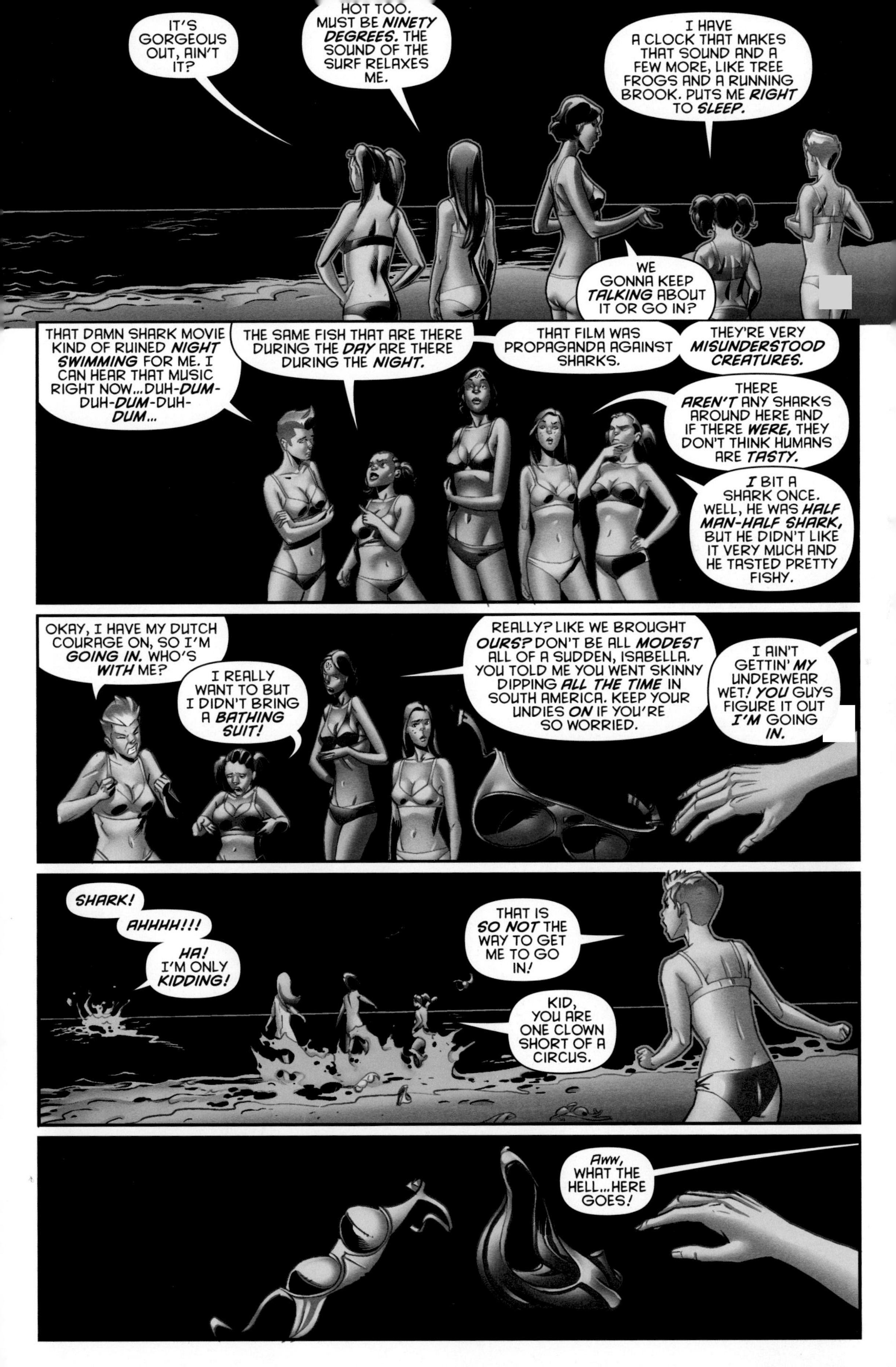
IT'S GORGEOUS OUT, AIN'T IT?
HOT TOO. MUST BE NINETY DEGREES. THE SOUND OF THE SURF RELAXES ME.
I HAVE A CLOCK THAT MAKES THAT SOUND AND A FEW MORE, LIKE TREE FROGS AND A RUNNING BROOK. PUTS ME RIGHT TO SLEEP.
WE GONNA KEEP TALKING ABOUT IT OR GO IN?
THAT DAMN SHARK MOVIE KIND OF RUINED NIGHT SWIMMING FOR ME. I CAN HEAR THAT MUSIC RIGHT NOW...DUH-DUM-DUH-DUM-DUH-DUM...
THE SAME FISH THAT ARE THERE DURING THE DAY ARE THERE DURING THE NIGHT.
THAT FILM WAS PROPAGANDA AGAINST SHARKS.
THEY'RE VERY MISUNDERSTOOD CREATURES.
THERE AREN'T ANY SHARKS AROUND HERE AND IF THERE WERE, THEY DON'T THINK HUMANS ARE TASTY.
I BIT A SHARK ONCE. WELL, HE WAS HALF MAN-HALF SHARK, BUT HE DIDN'T LIKE IT VERY MUCH AND HE TASTED PRETTY FISHY.
OKAY, I HAVE MY DUTCH COURAGE ON, SO I'M GOING IN. WHO'S WITH ME?
I REALLY WANT TO BUT I DIDN'T BRING A BATHING SUIT!
REALLY? LIKE WE BROUGHT OURS? DON'T BE ALL MODEST ALL OF A SUDDEN, ISABELLA. YOU TOLD ME YOU WENT SKINNY DIPPING ALL THE TIME IN SOUTH AMERICA. KEEP YOUR UNDIES ON IF YOU'RE SO WORRIED.
I AIN'T GETTIN' MY UNDERWEAR WET! YOU GUYS FIGURE IT OUT I'M GOING IN.
SHARK!
AHHHH!!!
HA! I'M ONLY KIDDING!
THAT IS SO NOT THE WAY TO GET ME TO GO IN!
KID, YOU ARE ONE CLOWN SHORT OF A CIRCUS.
Aww, WHAT THE HELL...HERE GOES!

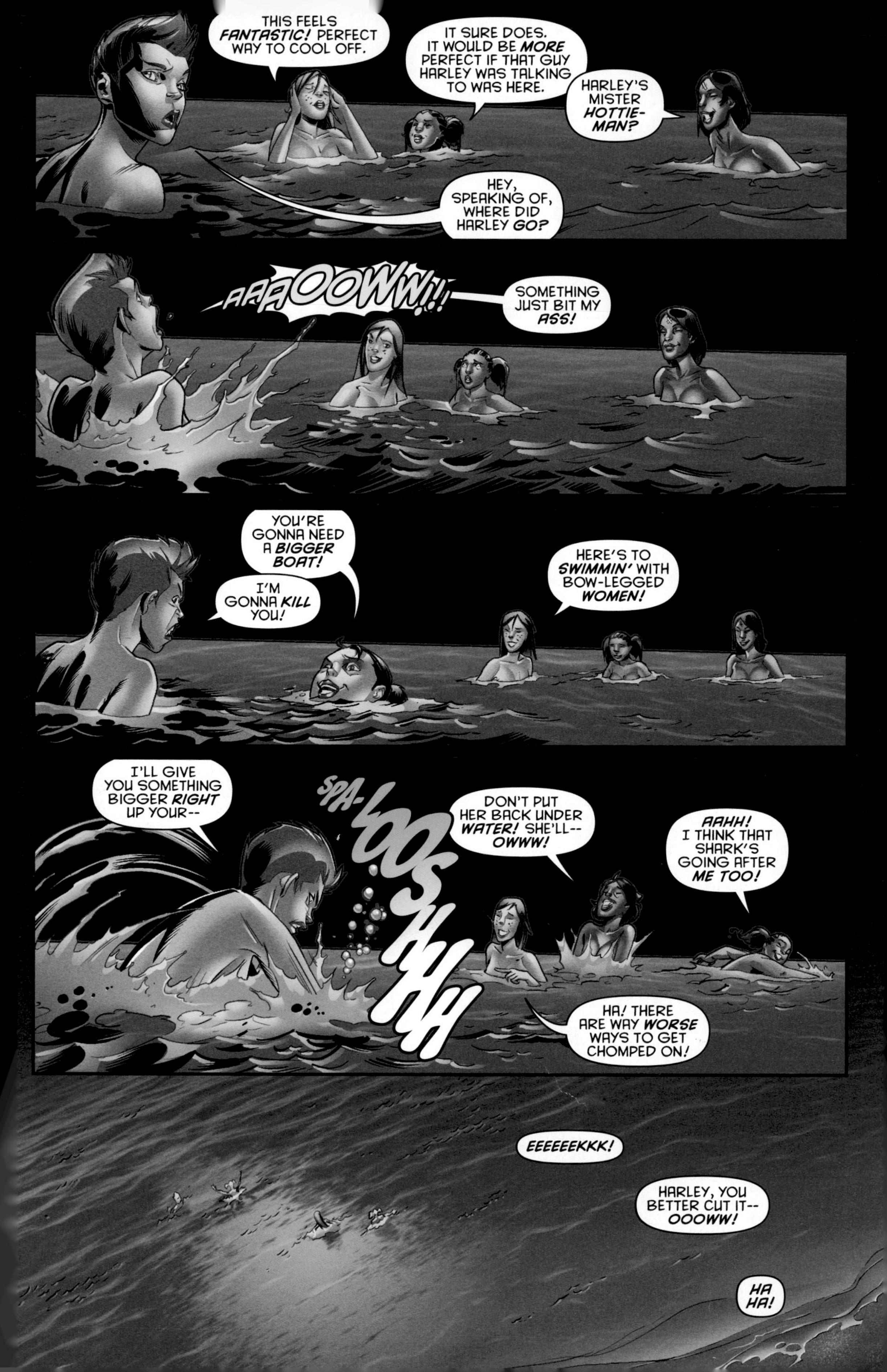
THIS FEELS FANTASTIC! PERFECT WAY TO COOL OFF.
IT SURE DOES. IT WOULD BE MORE PERFECT IF THAT GUY HARLEY WAS TALKING TO WAS HERE.
HARLEY'S MISTER HOTTIE-MAN?
HEY, SPEAKING OF, WHERE DID HARLEY GO?
AAAOOOWW!!!
SOMETHING JUST BIT MY ASS!
YOU'RE GONNA NEED A BIGGER BOAT!
I'M GONNA KILL YOU!
HERE'S TO SWIMMIN' WITH BOW-LEGGED WOMEN!
I'LL GIVE YOU SOMETHING BIGGER RIGHT UP YOUR--
SPA-LOOSHHH
DON'T PUT HER BACK UNDER WATER! SHE'LL-- OWWW!
AAHH! I THINK THAT SHARK'S GOING AFTER ME TOO!
HA! THERE ARE WAY WORSE WAYS TO GET CHOMPED ON!
EEEEEEKKK!
HARLEY, YOU BETTER CUT IT-- OOOWW!
HA HA!

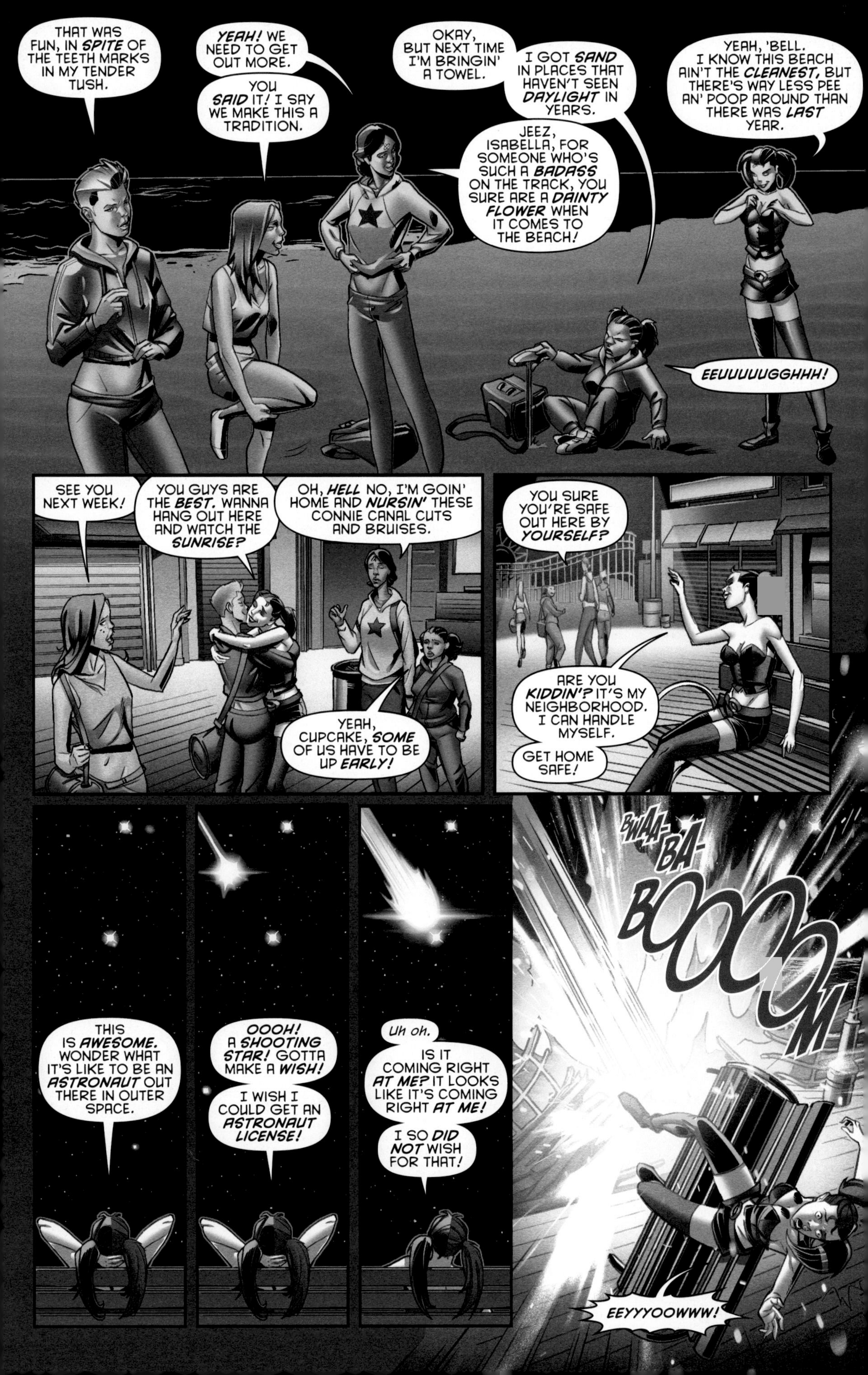
THAT WAS FUN, IN SPITE OF THE TEETH MARKS IN MY TENDER TUSH.
YEAH! WE NEED TO GET OUT MORE.
YOU SAID IT! I SAY WE MAKE THIS A TRADITION.
OKAY, BUT NEXT TIME I'M BRINGIN' A TOWEL.
I GOT SAND IN PLACES THAT HAVEN'T SEEN DAYLIGHT IN YEARS.
JEEZ, ISABELLA, FOR SOMEONE WHO'S SUCH A BADASS ON THE TRACK, YOU SURE ARE A DAINTY FLOWER WHEN IT COMES TO THE BEACH!
YEAH, 'BELL. I KNOW THIS BEACH AIN'T THE CLEANEST, BUT THERE'S WAY LESS PEE AN' POOP AROUND THAN THERE WAS LAST YEAR.
EEUUUUUGGHHH!
SEE YOU NEXT WEEK!
YOU GUYS ARE THE BEST. WANNA HANG OUT HERE AND WATCH THE SUNRISE?
OH, HELL NO, I'M GOIN' HOME AND NURSIN' THESE CONNIE CANAL CUTS AND BRUISES.
YEAH, CUPCAKE, SOME OF US HAVE TO BE UP EARLY!
YOU SURE YOU'RE SAFE OUT HERE BY YOURSELF?
ARE YOU KIDDIN'? IT'S MY NEIGHBORHOOD. I CAN HANDLE MYSELF.
GET HOME SAFE!
THIS IS AWESOME. WONDER WHAT IT'S LIKE TO BE AN ASTRONAUT OUT THERE IN OUTER SPACE.
OOOH! A SHOOTING STAR! GOTTA MAKE A WISH!
I WISH I COULD GET AN ASTRONAUT LICENSE!
Uh oh.
IS IT COMING RIGHT AT ME? IT LOOKS LIKE IT'S COMING RIGHT AT ME!
I SO DID NOT WISH FOR THAT!
BWAA-BA-BOOOOM
EEYYYOOWWW!

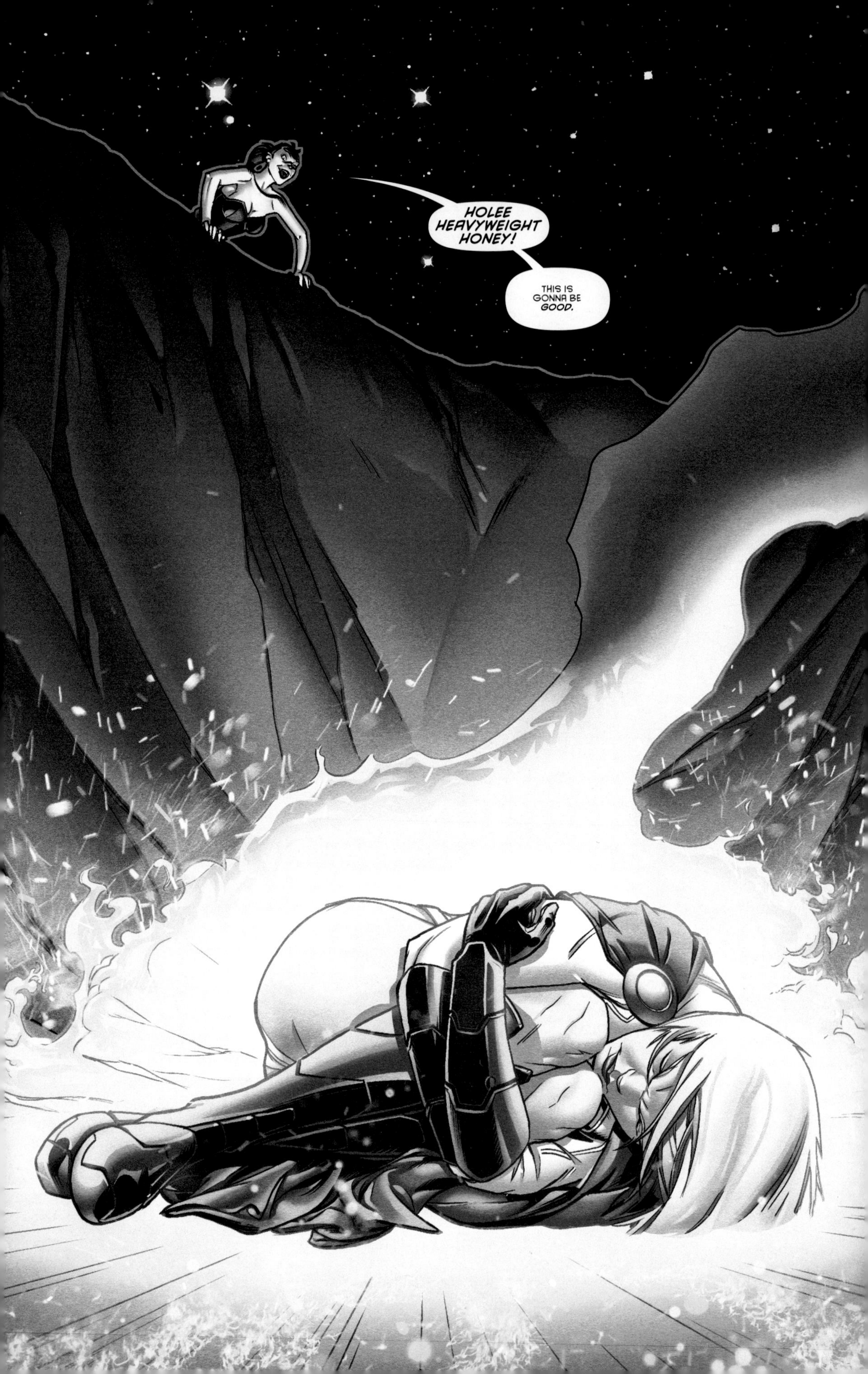
HOLEE HEAVYWEIGHT HONEY!
THIS IS GONNA BE GOOD.

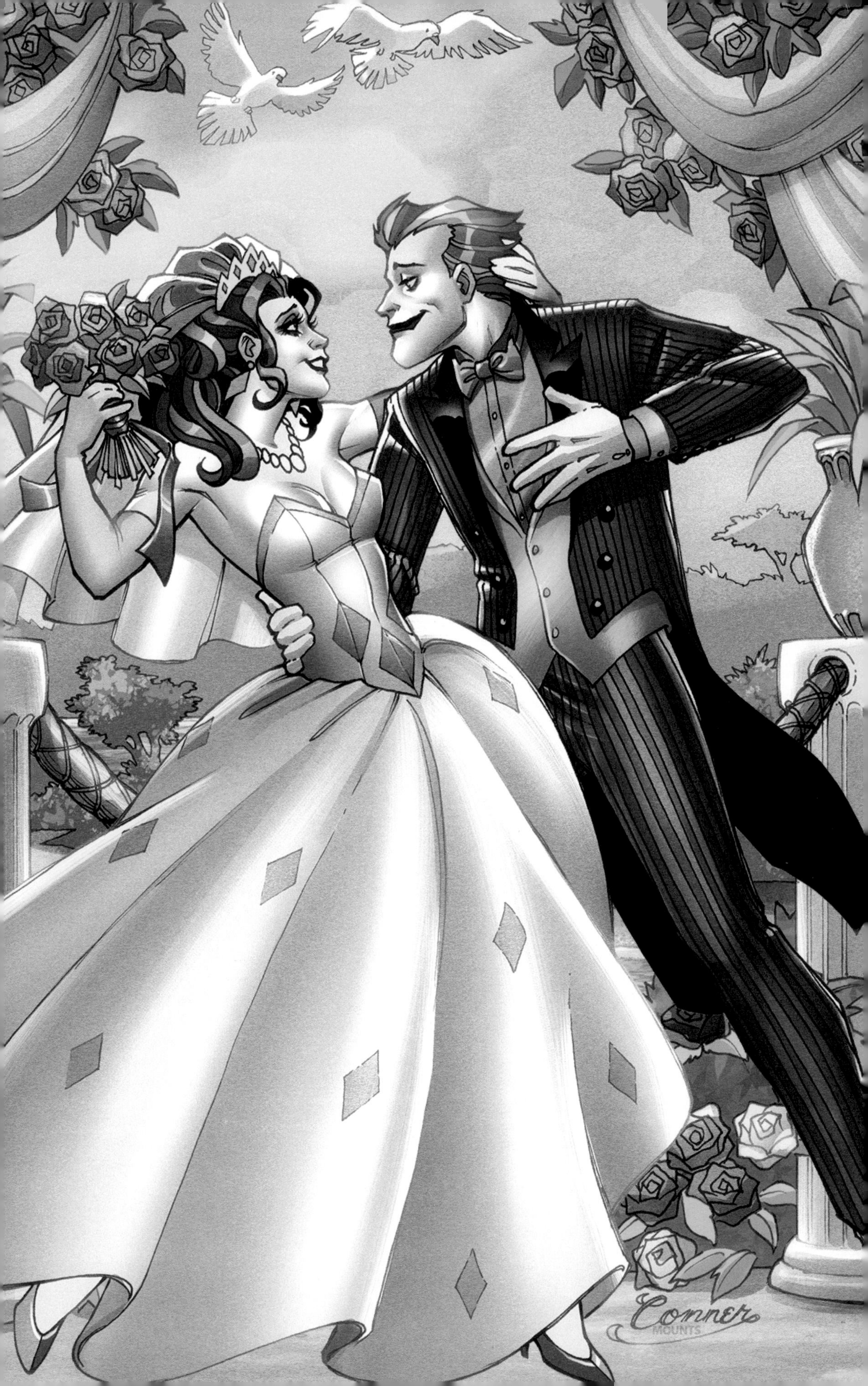
Conner
MOUNTS

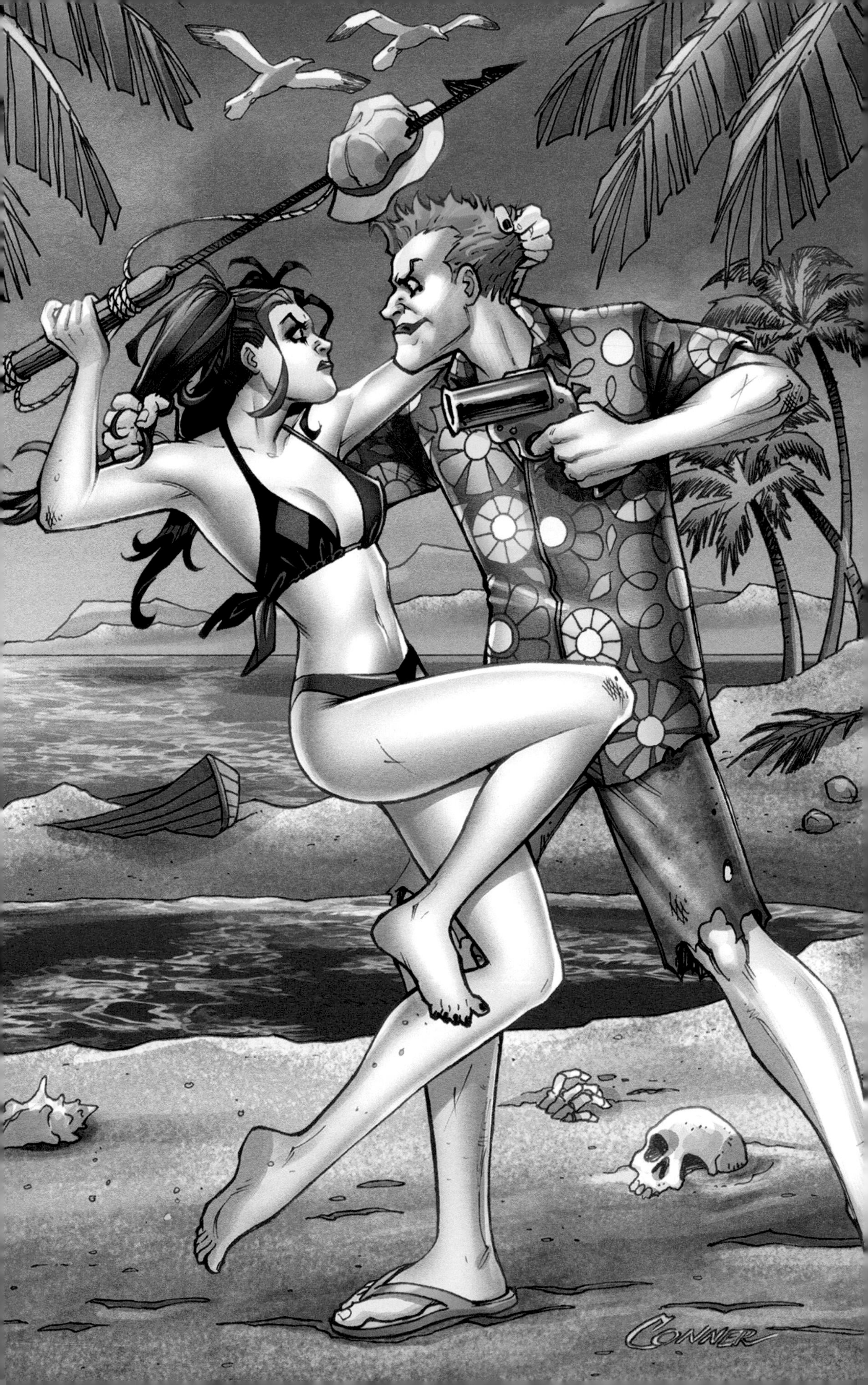
CONNER

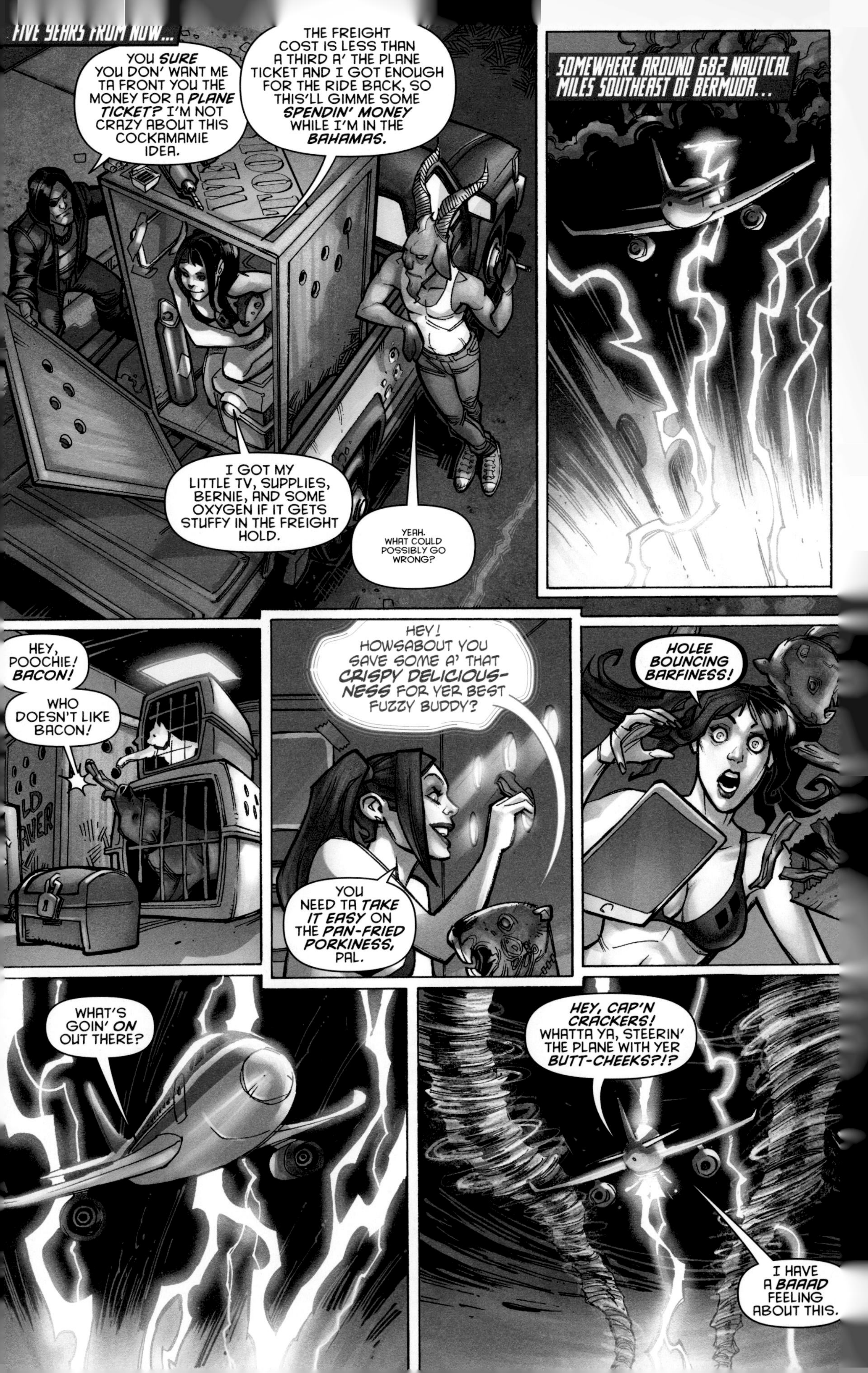
FIVE YEARS FROM NOW...
YOU SURE YOU DON' WANT ME TA FRONT YOU THE MONEY FOR A PLANE TICKET? I'M NOT CRAZY ABOUT THIS COCKAMAMIE IDEA.
THE FREIGHT COST IS LESS THAN A THIRD A' THE PLANE TICKET AND I GOT ENOUGH FOR THE RIDE BACK, SO THIS'LL GIMME SOME SPENDIN' MONEY WHILE I'M IN THE BAHAMAS.
I GOT MY LITTLE TV, SUPPLIES, BERNIE, AND SOME OXYGEN IF IT GETS STUFFY IN THE FREIGHT HOLD.
YEAH. WHAT COULD POSSIBLY GO WRONG?
SOMEWHERE AROUND 682 NAUTICAL MILES SOUTHEAST OF BERMUDA...
HEY, POOCHIE! BACON!
WHO DOESN'T LIKE BACON!
HEY! HOWSABOUT YOU SAVE SOME A' THAT CRISPY DELICIOUS-NESS FOR YER BEST FUZZY BUDDY?
YOU NEED TA TAKE IT EASY ON THE PAN-FRIED PORKINESS, PAL.
HOLEE BOUNCING BARFINESS!
WHAT'S GOIN' ON OUT THERE?
HEY, CAP'N CRACKERS! WHATTA YA, STEERIN' THE PLANE WITH YER BUTT-CHEEKS?!?
I HAVE A BAAAD FEELING ABOUT THIS.

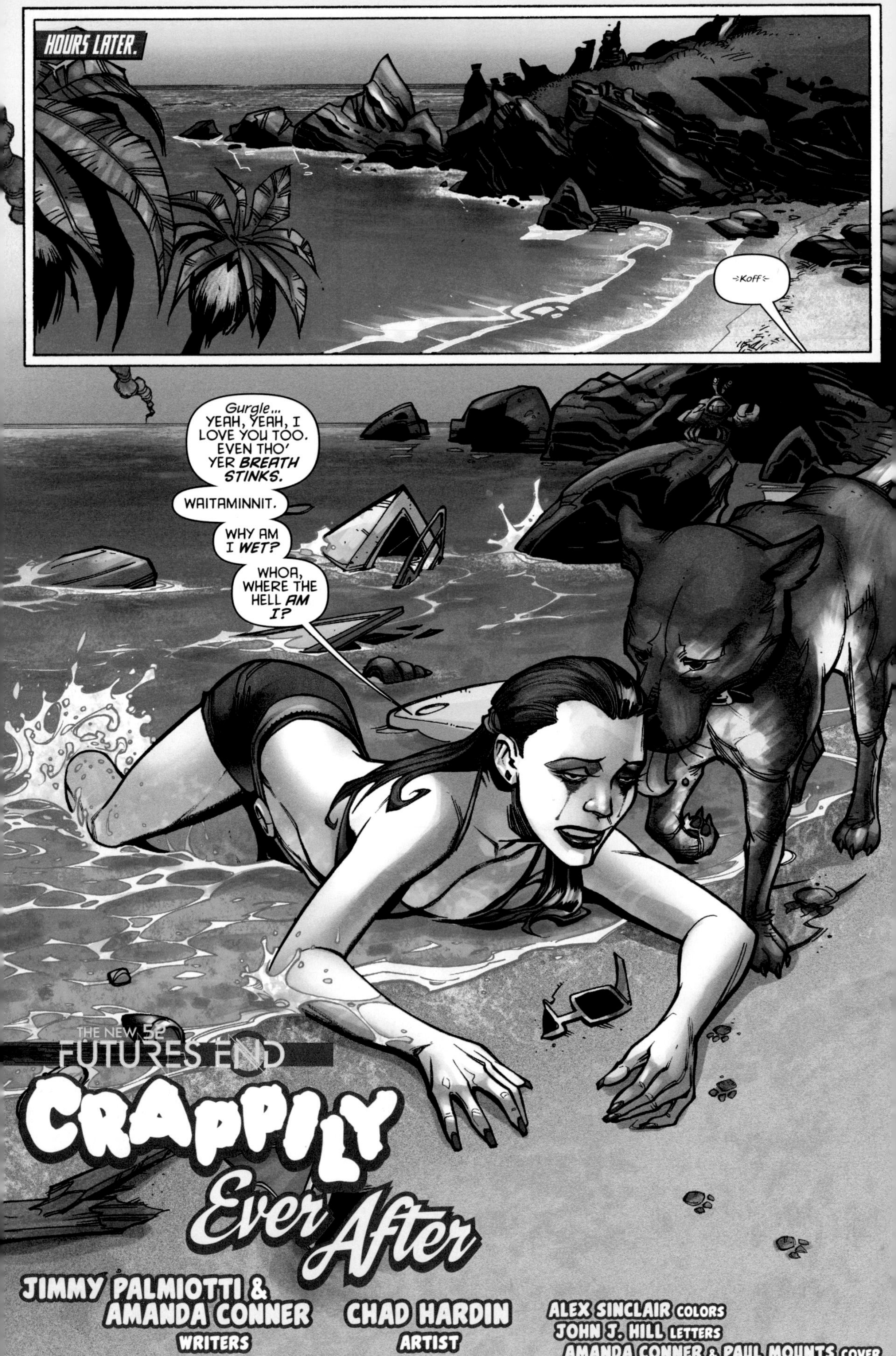
HOURS LATER.
KOFF
Gurgle... YEAH, YEAH, I LOVE YOU TOO. EVEN THO' YER BREATH STINKS.
WAITAMINNIT.
WHY AM I WET?
WHOA, WHERE THE HELL AM I?
THE NEW 52 FUTURES END
CRAPPILY Ever After
JIMMY PALMIOTTI & AMANDA CONNER WRITERS
CHAD HARDIN ARTIST
ALEX SINCLAIR COLORS
JOHN J. HILL LETTERS
AMANDA CONNER & PAUL MOUNTS COVER

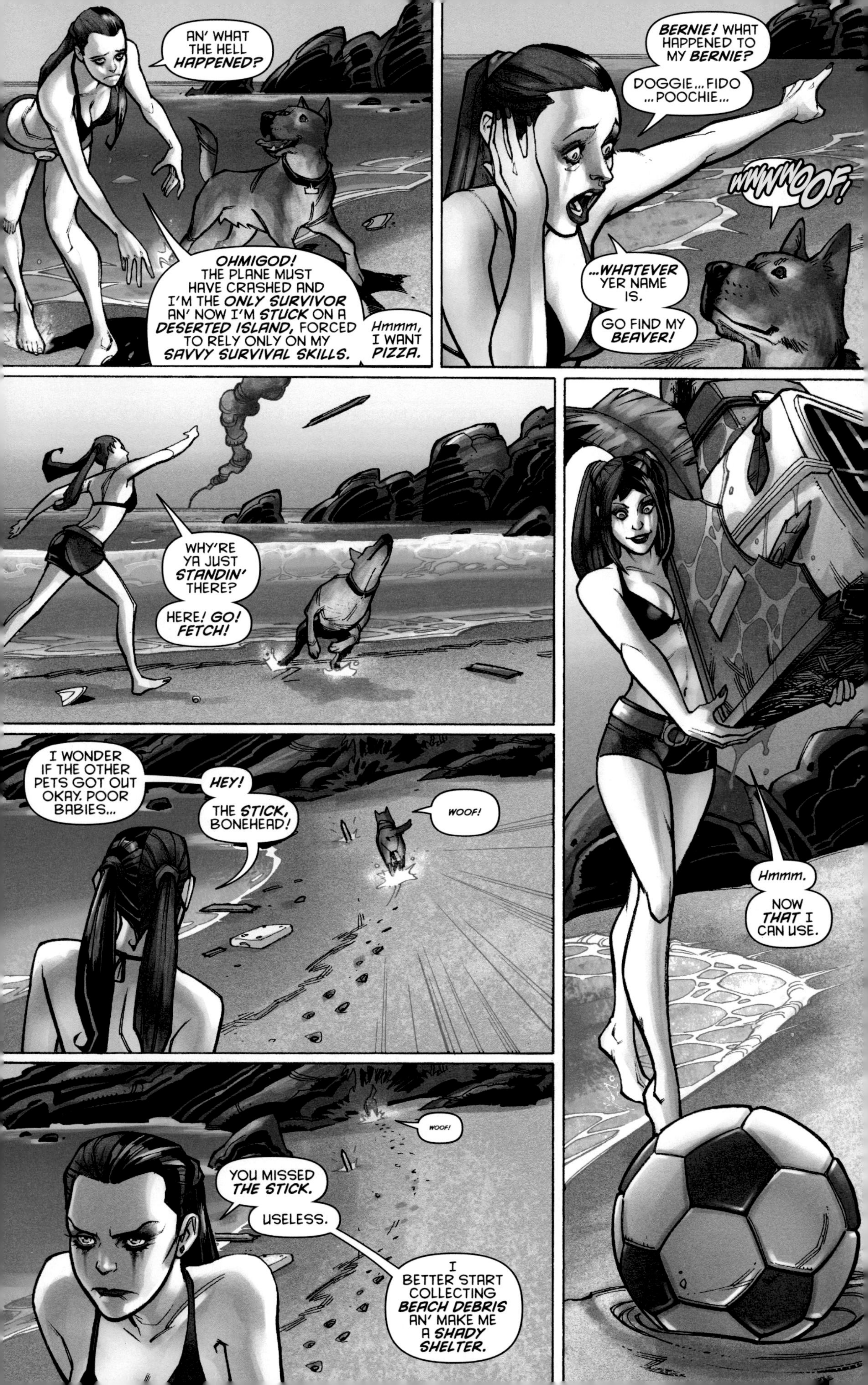
AN' WHAT THE HELL HAPPENED?
OHMIGOD! THE PLANE MUST HAVE CRASHED AND I'M THE ONLY SURVIVOR AN' NOW I'M STUCK ON A DESERTED ISLAND, FORCED TO RELY ONLY ON MY SAVVY SURVIVAL SKILLS.
Hmmm, I WANT PIZZA.
BERNIE! WHAT HAPPENED TO MY BERNIE?
DOGGIE... FIDO ...POOCHIE...
WWWWOOF!
...WHATEVER YER NAME IS.
GO FIND MY BEAVER!
WHY'RE YA JUST STANDIN' THERE?
HERE! GO! FETCH!
I WONDER IF THE OTHER PETS GOT OUT OKAY. POOR BABIES...
HEY!
THE STICK, BONEHEAD!
WOOF!
WOOF!
YOU MISSED THE STICK.
USELESS.
I BETTER START COLLECTING BEACH DEBRIS AN' MAKE ME A SHADY SHELTER.
Hmmm.
NOW THAT I CAN USE.

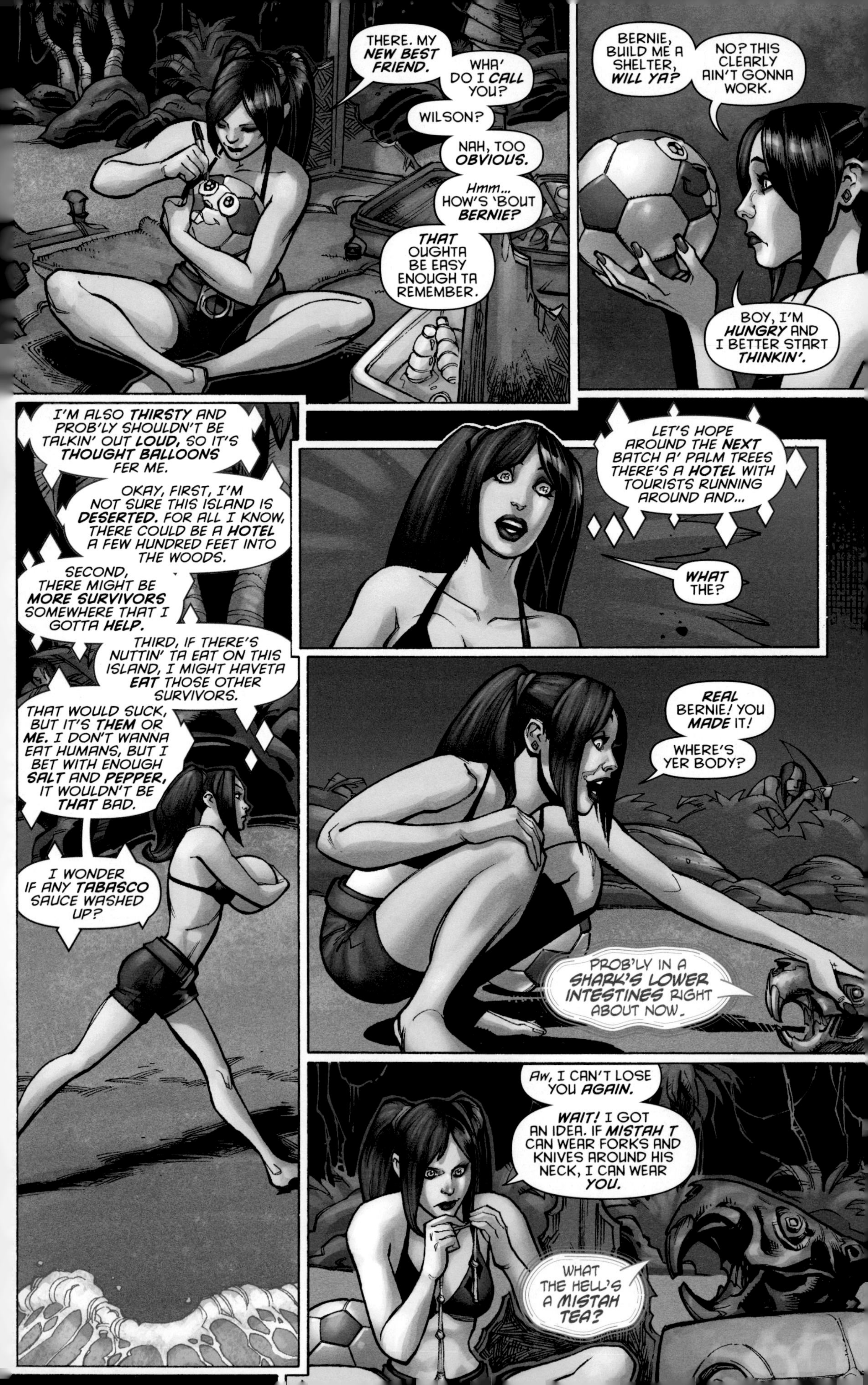
THERE. MY NEW BEST FRIEND.
WHA' DO I CALL YOU?
WILSON?
NAH, TOO OBVIOUS.
Hmm... HOW'S 'BOUT BERNIE?
THAT OUGHTA BE EASY ENOUGH TA REMEMBER.
BERNIE, BUILD ME A SHELTER, WILL YA?
NO? THIS CLEARLY AIN'T GONNA WORK.
BOY, I'M HUNGRY AND I BETTER START THINKIN'.
I'M ALSO THIRSTY AND PROB'LY SHOULDN'T BE TALKIN' OUT LOUD, SO IT'S THOUGHT BALLOONS FER ME.
OKAY, FIRST, I'M NOT SURE THIS ISLAND IS DESERTED. FOR ALL I KNOW, THERE COULD BE A HOTEL A FEW HUNDRED FEET INTO THE WOODS.
SECOND, THERE MIGHT BE MORE SURVIVORS SOMEWHERE THAT I GOTTA HELP.
THIRD, IF THERE'S NUTTIN' TA EAT ON THIS ISLAND, I MIGHT HAVETA EAT THOSE OTHER SURVIVORS.
THAT WOULD SUCK, BUT IT'S THEM OR ME. I DON'T WANNA EAT HUMANS, BUT I BET WITH ENOUGH SALT AND PEPPER, IT WOULDN'T BE THAT BAD.
I WONDER IF ANY TABASCO SAUCE WASHED UP?
LET'S HOPE AROUND THE NEXT BATCH A' PALM TREES THERE'S A HOTEL WITH TOURISTS RUNNING AROUND AND...
WHAT THE?
REAL BERNIE! YOU MADE IT!
WHERE'S YER BODY?
PROB'LY IN A SHARK'S LOWER INTESTINES RIGHT ABOUT NOW.
AW, I CAN'T LOSE YOU AGAIN.
WAIT! I GOT AN IDEA. IF MISTAH T CAN WEAR FORKS AND KNIVES AROUND HIS NECK, I CAN WEAR YOU.
WHAT THE HELL'S A MISTAH TEA?

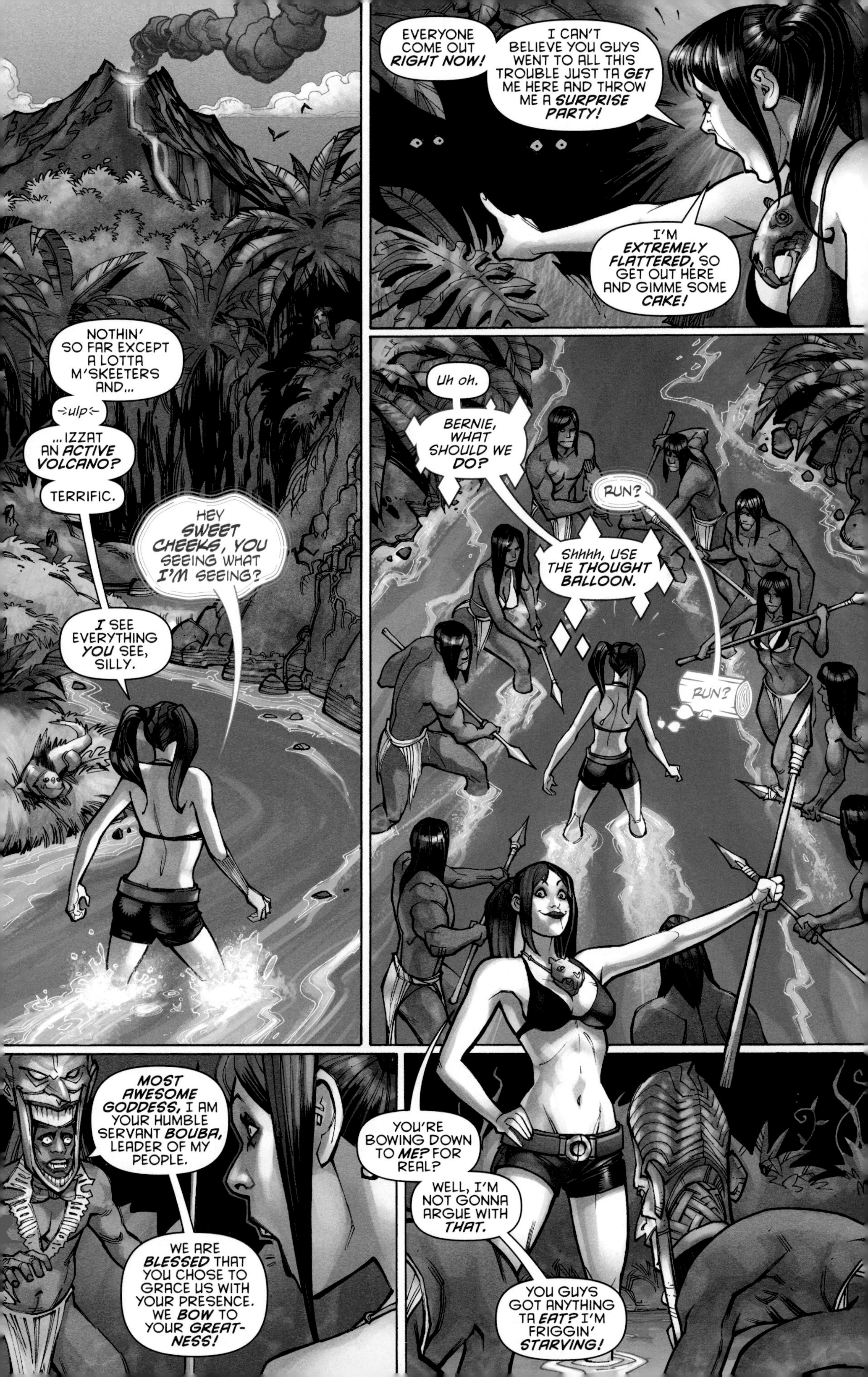
NOTHIN' SO FAR EXCEPT A LOTTA M'SKEETERS AND...
-ulp-
...IZZAT AN ACTIVE VOLCANO?
TERRIFIC.
HEY SWEET CHEEKS, YOU SEEING WHAT I'M SEEING?
I SEE EVERYTHING YOU SEE, SILLY.
EVERYONE COME OUT RIGHT NOW!
I CAN'T BELIEVE YOU GUYS WENT TO ALL THIS TROUBLE JUST TA GET ME HERE AND THROW ME A SURPRISE PARTY!
I'M EXTREMELY FLATTERED, SO GET OUT HERE AND GIMME SOME CAKE!
Uh oh.
BERNIE, WHAT SHOULD WE DO?
RUN?
Shhhh, USE THE THOUGHT BALLOON.
RUN?
MOST AWESOME GODDESS, I AM YOUR HUMBLE SERVANT BOUBA, LEADER OF MY PEOPLE.
WE ARE BLESSED THAT YOU CHOSE TO GRACE US WITH YOUR PRESENCE. WE BOW TO YOUR GREAT-NESS!
YOU'RE BOWING DOWN TO ME? FOR REAL?
WELL, I'M NOT GONNA ARGUE WITH THAT.
YOU GUYS GOT ANYTHING TA EAT? I'M FRIGGIN' STARVING!

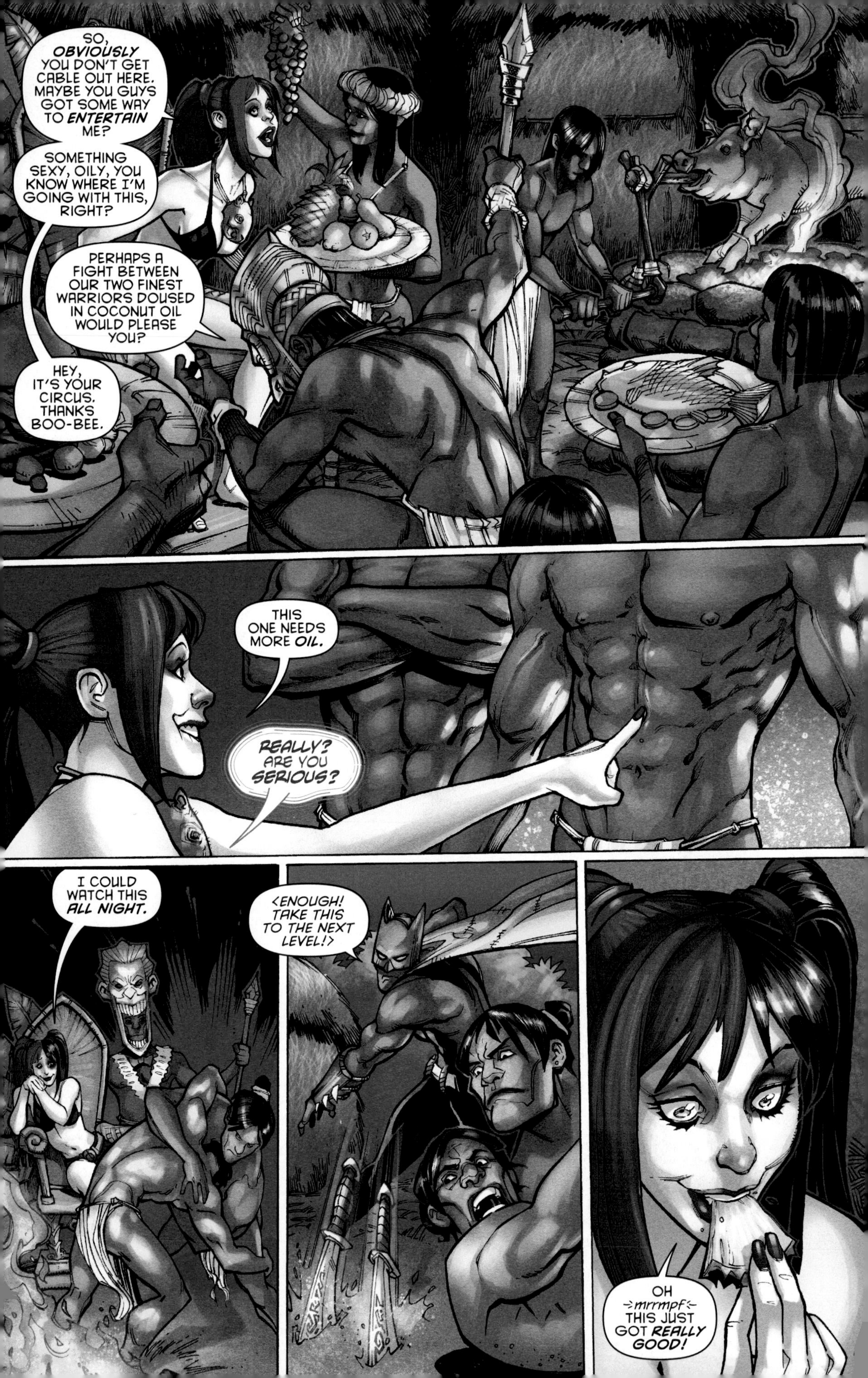
SO, OBVIOUSLY YOU DON'T GET CABLE OUT HERE. MAYBE YOU GUYS GOT SOME WAY TO ENTERTAIN ME?
SOMETHING SEXY, OILY, YOU KNOW WHERE I'M GOING WITH THIS, RIGHT?
PERHAPS A FIGHT BETWEEN OUR TWO FINEST WARRIORS DOUSED IN COCONUT OIL WOULD PLEASE YOU?
HEY, IT'S YOUR CIRCUS. THANKS BOO-BEE.
THIS ONE NEEDS MORE OIL.
REALLY? ARE YOU SERIOUS?
I COULD WATCH THIS ALL NIGHT.
<ENOUGH! TAKE THIS TO THE NEXT LEVEL!>
OH -mrrmpf- THIS JUST GOT REALLY GOOD!

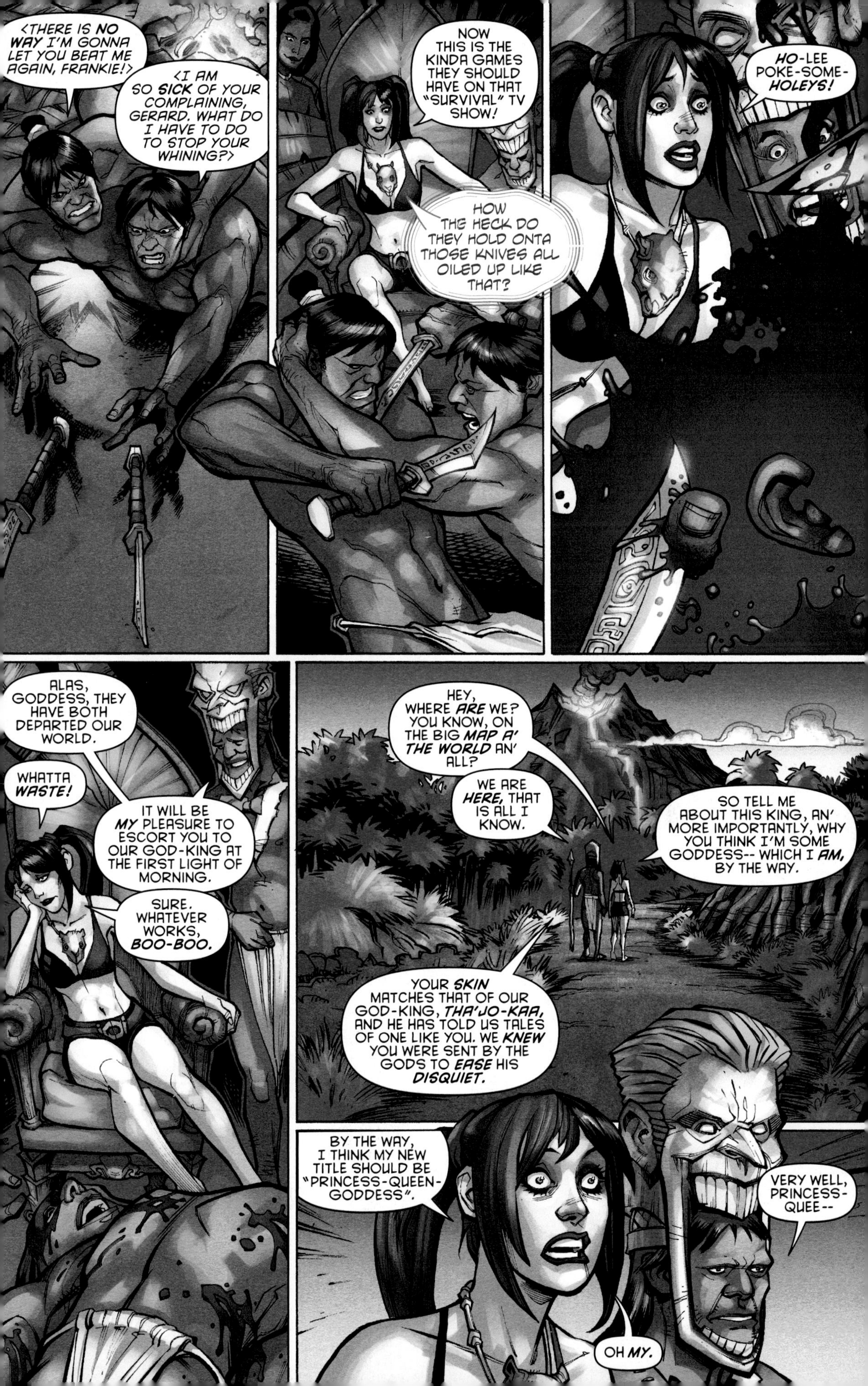
<THERE IS NO WAY I'M GONNA LET YOU BEAT ME AGAIN, FRANKIE!>
<I AM SO SICK OF YOUR COMPLAINING, GERARD. WHAT DO I HAVE TO DO TO STOP YOUR WHINING?>
NOW THIS IS THE KINDA GAMES THEY SHOULD HAVE ON THAT "SURVIVAL" TV SHOW!
HOW THE HECK DO THEY HOLD ONTA THOSE KNIVES ALL OILED UP LIKE THAT?
HO-LEE POKE-SOME-HOLEYS!
ALAS, GODDESS, THEY HAVE BOTH DEPARTED OUR WORLD.
WHATTA WASTE!
IT WILL BE MY PLEASURE TO ESCORT YOU TO OUR GOD-KING AT THE FIRST LIGHT OF MORNING.
SURE. WHATEVER WORKS, BOO-BOO.
HEY, WHERE ARE WE? YOU KNOW, ON THE BIG MAP A' THE WORLD AN' ALL?
WE ARE HERE, THAT IS ALL I KNOW.
SO TELL ME ABOUT THIS KING, AN' MORE IMPORTANTLY, WHY YOU THINK I'M SOME GODDESS-- WHICH I AM, BY THE WAY.
YOUR SKIN MATCHES THAT OF OUR GOD-KING, THA'JO-KAA, AND HE HAS TOLD US TALES OF ONE LIKE YOU. WE KNEW YOU WERE SENT BY THE GODS TO EASE HIS DISQUIET.
BY THE WAY, I THINK MY NEW TITLE SHOULD BE "PRINCESS-QUEEN-GODDESS".
VERY WELL, PRINCESS-QUEE--
OH MY.

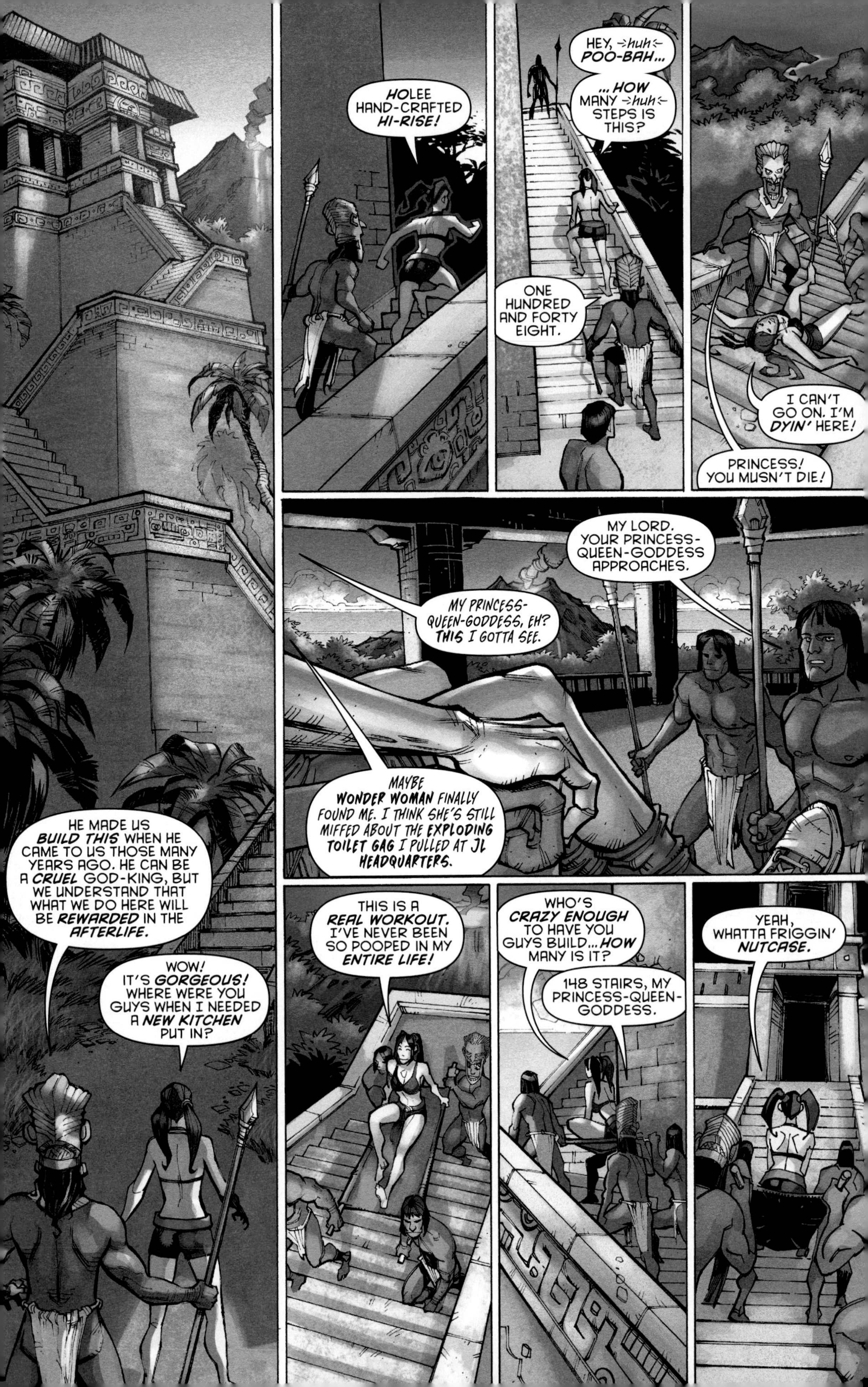
HOLEE HAND-CRAFTED HI-RISE!
HEY, ~huh~ POO-BAH...
...HOW MANY ~huh~ STEPS IS THIS?
ONE HUNDRED AND FORTY EIGHT.
I CAN'T GO ON. I'M DYIN' HERE!
PRINCESS! YOU MUSN'T DIE!
HE MADE US BUILD THIS WHEN HE CAME TO US THOSE MANY YEARS AGO. HE CAN BE A CRUEL GOD-KING, BUT WE UNDERSTAND THAT WHAT WE DO HERE WILL BE REWARDED IN THE AFTERLIFE.
WOW! IT'S GORGEOUS! WHERE WERE YOU GUYS WHEN I NEEDED A NEW KITCHEN PUT IN?
MY LORD. YOUR PRINCESS-QUEEN-GODDESS APPROACHES.
MY PRINCESS-QUEEN-GODDESS, EH? THIS I GOTTA SEE.
MAYBE WONDER WOMAN FINALLY FOUND ME. I THINK SHE'S STILL MIFFED ABOUT THE EXPLODING TOILET GAG I PULLED AT JL HEADQUARTERS.
THIS IS A REAL WORKOUT. I'VE NEVER BEEN SO POOPED IN MY ENTIRE LIFE!
WHO'S CRAZY ENOUGH TO HAVE YOU GUYS BUILD... HOW MANY IS IT?
148 STAIRS, MY PRINCESS-QUEEN-GODDESS.
YEAH, WHATTA FRIGGIN' NUTCASE.

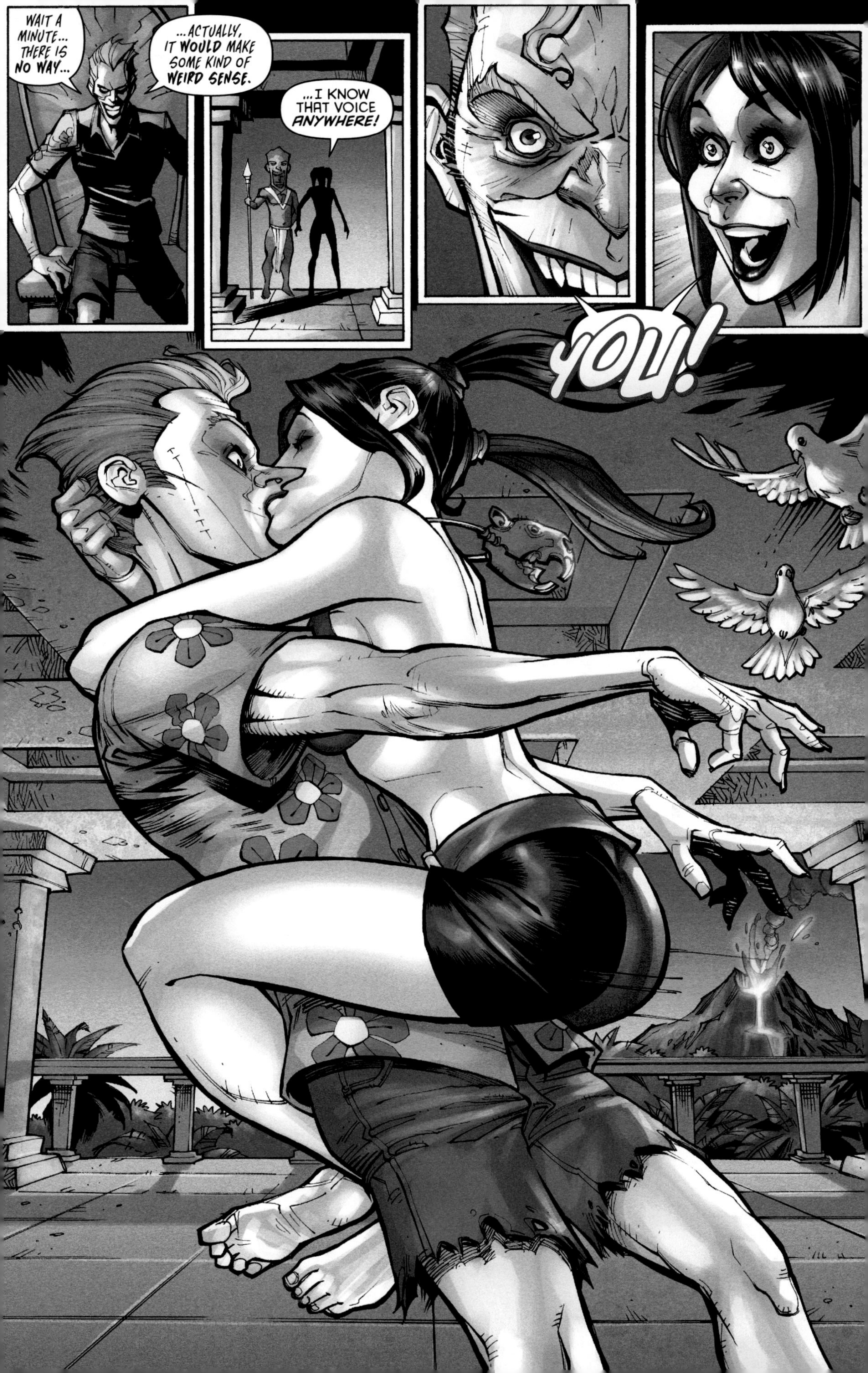
WAIT A MINUTE... THERE IS NO WAY...
...ACTUALLY, IT WOULD MAKE SOME KIND OF WEIRD SENSE.
...I KNOW THAT VOICE ANYWHERE!
YOU!

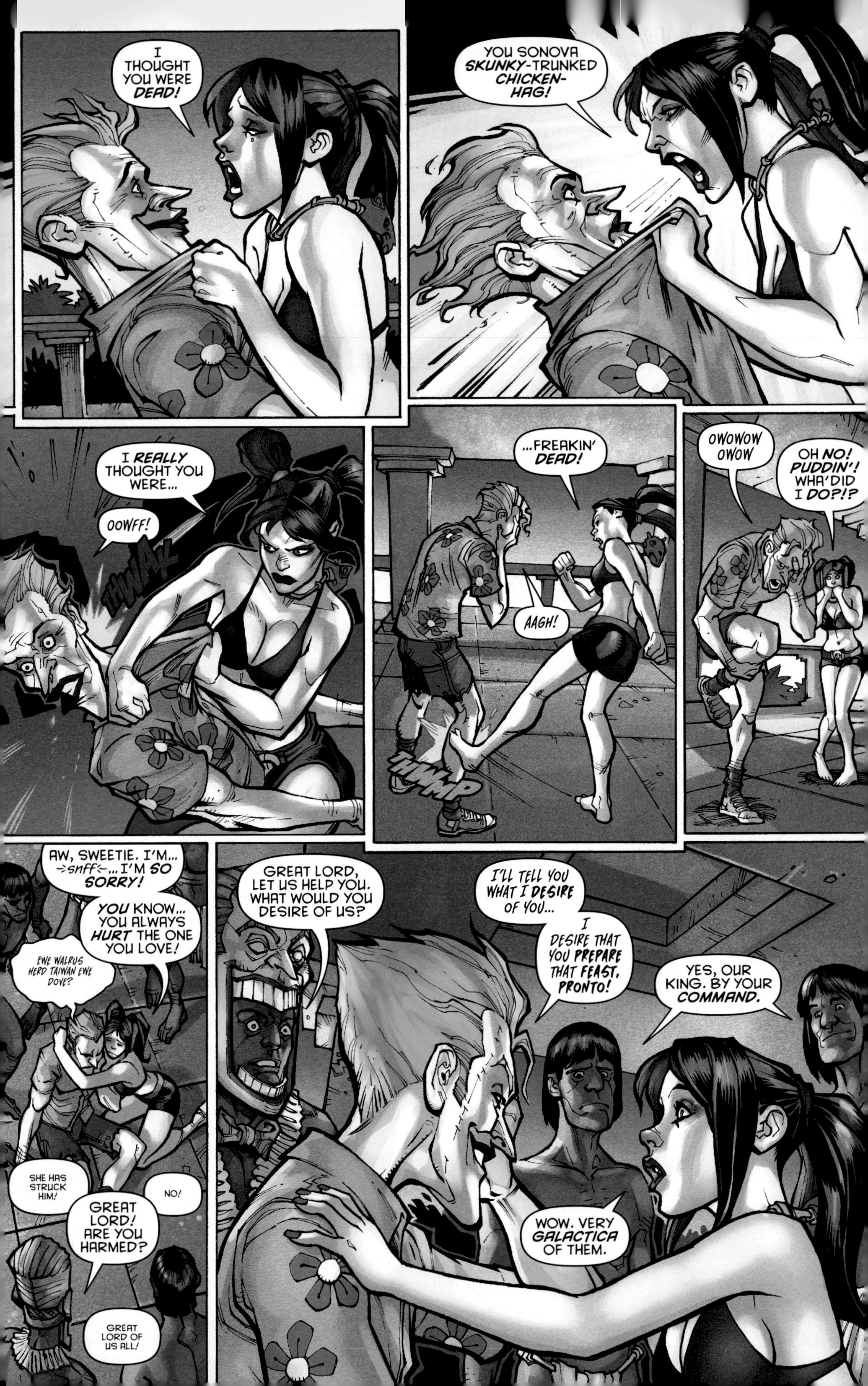
I THOUGHT YOU WERE DEAD!
YOU SONOVA SKUNKY-TRUNKED CHICKEN-HAG!
I REALLY THOUGHT YOU WERE...
OOWFF!
THWAK
...FREAKIN' DEAD!
AAGH!
THWMP
OWOWOW OWOW
OH NO! PUDDIN'! WHA'DID I DO?!?
AW, SWEETIE. I'M... ~snff~... I'M SO SORRY!
YOU KNOW... YOU ALWAYS HURT THE ONE YOU LOVE!
EWE WALRUS HERD TAIWAN EWE DOVE?
SHE HAS STRUCK HIM!
NO!
GREAT LORD! ARE YOU HARMED?
GREAT LORD OF US ALL!
GREAT LORD, LET US HELP YOU. WHAT WOULD YOU DESIRE OF US?
I'LL TELL YOU WHAT I DESIRE OF YOU...
I DESIRE THAT YOU PREPARE THAT FEAST, PRONTO!
YES, OUR KING. BY YOUR COMMAND.
WOW. VERY GALACTICA OF THEM.

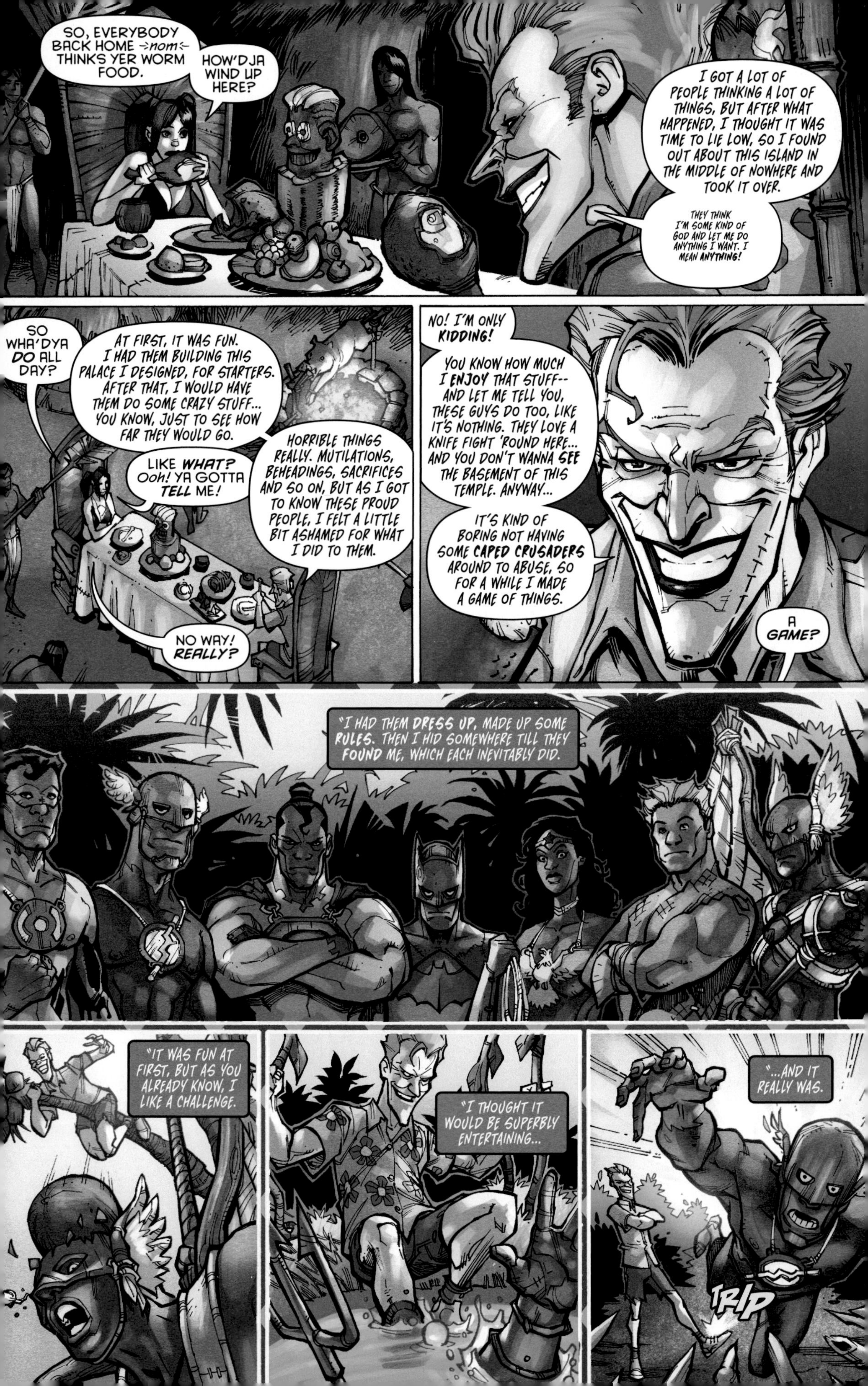
SO, EVERYBODY BACK HOME →nom← THINKS YER WORM FOOD.
HOW'DJA WIND UP HERE?
I GOT A LOT OF PEOPLE THINKING A LOT OF THINGS, BUT AFTER WHAT HAPPENED, I THOUGHT IT WAS TIME TO LIE LOW, SO I FOUND OUT ABOUT THIS ISLAND IN THE MIDDLE OF NOWHERE AND TOOK IT OVER.
THEY THINK I'M SOME KIND OF GOD AND LET ME DO ANYTHING I WANT. I MEAN ANYTHING!
SO WHA'DYA DO ALL DAY?
AT FIRST, IT WAS FUN. I HAD THEM BUILDING THIS PALACE I DESIGNED, FOR STARTERS. AFTER THAT, I WOULD HAVE THEM DO SOME CRAZY STUFF... YOU KNOW, JUST TO SEE HOW FAR THEY WOULD GO.
LIKE WHAT? Ooh! YA GOTTA TELL ME!
HORRIBLE THINGS REALLY. MUTILATIONS, BEHEADINGS, SACRIFICES AND SO ON, BUT AS I GOT TO KNOW THESE PROUD PEOPLE, I FELT A LITTLE BIT ASHAMED FOR WHAT I DID TO THEM.
NO WAY! REALLY?
NO! I'M ONLY KIDDING!
YOU KNOW HOW MUCH I ENJOY THAT STUFF-- AND LET ME TELL YOU, THESE GUYS DO TOO, LIKE IT'S NOTHING. THEY LOVE A KNIFE FIGHT 'ROUND HERE... AND YOU DON'T WANNA SEE THE BASEMENT OF THIS TEMPLE. ANYWAY...
IT'S KIND OF BORING NOT HAVING SOME CAPED CRUSADERS AROUND TO ABUSE, SO FOR A WHILE I MADE A GAME OF THINGS.
A GAME?
"I HAD THEM DRESS UP, MADE UP SOME RULES. THEN I HID SOMEWHERE TILL THEY FOUND ME, WHICH EACH INEVITABLY DID.
"IT WAS FUN AT FIRST, BUT AS YOU ALREADY KNOW, I LIKE A CHALLENGE.
"I THOUGHT IT WOULD BE SUPERBLY ENTERTAINING...
"...AND IT REALLY WAS.
TRIP

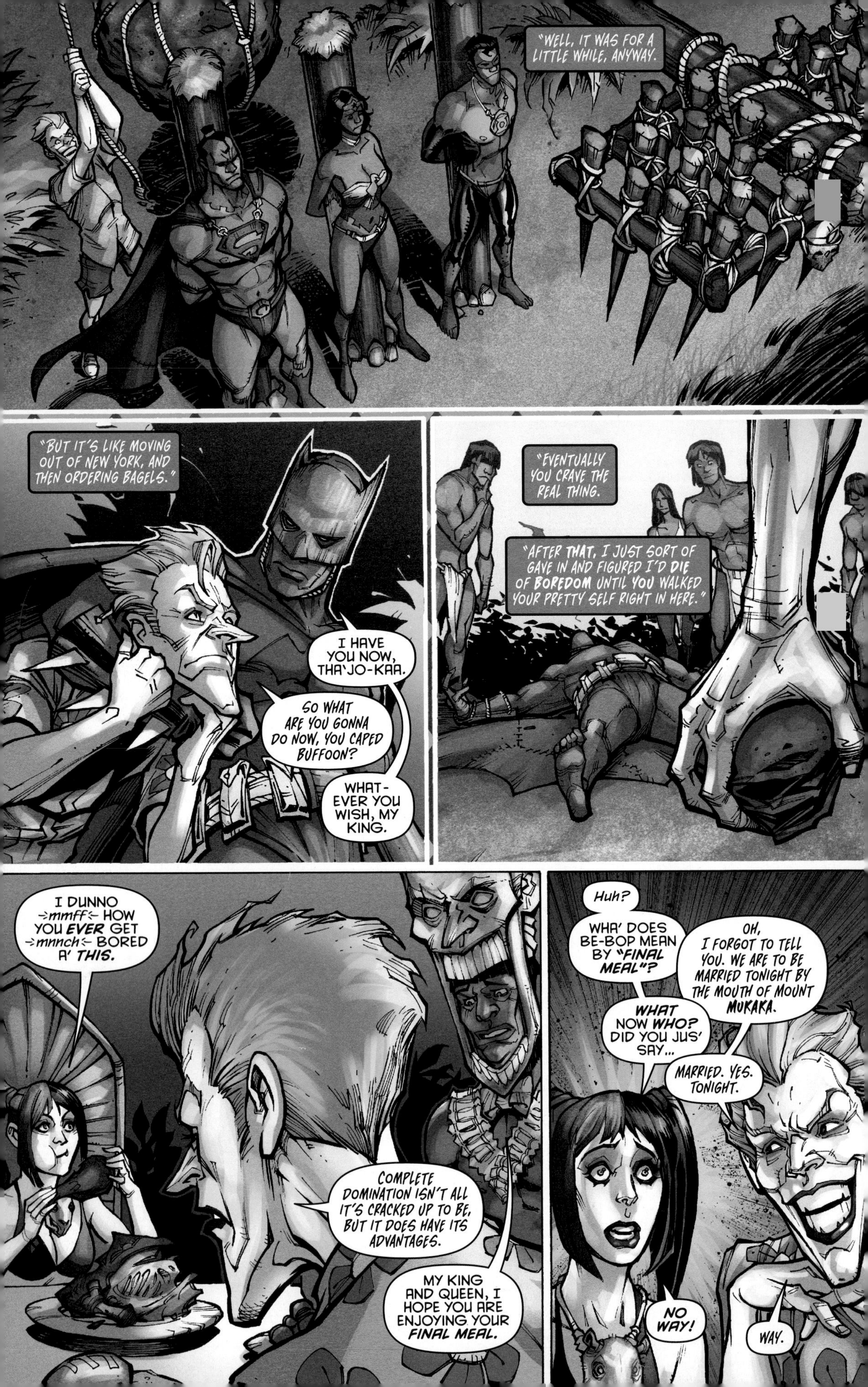
"WELL, IT WAS FOR A LITTLE WHILE, ANYWAY."
"BUT IT'S LIKE MOVING OUT OF NEW YORK, AND THEN ORDERING BAGELS."
I HAVE YOU NOW, THA'JO-KAA.
SO WHAT ARE YOU GONNA DO NOW, YOU CAPED BUFFOON?
WHAT-EVER YOU WISH, MY KING.
"EVENTUALLY YOU CRAVE THE REAL THING."
"AFTER THAT, I JUST SORT OF GAVE IN AND FIGURED I'D DIE OF BOREDOM UNTIL YOU WALKED YOUR PRETTY SELF RIGHT IN HERE."
I DUNNO ⇒mmff⇐ HOW YOU EVER GET ⇒mnnch⇐ BORED A' THIS.
COMPLETE DOMINATION ISN'T ALL IT'S CRACKED UP TO BE, BUT IT DOES HAVE ITS ADVANTAGES.
MY KING AND QUEEN, I HOPE YOU ARE ENJOYING YOUR FINAL MEAL.
Huh?
WHA' DOES BE-BOP MEAN BY "FINAL MEAL"?
OH, I FORGOT TO TELL YOU. WE ARE TO BE MARRIED TONIGHT BY THE MOUTH OF MOUNT MUKAKA.
WHAT NOW WHO? DID YOU JUS' SAY...
MARRIED. YES. TONIGHT.
NO WAY!
WAY.

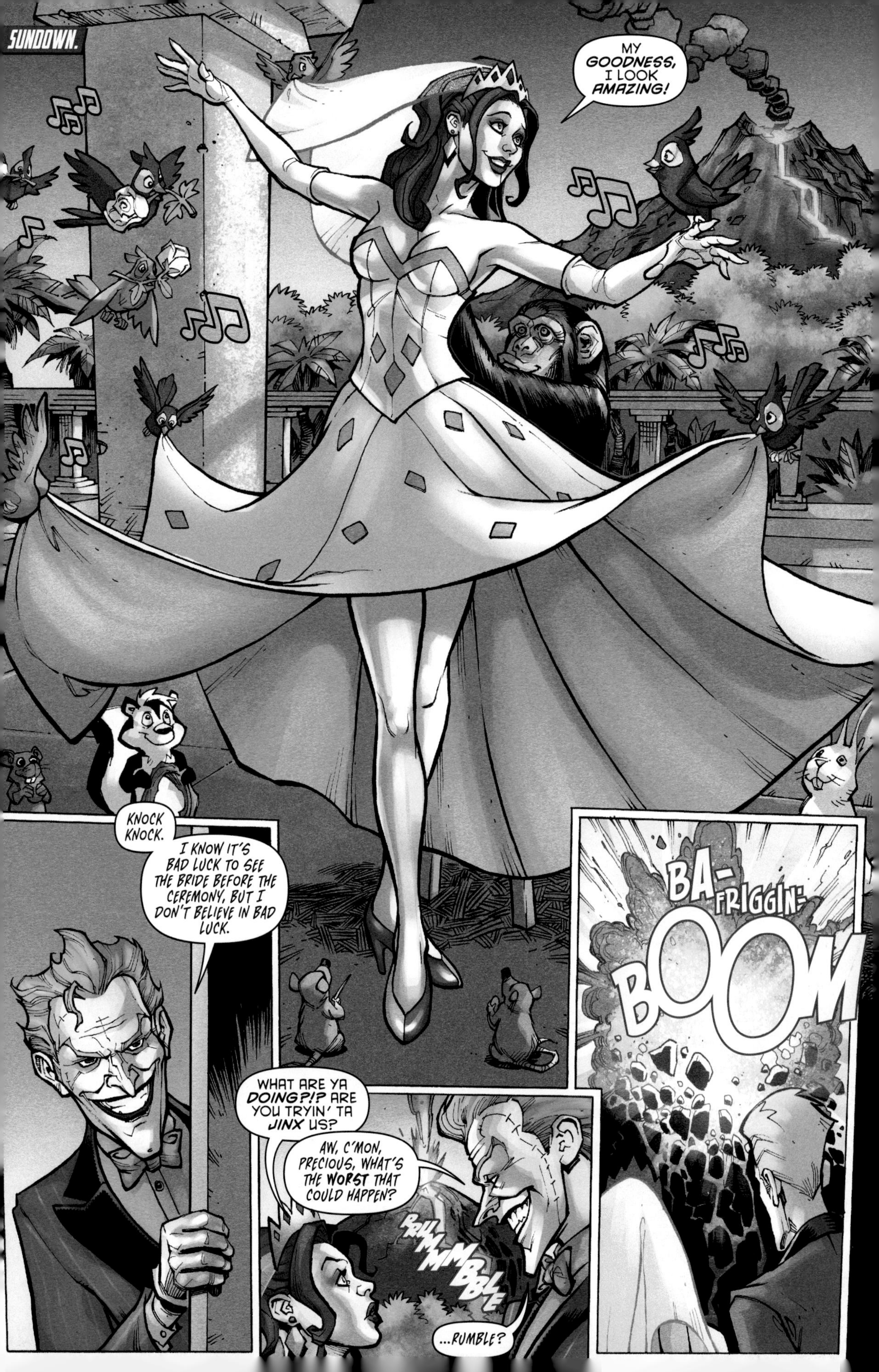
SUNDOWN.
MY GOODNESS, I LOOK AMAZING!
KNOCK KNOCK.
I KNOW IT'S BAD LUCK TO SEE THE BRIDE BEFORE THE CEREMONY, BUT I DON'T BELIEVE IN BAD LUCK.
WHAT ARE YA DOING?!? ARE YOU TRYIN' TA JINX US?
AW, C'MON, PRECIOUS, WHAT'S THE WORST THAT COULD HAPPEN?
RRUMMMBBLE
...RUMBLE?
BA-FRIGGIN-BOOM

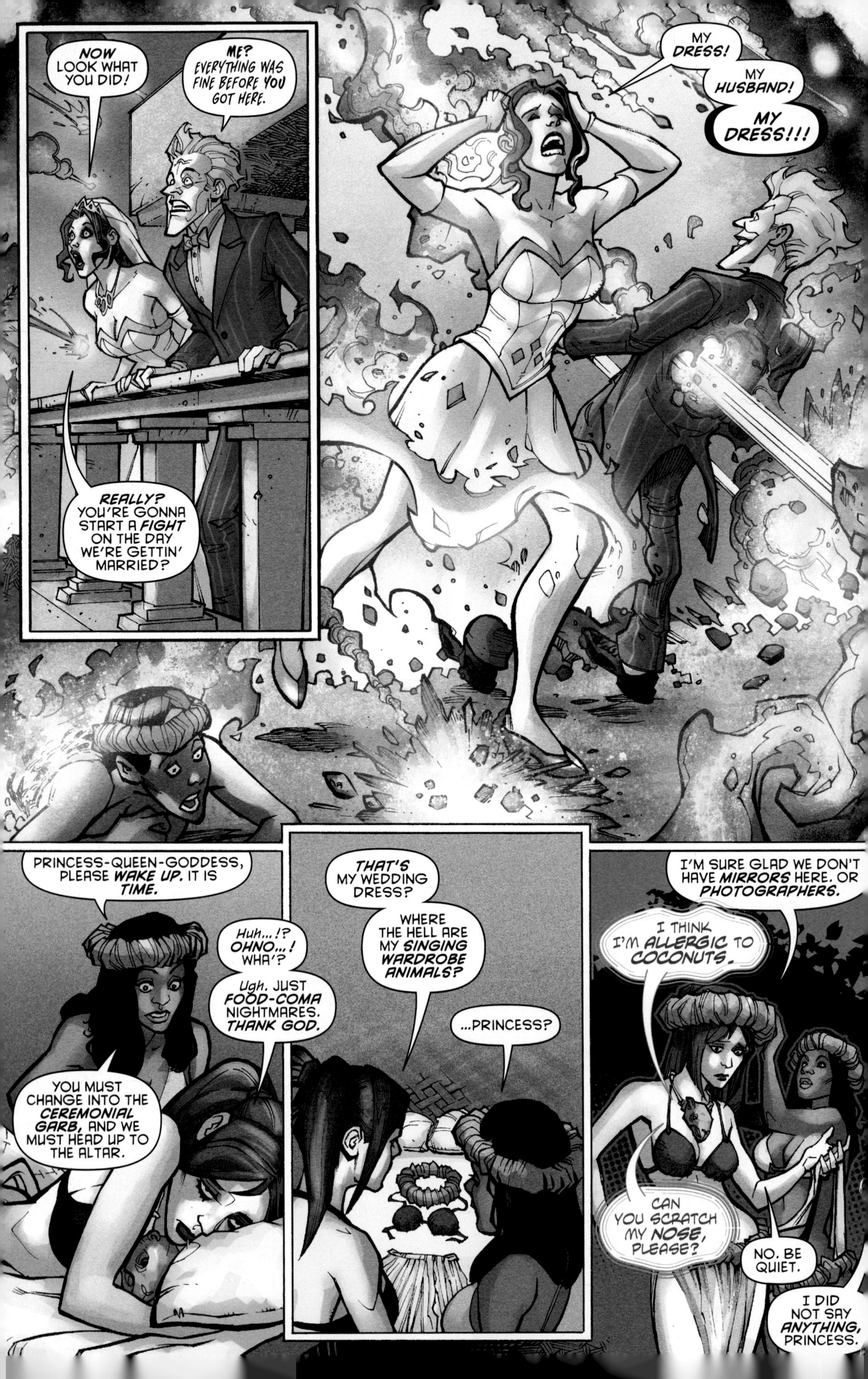
NOW LOOK WHAT YOU DID!
ME? EVERYTHING WAS FINE BEFORE YOU GOT HERE.
REALLY? YOU'RE GONNA START A FIGHT ON THE DAY WE'RE GETTIN' MARRIED?
MY DRESS!
MY HUSBAND!
MY DRESS!!!
PRINCESS-QUEEN-GODDESS, PLEASE WAKE UP. IT IS TIME.
Huh...!? OHNO...! WHA'?
Ugh. JUST FOOD-COMA NIGHTMARES. THANK GOD.
YOU MUST CHANGE INTO THE CEREMONIAL GARB, AND WE MUST HEAD UP TO THE ALTAR.
THAT'S MY WEDDING DRESS?
WHERE THE HELL ARE MY SINGING WARDROBE ANIMALS?
...PRINCESS?
I'M SURE GLAD WE DON'T HAVE MIRRORS HERE. OR PHOTOGRAPHERS.
I THINK I'M ALLERGIC TO COCONUTS.
CAN YOU SCRATCH MY NOSE, PLEASE?
NO. BE QUIET.
I DID NOT SAY ANYTHING, PRINCESS.

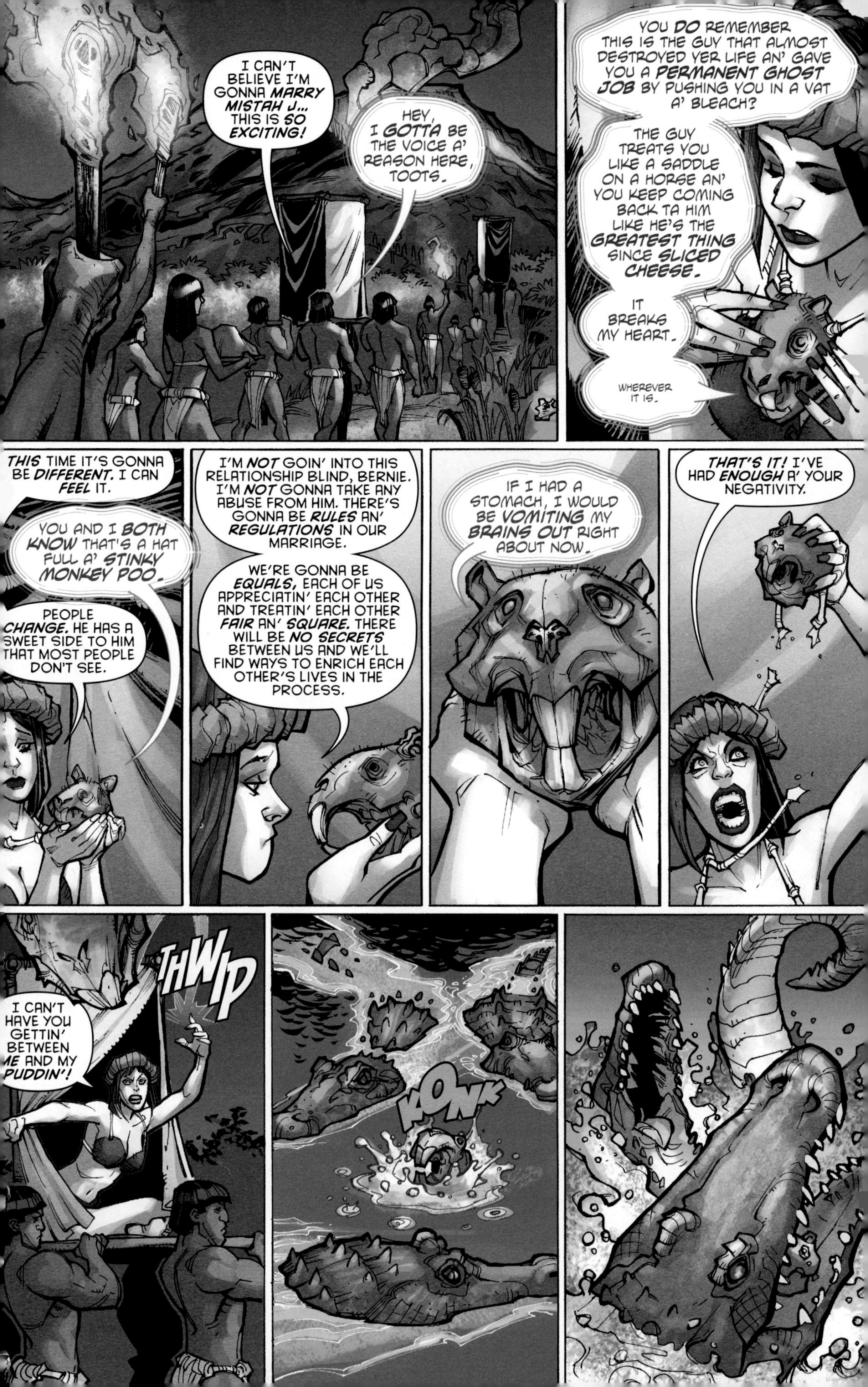
I CAN'T BELIEVE I'M GONNA MARRY MISTAH J... THIS IS SO EXCITING!
HEY, I GOTTA BE THE VOICE A' REASON HERE, TOOTS.
YOU DO REMEMBER THIS IS THE GUY THAT ALMOST DESTROYED YER LIFE AN' GAVE YOU A PERMANENT GHOST JOB BY PUSHING YOU IN A VAT A' BLEACH?
THE GUY TREATS YOU LIKE A SADDLE ON A HORSE AN' YOU KEEP COMING BACK TA HIM LIKE HE'S THE GREATEST THING SINCE SLICED CHEESE.
IT BREAKS MY HEART.
WHEREVER IT IS.
THIS TIME IT'S GONNA BE DIFFERENT. I CAN FEEL IT.
YOU AND I BOTH KNOW THAT'S A HAT FULL A' STINKY MONKEY POO.
PEOPLE CHANGE. HE HAS A SWEET SIDE TO HIM THAT MOST PEOPLE DON'T SEE.
I'M NOT GOIN' INTO THIS RELATIONSHIP BLIND, BERNIE. I'M NOT GONNA TAKE ANY ABUSE FROM HIM. THERE'S GONNA BE RULES AN' REGULATIONS IN OUR MARRIAGE.
WE'RE GONNA BE EQUALS, EACH OF US APPRECIATIN' EACH OTHER AND TREATIN' EACH OTHER FAIR AN' SQUARE. THERE WILL BE NO SECRETS BETWEEN US AND WE'LL FIND WAYS TO ENRICH EACH OTHER'S LIVES IN THE PROCESS.
IF I HAD A STOMACH, I WOULD BE VOMITING MY BRAINS OUT RIGHT ABOUT NOW.
THAT'S IT! I'VE HAD ENOUGH A' YOUR NEGATIVITY.
THWIP
I CAN'T HAVE YOU GETTIN' BETWEEN ME AND MY PUDDIN'!
KONK

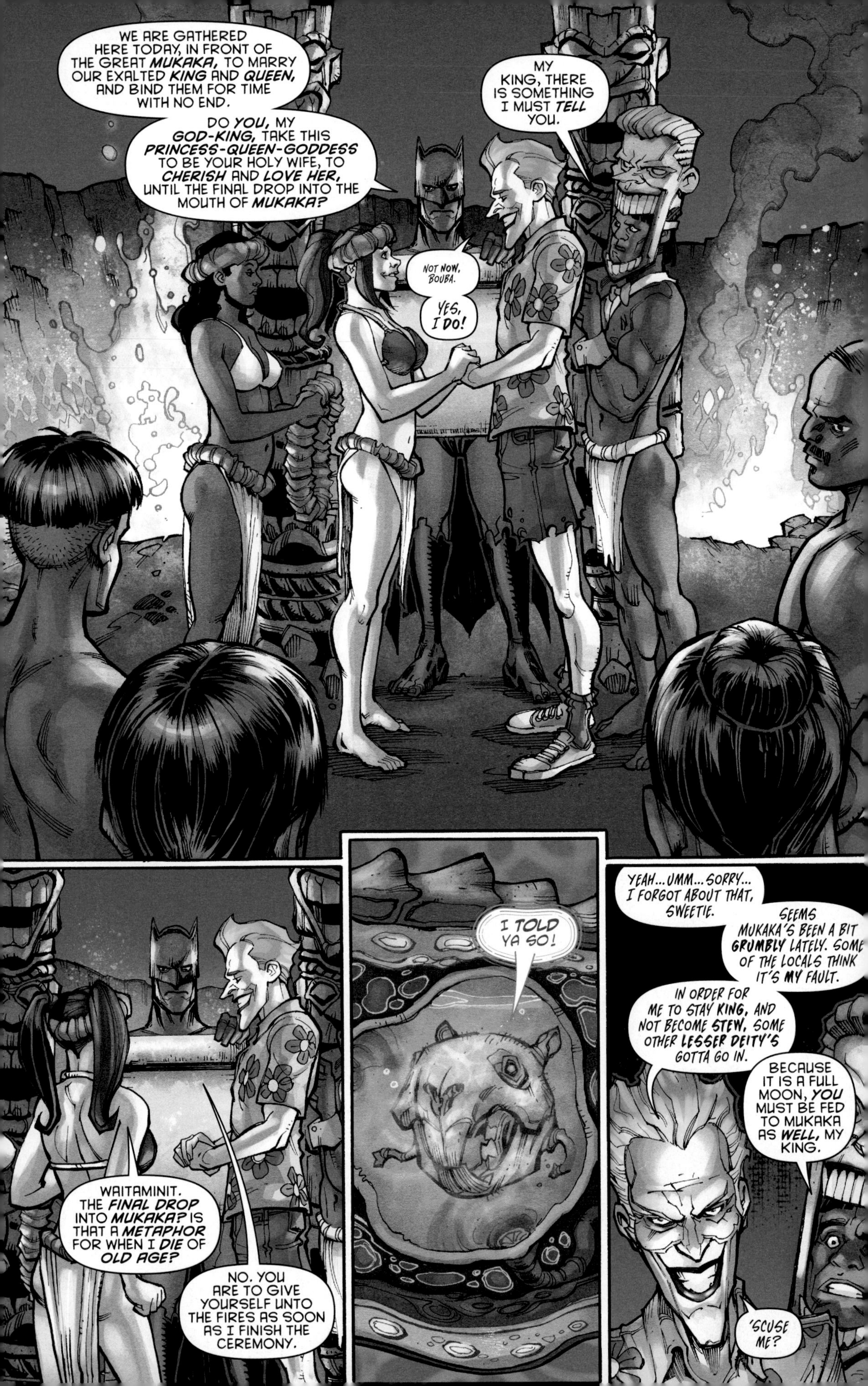
WE ARE GATHERED HERE TODAY, IN FRONT OF THE GREAT MUKAKA, TO MARRY OUR EXALTED KING AND QUEEN, AND BIND THEM FOR TIME WITH NO END.
DO YOU, MY GOD-KING, TAKE THIS PRINCESS-QUEEN-GODDESS TO BE YOUR HOLY WIFE, TO CHERISH AND LOVE HER, UNTIL THE FINAL DROP INTO THE MOUTH OF MUKAKA?
MY KING, THERE IS SOMETHING I MUST TELL YOU.
NOT NOW, BOUBA.
YES, I DO!
WAITAMINIT. THE FINAL DROP INTO MUKAKA? IS THAT A METAPHOR FOR WHEN I DIE OF OLD AGE?
NO. YOU ARE TO GIVE YOURSELF UNTO THE FIRES AS SOON AS I FINISH THE CEREMONY.
I TOLD YA SO!
YEAH... UMM... SORRY... I FORGOT ABOUT THAT, SWEETIE.
SEEMS MUKAKA'S BEEN A BIT GRUMBLY LATELY. SOME OF THE LOCALS THINK IT'S MY FAULT.
IN ORDER FOR ME TO STAY KING, AND NOT BECOME STEW, SOME OTHER LESSER DEITY'S GOTTA GO IN.
BECAUSE IT IS A FULL MOON, YOU MUST BE FED TO MUKAKA AS WELL, MY KING.
'SCUSE ME?

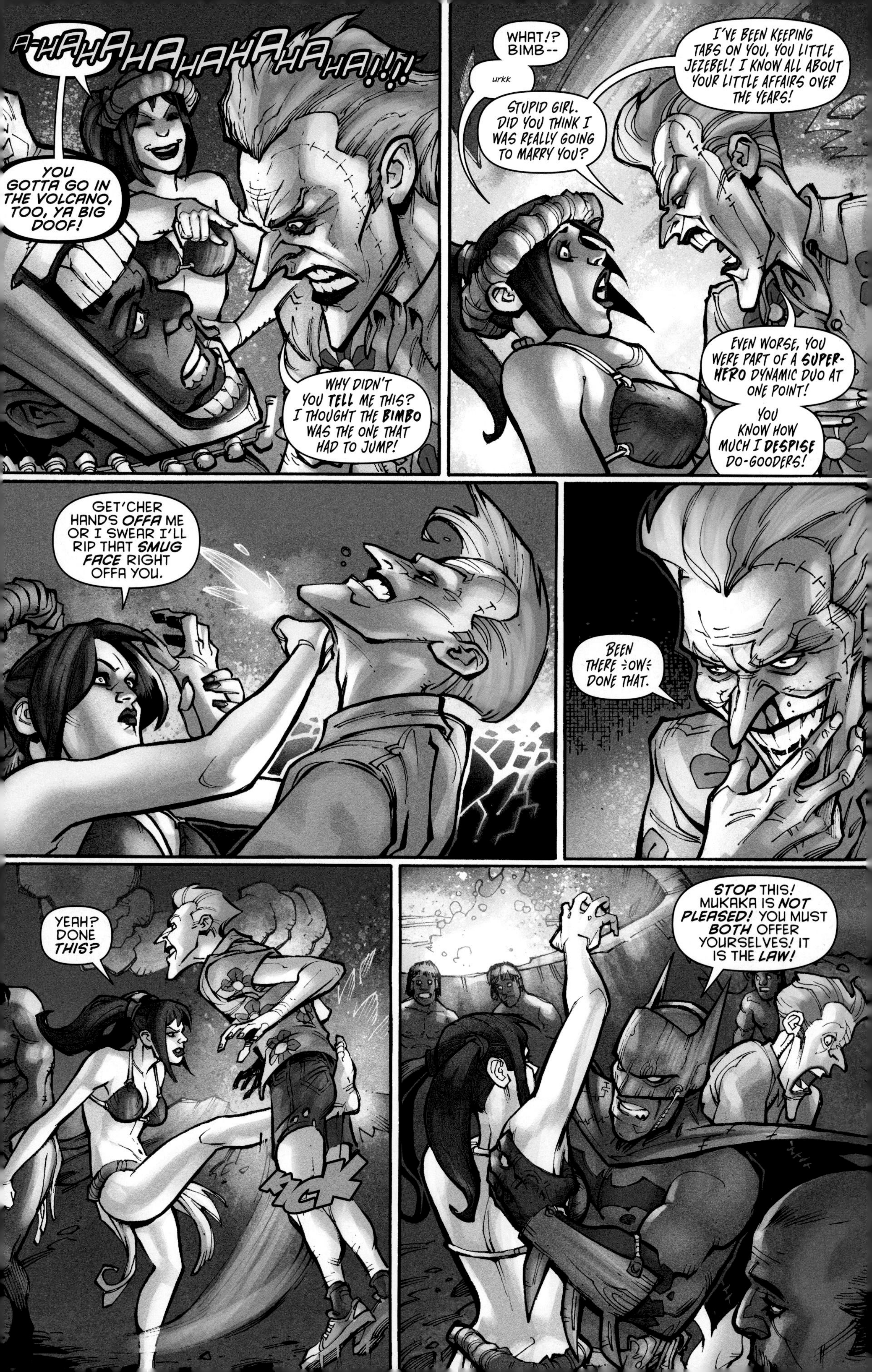
A-HAHAHAHAHAHAHAHAHA!!!!
YOU GOTTA GO IN THE VOLCANO, TOO, YA BIG DOOF!
WHY DIDN'T YOU TELL ME THIS? I THOUGHT THE BIMBO WAS THE ONE THAT HAD TO JUMP!
WHAT!? BIMB--
urkk
STUPID GIRL. DID YOU THINK I WAS REALLY GOING TO MARRY YOU?
I'VE BEEN KEEPING TABS ON YOU, YOU LITTLE JEZEBEL! I KNOW ALL ABOUT YOUR LITTLE AFFAIRS OVER THE YEARS!
EVEN WORSE, YOU WERE PART OF A SUPER-HERO DYNAMIC DUO AT ONE POINT!
YOU KNOW HOW MUCH I DESPISE DO-GOODERS!
GET'CHER HANDS OFFA ME OR I SWEAR I'LL RIP THAT SMUG FACE RIGHT OFFA YOU.
BEEN THERE OW DONE THAT.
YEAH? DONE THIS?
KICK
STOP THIS! MUKAKA IS NOT PLEASED! YOU MUST BOTH OFFER YOURSELVES! IT IS THE LAW!

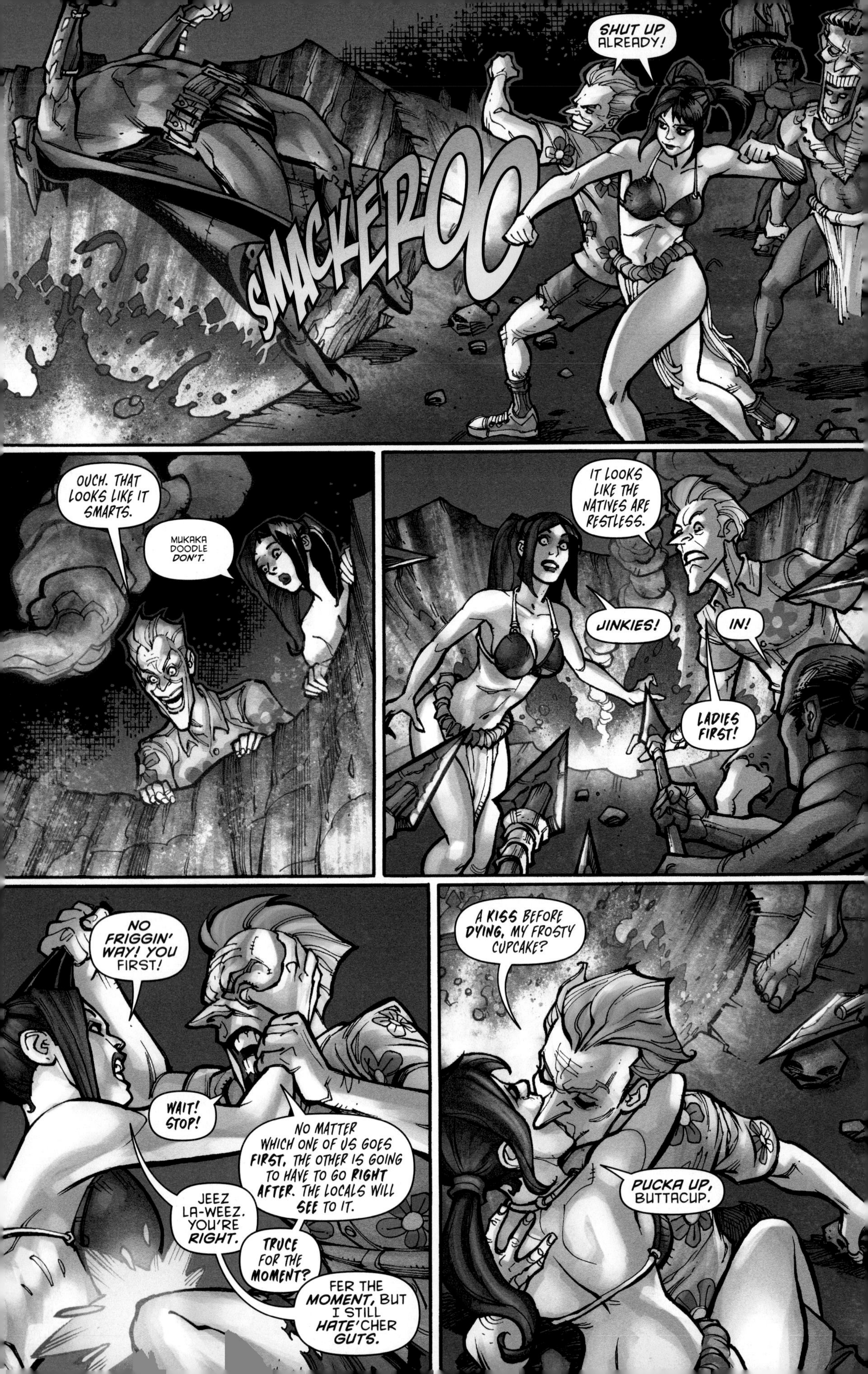
SHUT UP ALREADY!
SMACKEROO
OUCH. THAT LOOKS LIKE IT SMARTS.
MUKAKA DOODLE DON'T.
IT LOOKS LIKE THE NATIVES ARE RESTLESS.
JINKIES!
IN!
LADIES FIRST!
NO FRIGGIN' WAY! YOU FIRST!
WAIT! STOP!
NO MATTER WHICH ONE OF US GOES FIRST, THE OTHER IS GOING TO HAVE TO GO RIGHT AFTER. THE LOCALS WILL SEE TO IT.
JEEZ LA-WEEZ. YOU'RE RIGHT.
TRUCE FOR THE MOMENT?
FER THE MOMENT, BUT I STILL HATE'CHER GUTS.
A KISS BEFORE DYING, MY FROSTY CUPCAKE?
PUCKA UP, BUTTACUP.

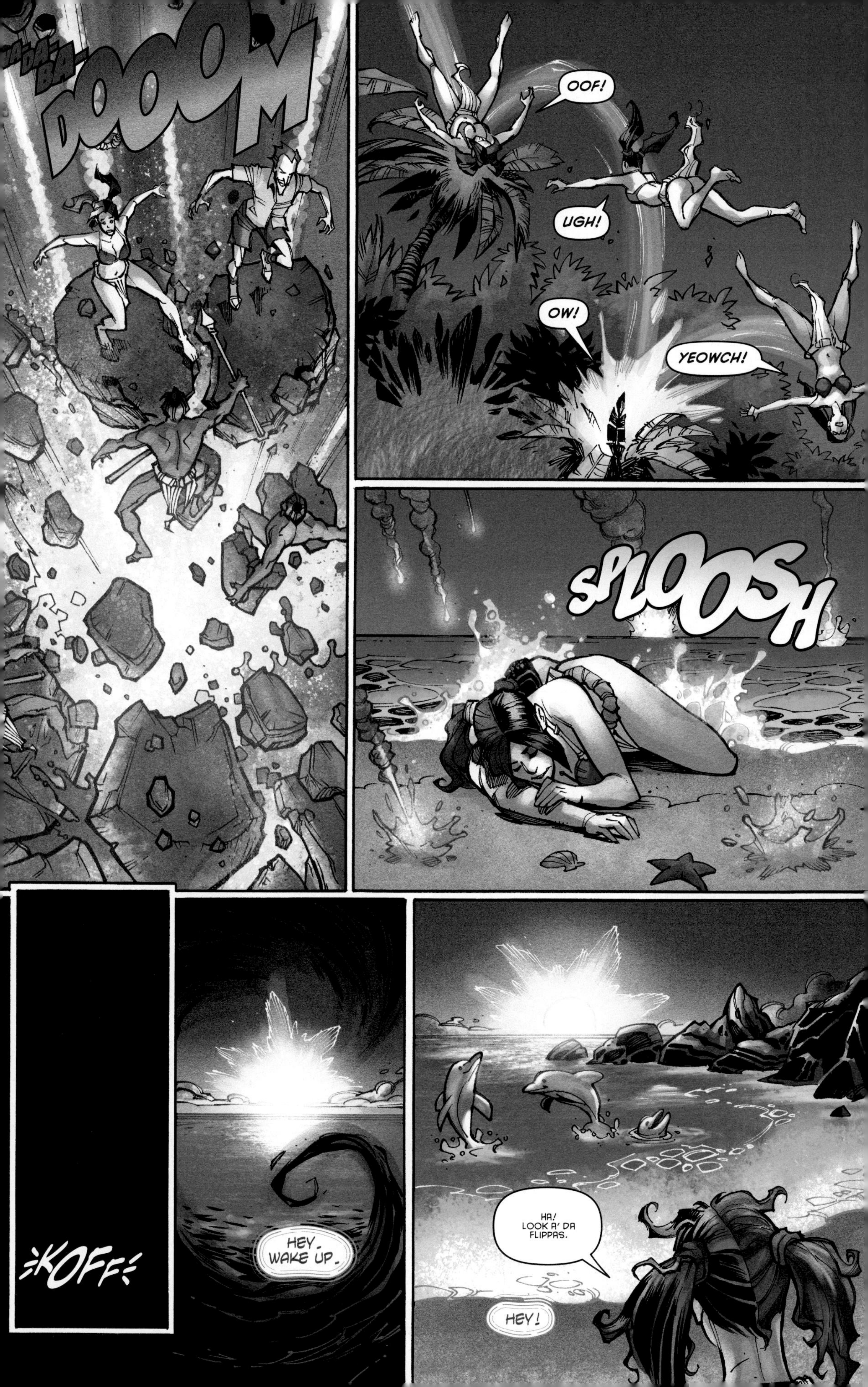
BA-DA-BA-DOOOM
OOF!
UGH!
OW!
YEOWCH!
SPLOOSH
KOFF
HEY. WAKE UP.
HA! LOOK A' DA FLIPPAS.
HEY!

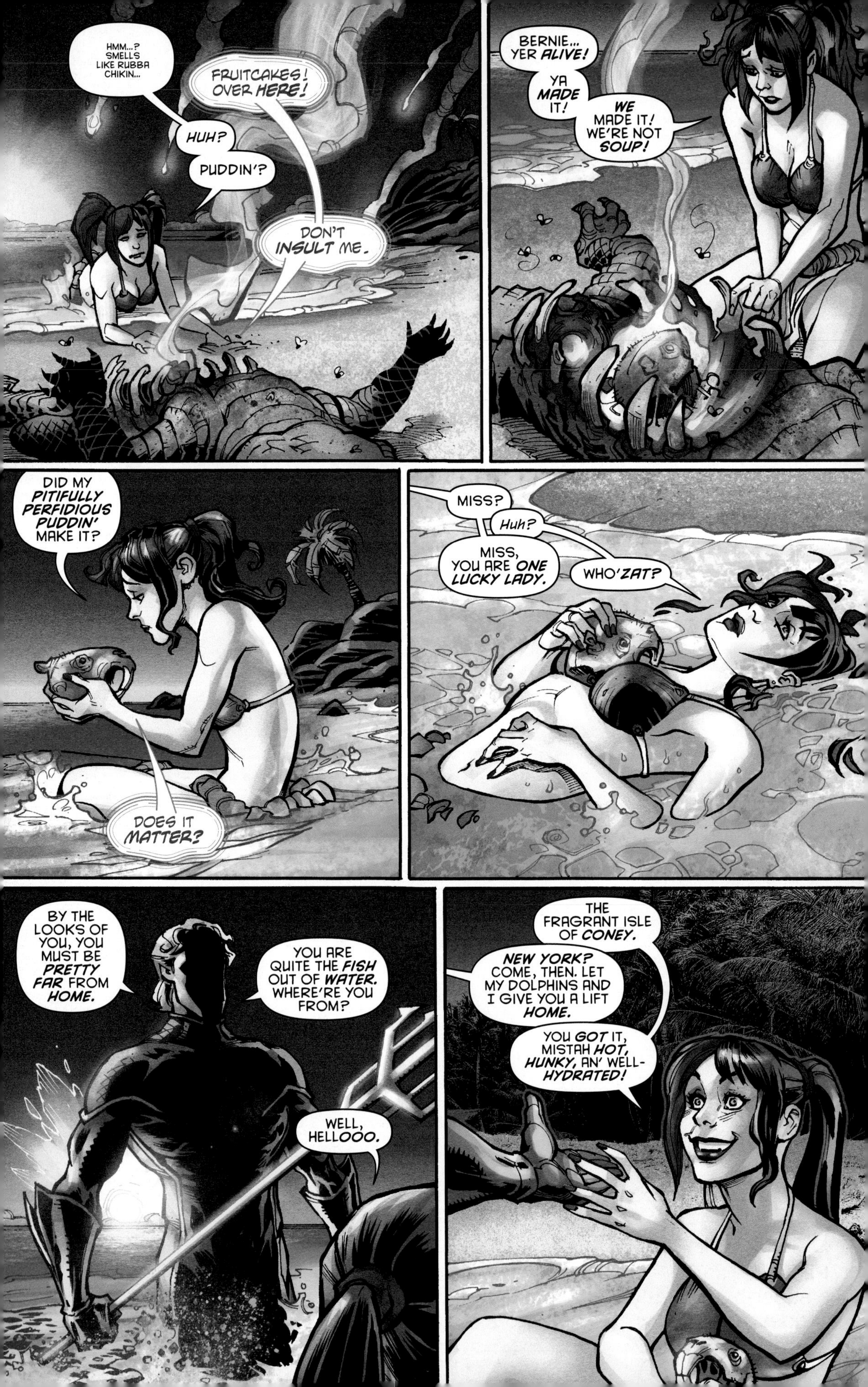
HMM...? SMELLS LIKE RUBBA CHIKIN...
FRUITCAKES! OVER HERE!
HUH?
PUDDIN'?
DON'T INSULT ME.
BERNIE... YER ALIVE!
YA MADE IT!
WE MADE IT! WE'RE NOT SOUP!
DID MY PITIFULLY PERFIDIOUS PUDDIN' MAKE IT?
DOES IT MATTER?
MISS?
Huh?
MISS, YOU ARE ONE LUCKY LADY.
WHO'ZAT?
BY THE LOOKS OF YOU, YOU MUST BE PRETTY FAR FROM HOME.
YOU ARE QUITE THE FISH OUT OF WATER. WHERE'RE YOU FROM?
WELL, HELLOOO.
THE FRAGRANT ISLE OF CONEY.
NEW YORK? COME, THEN. LET MY DOLPHINS AND I GIVE YOU A LIFT HOME.
YOU GOT IT, MISTAH HOT, HUNKY, AN' WELL-HYDRATED!

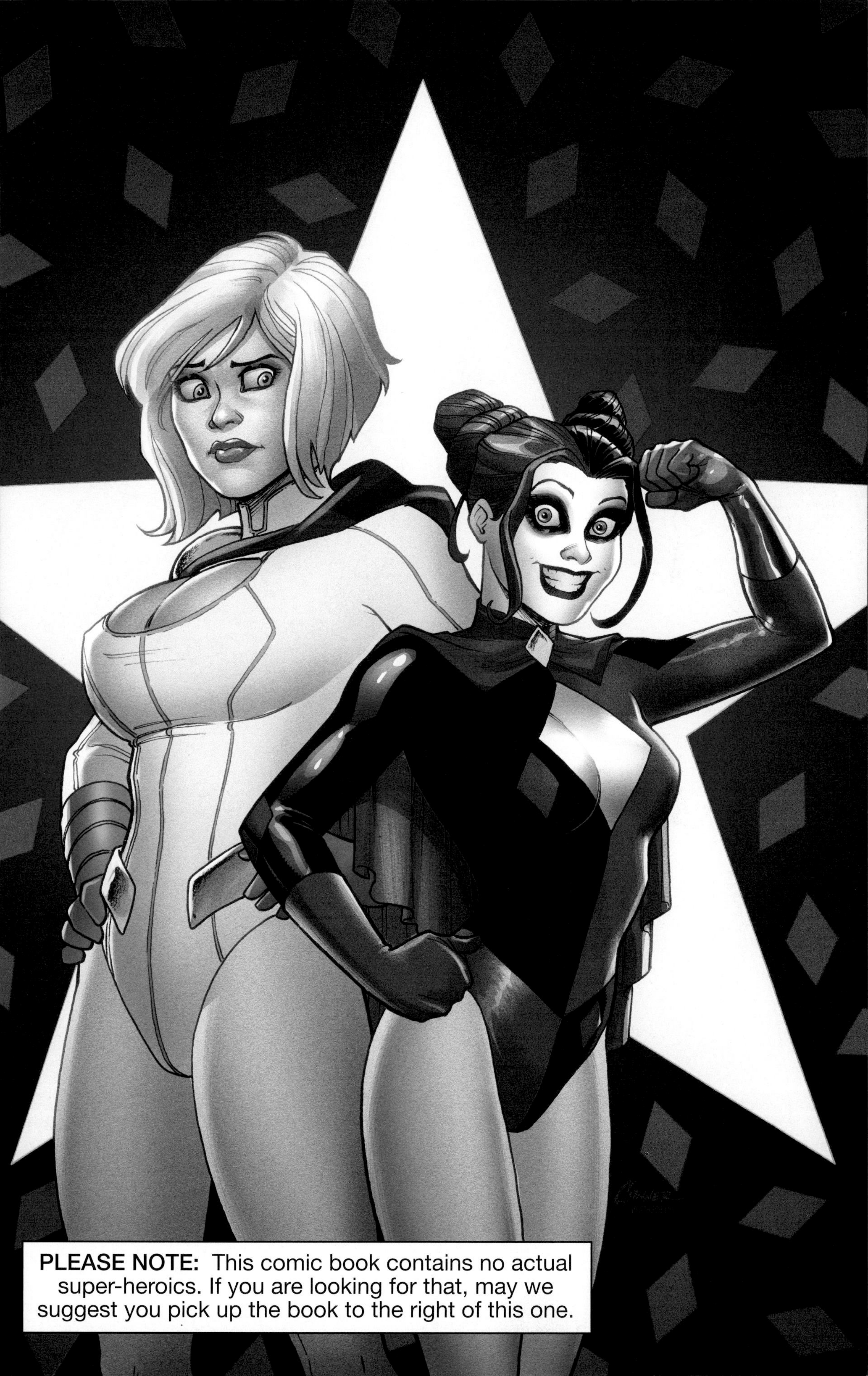
PLEASE NOTE: This comic book contains no actual super-heroics. If you are looking for that, may we suggest you pick up the book to the right of this one.

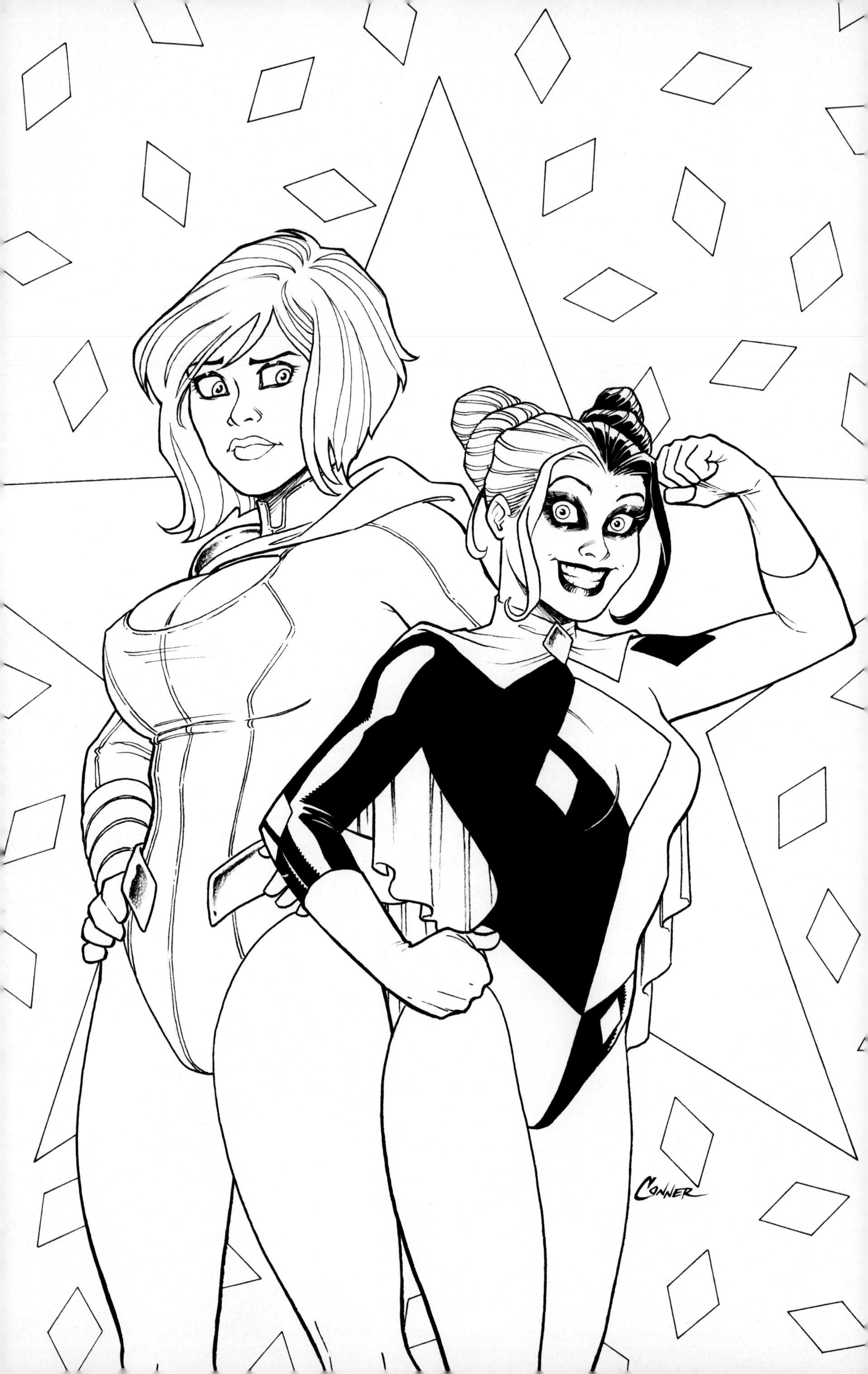
CONNER

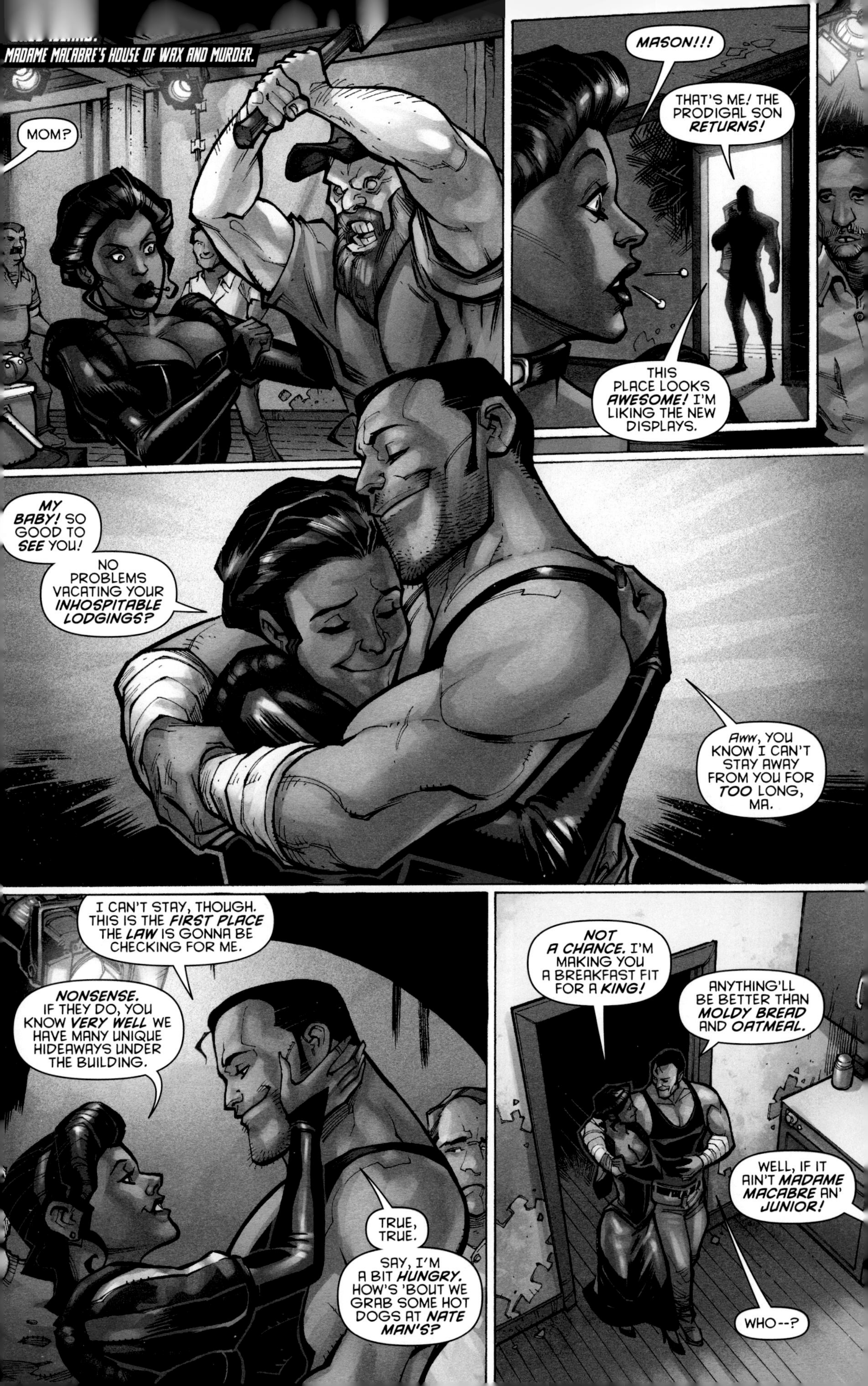
MADAME MACABRE'S HOUSE OF WAX AND MURDER.
MOM?
MASON!!!
THAT'S ME! THE PRODIGAL SON RETURNS!
THIS PLACE LOOKS AWESOME! I'M LIKING THE NEW DISPLAYS.
MY BABY! SO GOOD TO SEE YOU!
NO PROBLEMS VACATING YOUR INHOSPITABLE LODGINGS?
AWW, YOU KNOW I CAN'T STAY AWAY FROM YOU FOR TOO LONG, MA.
I CAN'T STAY, THOUGH. THIS IS THE FIRST PLACE THE LAW IS GONNA BE CHECKING FOR ME.
NONSENSE. IF THEY DO, YOU KNOW VERY WELL WE HAVE MANY UNIQUE HIDEAWAYS UNDER THE BUILDING.
TRUE, TRUE.
SAY, I'M A BIT HUNGRY. HOW'S 'BOUT WE GRAB SOME HOT DOGS AT NATE MAN'S?
NOT A CHANCE. I'M MAKING YOU A BREAKFAST FIT FOR A KING!
ANYTHING'LL BE BETTER THAN MOLDY BREAD AND OATMEAL.
WELL, IF IT AIN'T MADAME MACABRE AN' JUNIOR!
WHO--?

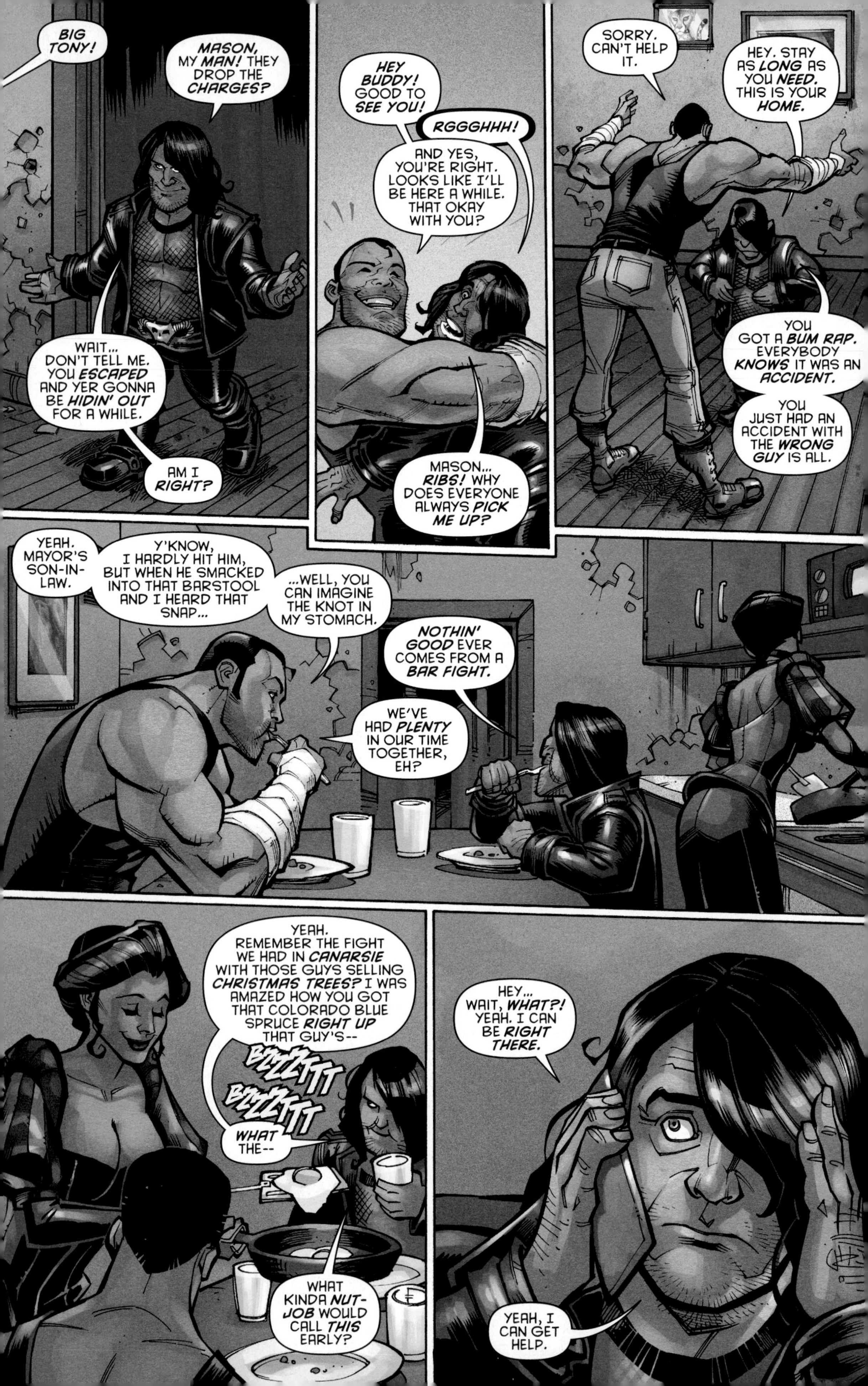
BIG TONY!
MASON, MY MAN! THEY DROP THE CHARGES?
WAIT... DON'T TELL ME. YOU ESCAPED AND YER GONNA BE HIDIN' OUT FOR A WHILE.
AM I RIGHT?
HEY BUDDY! GOOD TO SEE YOU!
RGGGHHH!
AND YES, YOU'RE RIGHT. LOOKS LIKE I'LL BE HERE A WHILE. THAT OKAY WITH YOU?
MASON... RIBS! WHY DOES EVERYONE ALWAYS PICK ME UP?
SORRY. CAN'T HELP IT.
HEY. STAY AS LONG AS YOU NEED. THIS IS YOUR HOME.
YOU GOT A BUM RAP. EVERYBODY KNOWS IT WAS AN ACCIDENT.
YOU JUST HAD AN ACCIDENT WITH THE WRONG GUY IS ALL.
YEAH. MAYOR'S SON-IN-LAW.
Y'KNOW, I HARDLY HIT HIM, BUT WHEN HE SMACKED INTO THAT BARSTOOL AND I HEARD THAT SNAP...
...WELL, YOU CAN IMAGINE THE KNOT IN MY STOMACH.
NOTHIN' GOOD EVER COMES FROM A BAR FIGHT.
WE'VE HAD PLENTY IN OUR TIME TOGETHER, EH?
YEAH. REMEMBER THE FIGHT WE HAD IN CANARSIE WITH THOSE GUYS SELLING CHRISTMAS TREES? I WAS AMAZED HOW YOU GOT THAT COLORADO BLUE SPRUCE RIGHT UP THAT GUY'S--
BZZZZTTT
BZZZZTTT
WHAT THE--
WHAT KINDA NUT-JOB WOULD CALL THIS EARLY?
HEY... WAIT, WHAT?! YEAH. I CAN BE RIGHT THERE.
YEAH, I CAN GET HELP.

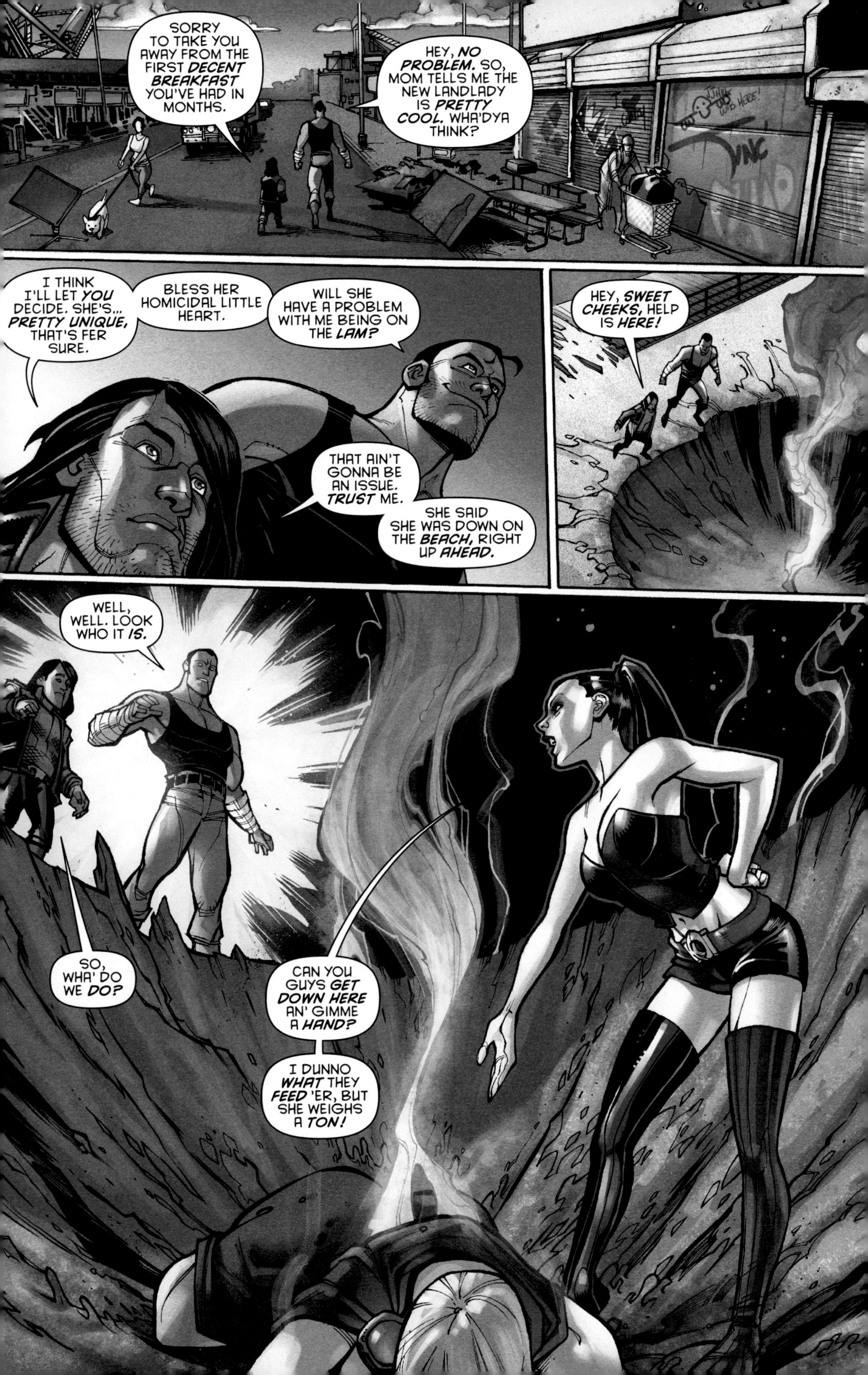
SORRY TO TAKE YOU AWAY FROM THE FIRST DECENT BREAKFAST YOU'VE HAD IN MONTHS.
HEY, NO PROBLEM. SO, MOM TELLS ME THE NEW LANDLADY IS PRETTY COOL. WHA'DYA THINK?
I THINK I'LL LET YOU DECIDE. SHE'S... PRETTY UNIQUE, THAT'S FER SURE.
BLESS HER HOMICIDAL LITTLE HEART.
WILL SHE HAVE A PROBLEM WITH ME BEING ON THE LAM?
THAT AIN'T GONNA BE AN ISSUE. TRUST ME.
SHE SAID SHE WAS DOWN ON THE BEACH, RIGHT UP AHEAD.
HEY, SWEET CHEEKS, HELP IS HERE!
WELL, WELL. LOOK WHO IT IS.
SO, WHA' DO WE DO?
CAN YOU GUYS GET DOWN HERE AN' GIMME A HAND?
I DUNNO WHAT THEY FEED 'ER, BUT SHE WEIGHS A TON!

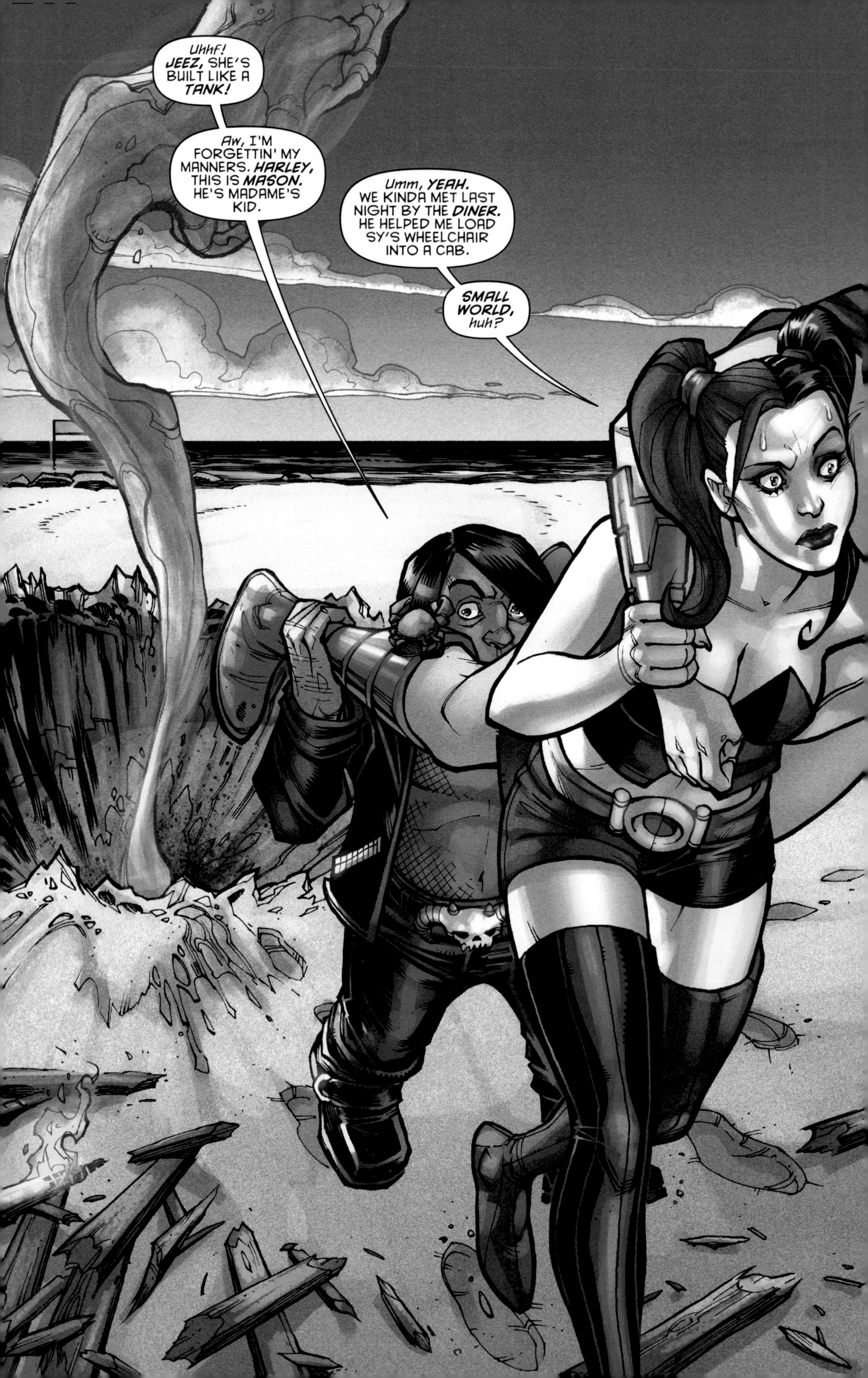
Uhhf! JEEZ, SHE'S BUILT LIKE A TANK!
Aw, I'M FORGETTIN' MY MANNERS. HARLEY, THIS IS MASON. HE'S MADAME'S KID.
Umm, YEAH. WE KINDA MET LAST NIGHT BY THE DINER. HE HELPED ME LOAD SY'S WHEELCHAIR INTO A CAB.
SMALL WORLD, huh?

SOUNDS LIKE FATE TO ME.
SO, WHAT HAPPENED TO YOUR COSTUMED FRIEND HERE?
I DUNNO. WHEN WE GET HER BACK TO MY PLACE WE CAN TRY AN' WAKE HER UP AN' FIND OUT.
POWER OUTAGE
AMANDA CONNER & JIMMY PALMIOTTI WRITERS
CHAD HARDIN ARTIST
ALEX SINCLAIR COLORS
JOHN J. HILL LETTERS
AMANDA CONNER WITH PAUL MOUNTS COVER

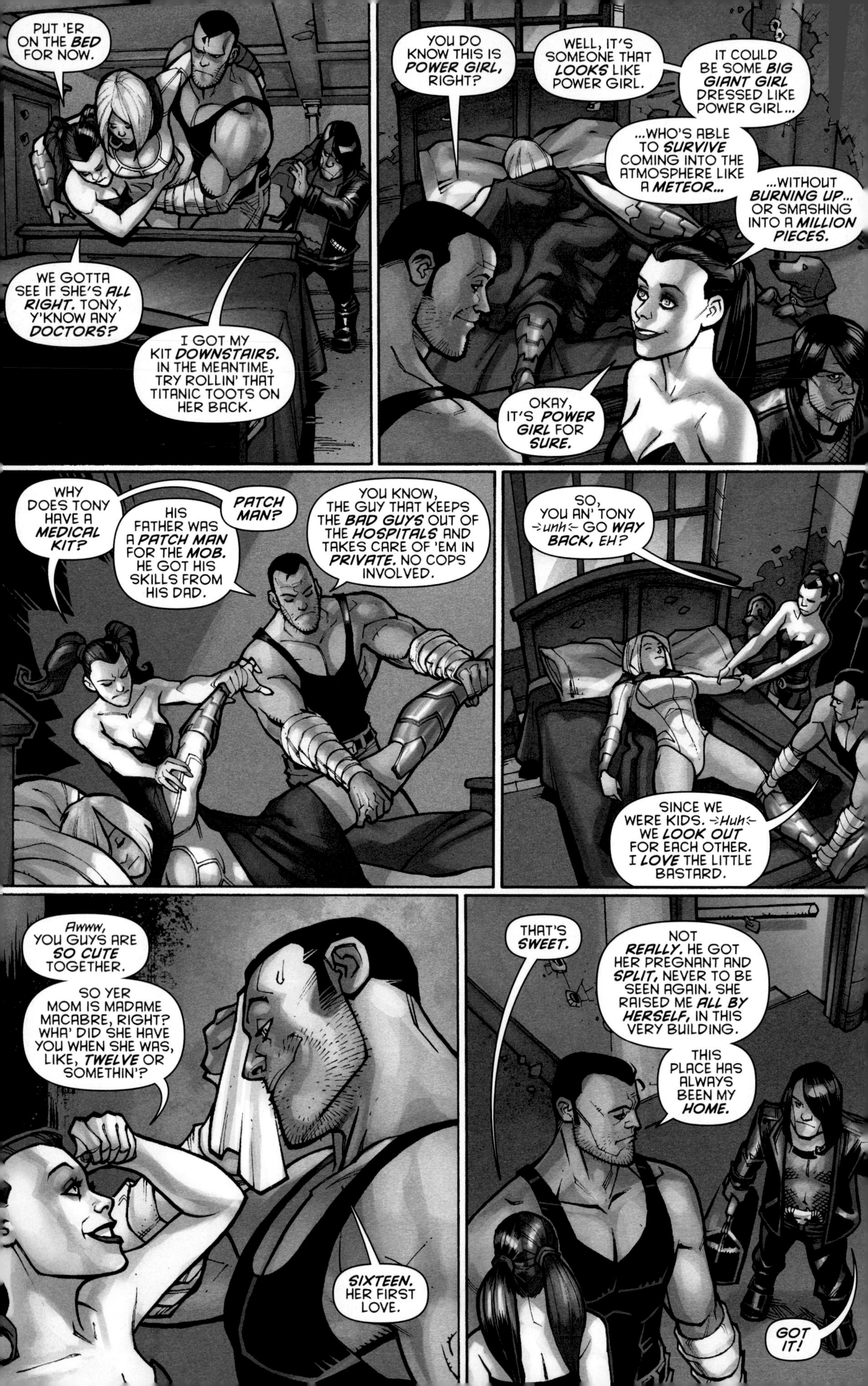

PUT 'ER ON THE BED FOR NOW.
WE GOTTA SEE IF SHE'S ALL RIGHT. TONY, Y'KNOW ANY DOCTORS?
I GOT MY KIT DOWNSTAIRS. IN THE MEANTIME, TRY ROLLIN' THAT TITANIC TOOTS ON HER BACK.
YOU DO KNOW THIS IS POWER GIRL, RIGHT?
WELL, IT'S SOMEONE THAT LOOKS LIKE POWER GIRL.
IT COULD BE SOME BIG GIANT GIRL DRESSED LIKE POWER GIRL...
...WHO'S ABLE TO SURVIVE COMING INTO THE ATMOSPHERE LIKE A METEOR...
...WITHOUT BURNING UP... OR SMASHING INTO A MILLION PIECES.
OKAY, IT'S POWER GIRL FOR SURE.
WHY DOES TONY HAVE A MEDICAL KIT?
HIS FATHER WAS A PATCH MAN FOR THE MOB. HE GOT HIS SKILLS FROM HIS DAD.
PATCH MAN?
YOU KNOW, THE GUY THAT KEEPS THE BAD GUYS OUT OF THE HOSPITALS AND TAKES CARE OF 'EM IN PRIVATE. NO COPS INVOLVED.
SO, YOU AN' TONY -unh- GO WAY BACK, EH?
SINCE WE WERE KIDS. -Huh- WE LOOK OUT FOR EACH OTHER. I LOVE THE LITTLE BASTARD.
Awww, YOU GUYS ARE SO CUTE TOGETHER.
SO YER MOM IS MADAME MACABRE, RIGHT? WHA' DID SHE HAVE YOU WHEN SHE WAS, LIKE, TWELVE OR SOMETHIN'?
SIXTEEN. HER FIRST LOVE.
THAT'S SWEET.
NOT REALLY. HE GOT HER PREGNANT AND SPLIT, NEVER TO BE SEEN AGAIN. SHE RAISED ME ALL BY HERSELF, IN THIS VERY BUILDING.
THIS PLACE HAS ALWAYS BEEN MY HOME.
GOT IT!

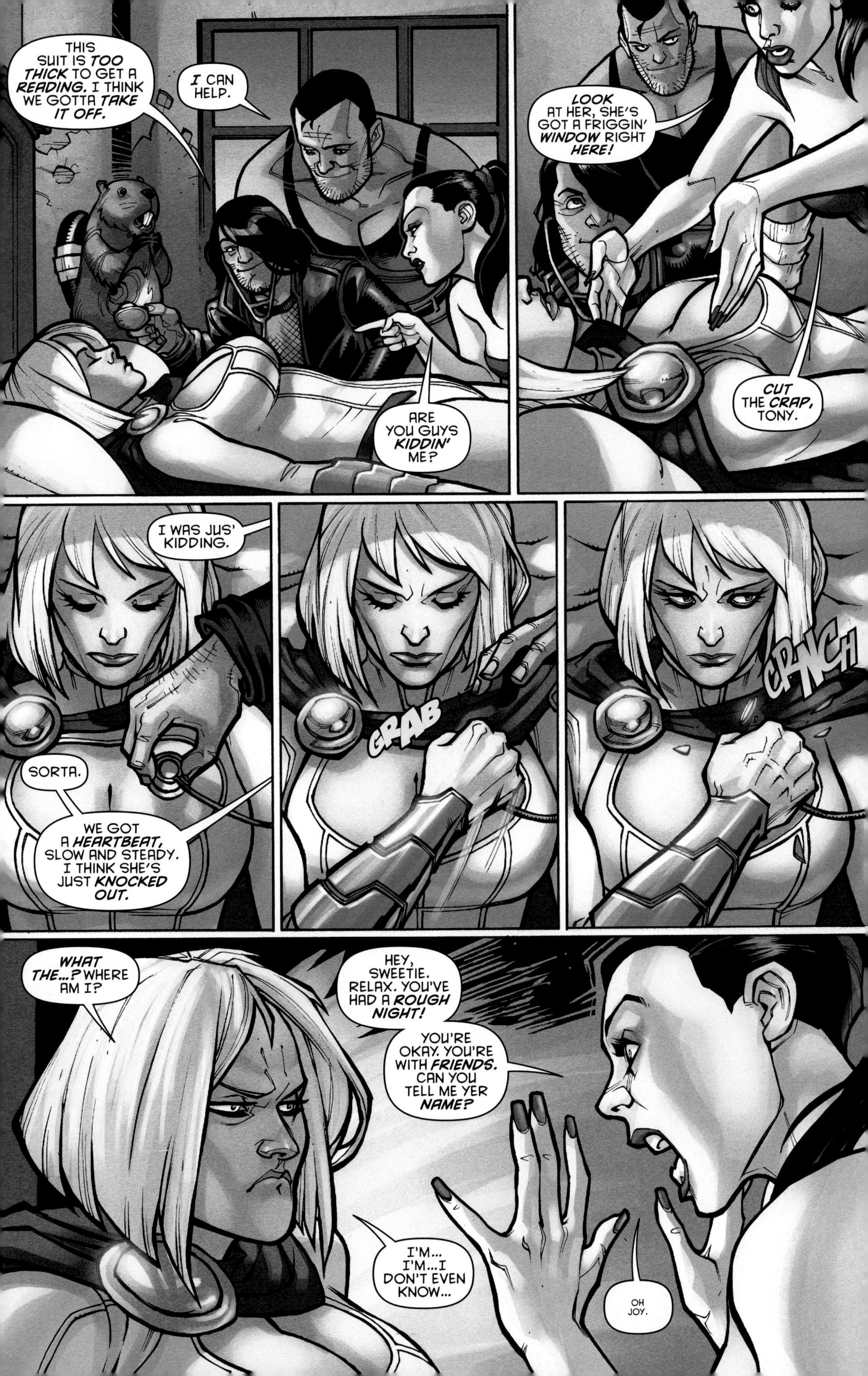
THIS SUIT IS TOO THICK TO GET A READING. I THINK WE GOTTA TAKE IT OFF.
I CAN HELP.
ARE YOU GUYS KIDDIN' ME?
LOOK AT HER, SHE'S GOT A FRIGGIN' WINDOW RIGHT HERE!
CUT THE CRAP, TONY.
I WAS JUS' KIDDING.
SORTA.
WE GOT A HEARTBEAT, SLOW AND STEADY. I THINK SHE'S JUST KNOCKED OUT.
GRAB
CRNCH
WHAT THE...? WHERE AM I?
HEY, SWEETIE. RELAX. YOU'VE HAD A ROUGH NIGHT!
YOU'RE OKAY. YOU'RE WITH FRIENDS. CAN YOU TELL ME YER NAME?
I'M... I'M...I DON'T EVEN KNOW...
OH JOY.

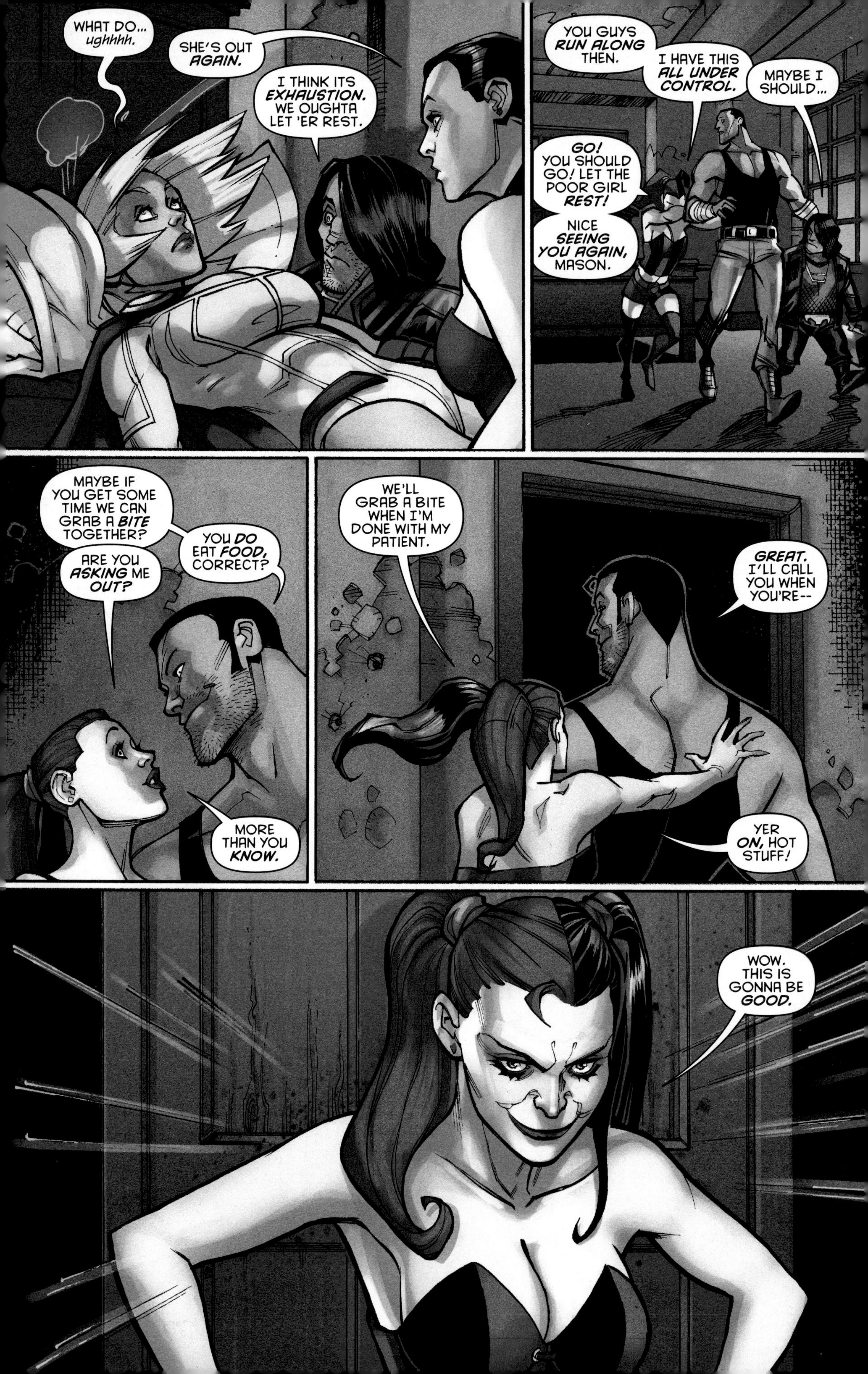
WHAT DO... *ughhhh.*
SHE'S OUT ***AGAIN.***
I THINK ITS ***EXHAUSTION.*** WE OUGHTA LET 'ER REST.
YOU GUYS ***RUN ALONG*** THEN.
I HAVE THIS ***ALL UNDER CONTROL.***
MAYBE I SHOULD...
GO! YOU SHOULD GO! LET THE POOR GIRL ***REST!***
NICE ***SEEING YOU AGAIN,*** MASON.
MAYBE IF YOU GET SOME TIME WE CAN GRAB A ***BITE*** TOGETHER?
YOU ***DO*** EAT ***FOOD,*** CORRECT?
ARE YOU ***ASKING*** ME ***OUT?***
MORE THAN YOU ***KNOW.***
WE'LL GRAB A BITE WHEN I'M DONE WITH MY PATIENT.
GREAT. I'LL CALL YOU WHEN YOU'RE--
YER ***ON,*** HOT STUFF!
WOW. THIS IS GONNA BE ***GOOD.***

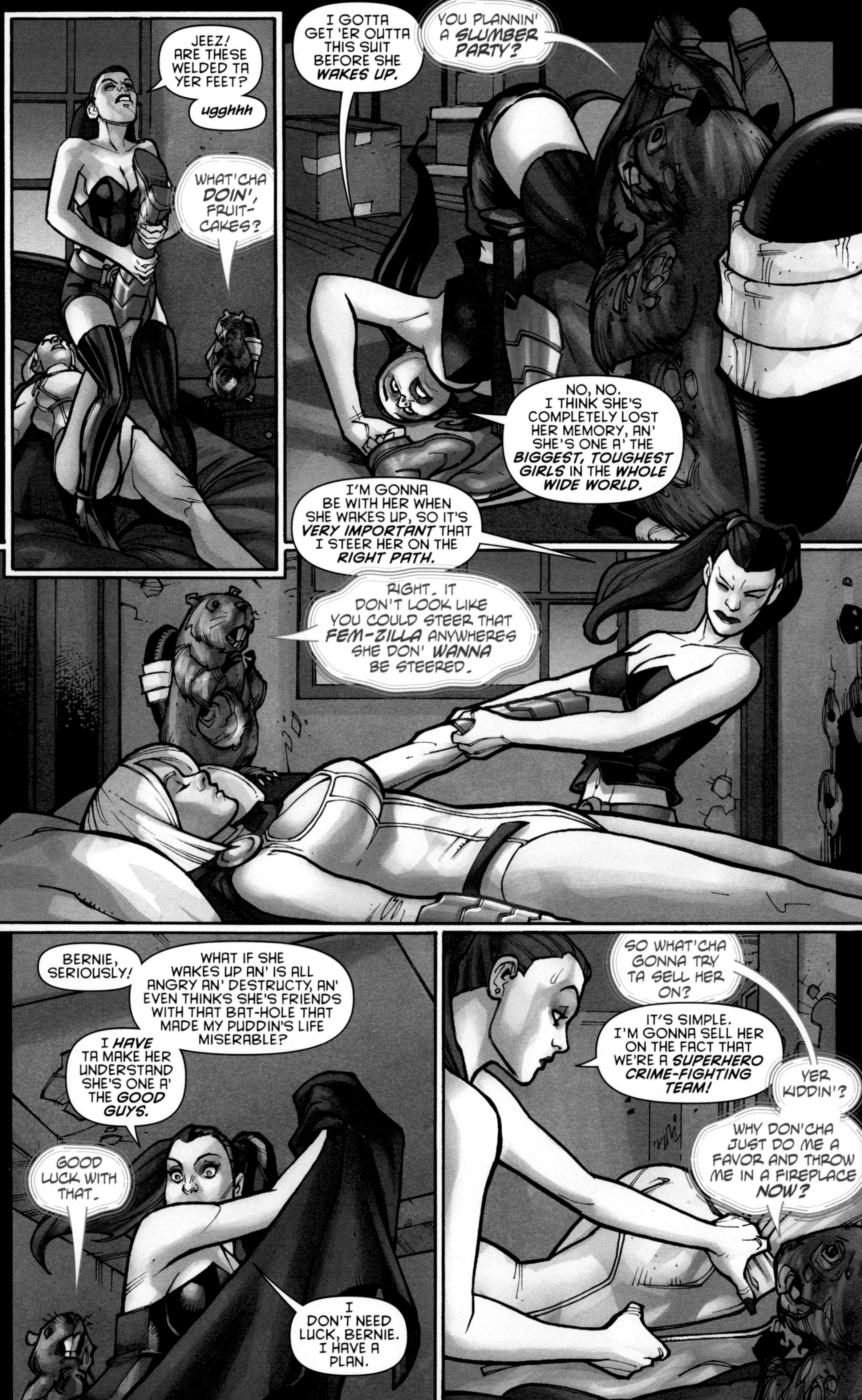
JEEZ! ARE THESE WELDED TA YER FEET?
ugghhh
WHAT'CHA DOIN', FRUIT-CAKES?
I GOTTA GET 'ER OUTTA THIS SUIT BEFORE SHE WAKES UP.
YOU PLANNIN' A SLUMBER PARTY?
NO, NO. I THINK SHE'S COMPLETELY LOST HER MEMORY, AN' SHE'S ONE A' THE BIGGEST, TOUGHEST GIRLS IN THE WHOLE WIDE WORLD.
I'M GONNA BE WITH HER WHEN SHE WAKES UP, SO IT'S VERY IMPORTANT THAT I STEER HER ON THE RIGHT PATH.
RIGHT. IT DON'T LOOK LIKE YOU COULD STEER THAT FEM-ZILLA ANYWHERES SHE DON' WANNA BE STEERED.
BERNIE, SERIOUSLY!
WHAT IF SHE WAKES UP AN' IS ALL ANGRY AN' DESTRUCTY, AN' EVEN THINKS SHE'S FRIENDS WITH THAT BAT-HOLE THAT MADE MY PUDDIN'S LIFE MISERABLE?
I HAVE TA MAKE HER UNDERSTAND SHE'S ONE A' THE GOOD GUYS.
GOOD LUCK WITH THAT.
I DON'T NEED LUCK, BERNIE. I HAVE A PLAN.
SO WHAT'CHA GONNA TRY TA SELL HER ON?
IT'S SIMPLE. I'M GONNA SELL HER ON THE FACT THAT WE'RE A SUPERHERO CRIME-FIGHTING TEAM!
YER KIDDIN'?
WHY DON'CHA JUST DO ME A FAVOR AND THROW ME IN A FIREPLACE NOW?

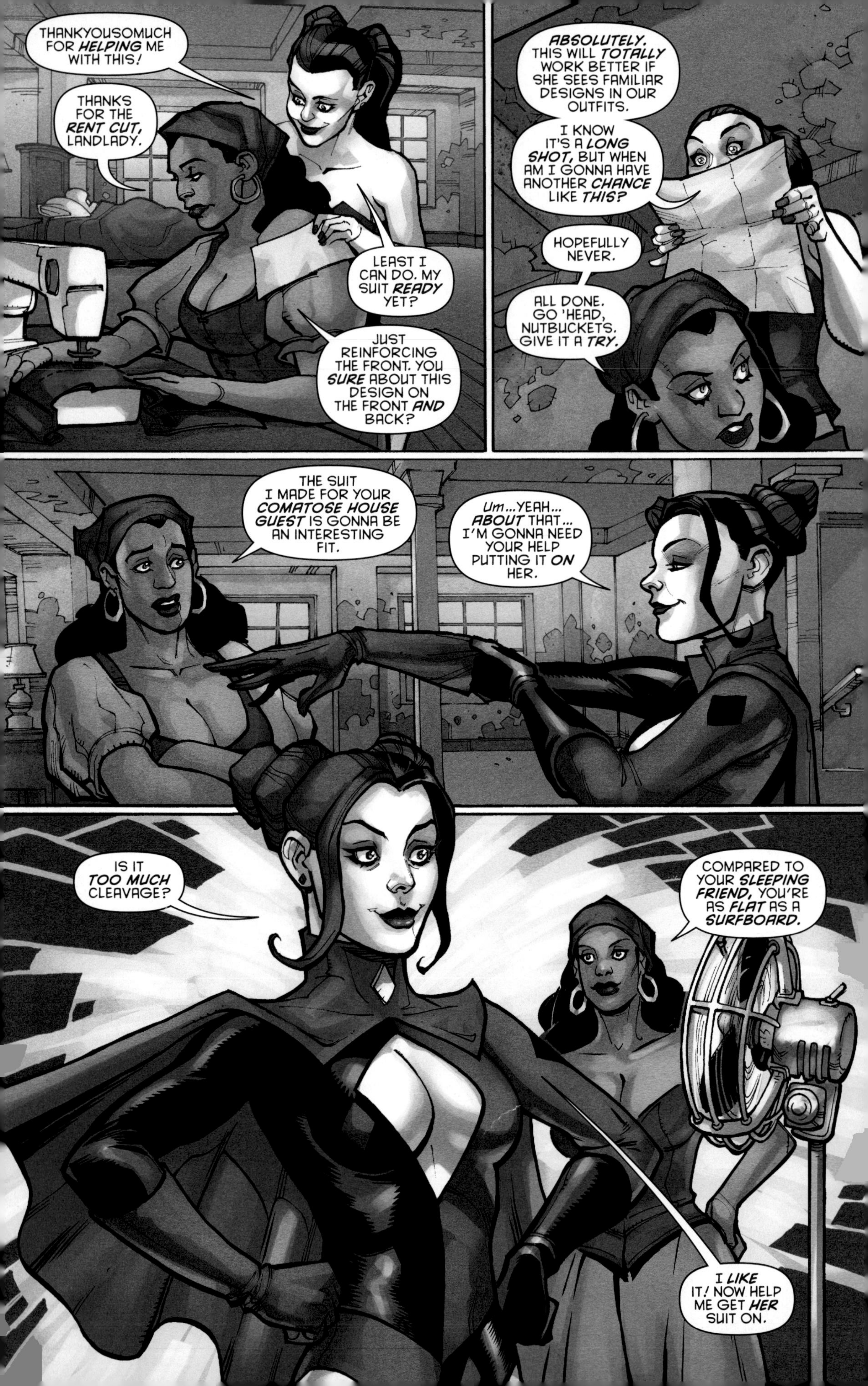
THANKYOUSOMUCH FOR *HELPING* ME WITH THIS!
THANKS FOR THE *RENT CUT,* LANDLADY.
LEAST I CAN DO. MY SUIT *READY* YET?
JUST REINFORCING THE FRONT. YOU *SURE* ABOUT THIS DESIGN ON THE FRONT *AND* BACK?
ABSOLUTELY. THIS WILL *TOTALLY* WORK BETTER IF SHE SEES FAMILIAR DESIGNS IN OUR OUTFITS.
I KNOW IT'S A *LONG SHOT,* BUT WHEN AM I GONNA HAVE ANOTHER *CHANCE* LIKE *THIS?*
HOPEFULLY NEVER.
ALL DONE. GO 'HEAD, NUTBUCKETS. GIVE IT A *TRY.*
THE SUIT I MADE FOR YOUR *COMATOSE HOUSE GUEST* IS GONNA BE AN INTERESTING FIT.
Um...YEAH... *ABOUT* THAT... I'M GONNA NEED YOUR HELP PUTTING IT *ON* HER.
IS IT *TOO MUCH* CLEAVAGE?
COMPARED TO YOUR *SLEEPING FRIEND,* YOU'RE AS *FLAT* AS A *SURFBOARD.*
I *LIKE* IT! NOW HELP ME GET *HER* SUIT ON.

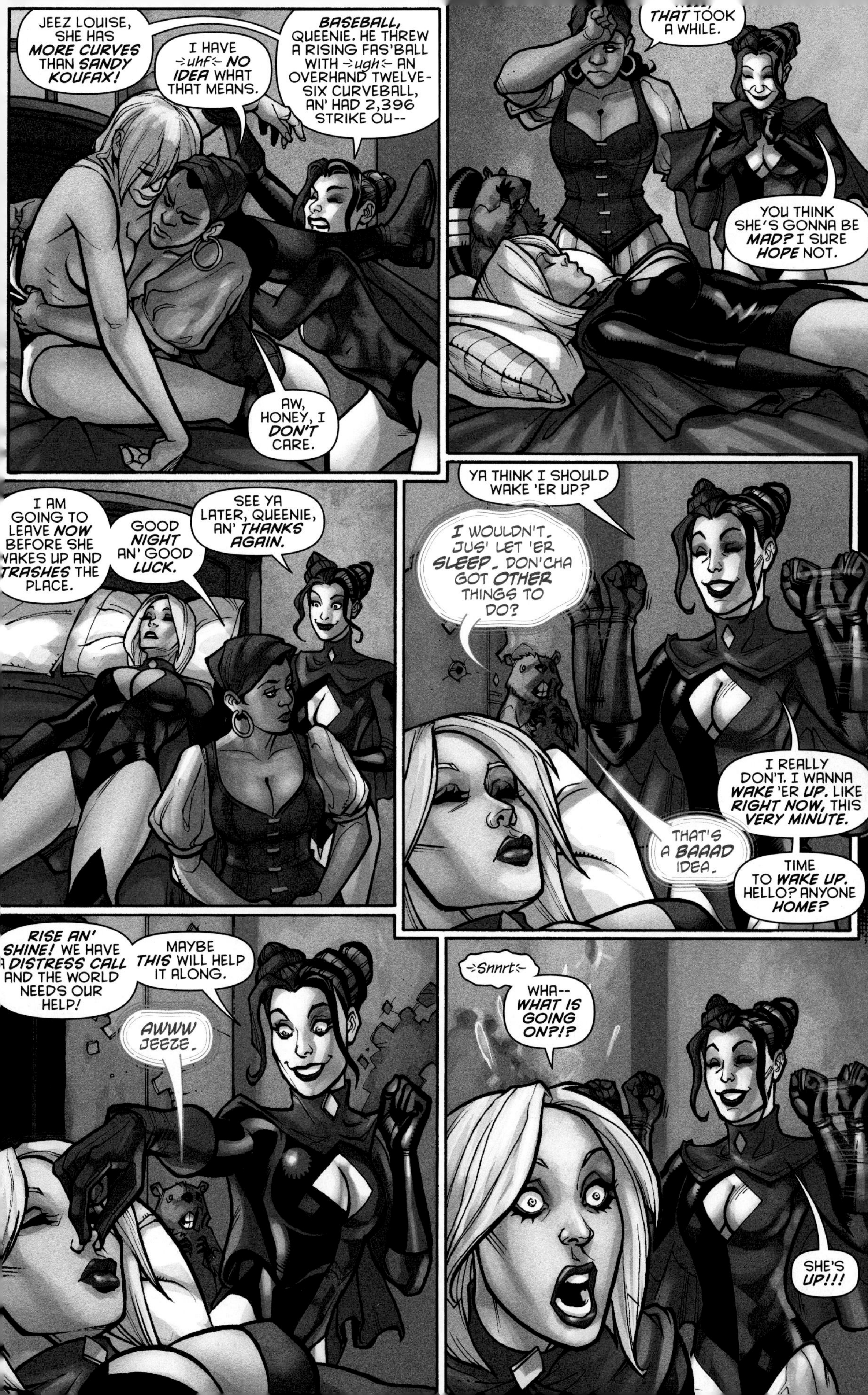
JEEZ LOUISE, SHE HAS MORE CURVES THAN SANDY KOUFAX!
I HAVE ⇒uhf⇐ NO IDEA WHAT THAT MEANS.
BASEBALL, QUEENIE. HE THREW A RISING FAS'BALL WITH ⇒ugh⇐ AN OVERHAND TWELVE-SIX CURVEBALL, AN' HAD 2,396 STRIKE OU--
AW, HONEY, I DON'T CARE.
THAT TOOK A WHILE.
YOU THINK SHE'S GONNA BE MAD? I SURE HOPE NOT.
I AM GOING TO LEAVE NOW BEFORE SHE WAKES UP AND TRASHES THE PLACE.
GOOD NIGHT AN' GOOD LUCK.
SEE YA LATER, QUEENIE, AN' THANKS AGAIN.
YA THINK I SHOULD WAKE 'ER UP?
I WOULDN'T. JUS' LET 'ER SLEEP. DON'CHA GOT OTHER THINGS TO DO?
I REALLY DON'T. I WANNA WAKE 'ER UP. LIKE RIGHT NOW, THIS VERY MINUTE.
THAT'S A BAAAD IDEA.
TIME TO WAKE UP. HELLO? ANYONE HOME?
RISE AN' SHINE! WE HAVE A DISTRESS CALL AND THE WORLD NEEDS OUR HELP!
MAYBE THIS WILL HELP IT ALONG.
AWWW JEEZE.
⇒Snnrt⇐
WHA-- WHAT IS GOING ON?!?
SHE'S UP!!!

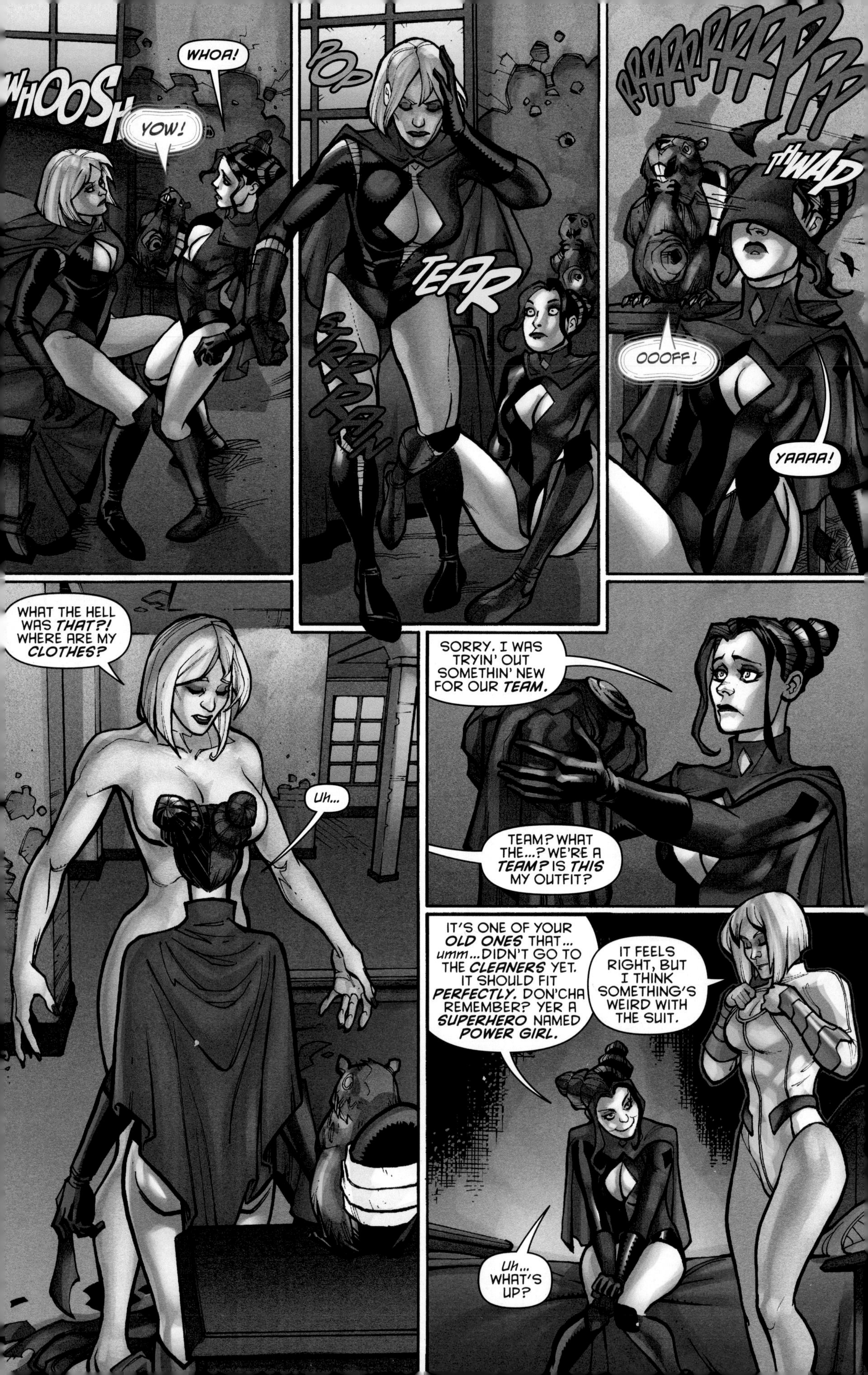
WHOOSH
WHOA!
YOW!
POP
TEAR
SKRRRRN
RRRRRRRRRRRRR
THWAP
OOOFF!
YAAAA!
WHAT THE HELL WAS THAT?! WHERE ARE MY CLOTHES?
UH...
SORRY. I WAS TRYIN' OUT SOMETHIN' NEW FOR OUR TEAM.
TEAM? WHAT THE...? WE'RE A TEAM? IS THIS MY OUTFIT?
IT'S ONE OF YOUR OLD ONES THAT... umm...DIDN'T GO TO THE CLEANERS YET. IT SHOULD FIT PERFECTLY. DON'CHA REMEMBER? YER A SUPERHERO NAMED POWER GIRL.
IT FEELS RIGHT, BUT I THINK SOMETHING'S WEIRD WITH THE SUIT.
UH... WHAT'S UP?

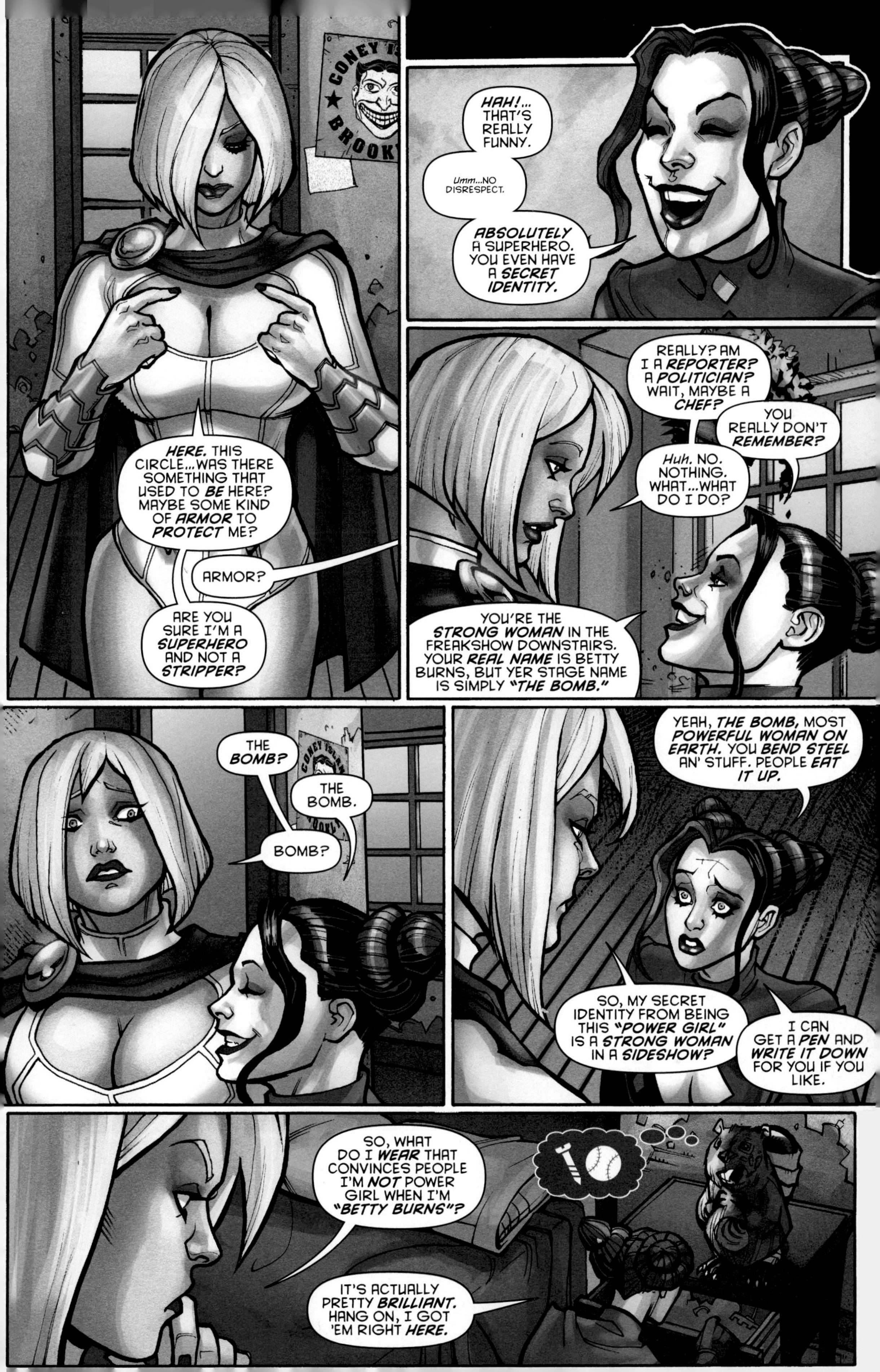
CONEY IS
BROOKL
HAH!... THAT'S REALLY FUNNY.
Umm...NO DISRESPECT.
ABSOLUTELY A SUPERHERO. YOU EVEN HAVE A SECRET IDENTITY.
HERE. THIS CIRCLE...WAS THERE SOMETHING THAT USED TO BE HERE? MAYBE SOME KIND OF ARMOR TO PROTECT ME?
ARMOR?
ARE YOU SURE I'M A SUPERHERO AND NOT A STRIPPER?
REALLY? AM I A REPORTER? A POLITICIAN? WAIT, MAYBE A CHEF?
YOU REALLY DON'T REMEMBER?
Huh. NO. NOTHING. WHAT...WHAT DO I DO?
YOU'RE THE STRONG WOMAN IN THE FREAKSHOW DOWNSTAIRS. YOUR REAL NAME IS BETTY BURNS, BUT YER STAGE NAME IS SIMPLY "THE BOMB."
THE BOMB?
THE BOMB.
BOMB?
YEAH, THE BOMB, MOST POWERFUL WOMAN ON EARTH. YOU BEND STEEL AN' STUFF. PEOPLE EAT IT UP.
SO, MY SECRET IDENTITY FROM BEING THIS "POWER GIRL" IS A STRONG WOMAN IN A SIDESHOW?
I CAN GET A PEN AND WRITE IT DOWN FOR YOU IF YOU LIKE.
SO, WHAT DO I WEAR THAT CONVINCES PEOPLE I'M NOT POWER GIRL WHEN I'M "BETTY BURNS"?
IT'S ACTUALLY PRETTY BRILLIANT. HANG ON, I GOT 'EM RIGHT HERE.

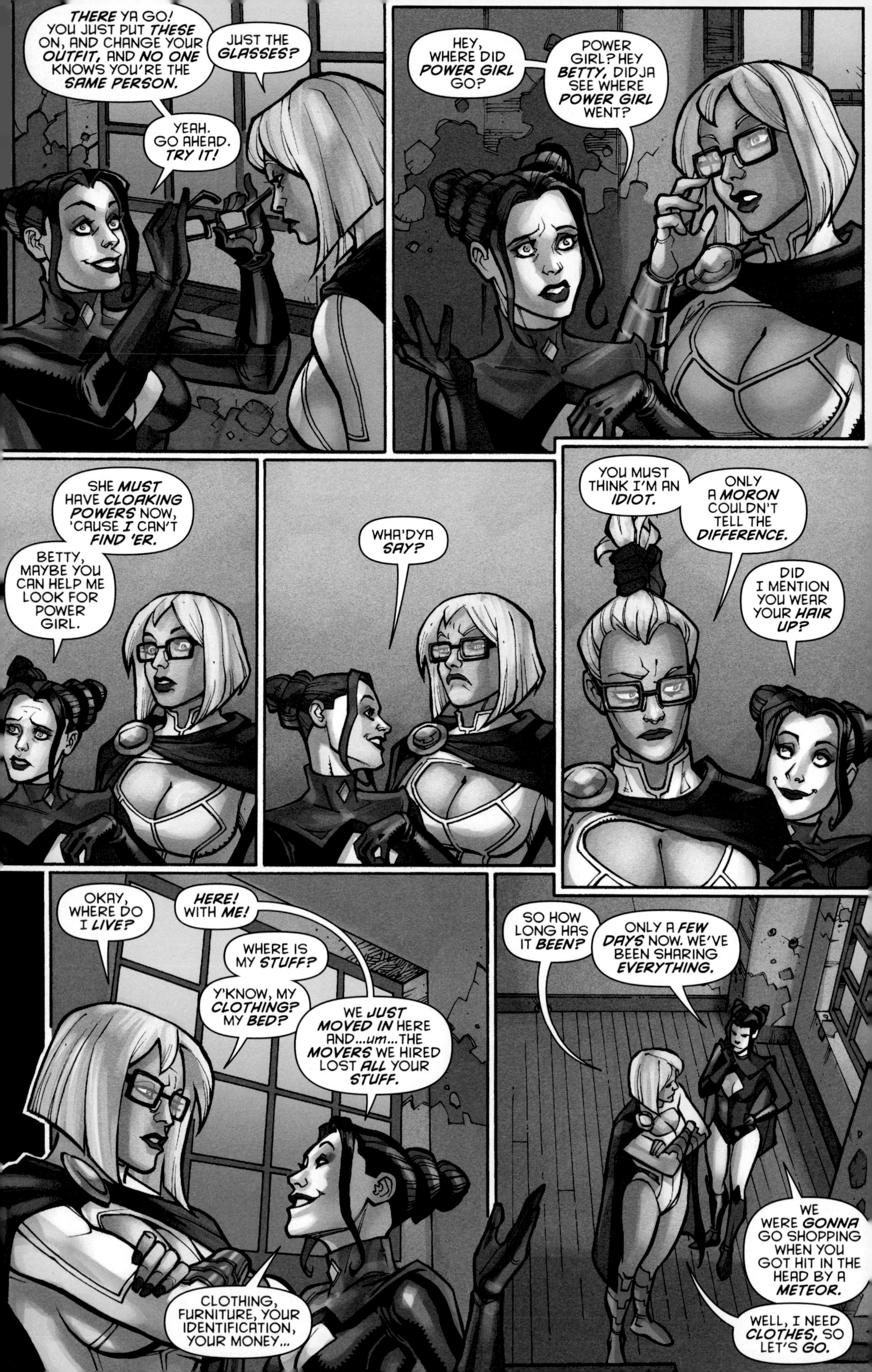
THERE YA GO! YOU JUST PUT THESE ON, AND CHANGE YOUR OUTFIT, AND NO ONE KNOWS YOU'RE THE SAME PERSON.
JUST THE GLASSES?
YEAH. GO AHEAD. TRY IT!
HEY, WHERE DID POWER GIRL GO?
POWER GIRL? HEY BETTY, DIDJA SEE WHERE POWER GIRL WENT?
SHE MUST HAVE CLOAKING POWERS NOW, 'CAUSE I CAN'T FIND 'ER.
BETTY, MAYBE YOU CAN HELP ME LOOK FOR POWER GIRL.
WHA'DYA SAY?
YOU MUST THINK I'M AN IDIOT.
ONLY A MORON COULDN'T TELL THE DIFFERENCE.
DID I MENTION YOU WEAR YOUR HAIR UP?
OKAY, WHERE DO I LIVE?
HERE! WITH ME!
WHERE IS MY STUFF?
Y'KNOW, MY CLOTHING? MY BED?
WE JUST MOVED IN HERE AND...um...THE MOVERS WE HIRED LOST ALL YOUR STUFF.
CLOTHING, FURNITURE, YOUR IDENTIFICATION, YOUR MONEY...
SO HOW LONG HAS IT BEEN?
ONLY A FEW DAYS NOW. WE'VE BEEN SHARING EVERYTHING.
WE WERE GONNA GO SHOPPING WHEN YOU GOT HIT IN THE HEAD BY A METEOR.
WELL, I NEED CLOTHES, SO LET'S GO.

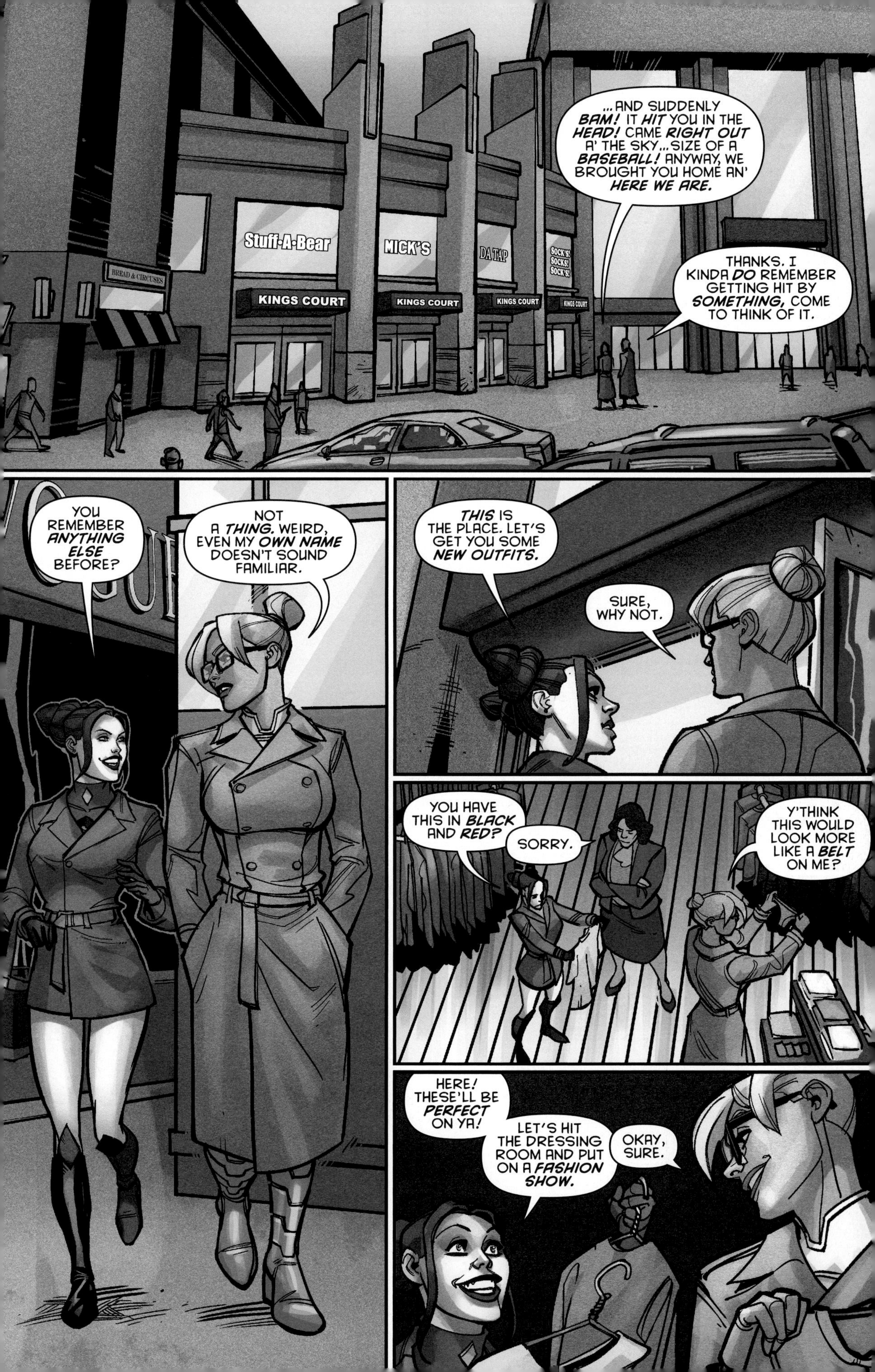
...AND SUDDENLY BAM! IT HIT YOU IN THE HEAD! CAME RIGHT OUT A' THE SKY...SIZE OF A BASEBALL! ANYWAY, WE BROUGHT YOU HOME AN' HERE WE ARE.
THANKS. I KINDA DO REMEMBER GETTING HIT BY SOMETHING, COME TO THINK OF IT.
Stuff-A-Bear
MICK'S
DA TAP
SOCK'S! SOCKS! SOCK'S!
BREAD & CIRCUSES
KINGS COURT
KINGS COURT
KINGS COURT
KINGS COURT
YOU REMEMBER ANYTHING ELSE BEFORE?
NOT A THING. WEIRD, EVEN MY OWN NAME DOESN'T SOUND FAMILIAR.
THIS IS THE PLACE. LET'S GET YOU SOME NEW OUTFITS.
SURE, WHY NOT.
YOU HAVE THIS IN BLACK AND RED?
SORRY.
Y'THINK THIS WOULD LOOK MORE LIKE A BELT ON ME?
HERE! THESE'LL BE PERFECT ON YA!
LET'S HIT THE DRESSING ROOM AND PUT ON A FASHION SHOW.
OKAY, SURE.

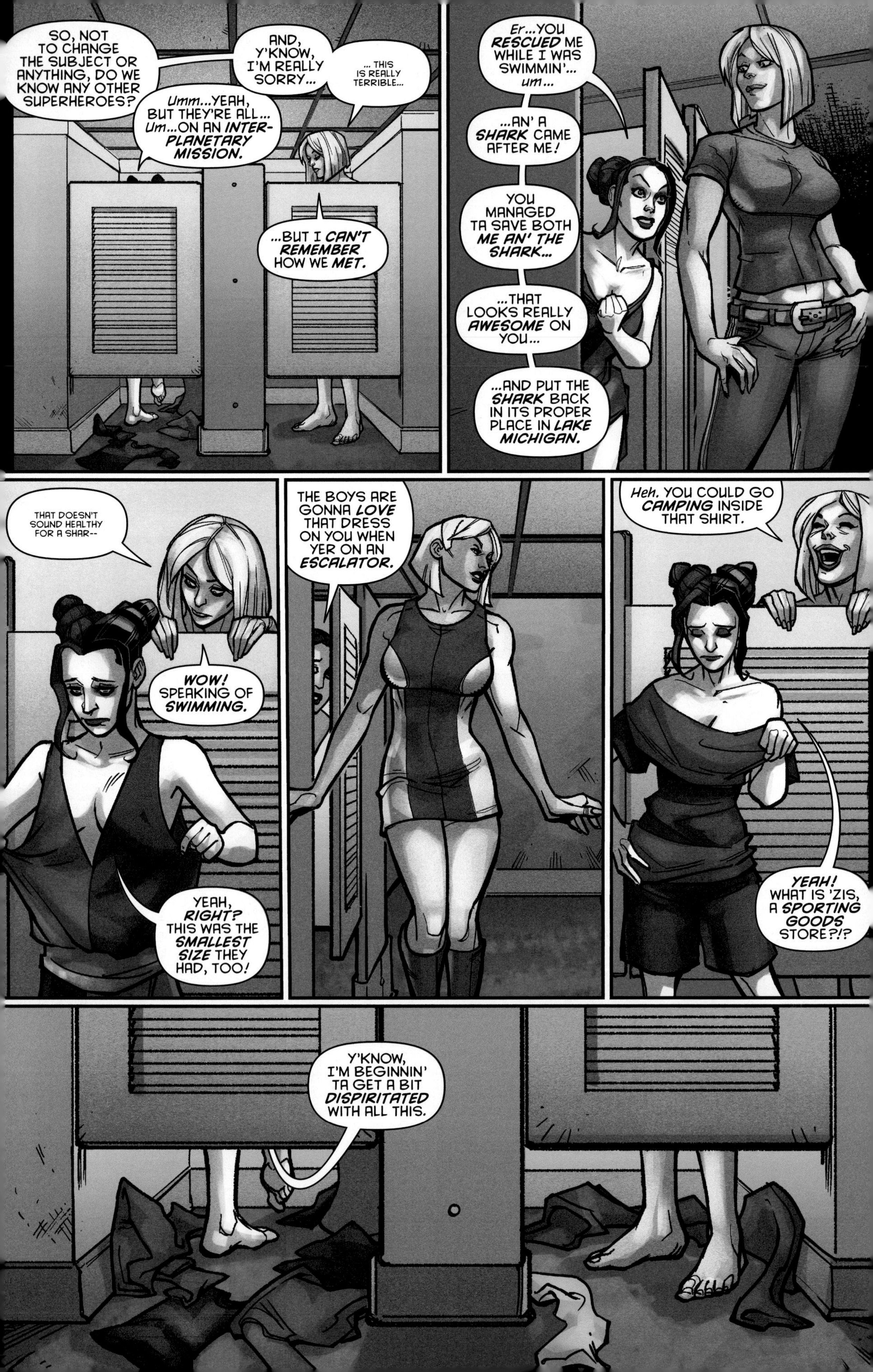
SO, NOT TO CHANGE THE SUBJECT OR ANYTHING, DO WE KNOW ANY OTHER SUPERHEROES?
AND, Y'KNOW, I'M REALLY SORRY...
... THIS IS REALLY TERRIBLE...
Umm...YEAH, BUT THEY'RE ALL... Um...ON AN INTER-PLANETARY MISSION.
...BUT I CAN'T REMEMBER HOW WE MET.
Er...YOU RESCUED ME WHILE I WAS SWIMMIN'... um...
...AN' A SHARK CAME AFTER ME!
YOU MANAGED TA SAVE BOTH ME AN' THE SHARK...
...THAT LOOKS REALLY AWESOME ON YOU...
...AND PUT THE SHARK BACK IN ITS PROPER PLACE IN LAKE MICHIGAN.
THAT DOESN'T SOUND HEALTHY FOR A SHAR--
WOW! SPEAKING OF SWIMMING.
YEAH, RIGHT? THIS WAS THE SMALLEST SIZE THEY HAD, TOO!
THE BOYS ARE GONNA LOVE THAT DRESS ON YOU WHEN YER ON AN ESCALATOR.
Heh. YOU COULD GO CAMPING INSIDE THAT SHIRT.
YEAH! WHAT IS 'ZIS, A SPORTING GOODS STORE?!?
Y'KNOW, I'M BEGINNIN' TA GET A BIT DISPIRITATED WITH ALL THIS.

A'RIGHT, *THAT'S* IT! I'VE HAD *ENOUGH* A' THIS PLACE!

HEY! MY *PAL* HERE DID OKAY, BUT NOTHING IN THIS PLACE FITS *ME!*

THAT'S BECAUSE THIS IS *"HUSKY HONEYS."*

YOU'D BE BETTER OFF GOING NEXT DOOR TO *"DAINTY DIVAS."*

Dainty Divas

YEAH, WELL I *AM* UNDENIABLY *DAINTY* IF I *DO SAY* SO MYSELF.

Hah! NOW *THIS* IS MORE LIKE IT!

JINKIES, THIS DRESSING ROOM IS *TINY!*

WELL, THIS IS GOING TO BE A BIG, FAT *NO WAY.*

YES WAY!

OKAY...I'M KINDA *DONE* HERE.

YOU *HUNGRY?*

ALWAYS!

IF YOU CAN READ THIS YOU'RE A PERV

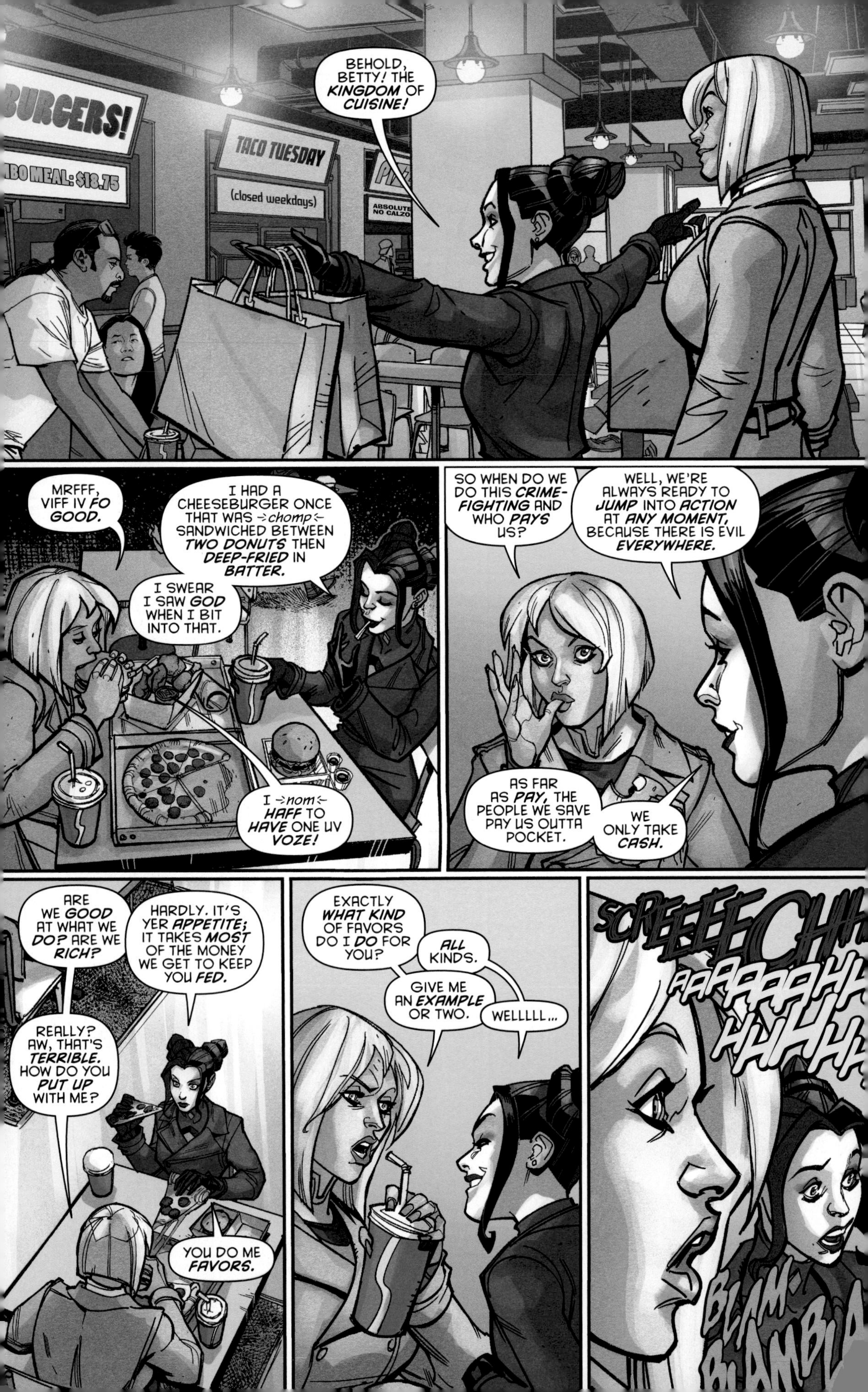
BURGERS!
BO MEAL: $18.75
TACO TUESDAY
(closed weekdays)
ABSOLUTE NO CALZO
BEHOLD, BETTY! THE KINGDOM OF CUISINE!
MRFFF, VIFF IV FO GOOD.
I HAD A CHEESEBURGER ONCE THAT WAS →chomp← SANDWICHED BETWEEN TWO DONUTS THEN DEEP-FRIED IN BATTER.
I SWEAR I SAW GOD WHEN I BIT INTO THAT.
I →nom← HAFF TO HAVE ONE UV VOZE!
SO WHEN DO WE DO THIS CRIME-FIGHTING AND WHO PAYS US?
WELL, WE'RE ALWAYS READY TO JUMP INTO ACTION AT ANY MOMENT, BECAUSE THERE IS EVIL EVERYWHERE.
AS FAR AS PAY, THE PEOPLE WE SAVE PAY US OUTTA POCKET.
WE ONLY TAKE CASH.
ARE WE GOOD AT WHAT WE DO? ARE WE RICH?
HARDLY. IT'S YER APPETITE; IT TAKES MOST OF THE MONEY WE GET TO KEEP YOU FED.
REALLY? AW, THAT'S TERRIBLE. HOW DO YOU PUT UP WITH ME?
YOU DO ME FAVORS.
EXACTLY WHAT KIND OF FAVORS DO I DO FOR YOU?
ALL KINDS.
GIVE ME AN EXAMPLE OR TWO.
WELLLLL...
SCREEEEECHH
AAAAAAHH
HHHHH
BLAM BLAMBLA

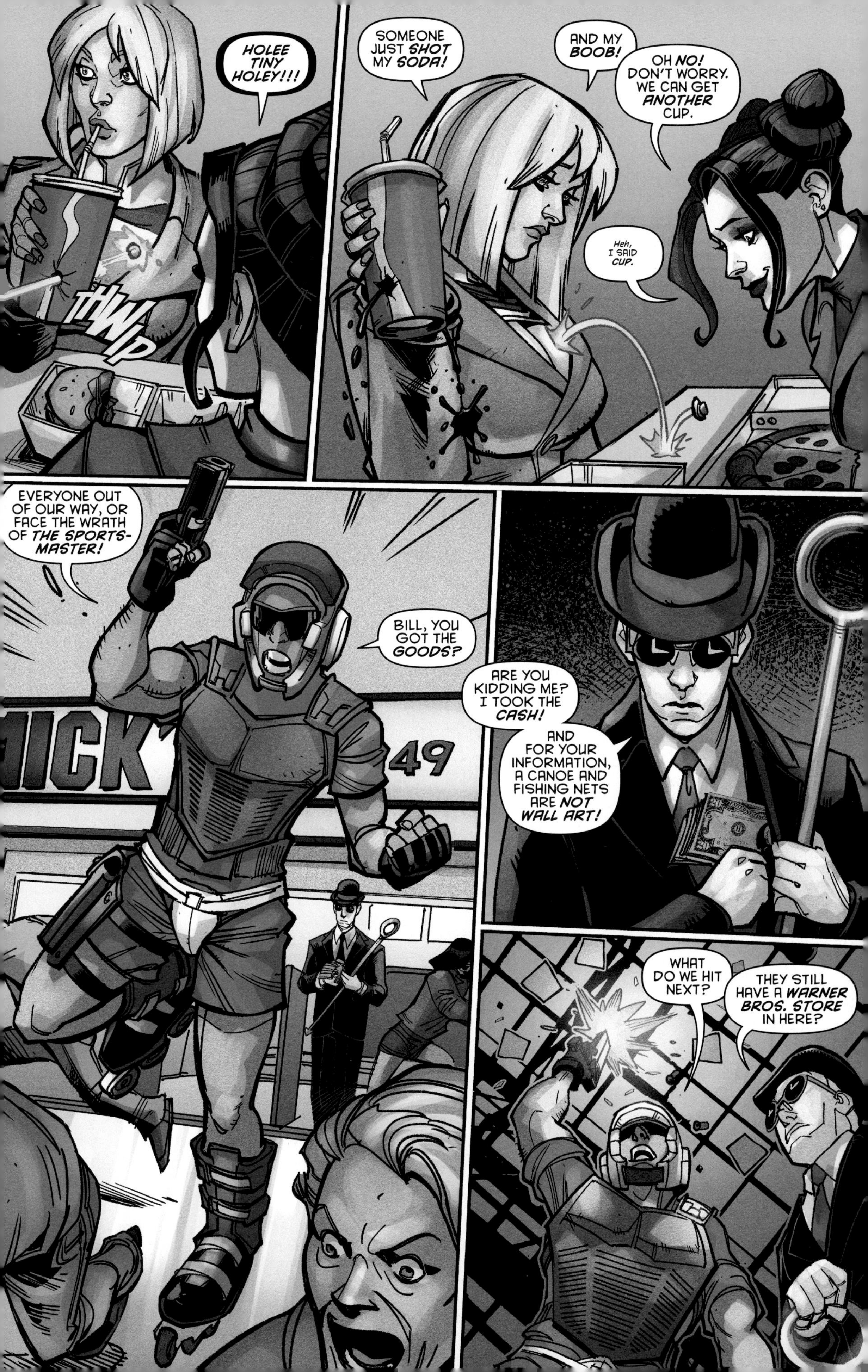
HOLEE TINY HOLEY!!!
THWIP
SOMEONE JUST SHOT MY SODA!
AND MY BOOB!
OH NO! DON'T WORRY. WE CAN GET ANOTHER CUP.
Heh, I SAID CUP.
EVERYONE OUT OF OUR WAY, OR FACE THE WRATH OF THE SPORTS-MASTER!
BILL, YOU GOT THE GOODS?
ARE YOU KIDDING ME? I TOOK THE CASH!
AND FOR YOUR INFORMATION, A CANOE AND FISHING NETS ARE NOT WALL ART!
WHAT DO WE HIT NEXT?
THEY STILL HAVE A WARNER BROS. STORE IN HERE?

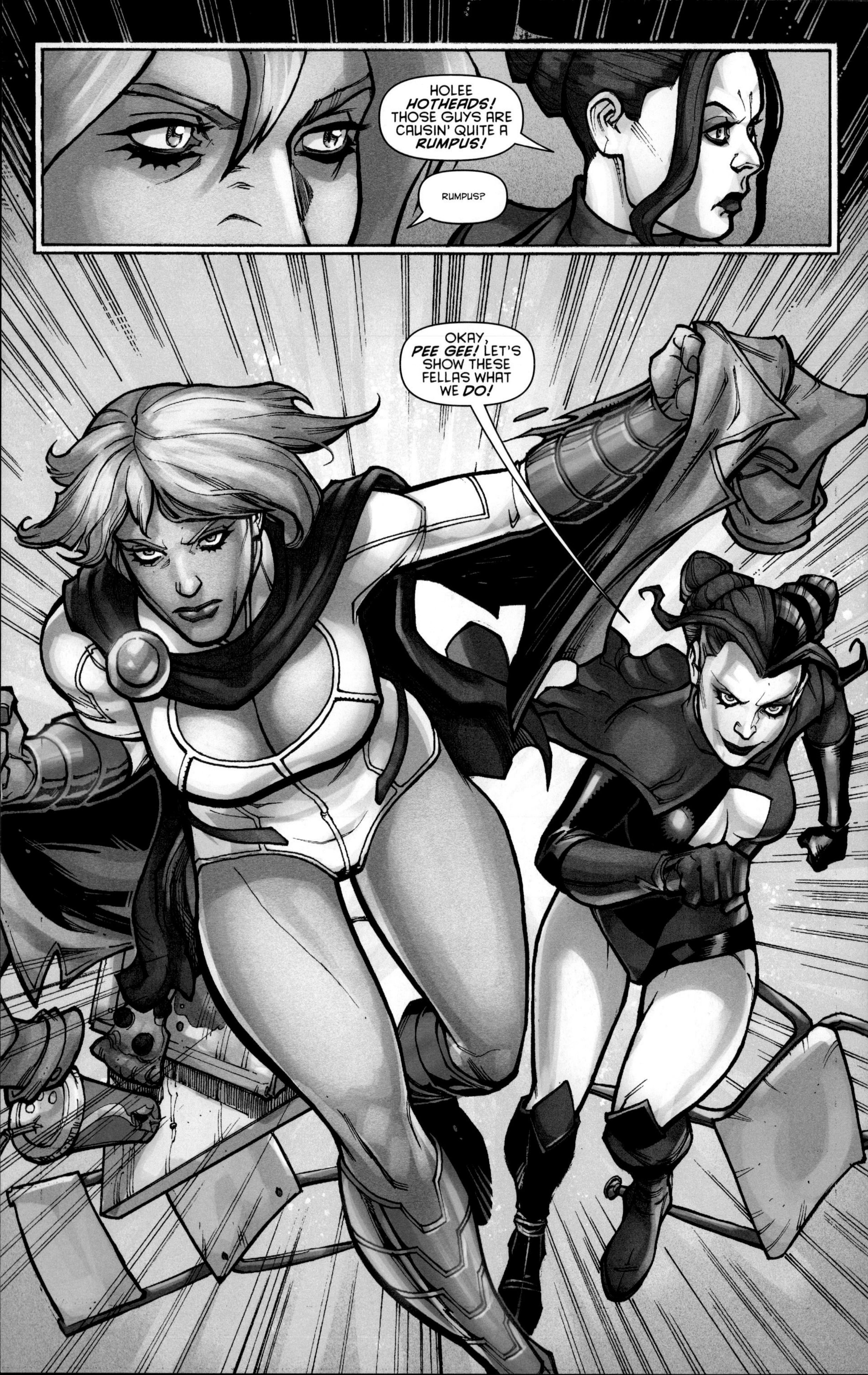
HOLEE HOTHEADS! THOSE GUYS ARE CAUSIN' QUITE A RUMPUS!
RUMPUS?
OKAY, PEE GEE! LET'S SHOW THESE FELLAS WHAT WE DO!

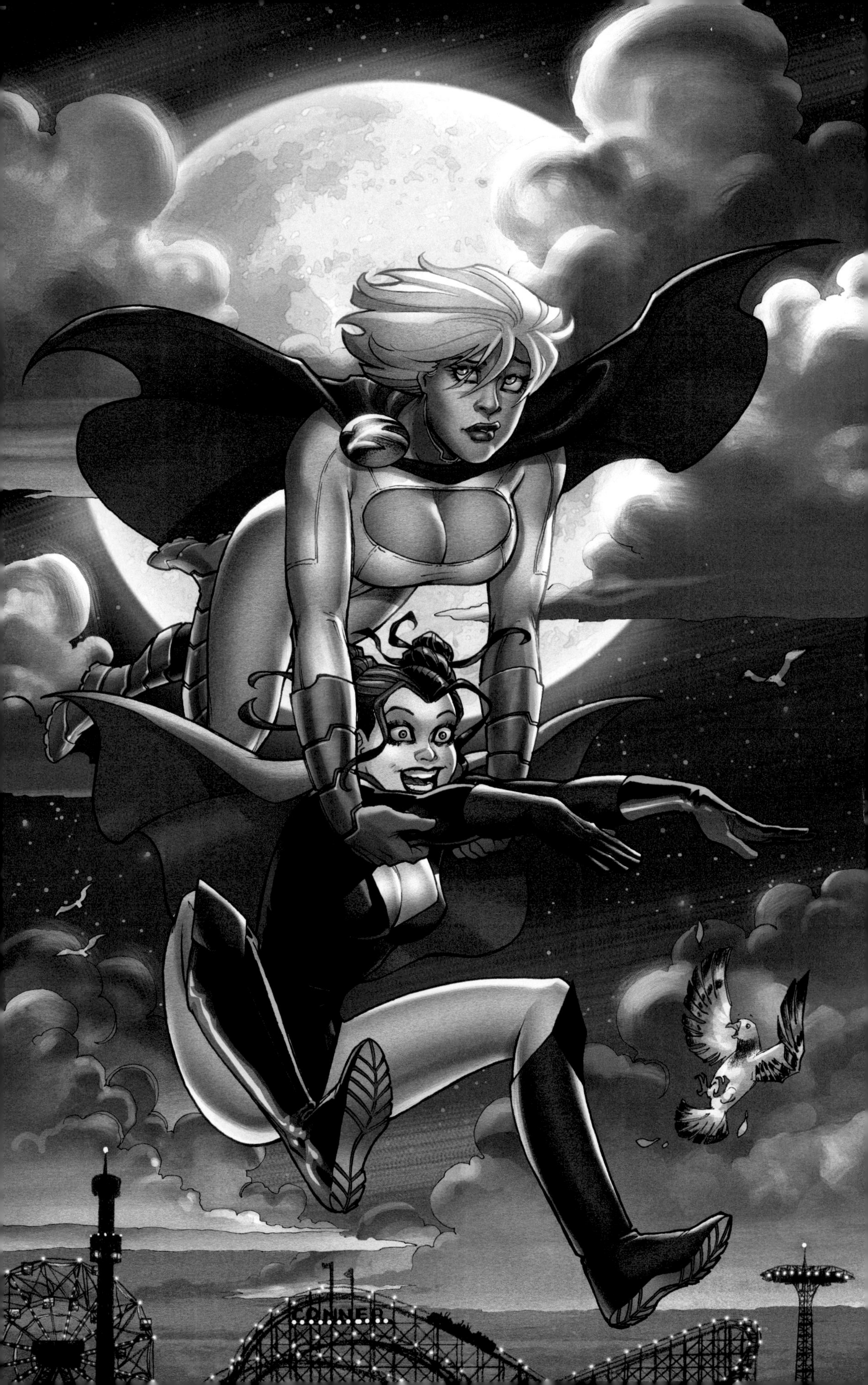
CONNER

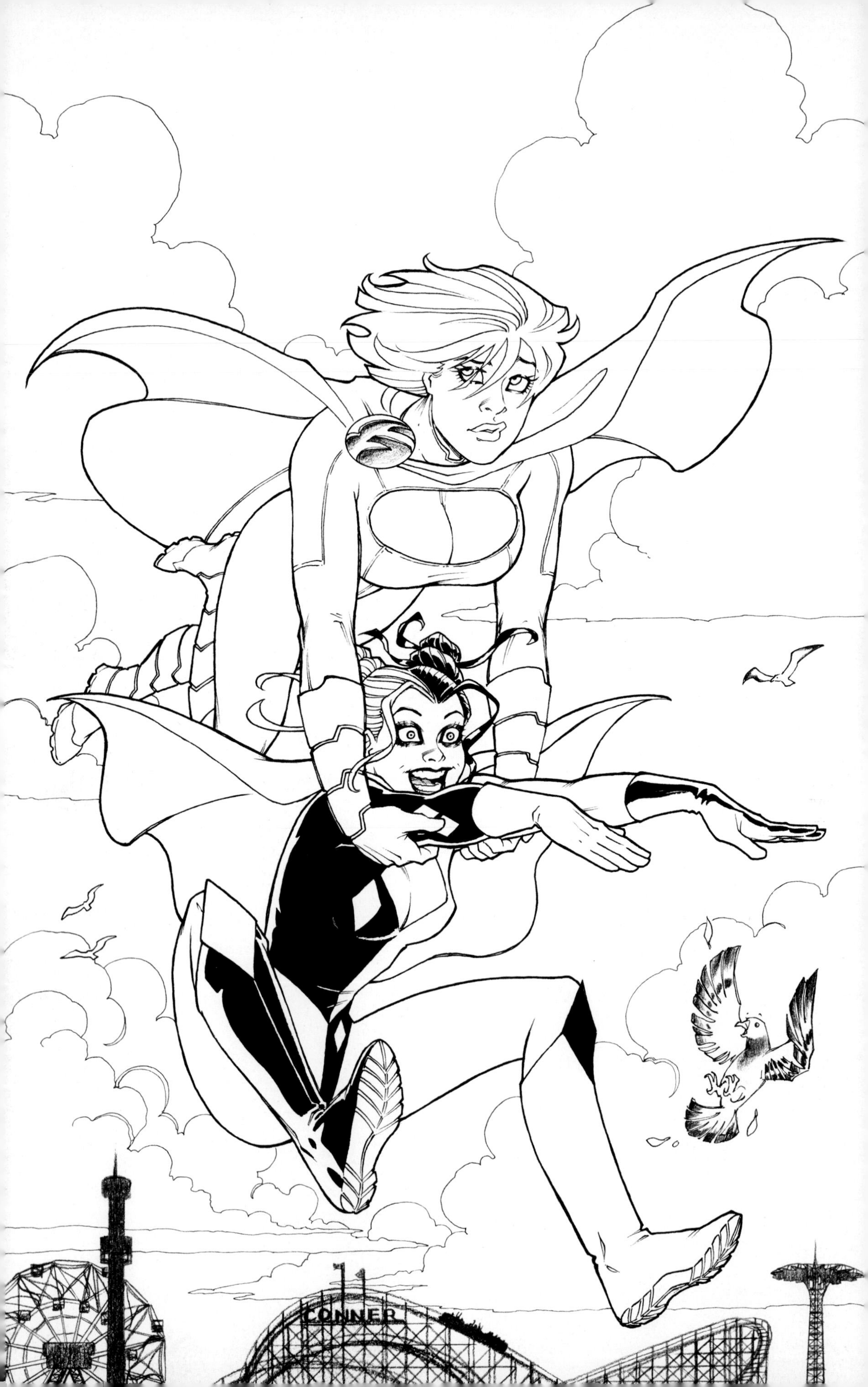
CONNER

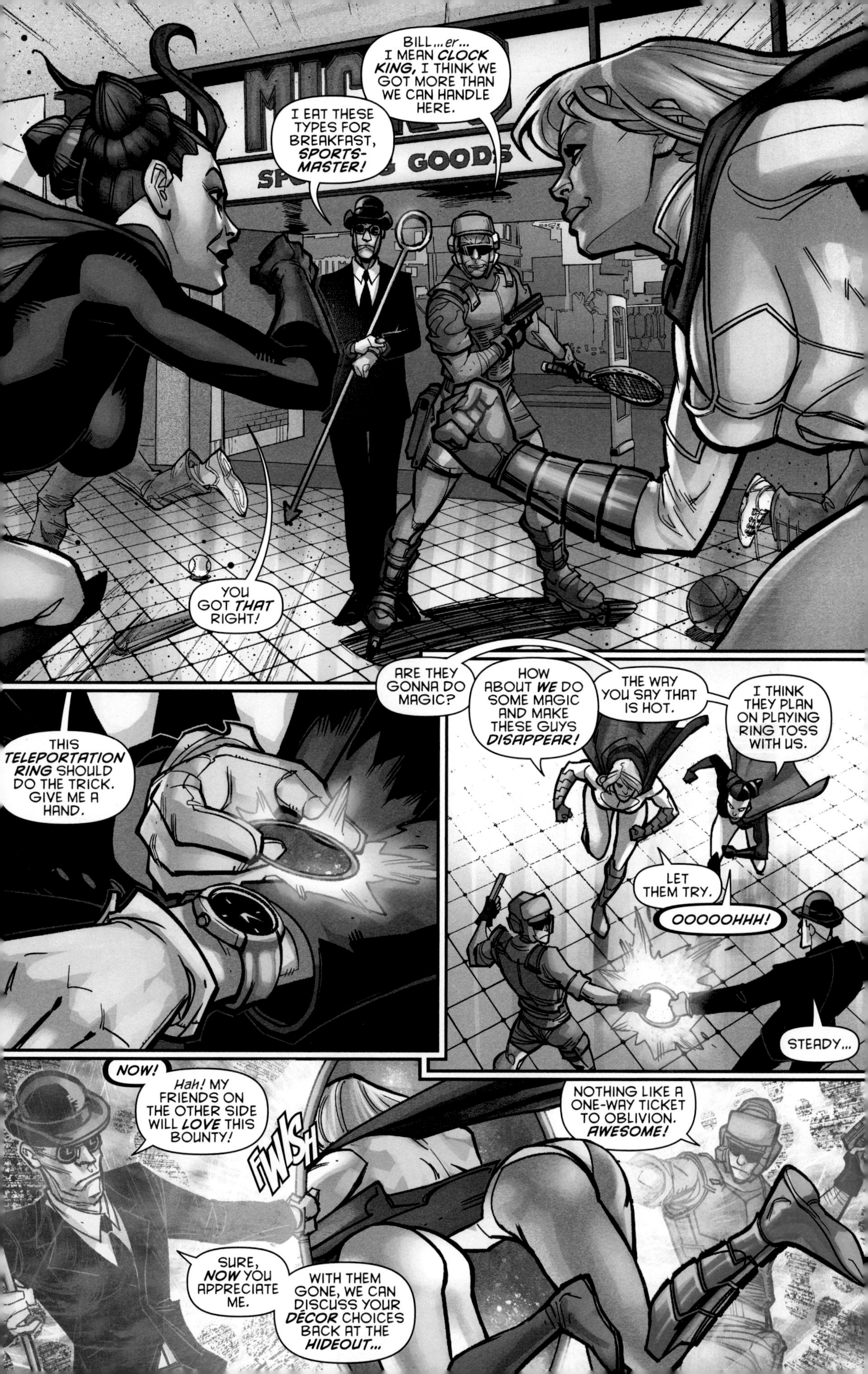

MIC
SPO G GOODS
I EAT THESE TYPES FOR BREAKFAST, SPORTSMASTER!
BILL...er... I MEAN CLOCK KING, I THINK WE GOT MORE THAN WE CAN HANDLE HERE.
YOU GOT THAT RIGHT!
THIS TELEPORTATION RING SHOULD DO THE TRICK. GIVE ME A HAND.
ARE THEY GONNA DO MAGIC?
HOW ABOUT WE DO SOME MAGIC AND MAKE THESE GUYS DISAPPEAR!
THE WAY YOU SAY THAT IS HOT.
I THINK THEY PLAN ON PLAYING RING TOSS WITH US.
LET THEM TRY.
OOOOOHHH!
STEADY...
NOW!
Hah! MY FRIENDS ON THE OTHER SIDE WILL LOVE THIS BOUNTY!
FWISH
NOTHING LIKE A ONE-WAY TICKET TO OBLIVION. AWESOME!
SURE, NOW YOU APPRECIATE ME.
WITH THEM GONE, WE CAN DISCUSS YOUR DÉCOR CHOICES BACK AT THE HIDEOUT...

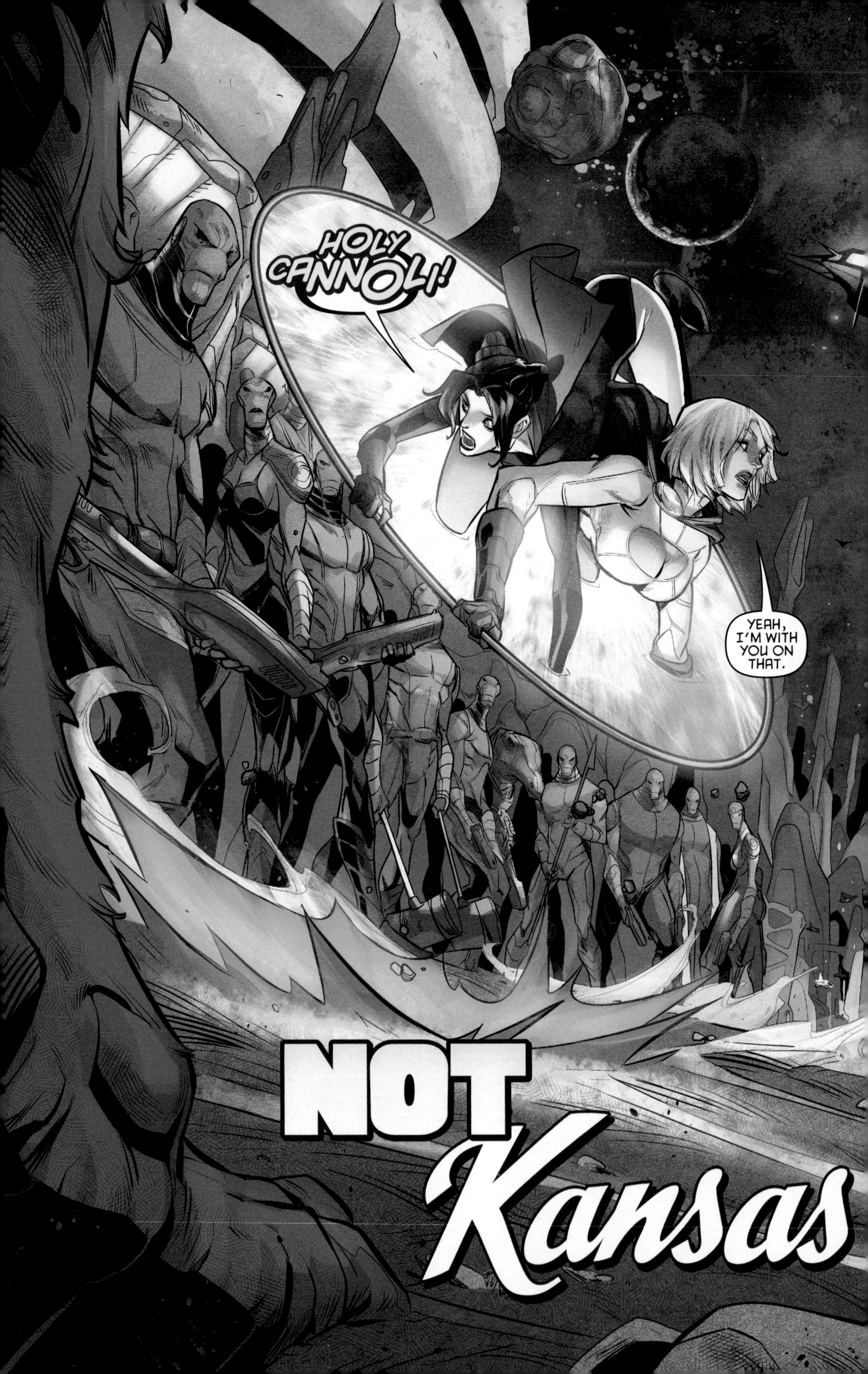
HOLY CANNOLI!
YEAH, I'M WITH YOU ON THAT.
NOT Kansas

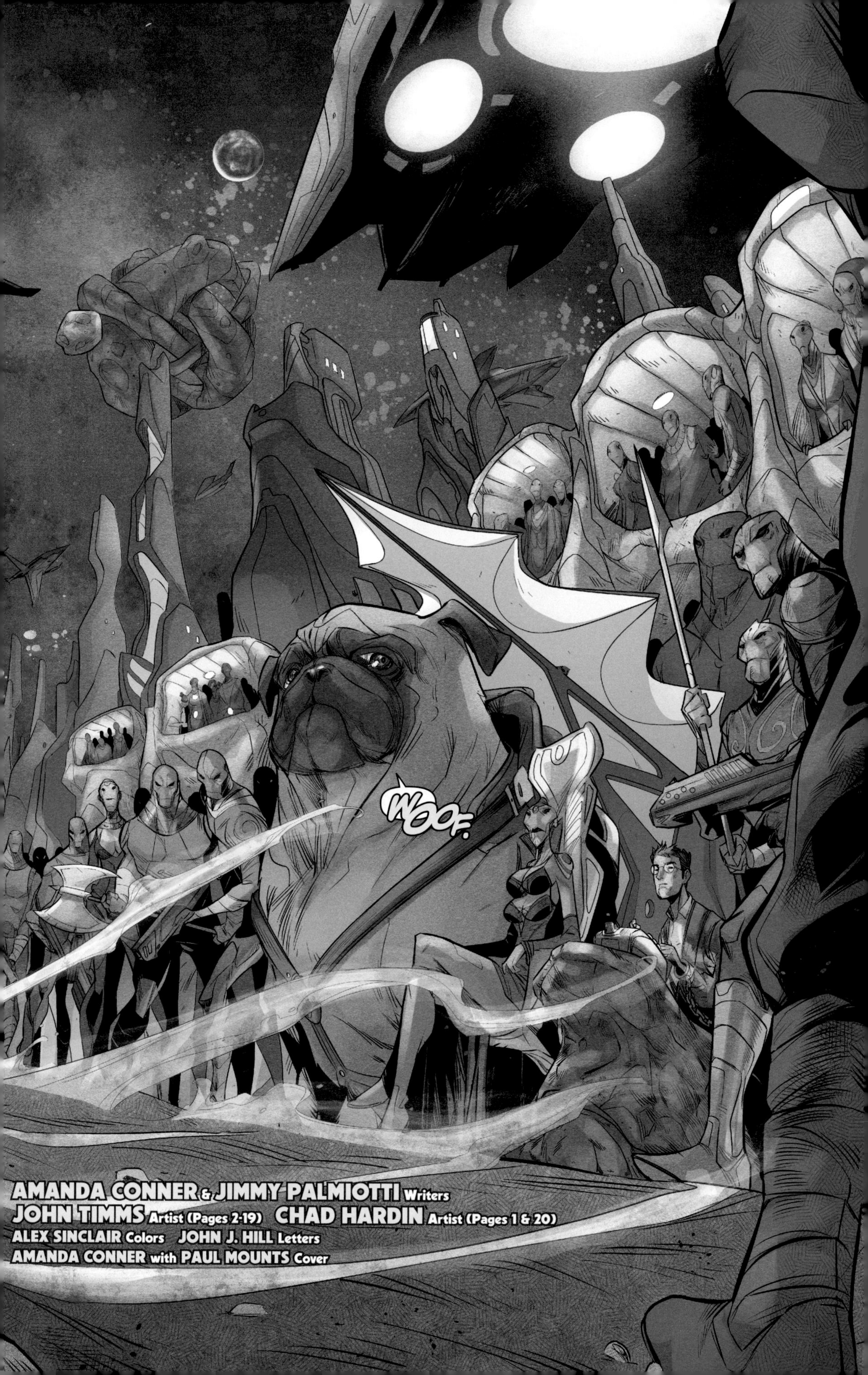
WOOF.
AMANDA CONNER & JIMMY PALMIOTTI Writers
JOHN TIMMS Artist (Pages 2-19) CHAD HARDIN Artist (Pages 1 & 20)
ALEX SINCLAIR Colors JOHN J. HILL Letters
AMANDA CONNER with PAUL MOUNTS Cover

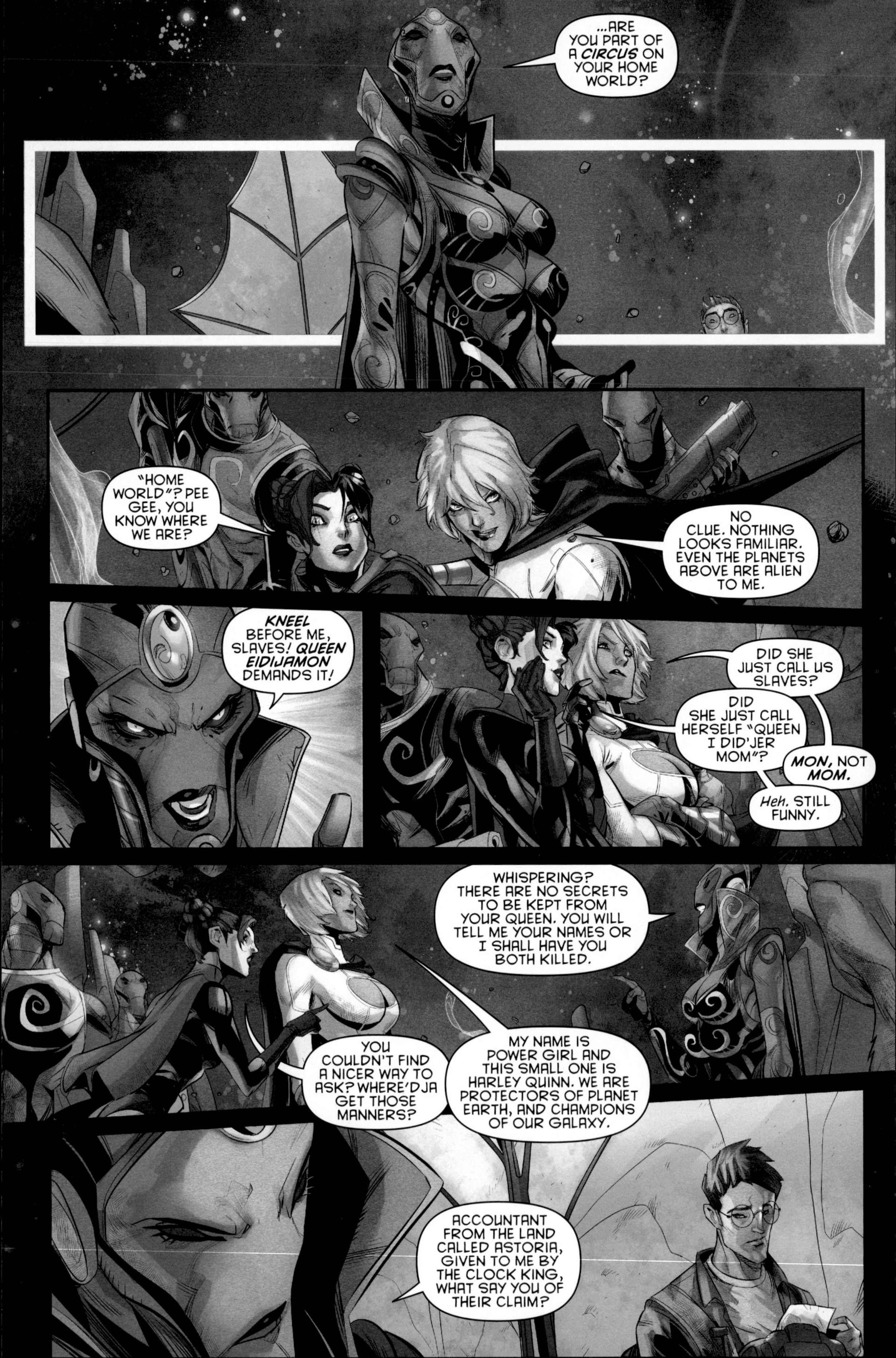

...ARE YOU PART OF A *CIRCUS* ON YOUR HOME WORLD?
"HOME WORLD"? PEE GEE, YOU KNOW WHERE WE ARE?
NO CLUE. NOTHING LOOKS FAMILIAR. EVEN THE PLANETS ABOVE ARE ALIEN TO ME.
KNEEL BEFORE ME, SLAVES! *QUEEN EIDIJAMON* DEMANDS IT!
DID SHE JUST CALL US SLAVES?
DID SHE JUST CALL HERSELF "QUEEN I DID'JER MOM"?
MON, NOT ***MOM.***
Heh. STILL FUNNY.
WHISPERING? THERE ARE NO SECRETS TO BE KEPT FROM YOUR QUEEN. YOU WILL TELL ME YOUR NAMES OR I SHALL HAVE YOU BOTH KILLED.
YOU COULDN'T FIND A NICER WAY TO ASK? WHERE'DJA GET THOSE MANNERS?
MY NAME IS POWER GIRL AND THIS SMALL ONE IS HARLEY QUINN. WE ARE PROTECTORS OF PLANET EARTH, AND CHAMPIONS OF OUR GALAXY.
ACCOUNTANT FROM THE LAND CALLED ASTORIA, GIVEN TO ME BY THE CLOCK KING, WHAT SAY YOU OF THEIR CLAIM?

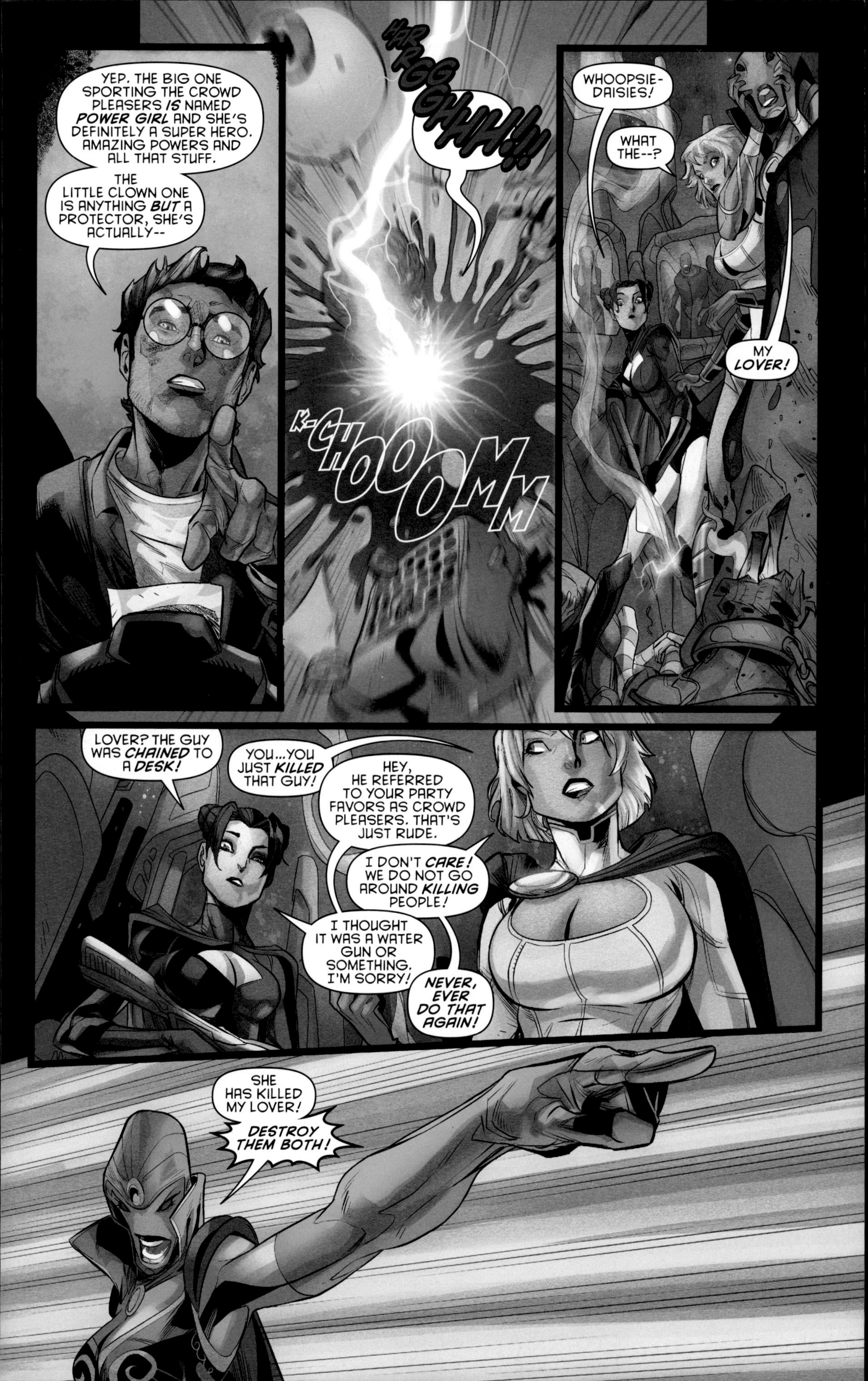
YEP. THE BIG ONE SPORTING THE CROWD PLEASERS *IS* NAMED **POWER GIRL** AND SHE'S DEFINITELY A SUPER HERO. AMAZING POWERS AND ALL THAT STUFF.
THE LITTLE CLOWN ONE IS ANYTHING *BUT* A PROTECTOR, SHE'S ACTUALLY--
HARRGGHHHH!!!
K-CHOOOOMMM
WHOOPSIE-DAISIES!
WHAT THE--?
MY **LOVER!**
LOVER? THE GUY WAS ***CHAINED*** TO A ***DESK!***
YOU...YOU JUST ***KILLED*** THAT GUY!
HEY, HE REFERRED TO YOUR PARTY FAVORS AS CROWD PLEASERS. THAT'S JUST RUDE.
I DON'T ***CARE!*** WE DO NOT GO AROUND ***KILLING*** PEOPLE!
I THOUGHT IT WAS A WATER GUN OR SOMETHING. I'M SORRY!
NEVER, EVER DO THAT AGAIN!
SHE HAS KILLED MY LOVER!
DESTROY THEM BOTH!

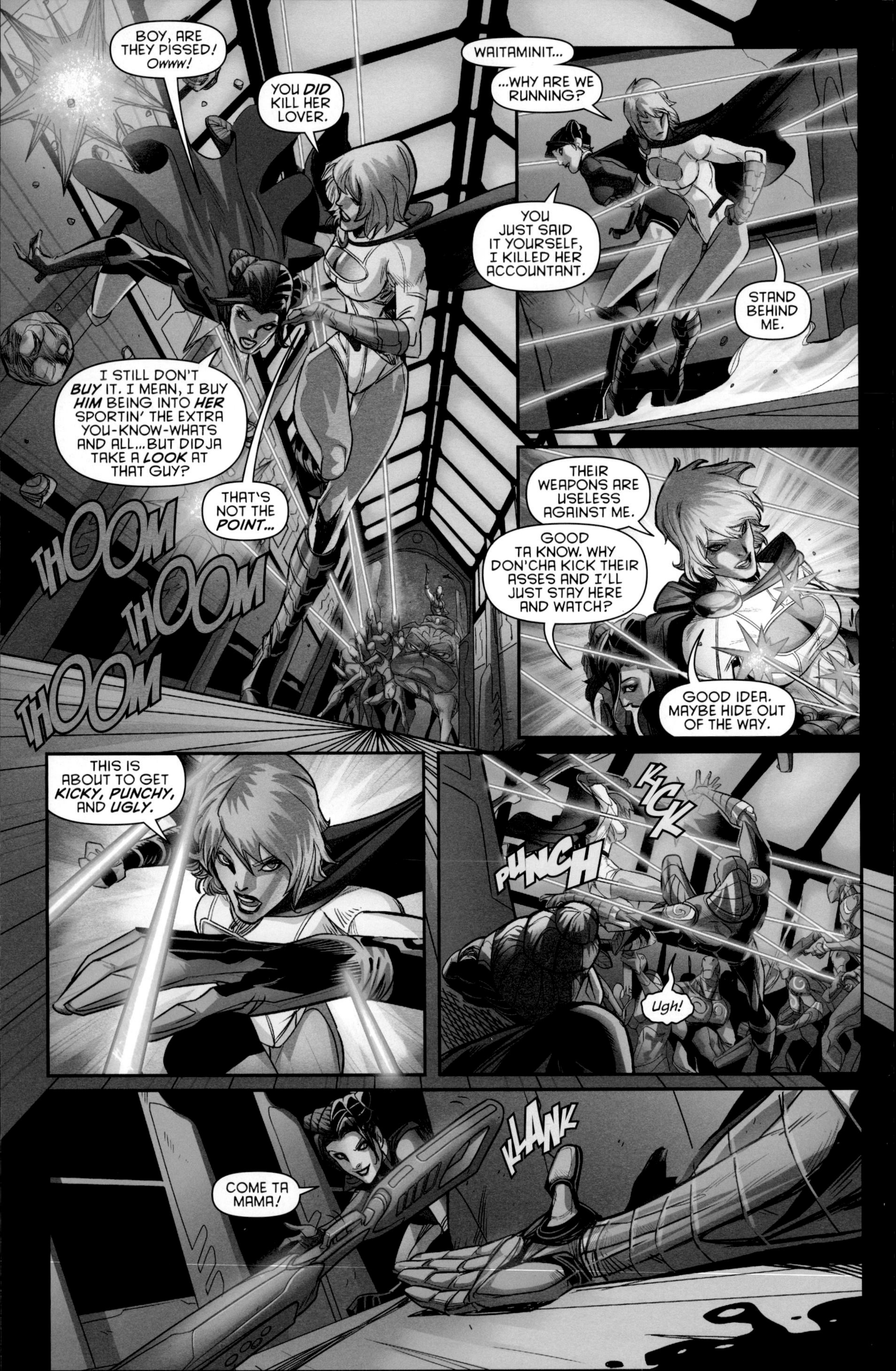
BOY, ARE THEY PISSED! *Owww!*
YOU *DID* KILL HER LOVER.
I STILL DON'T *BUY* IT. I MEAN, I BUY *HIM* BEING INTO *HER* SPORTIN' THE EXTRA YOU-KNOW-WHATS AND ALL...BUT DIDJA TAKE A *LOOK* AT THAT GUY?
THAT'S NOT THE *POINT...*
THOOM
THOOM
THOOM
WAITAMINIT...
...WHY ARE WE RUNNING?
YOU JUST SAID IT YOURSELF, I KILLED HER ACCOUNTANT.
STAND BEHIND ME.
THEIR WEAPONS ARE USELESS AGAINST ME.
GOOD TA KNOW. WHY DON'CHA KICK THEIR ASSES AND I'LL JUST STAY HERE AND WATCH?
GOOD IDEA. MAYBE HIDE OUT OF THE WAY.
THIS IS ABOUT TO GET *KICKY, PUNCHY,* AND *UGLY.*
KICK
PUNCH
Ugh!
KLANK
COME TA MAMA!

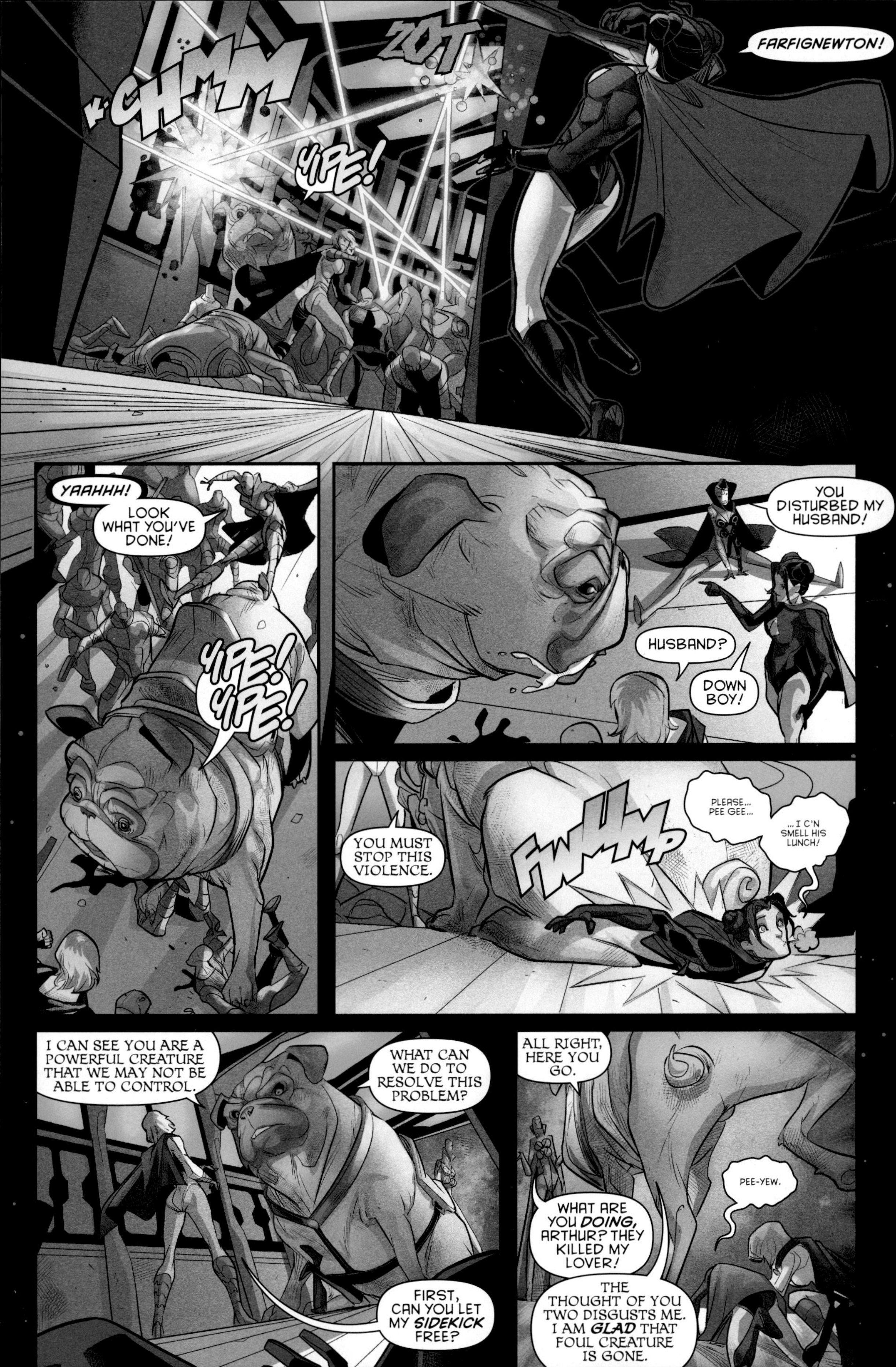
K-CHMM
ZOT
FARFIGNEWTON!
YIPE!
YAAHHH!
LOOK WHAT YOU'VE DONE!
YIPE! YIPE!
YOU DISTURBED MY HUSBAND!
HUSBAND?
DOWN BOY!
YOU MUST STOP THIS VIOLENCE.
FWUMP
PLEASE... PEE GEE...
...I C'N SMELL HIS LUNCH!
I CAN SEE YOU ARE A POWERFUL CREATURE THAT WE MAY NOT BE ABLE TO CONTROL.
WHAT CAN WE DO TO RESOLVE THIS PROBLEM?
FIRST, CAN YOU LET MY SIDEKICK FREE?
ALL RIGHT, HERE YOU GO.
PEE-YEW.
WHAT ARE YOU DOING, ARTHUR? THEY KILLED MY LOVER!
THE THOUGHT OF YOU TWO DISGUSTS ME. I AM GLAD THAT FOUL CREATURE IS GONE.

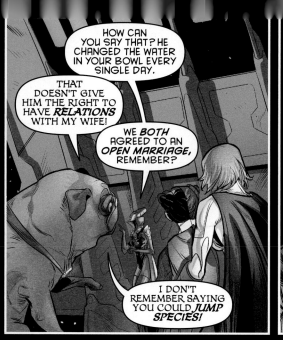

HOW CAN YOU SAY THAT? HE CHANGED THE WATER IN YOUR BOWL EVERY SINGLE DAY.

THAT DOESN'T GIVE HIM THE RIGHT TO HAVE *RELATIONS* WITH MY WIFE!

WE *BOTH* AGREED TO AN *OPEN MARRIAGE*, REMEMBER?

I DON'T REMEMBER SAYING YOU COULD *JUMP SPECIES!*

DO ME A FAVOR AND *PINCH ME.*

IN *BROOKLYN* WOULD BE NICE.

WHAT PART OF YOU IS "BROOKLYN"?

FERGET IT. I CAN'T BE DREAMING SOMETHING *THIS* RIDICULOUS. IT'S JUST IMPOSSIBLE.

DON'T ACT LIKE THAT WAS YOUR *ONLY* INDISCRETION! YOU *SICKEN* ME!

I SICKEN *YOU?* YOU THINK IT'S EASY WATCHING YOU LICK YOURSELF FOR HOURS YOU KNOW WHERE...

ENOUGH! I WILL HAVE NO MORE OF THIS.

SHOMP

GLOMP GLOMP

GULP

ANYWAY, WHERE WERE WE?

BURRRP

OH, RIGHT, WHAT WAS THE *OTHER* THING YOU WANTED?

UH...

WHA...

UH...OUT OF HERE. HOW DO WE GET BACK TO WHERE WE *CAME FROM?*

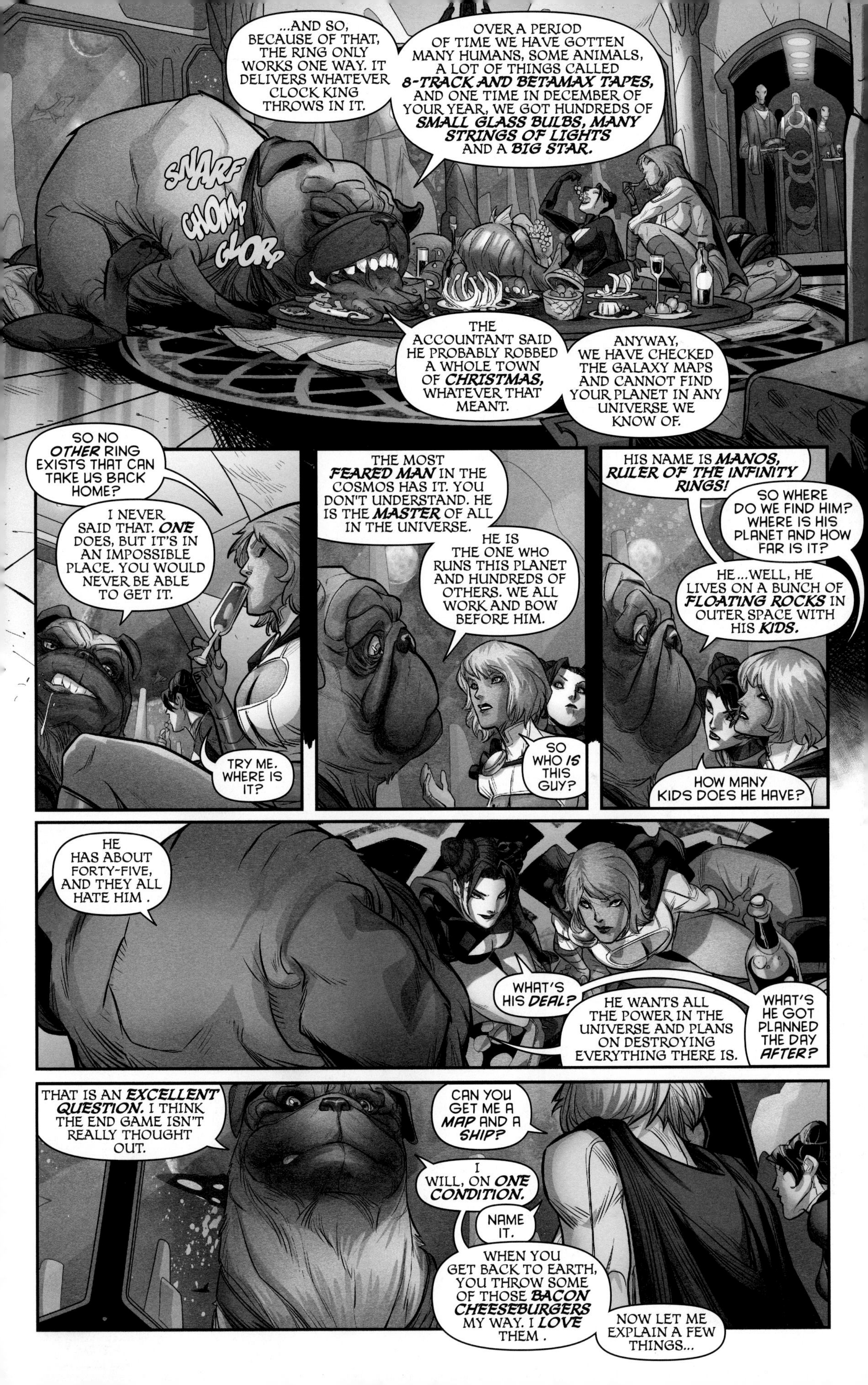
...AND SO, BECAUSE OF THAT, THE RING ONLY WORKS ONE WAY. IT DELIVERS WHATEVER CLOCK KING THROWS IN IT.
OVER A PERIOD OF TIME WE HAVE GOTTEN MANY HUMANS, SOME ANIMALS, A LOT OF THINGS CALLED 8-TRACK AND BETAMAX TAPES, AND ONE TIME IN DECEMBER OF YOUR YEAR, WE GOT HUNDREDS OF SMALL GLASS BULBS, MANY STRINGS OF LIGHTS AND A BIG STAR.
SNARF
CHOMP
GLORP
THE ACCOUNTANT SAID HE PROBABLY ROBBED A WHOLE TOWN OF CHRISTMAS, WHATEVER THAT MEANT.
ANYWAY, WE HAVE CHECKED THE GALAXY MAPS AND CANNOT FIND YOUR PLANET IN ANY UNIVERSE WE KNOW OF.
SO NO OTHER RING EXISTS THAT CAN TAKE US BACK HOME?
I NEVER SAID THAT. ONE DOES, BUT IT'S IN AN IMPOSSIBLE PLACE. YOU WOULD NEVER BE ABLE TO GET IT.
TRY ME. WHERE IS IT?
THE MOST FEARED MAN IN THE COSMOS HAS IT. YOU DON'T UNDERSTAND. HE IS THE MASTER OF ALL IN THE UNIVERSE.
HE IS THE ONE WHO RUNS THIS PLANET AND HUNDREDS OF OTHERS. WE ALL WORK AND BOW BEFORE HIM.
SO WHO IS THIS GUY?
HIS NAME IS MANOS, RULER OF THE INFINITY RINGS!
SO WHERE DO WE FIND HIM? WHERE IS HIS PLANET AND HOW FAR IS IT?
HE...WELL, HE LIVES ON A BUNCH OF FLOATING ROCKS IN OUTER SPACE WITH HIS KIDS.
HOW MANY KIDS DOES HE HAVE?
HE HAS ABOUT FORTY-FIVE, AND THEY ALL HATE HIM .
WHAT'S HIS DEAL?
HE WANTS ALL THE POWER IN THE UNIVERSE AND PLANS ON DESTROYING EVERYTHING THERE IS.
WHAT'S HE GOT PLANNED THE DAY AFTER?
THAT IS AN EXCELLENT QUESTION. I THINK THE END GAME ISN'T REALLY THOUGHT OUT.
CAN YOU GET ME A MAP AND A SHIP?
I WILL, ON ONE CONDITION.
NAME IT.
WHEN YOU GET BACK TO EARTH, YOU THROW SOME OF THOSE BACON CHEESEBURGERS MY WAY. I LOVE THEM .
NOW LET ME EXPLAIN A FEW THINGS...

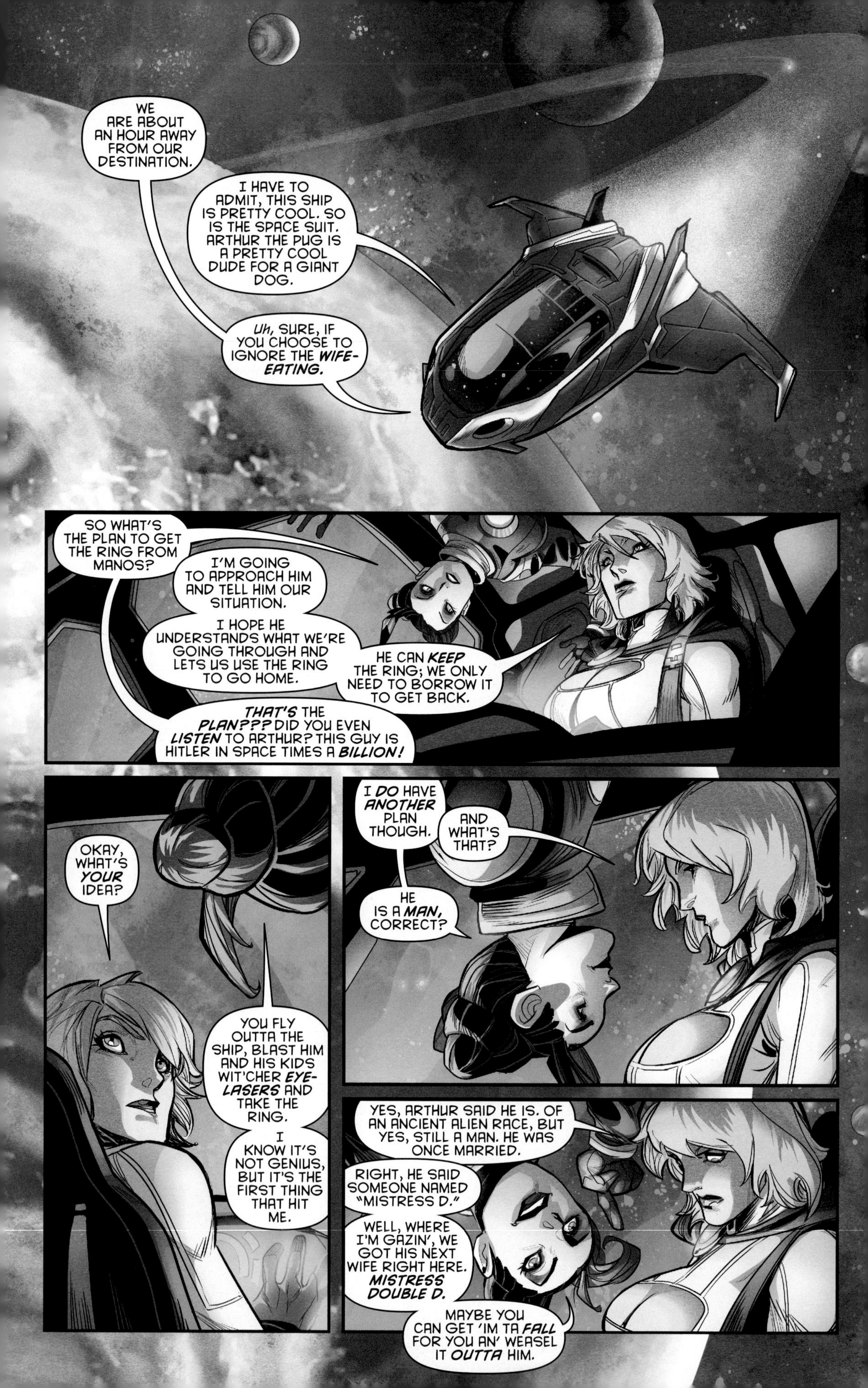
WE ARE ABOUT AN HOUR AWAY FROM OUR DESTINATION.
I HAVE TO ADMIT, THIS SHIP IS PRETTY COOL. SO IS THE SPACE SUIT. ARTHUR THE PUG IS A PRETTY COOL DUDE FOR A GIANT DOG.
UH, SURE, IF YOU CHOOSE TO IGNORE THE ***WIFE-EATING.***
SO WHAT'S THE PLAN TO GET THE RING FROM MANOS?
I'M GOING TO APPROACH HIM AND TELL HIM OUR SITUATION.
I HOPE HE UNDERSTANDS WHAT WE'RE GOING THROUGH AND LETS US USE THE RING TO GO HOME.
HE CAN ***KEEP*** THE RING; WE ONLY NEED TO BORROW IT TO GET BACK.
THAT'S THE ***PLAN???*** DID YOU EVEN ***LISTEN*** TO ARTHUR? THIS GUY IS HITLER IN SPACE TIMES A ***BILLION!***
OKAY, WHAT'S ***YOUR*** IDEA?
YOU FLY OUTTA THE SHIP, BLAST HIM AND HIS KIDS WIT'CHER ***EYE-LASERS*** AND TAKE THE RING.
I KNOW IT'S NOT GENIUS, BUT IT'S THE FIRST THING THAT HIT ME.
I ***DO*** HAVE ***ANOTHER*** PLAN THOUGH.
AND WHAT'S THAT?
HE IS A ***MAN,*** CORRECT?
YES, ARTHUR SAID HE IS. OF AN ANCIENT ALIEN RACE, BUT YES, STILL A MAN. HE WAS ONCE MARRIED.
RIGHT, HE SAID SOMEONE NAMED "MISTRESS D."
WELL, WHERE I'M GAZIN', WE GOT HIS NEXT WIFE RIGHT HERE. ***MISTRESS DOUBLE D.***
MAYBE YOU CAN GET 'IM TA ***FALL*** FOR YOU AN' WEASEL IT ***OUTTA*** HIM.

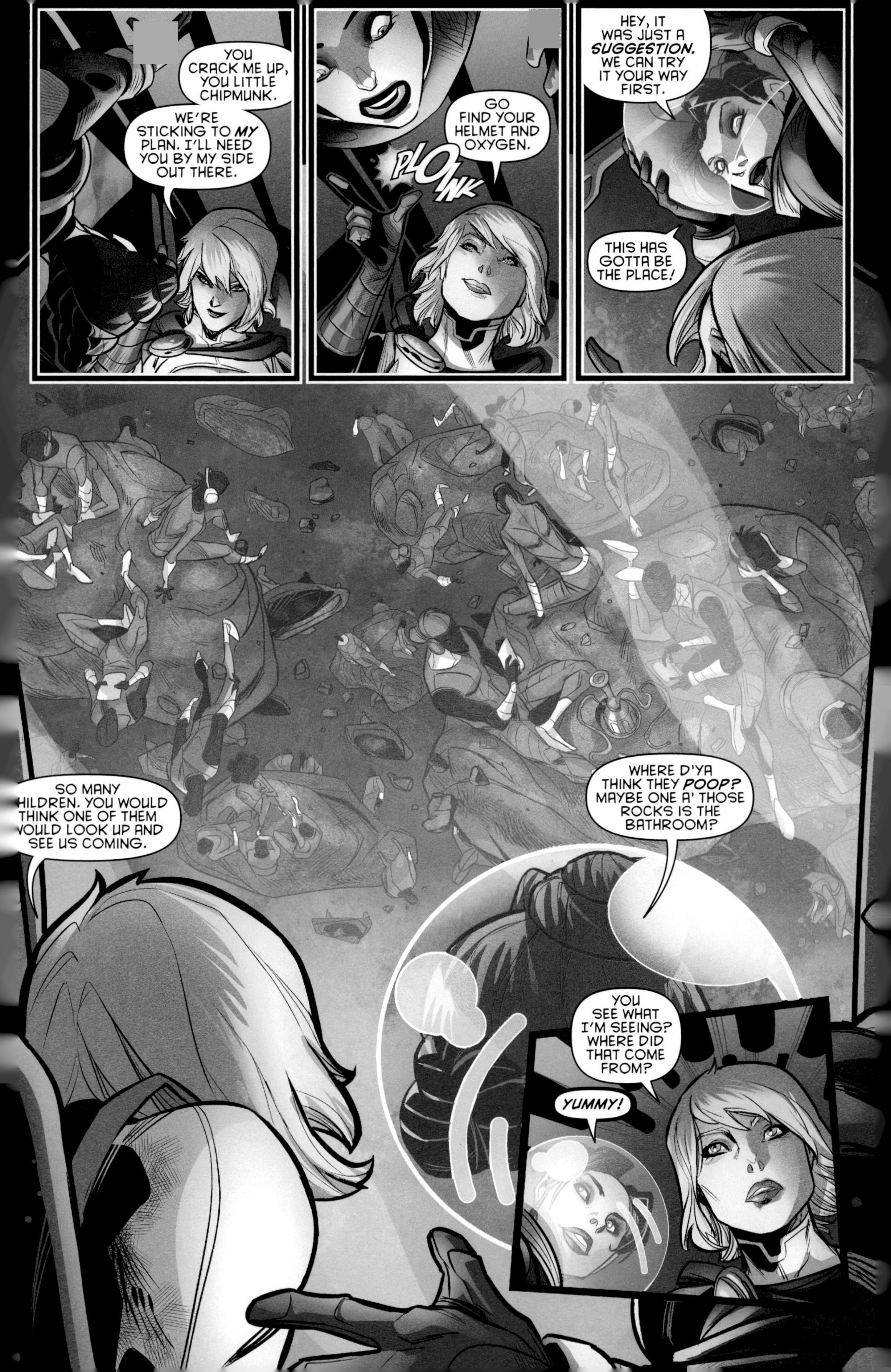
YOU CRACK ME UP, YOU LITTLE CHIPMUNK.
WE'RE STICKING TO *MY* PLAN. I'LL NEED YOU BY MY SIDE OUT THERE.
GO FIND YOUR HELMET AND OXYGEN.
PLONK
HEY, IT WAS JUST A *SUGGESTION.* WE CAN TRY IT YOUR WAY FIRST.
THIS HAS GOTTA BE THE PLACE!
SO MANY HILDREN. YOU WOULD THINK ONE OF THEM WOULD LOOK UP AND SEE US COMING.
WHERE D'YA THINK THEY *POOP?* MAYBE ONE A' THOSE ROCKS IS THE BATHROOM?
YOU SEE WHAT I'M SEEING? WHERE DID THAT COME FROM?
YUMMY!

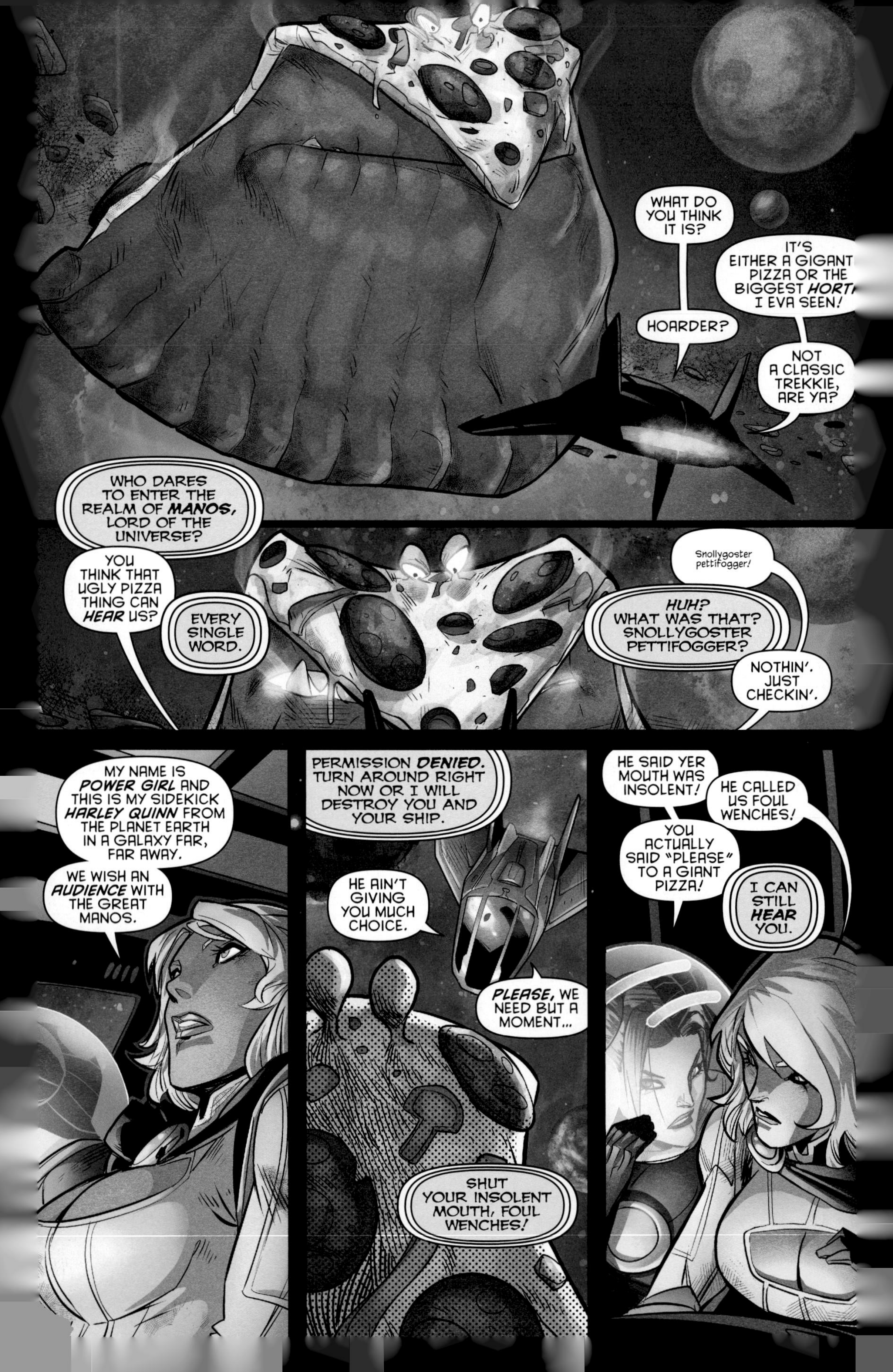
WHAT DO YOU THINK IT IS?
IT'S EITHER A GIGANT PIZZA OR THE BIGGEST HORT I EVA SEEN!
HOARDER?
NOT A CLASSIC TREKKIE, ARE YA?
WHO DARES TO ENTER THE REALM OF MANOS, LORD OF THE UNIVERSE?
YOU THINK THAT UGLY PIZZA THING CAN HEAR US?
EVERY SINGLE WORD.
Snollygoster pettifogger!
HUH? WHAT WAS THAT? SNOLLYGOSTER PETTIFOGGER?
NOTHIN'. JUST CHECKIN'.
MY NAME IS POWER GIRL AND THIS IS MY SIDEKICK HARLEY QUINN FROM THE PLANET EARTH IN A GALAXY FAR, FAR AWAY.
WE WISH AN AUDIENCE WITH THE GREAT MANOS.
PERMISSION DENIED. TURN AROUND RIGHT NOW OR I WILL DESTROY YOU AND YOUR SHIP.
HE AIN'T GIVING YOU MUCH CHOICE.
PLEASE, WE NEED BUT A MOMENT...
SHUT YOUR INSOLENT MOUTH, FOUL WENCHES!
HE SAID YER MOUTH WAS INSOLENT!
HE CALLED US FOUL WENCHES!
YOU ACTUALLY SAID "PLEASE" TO A GIANT PIZZA!
I CAN STILL HEAR YOU.

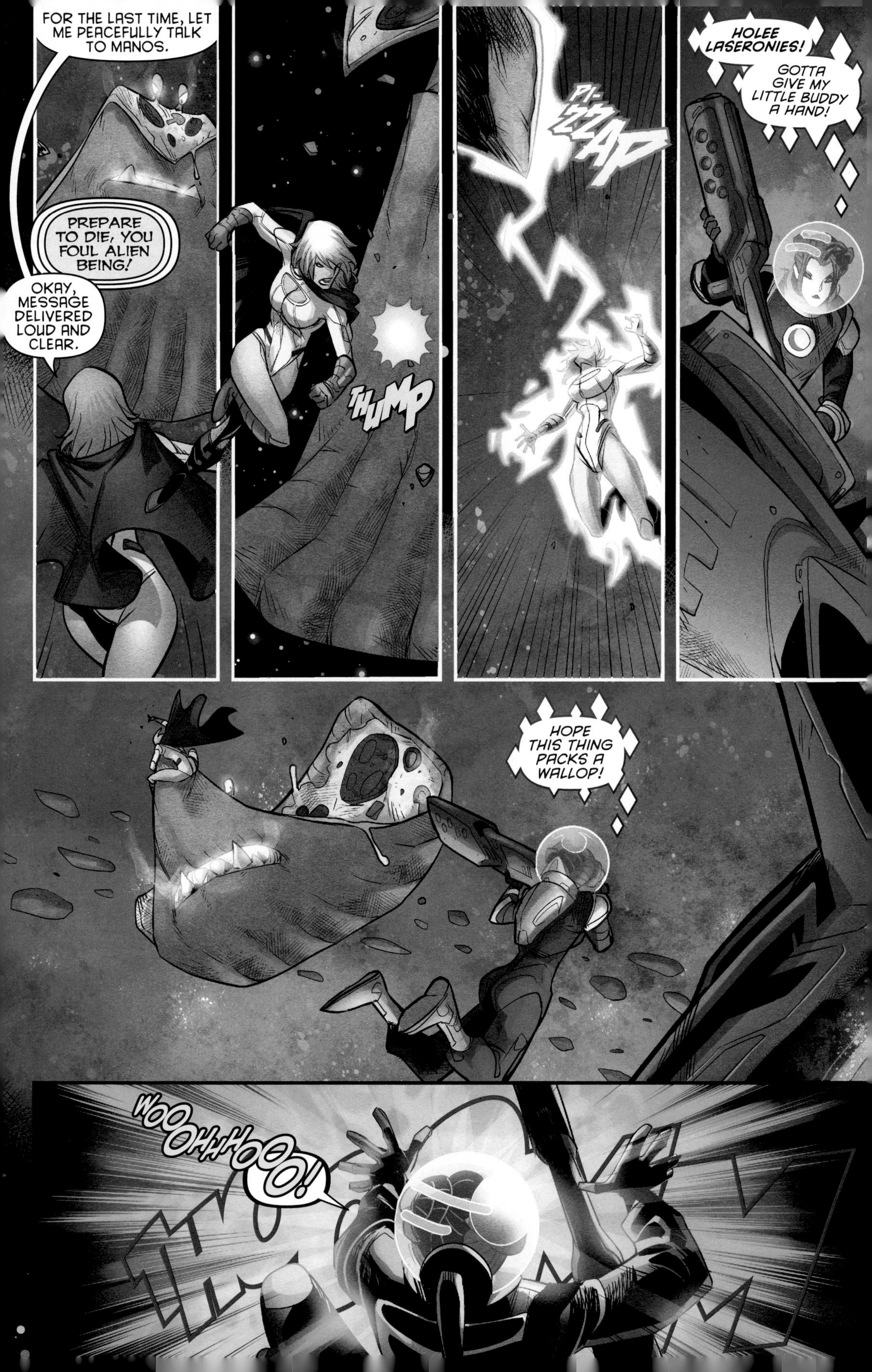
FOR THE LAST TIME, LET ME PEACEFULLY TALK TO MANOS.
PREPARE TO DIE, YOU FOUL ALIEN BEING!
OKAY, MESSAGE DELIVERED LOUD AND CLEAR.
THUMP
PI-ZZZAP
HOLEE LASERONIES!
GOTTA GIVE MY LITTLE BUDDY A HAND!
HOPE THIS THING PACKS A WALLOP!
WOOOHHHOOOO!

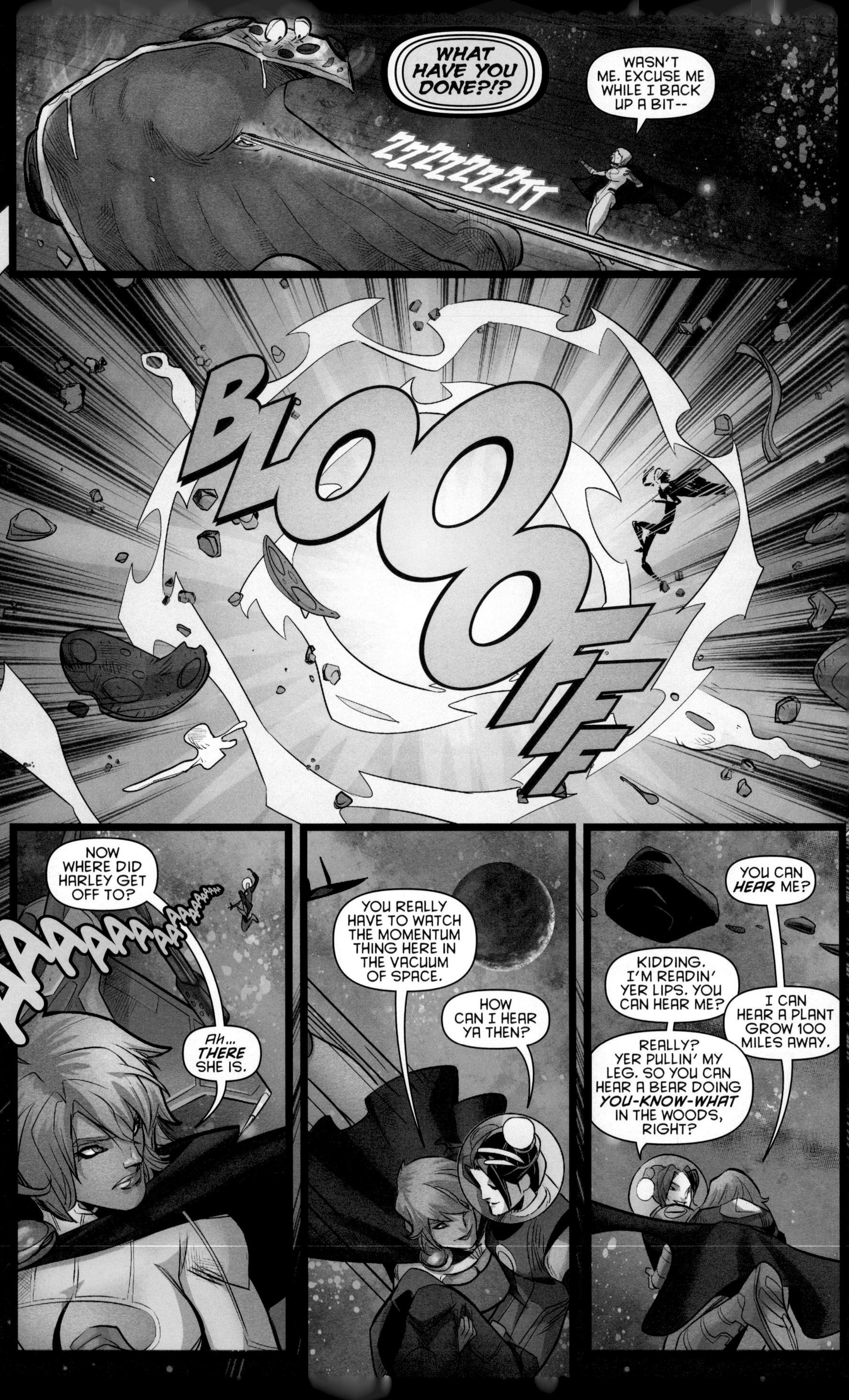
WHAT HAVE YOU DONE?!?
WASN'T ME. EXCUSE ME WHILE I BACK UP A BIT--
ZZZZZZZZTT
BLOOOOFFF
NOW WHERE DID HARLEY GET OFF TO?
AAAAAAAAAAAAAAAA
Ah... THERE SHE IS.
YOU REALLY HAVE TO WATCH THE MOMENTUM THING HERE IN THE VACUUM OF SPACE.
HOW CAN I HEAR YA THEN?
YOU CAN HEAR ME?
KIDDING. I'M READIN' YER LIPS. YOU CAN HEAR ME?
I CAN HEAR A PLANT GROW 100 MILES AWAY.
REALLY? YER PULLIN' MY LEG. SO YOU CAN HEAR A BEAR DOING YOU-KNOW-WHAT IN THE WOODS, RIGHT?

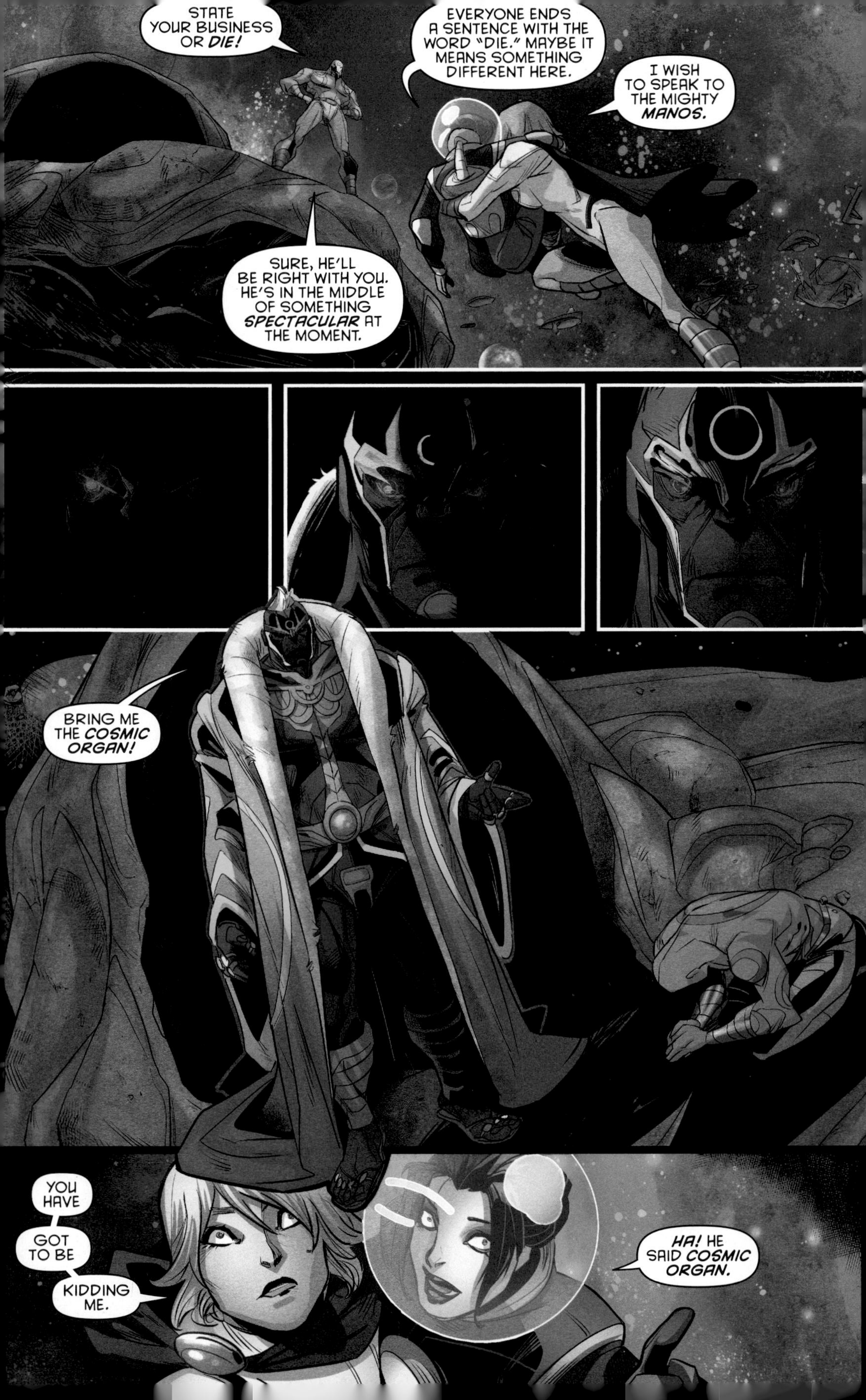
STATE YOUR BUSINESS OR DIE!
EVERYONE ENDS A SENTENCE WITH THE WORD "DIE." MAYBE IT MEANS SOMETHING DIFFERENT HERE.
I WISH TO SPEAK TO THE MIGHTY MANOS.
SURE, HE'LL BE RIGHT WITH YOU. HE'S IN THE MIDDLE OF SOMETHING SPECTACULAR AT THE MOMENT.
BRING ME THE COSMIC ORGAN!
YOU HAVE
GOT TO BE
KIDDING ME.
HA! HE SAID COSMIC ORGAN.

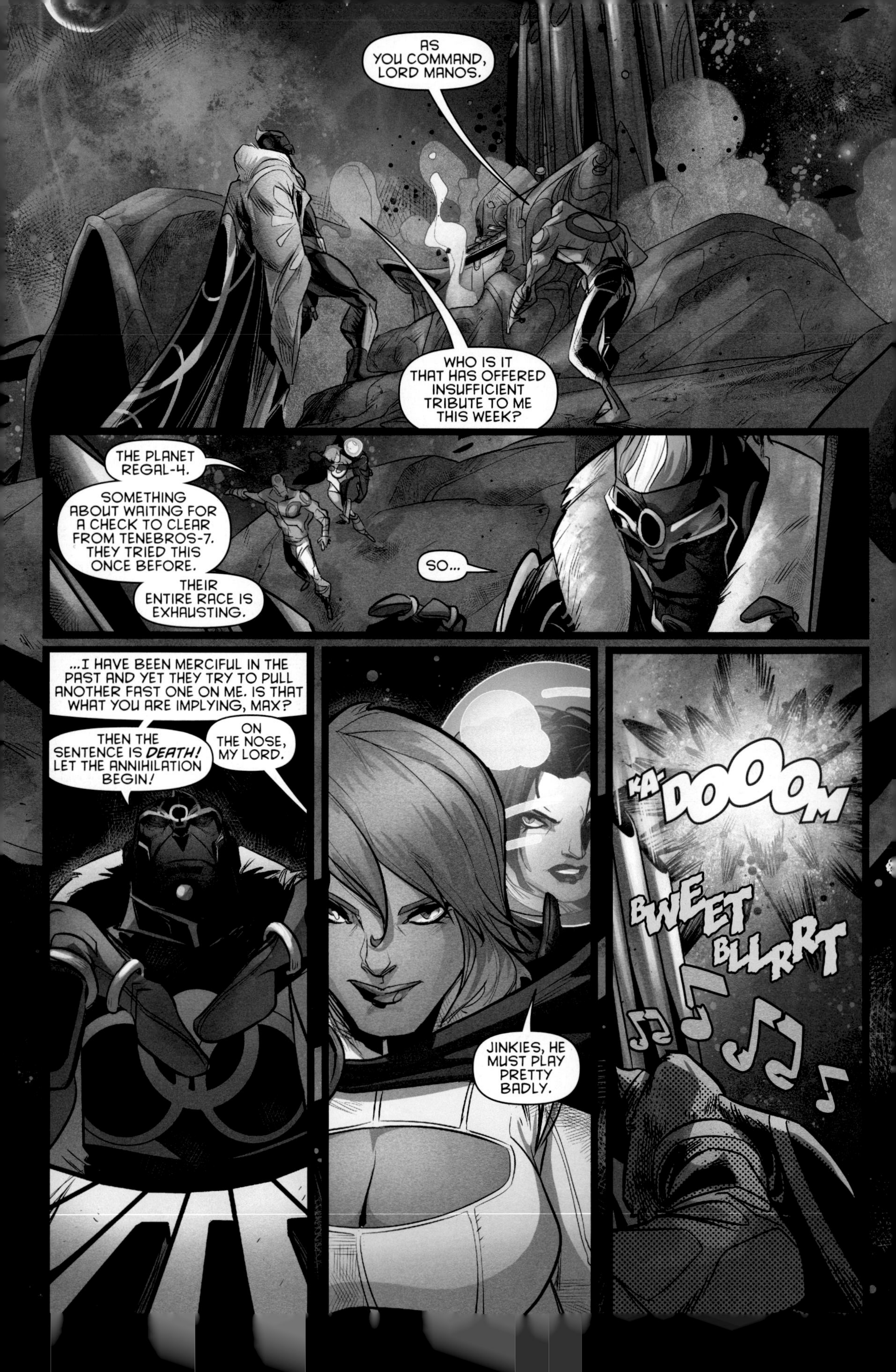

AS YOU COMMAND, LORD MANOS.
WHO IS IT THAT HAS OFFERED INSUFFICIENT TRIBUTE TO ME THIS WEEK?
THE PLANET REGAL-4.
SOMETHING ABOUT WAITING FOR A CHECK TO CLEAR FROM TENEBROS-7. THEY TRIED THIS ONCE BEFORE.
THEIR ENTIRE RACE IS EXHAUSTING.
SO...
...I HAVE BEEN MERCIFUL IN THE PAST AND YET THEY TRY TO PULL ANOTHER FAST ONE ON ME. IS THAT WHAT YOU ARE IMPLYING, MAX?
ON THE NOSE, MY LORD.
THEN THE SENTENCE IS *DEATH!* LET THE ANNIHILATION BEGIN!
JINKIES, HE MUST PLAY PRETTY BADLY.
KA-DOOOOM
BWEET BLLRRRT

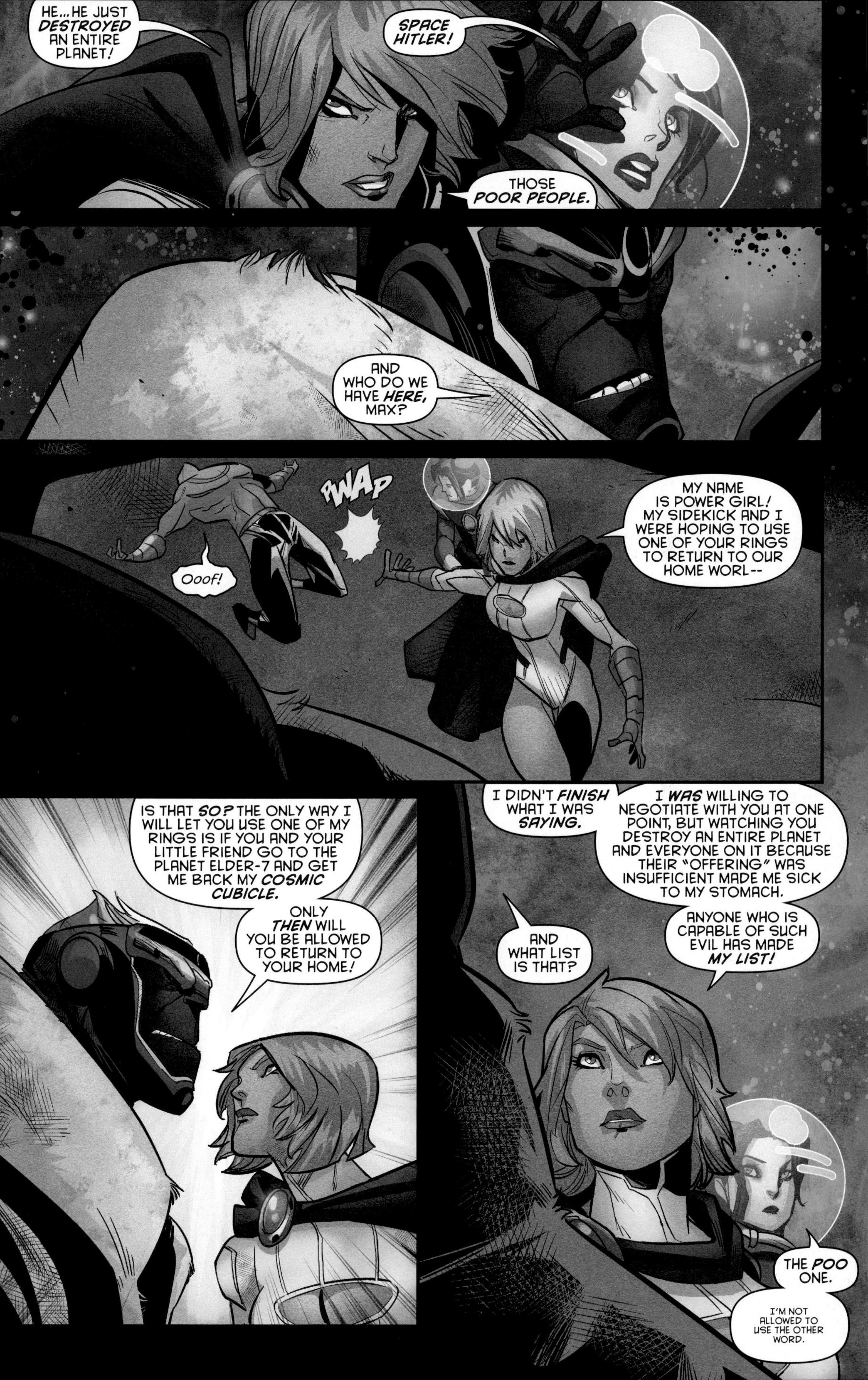
HE...HE JUST DESTROYED AN ENTIRE PLANET!
SPACE HITLER!
THOSE POOR PEOPLE.
AND WHO DO WE HAVE HERE, MAX?
PWAP
Ooof!
MY NAME IS POWER GIRL! MY SIDEKICK AND I WERE HOPING TO USE ONE OF YOUR RINGS TO RETURN TO OUR HOME WORL--
IS THAT SO? THE ONLY WAY I WILL LET YOU USE ONE OF MY RINGS IS IF YOU AND YOUR LITTLE FRIEND GO TO THE PLANET ELDER-7 AND GET ME BACK MY COSMIC CUBICLE.
ONLY THEN WILL YOU BE ALLOWED TO RETURN TO YOUR HOME!
I DIDN'T FINISH WHAT I WAS SAYING.
I WAS WILLING TO NEGOTIATE WITH YOU AT ONE POINT, BUT WATCHING YOU DESTROY AN ENTIRE PLANET AND EVERYONE ON IT BECAUSE THEIR "OFFERING" WAS INSUFFICIENT MADE ME SICK TO MY STOMACH.
ANYONE WHO IS CAPABLE OF SUCH EVIL HAS MADE MY LIST!
AND WHAT LIST IS THAT?
THE POO ONE.
I'M NOT ALLOWED TO USE THE OTHER WORD.

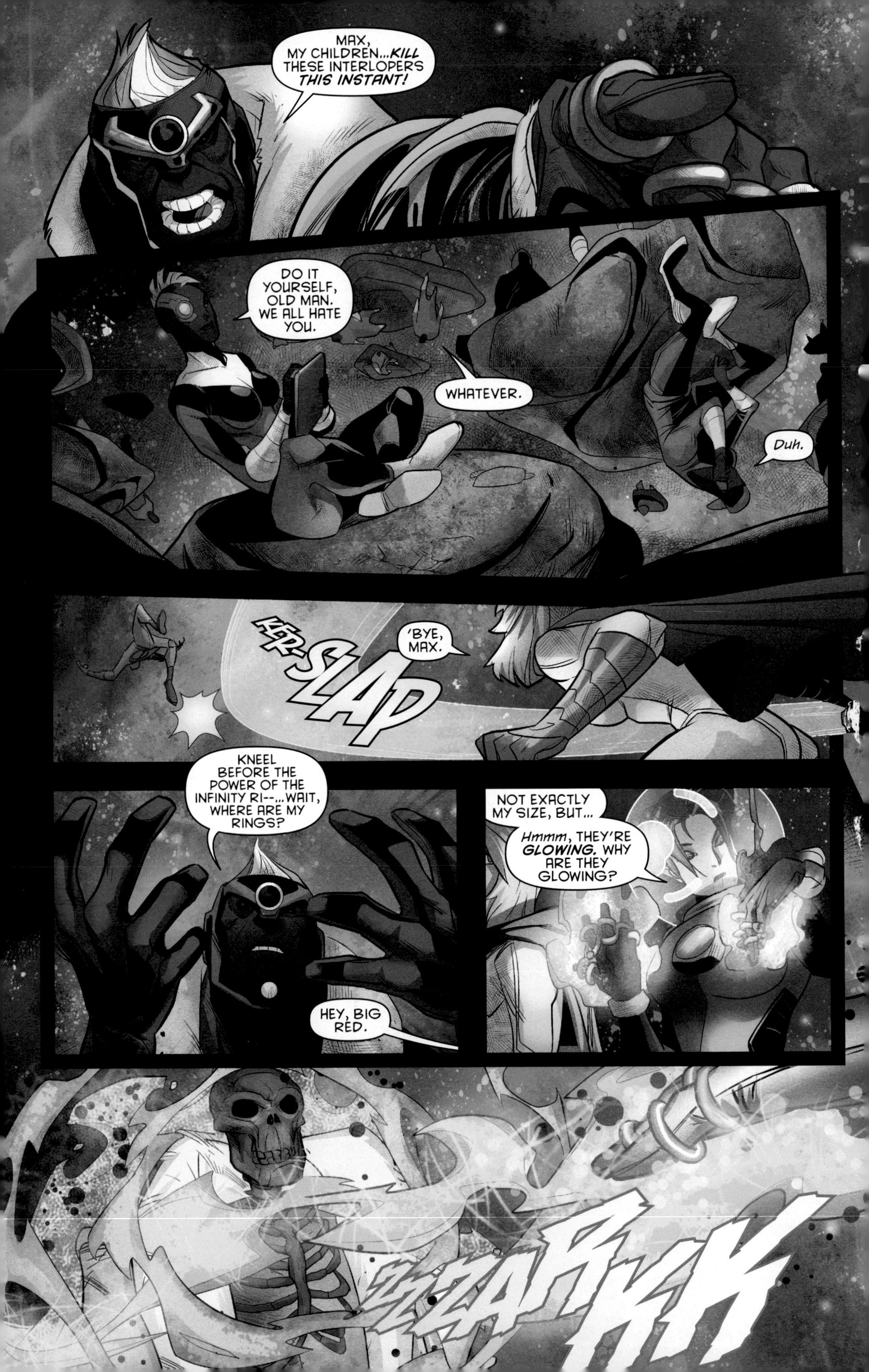
MAX, MY CHILDREN...KILL THESE INTERLOPERS THIS INSTANT!
DO IT YOURSELF, OLD MAN. WE ALL HATE YOU.
WHATEVER.
Duh.
KER-SLAP
'BYE, MAX.
KNEEL BEFORE THE POWER OF THE INFINITY RI--...WAIT, WHERE ARE MY RINGS?
HEY, BIG RED.
NOT EXACTLY MY SIZE, BUT...
Hmmm, THEY'RE GLOWING. WHY ARE THEY GLOWING?
ZZZAKKK

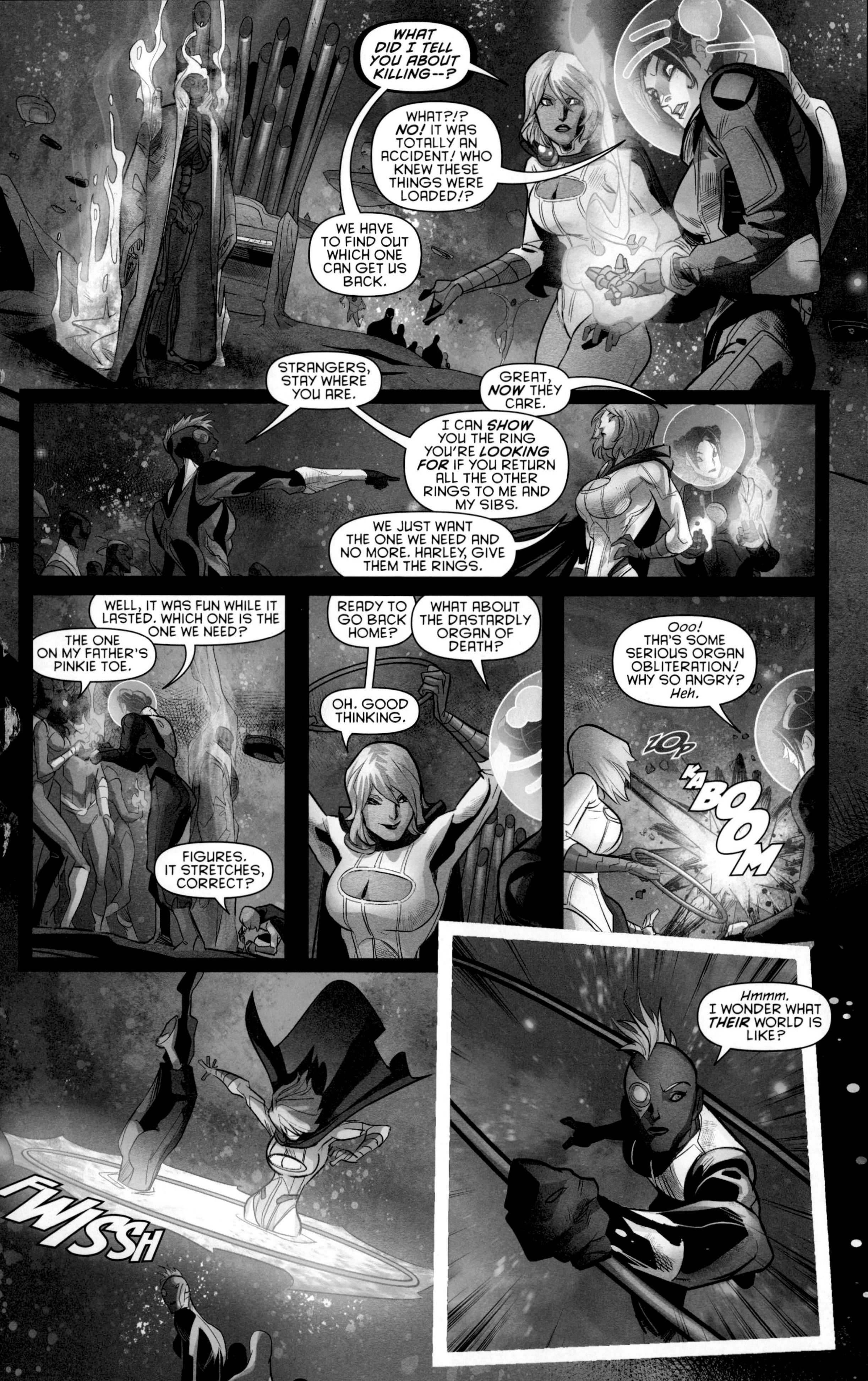
WHAT DID I TELL YOU ABOUT KILLING--?
WHAT?!? NO! IT WAS TOTALLY AN ACCIDENT! WHO KNEW THESE THINGS WERE LOADED!?
WE HAVE TO FIND OUT WHICH ONE CAN GET US BACK.
STRANGERS, STAY WHERE YOU ARE.
GREAT, NOW THEY CARE.
I CAN SHOW YOU THE RING YOU'RE LOOKING FOR IF YOU RETURN ALL THE OTHER RINGS TO ME AND MY SIBS.
WE JUST WANT THE ONE WE NEED AND NO MORE. HARLEY, GIVE THEM THE RINGS.
WELL, IT WAS FUN WHILE IT LASTED. WHICH ONE IS THE ONE WE NEED?
THE ONE ON MY FATHER'S PINKIE TOE.
FIGURES. IT STRETCHES, CORRECT?
READY TO GO BACK HOME?
WHAT ABOUT THE DASTARDLY ORGAN OF DEATH?
OH. GOOD THINKING.
Ooo! THA'S SOME SERIOUS ORGAN OBLITERATION! WHY SO ANGRY? Heh.
ZOP
KABOOOM
FWISSH
Hmmm. I WONDER WHAT THEIR WORLD IS LIKE?

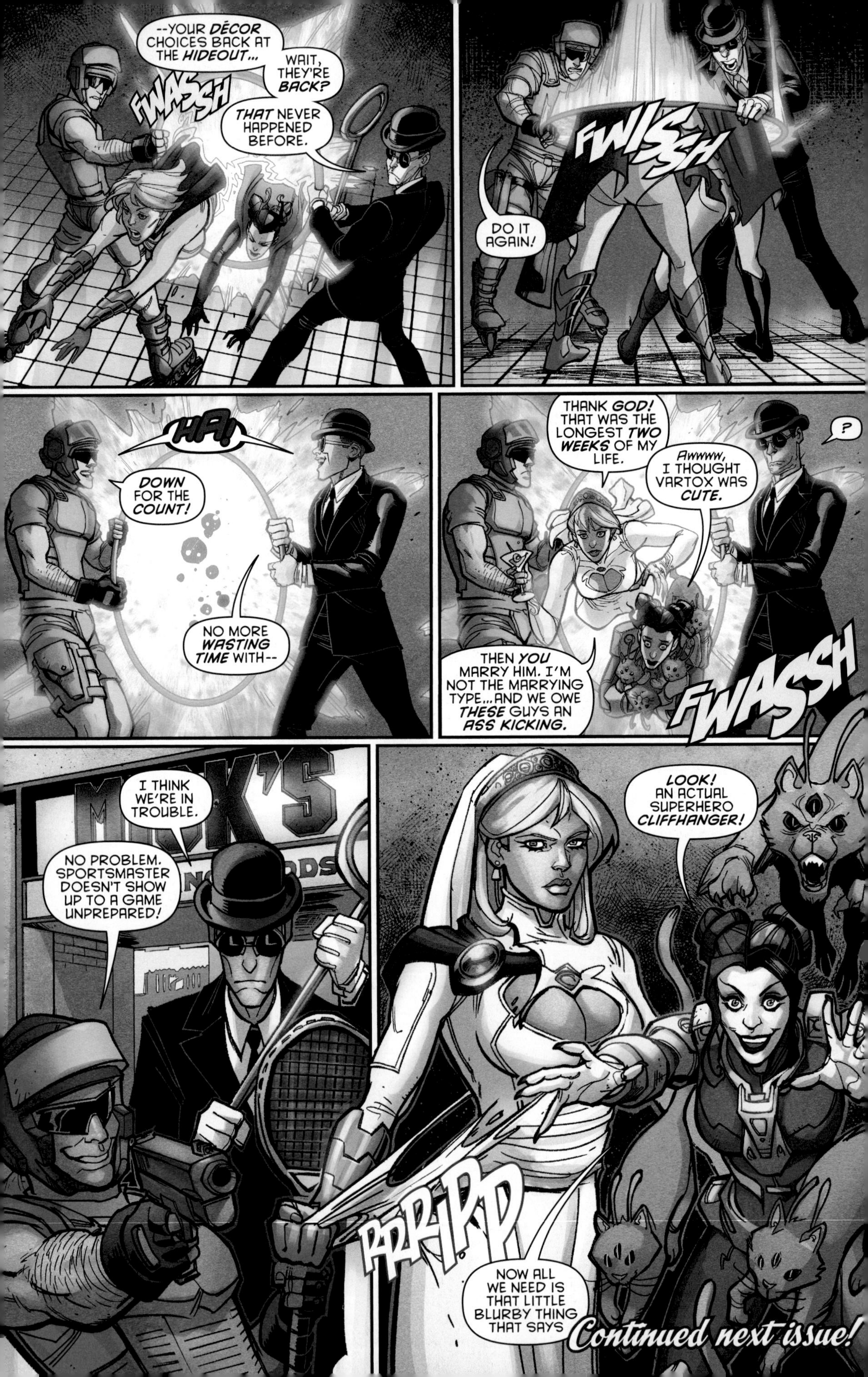
--YOUR DÉCOR CHOICES BACK AT THE HIDEOUT...
FWASSH
WAIT, THEY'RE BACK?
THAT NEVER HAPPENED BEFORE.
FWISSH
DO IT AGAIN!
HA!
DOWN FOR THE COUNT!
NO MORE WASTING TIME WITH--
THANK GOD! THAT WAS THE LONGEST TWO WEEKS OF MY LIFE.
?
AWWWW, I THOUGHT VARTOX WAS CUTE.
THEN YOU MARRY HIM. I'M NOT THE MARRYING TYPE...AND WE OWE THESE GUYS AN ASS KICKING.
FWASSH
I THINK WE'RE IN TROUBLE.
NO PROBLEM. SPORTSMASTER DOESN'T SHOW UP TO A GAME UNPREPARED!
LOOK! AN ACTUAL SUPERHERO CLIFFHANGER!
RRRIPP
NOW ALL WE NEED IS THAT LITTLE BLURBY THING THAT SAYS
Continued next issue!

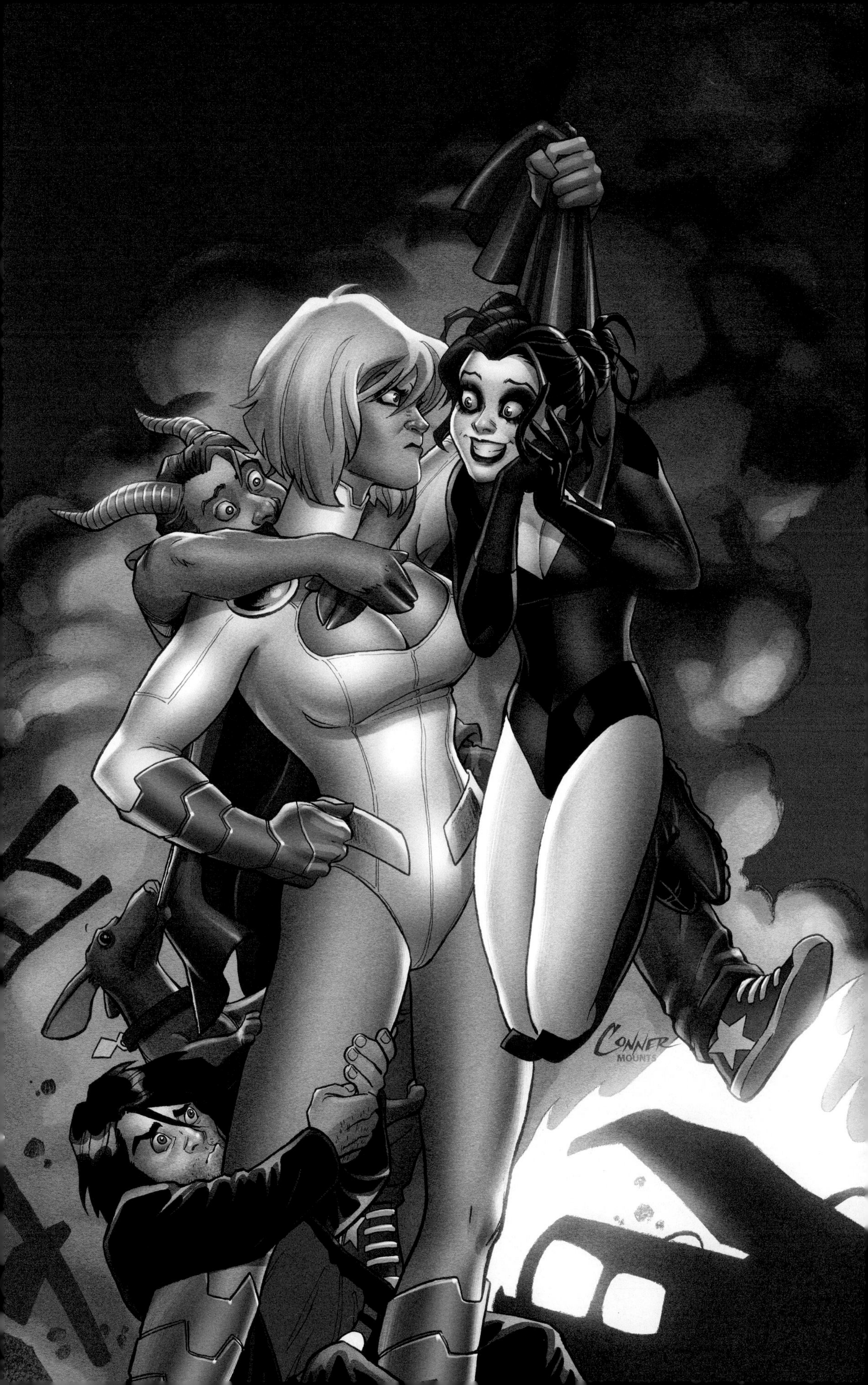
CONNER
MOUNTS

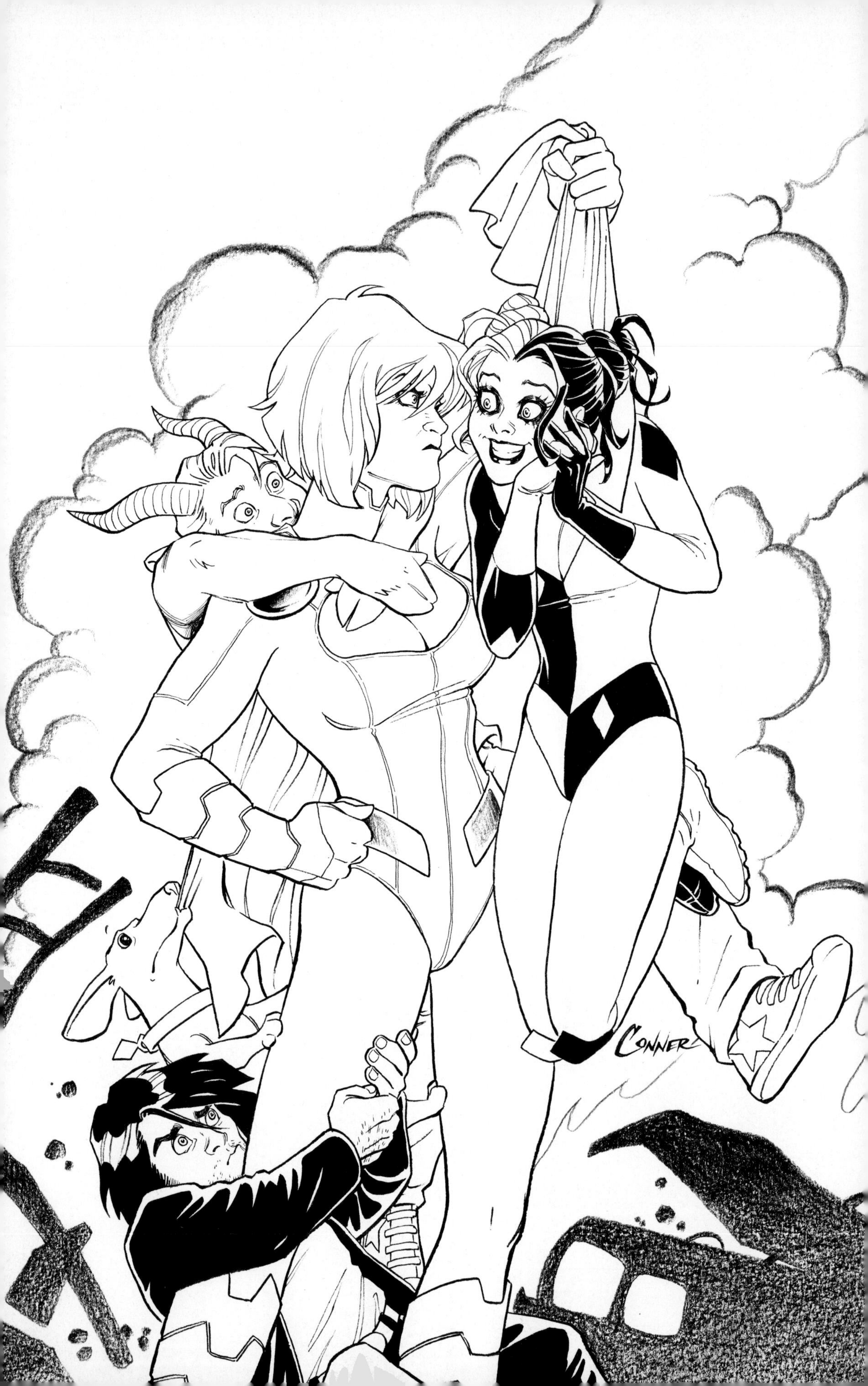

CONNER

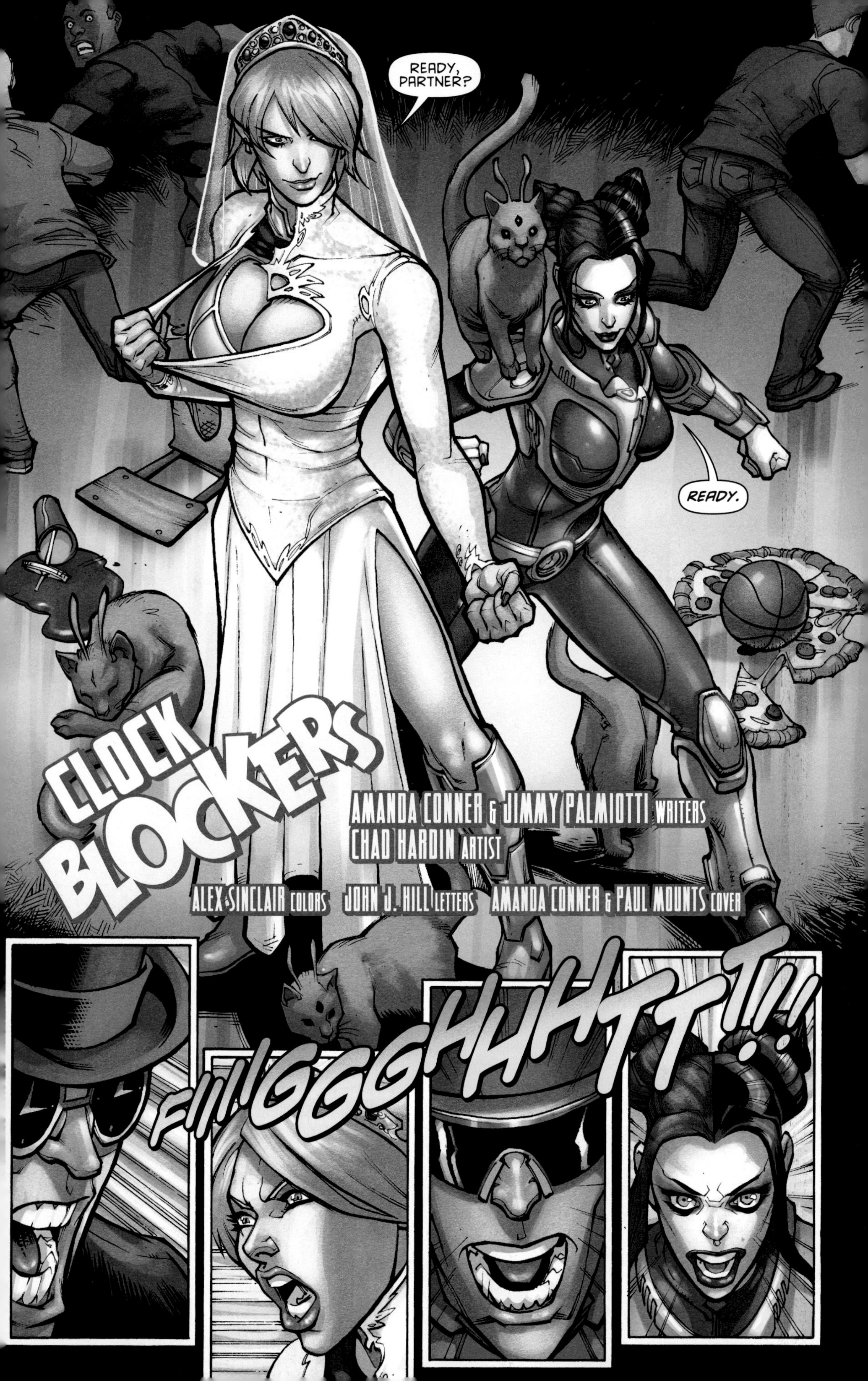

READY, PARTNER?
READY.
CLOCK BLOCKERS
AMANDA CONNER & JIMMY PALMIOTTI WRITERS
CHAD HARDIN ARTIST
ALEX SINCLAIR COLORS
JOHN J. HILL LETTERS
AMANDA CONNER & PAUL MOUNTS COVER
FIIIGGGGHHHTT!!!

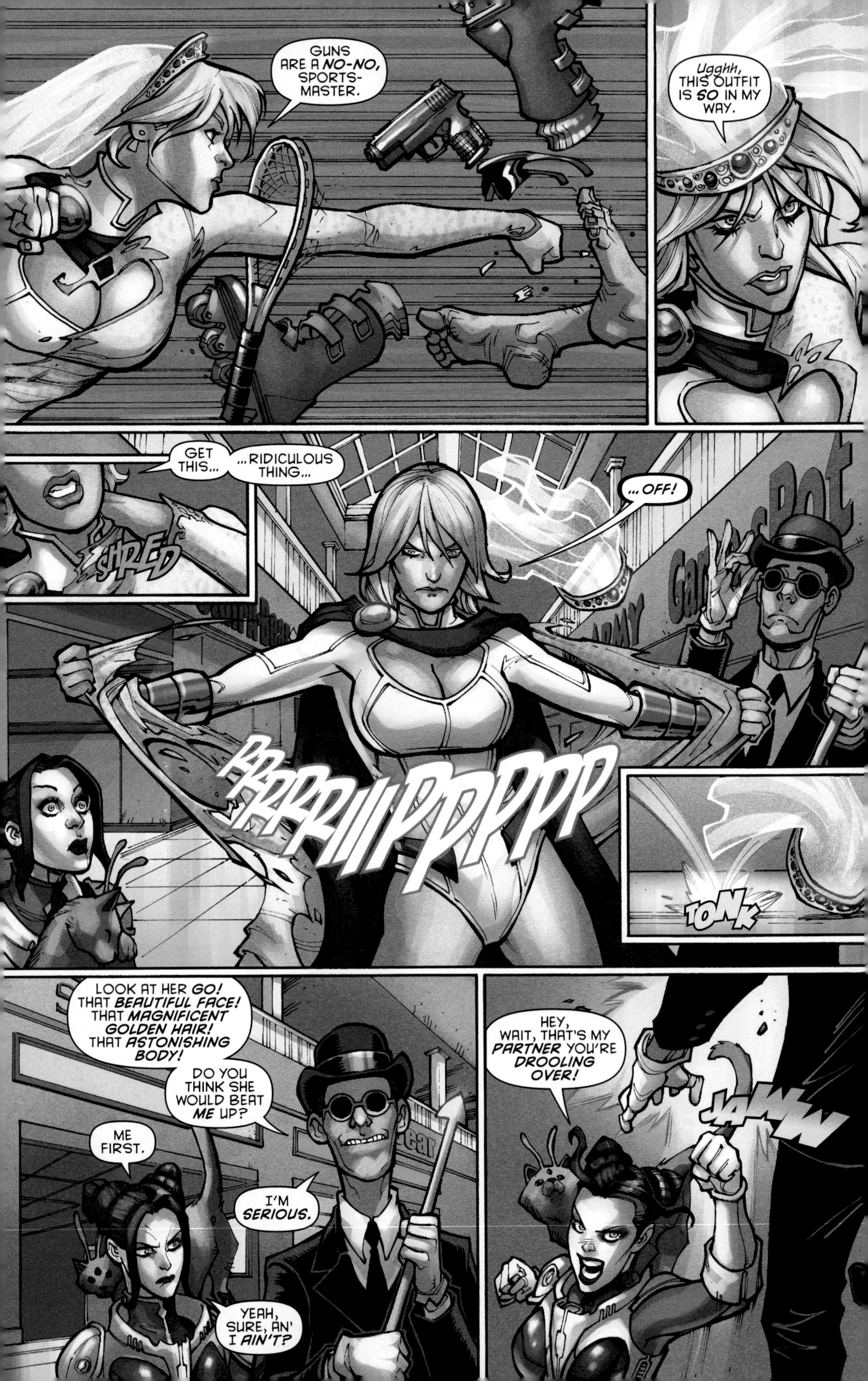
GUNS ARE A NO-NO, SPORTS-MASTER.
Ugghh, THIS OUTFIT IS SO IN MY WAY.
GET THIS...
...RIDICULOUS THING...
SHRED
...OFF!
RRRRRIIIPPPPPP
TONK
LOOK AT HER GO! THAT BEAUTIFUL FACE! THAT MAGNIFICENT GOLDEN HAIR! THAT ASTONISHING BODY!
DO YOU THINK SHE WOULD BEAT ME UP?
ME FIRST.
I'M SERIOUS.
YEAH, SURE, AN' I AIN'T?
HEY, WAIT, THAT'S MY PARTNER YOU'RE DROOLING OVER!
JAWW

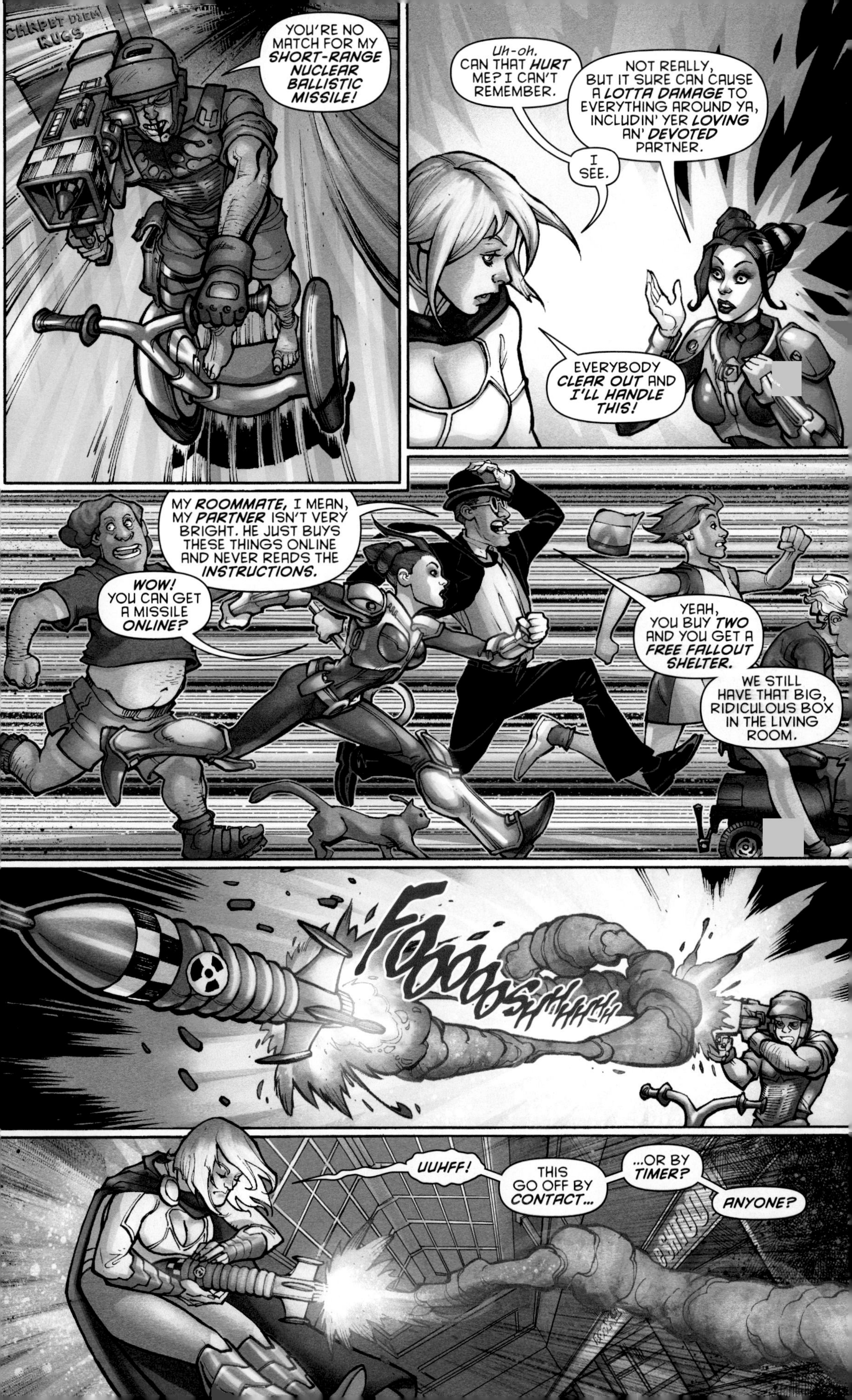
CARPET DIEM RUGS
YOU'RE NO MATCH FOR MY SHORT-RANGE NUCLEAR BALLISTIC MISSILE!
Uh-oh. CAN THAT HURT ME? I CAN'T REMEMBER.
NOT REALLY, BUT IT SURE CAN CAUSE A LOTTA DAMAGE TO EVERYTHING AROUND YA, INCLUDIN' YER LOVING AN' DEVOTED PARTNER.
I SEE.
EVERYBODY CLEAR OUT AND I'LL HANDLE THIS!
MY ROOMMATE, I MEAN, MY PARTNER ISN'T VERY BRIGHT. HE JUST BUYS THESE THINGS ONLINE AND NEVER READS THE INSTRUCTIONS.
WOW! YOU CAN GET A MISSILE ONLINE?
YEAH, YOU BUY TWO AND YOU GET A FREE FALLOUT SHELTER.
WE STILL HAVE THAT BIG, RIDICULOUS BOX IN THE LIVING ROOM.
FOOOOSHHHH
UUHFF!
THIS GO OFF BY CONTACT...
...OR BY TIMER?
ANYONE?

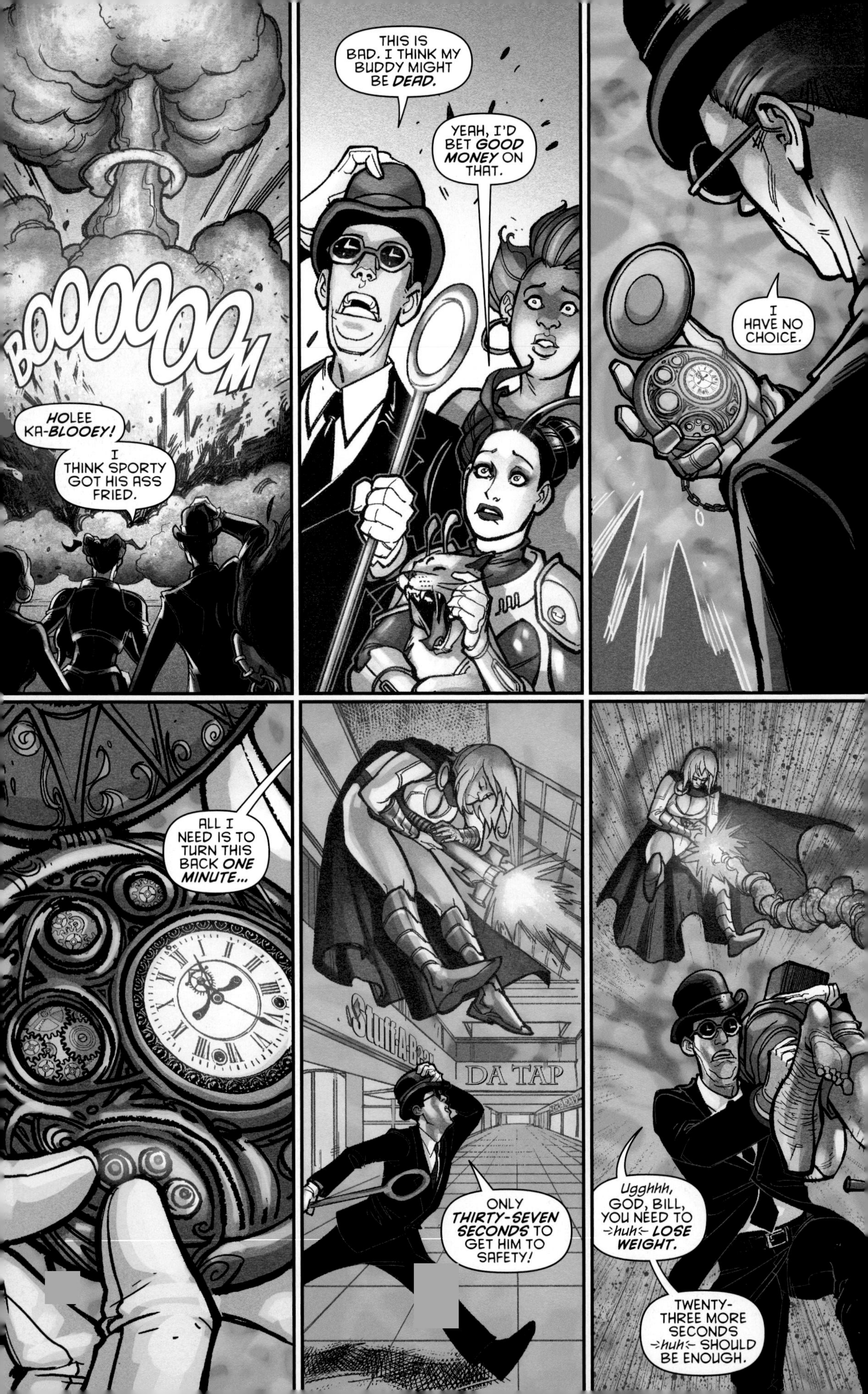
BOOOOOOM
HOLEE KA-BLOOEY!
I THINK SPORTY GOT HIS ASS FRIED.
THIS IS BAD. I THINK MY BUDDY MIGHT BE DEAD.
YEAH, I'D BET GOOD MONEY ON THAT.
I HAVE NO CHOICE.
ALL I NEED IS TO TURN THIS BACK ONE MINUTE...
Stuff-A-Bear
DA TAP
ONLY THIRTY-SEVEN SECONDS TO GET HIM TO SAFETY!
Ugghhh, GOD, BILL, YOU NEED TO -huh- LOSE WEIGHT.
TWENTY-THREE MORE SECONDS -huh- SHOULD BE ENOUGH.

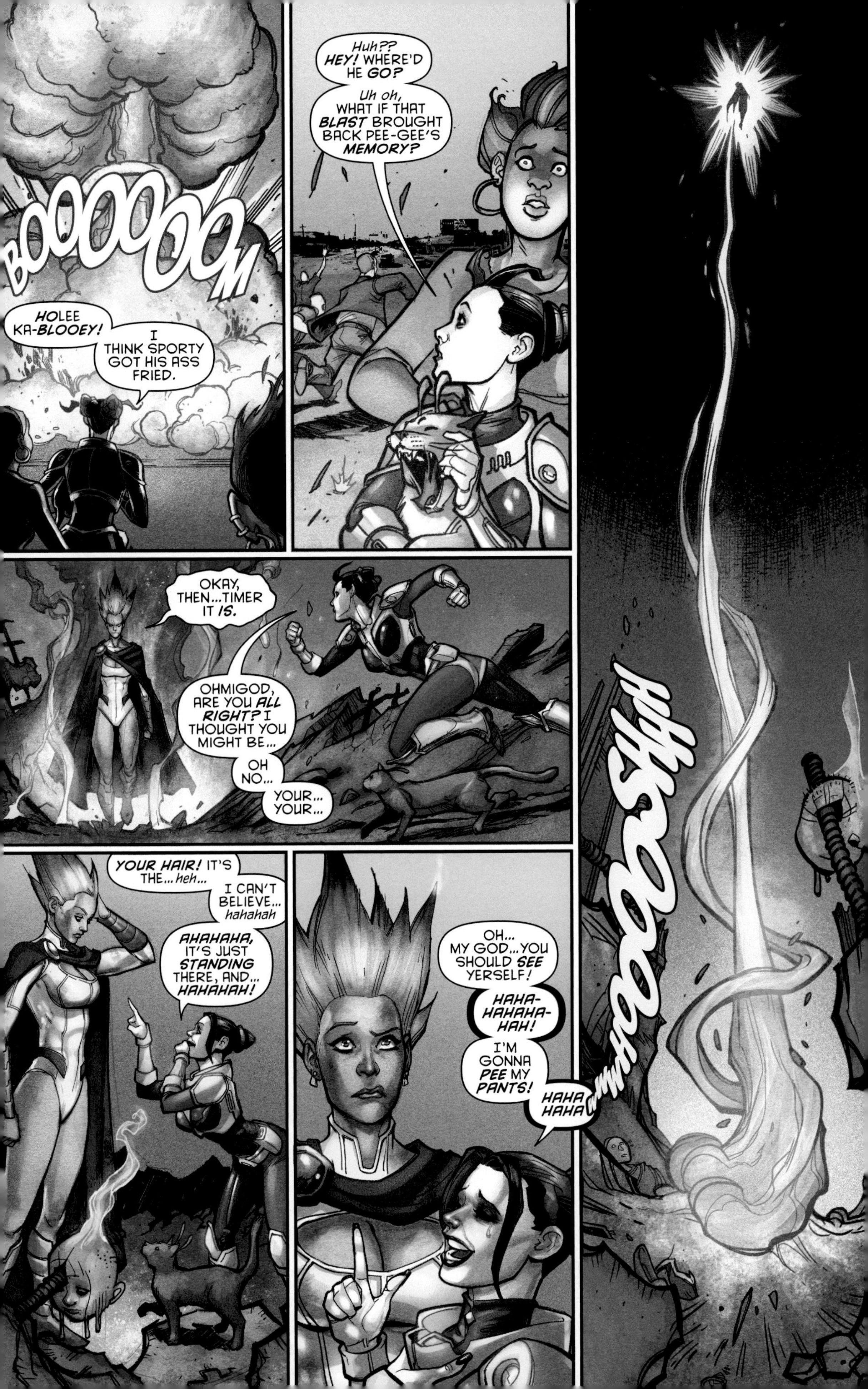
BOOOOOOM
HOLEE KA-BLOOEY!
I THINK SPORTY GOT HIS ASS FRIED.
Huh?? HEY! WHERE'D HE GO?
Uh oh, WHAT IF THAT BLAST BROUGHT BACK PEE-GEE'S MEMORY?
OKAY, THEN...TIMER IT IS.
OHMIGOD, ARE YOU ALL RIGHT? I THOUGHT YOU MIGHT BE...
OH NO...
YOUR... YOUR...
YOUR HAIR! IT'S THE... heh...
I CAN'T BELIEVE... hahahah
AHAHAHA, IT'S JUST STANDING THERE, AND... HAHAHAH!
OH... MY GOD...YOU SHOULD SEE YERSELF!
HAHA-HAHAHA-HAH!
I'M GONNA PEE MY PANTS!
HAHA HAHA
HHHHHOOOOOSSSHHHHH

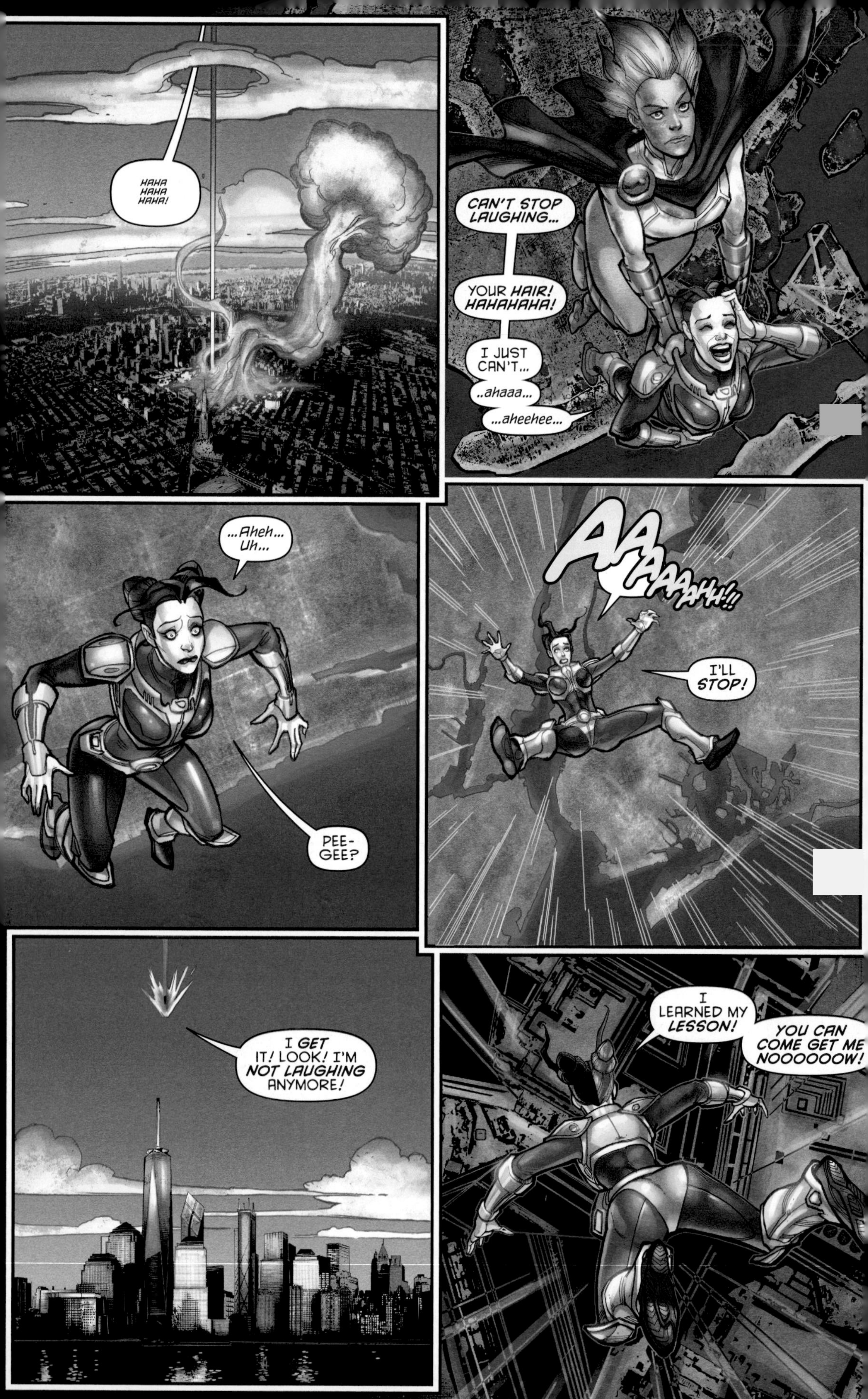
HAHA HAHA HAHA!
CAN'T STOP LAUGHING...
YOUR HAIR! HAHAHAHA!
I JUST CAN'T...
..ahaaa...
...aheehee...
...Aheh... Uh...
PEE-GEE?
AAAAAAHH!!
I'LL STOP!
I GET IT! LOOK! I'M NOT LAUGHING ANYMORE!
I LEARNED MY LESSON!
YOU CAN COME GET ME NOOOOOOW!

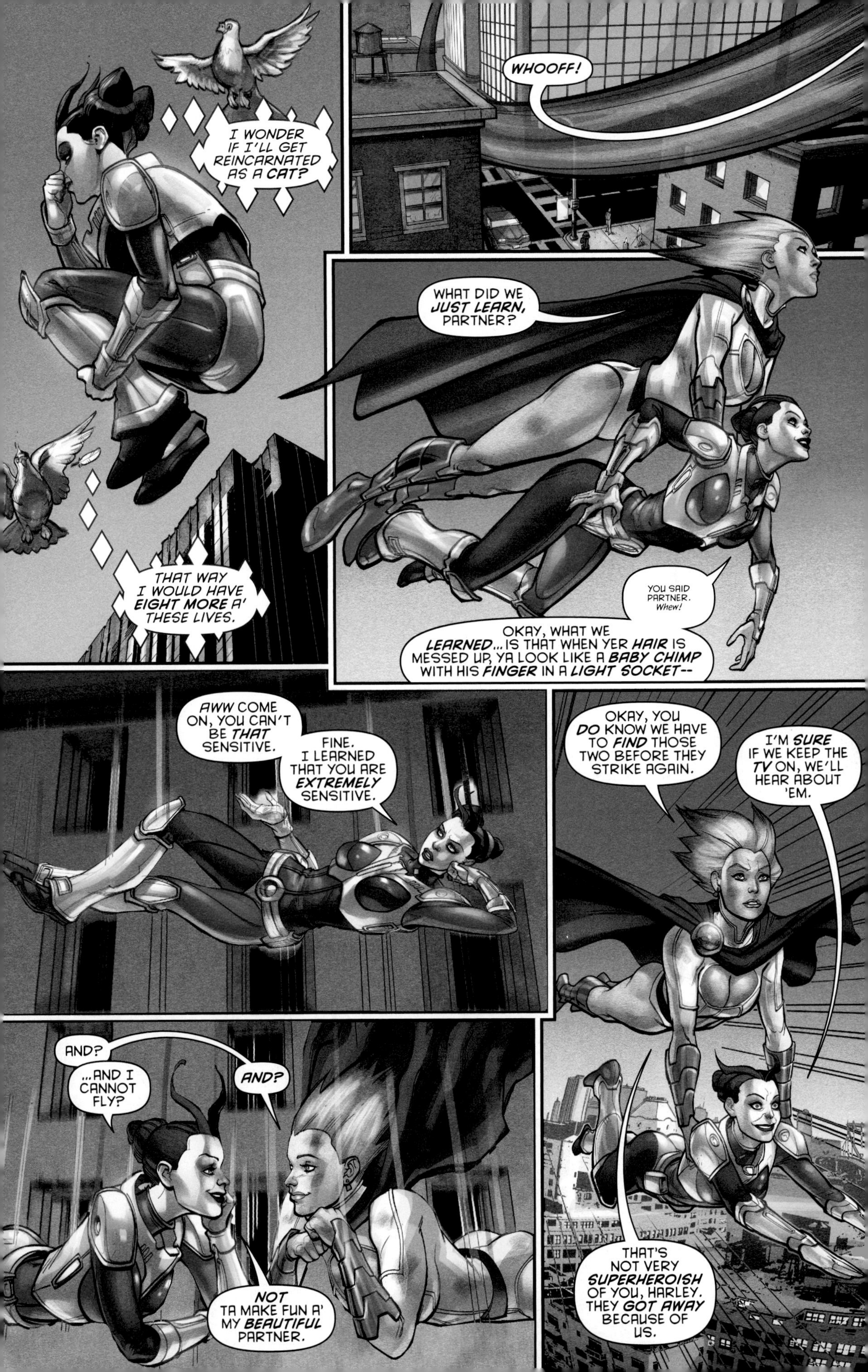
I WONDER IF I'LL GET REINCARNATED AS A CAT?
THAT WAY I WOULD HAVE EIGHT MORE A' THESE LIVES.
WHOOFF!
WHAT DID WE JUST LEARN, PARTNER?
YOU SAID PARTNER. Whew!
OKAY, WHAT WE LEARNED... IS THAT WHEN YER HAIR IS MESSED UP, YA LOOK LIKE A BABY CHIMP WITH HIS FINGER IN A LIGHT SOCKET--
AWW COME ON, YOU CAN'T BE THAT SENSITIVE.
FINE. I LEARNED THAT YOU ARE EXTREMELY SENSITIVE.
OKAY, YOU DO KNOW WE HAVE TO FIND THOSE TWO BEFORE THEY STRIKE AGAIN.
I'M SURE IF WE KEEP THE TV ON, WE'LL HEAR ABOUT 'EM.
AND?
...AND I CANNOT FLY?
AND?
NOT TA MAKE FUN A' MY BEAUTIFUL PARTNER.
THAT'S NOT VERY SUPERHEROISH OF YOU, HARLEY. THEY GOT AWAY BECAUSE OF US.

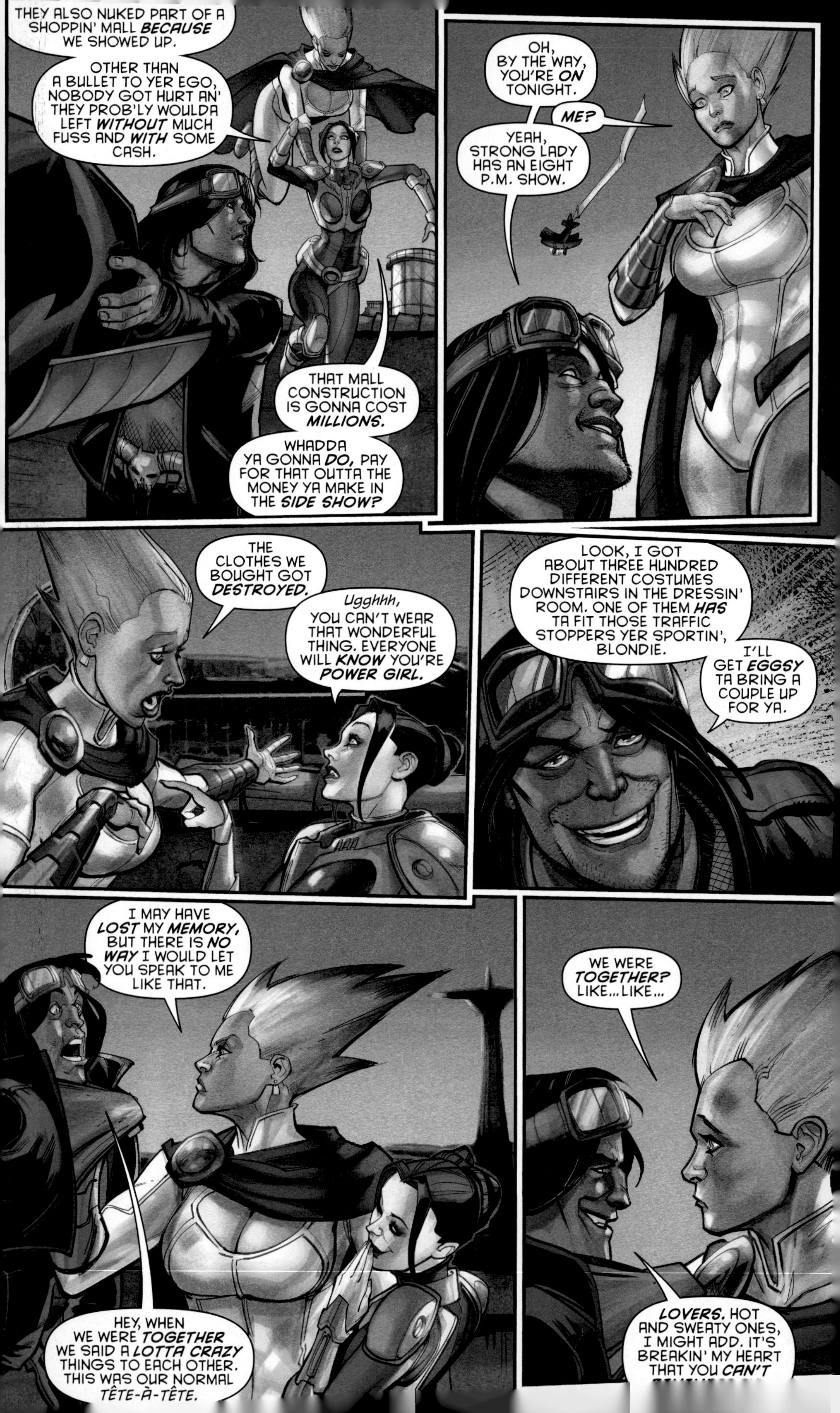
THEY ALSO NUKED PART OF A SHOPPIN' MALL *BECAUSE* WE SHOWED UP.
OTHER THAN A BULLET TO YER EGO, NOBODY GOT HURT AN' THEY PROB'LY WOULDA LEFT *WITHOUT* MUCH FUSS AND *WITH* SOME CASH.
THAT MALL CONSTRUCTION IS GONNA COST *MILLIONS.*
WHADDA YA GONNA *DO,* PAY FOR THAT OUTTA THE MONEY YA MAKE IN THE *SIDE SHOW?*
OH, BY THE WAY, YOU'RE *ON* TONIGHT.
ME?
YEAH, STRONG LADY HAS AN EIGHT P.M. SHOW.
THE CLOTHES WE BOUGHT GOT *DESTROYED.*
Ugghhh, YOU CAN'T WEAR THAT WONDERFUL THING. EVERYONE WILL *KNOW* YOU'RE *POWER GIRL.*
LOOK, I GOT ABOUT THREE HUNDRED DIFFERENT COSTUMES DOWNSTAIRS IN THE DRESSIN' ROOM. ONE OF THEM *HAS* TA FIT THOSE TRAFFIC STOPPERS YER SPORTIN', BLONDIE.
I'LL GET *EGGSY* TA BRING A COUPLE UP FOR YA.
I MAY HAVE *LOST* MY *MEMORY,* BUT THERE IS *NO WAY* I WOULD LET YOU SPEAK TO ME LIKE THAT.
HEY, WHEN WE WERE *TOGETHER* WE SAID A *LOTTA CRAZY* THINGS TO EACH OTHER. THIS WAS OUR NORMAL *TÊTE-À-TÊTE.*
WE WERE *TOGETHER?* LIKE... LIKE...
LOVERS. HOT AND SWEATY ONES, I MIGHT ADD. IT'S BREAKIN' MY HEART THAT YOU *CAN'T*

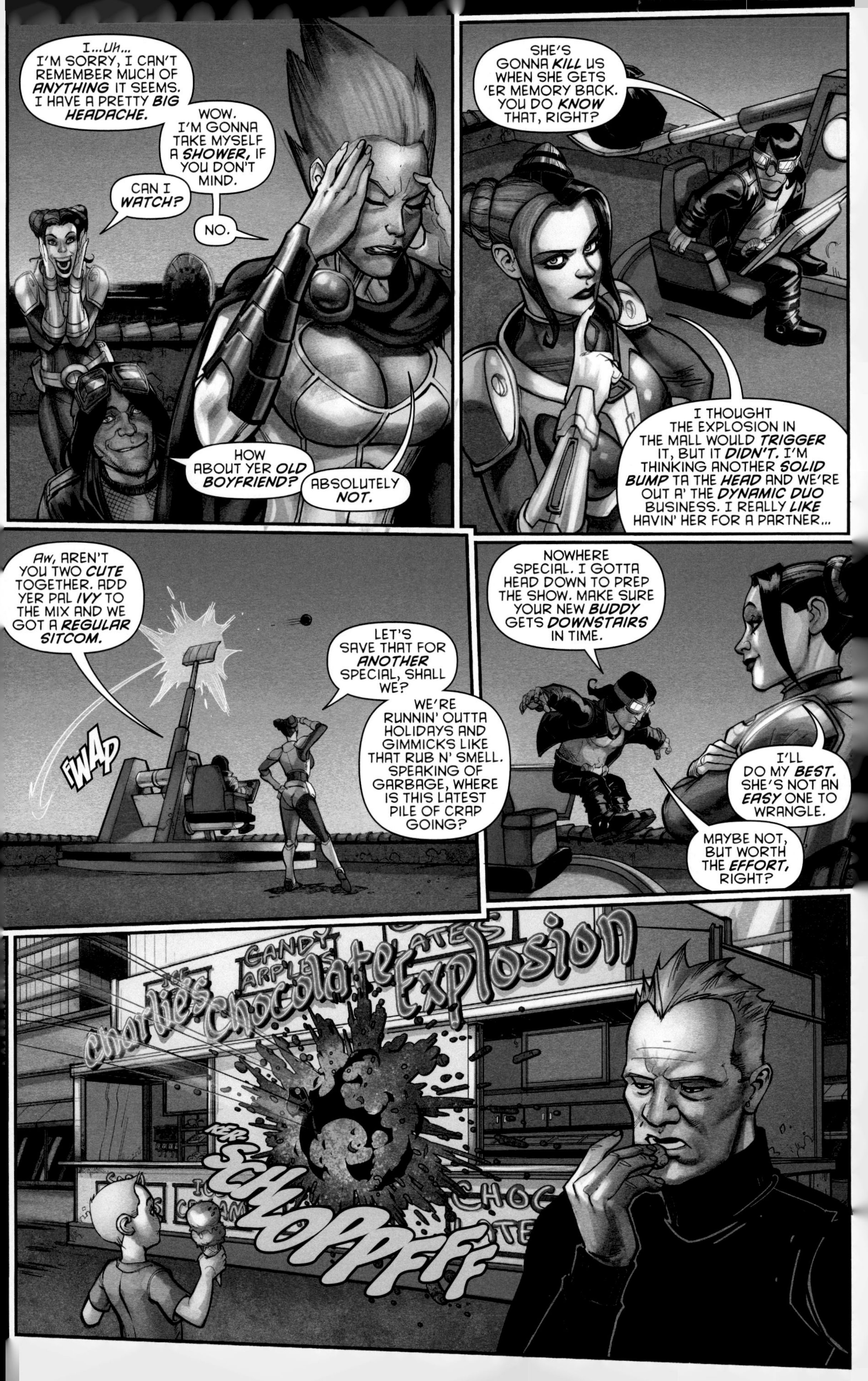
I...Uh...
I'M SORRY, I CAN'T REMEMBER MUCH OF ANYTHING IT SEEMS. I HAVE A PRETTY BIG HEADACHE.
WOW. I'M GONNA TAKE MYSELF A SHOWER, IF YOU DON'T MIND.
CAN I WATCH?
NO.
HOW ABOUT YER OLD BOYFRIEND?
ABSOLUTELY NOT.
SHE'S GONNA KILL US WHEN SHE GETS 'ER MEMORY BACK. YOU DO KNOW THAT, RIGHT?
I THOUGHT THE EXPLOSION IN THE MALL WOULD TRIGGER IT, BUT IT DIDN'T. I'M THINKING ANOTHER SOLID BUMP TA THE HEAD AND WE'RE OUT A' THE DYNAMIC DUO BUSINESS. I REALLY LIKE HAVIN' HER FOR A PARTNER...
Aw, AREN'T YOU TWO CUTE TOGETHER. ADD YER PAL IVY TO THE MIX AND WE GOT A REGULAR SITCOM.
fWAP
LET'S SAVE THAT FOR ANOTHER SPECIAL, SHALL WE?
WE'RE RUNNIN' OUTTA HOLIDAYS AND GIMMICKS LIKE THAT RUB N' SMELL. SPEAKING OF GARBAGE, WHERE IS THIS LATEST PILE OF CRAP GOING?
NOWHERE SPECIAL. I GOTTA HEAD DOWN TO PREP THE SHOW. MAKE SURE YOUR NEW BUDDY GETS DOWNSTAIRS IN TIME.
I'LL DO MY BEST. SHE'S NOT AN EASY ONE TO WRANGLE.
MAYBE NOT, BUT WORTH THE EFFORT, RIGHT?
CANDY
APPLES
Charlie's Chocolate Explosion
KER SCHWOPPFFF
ICE CREAM
CHOC LATE

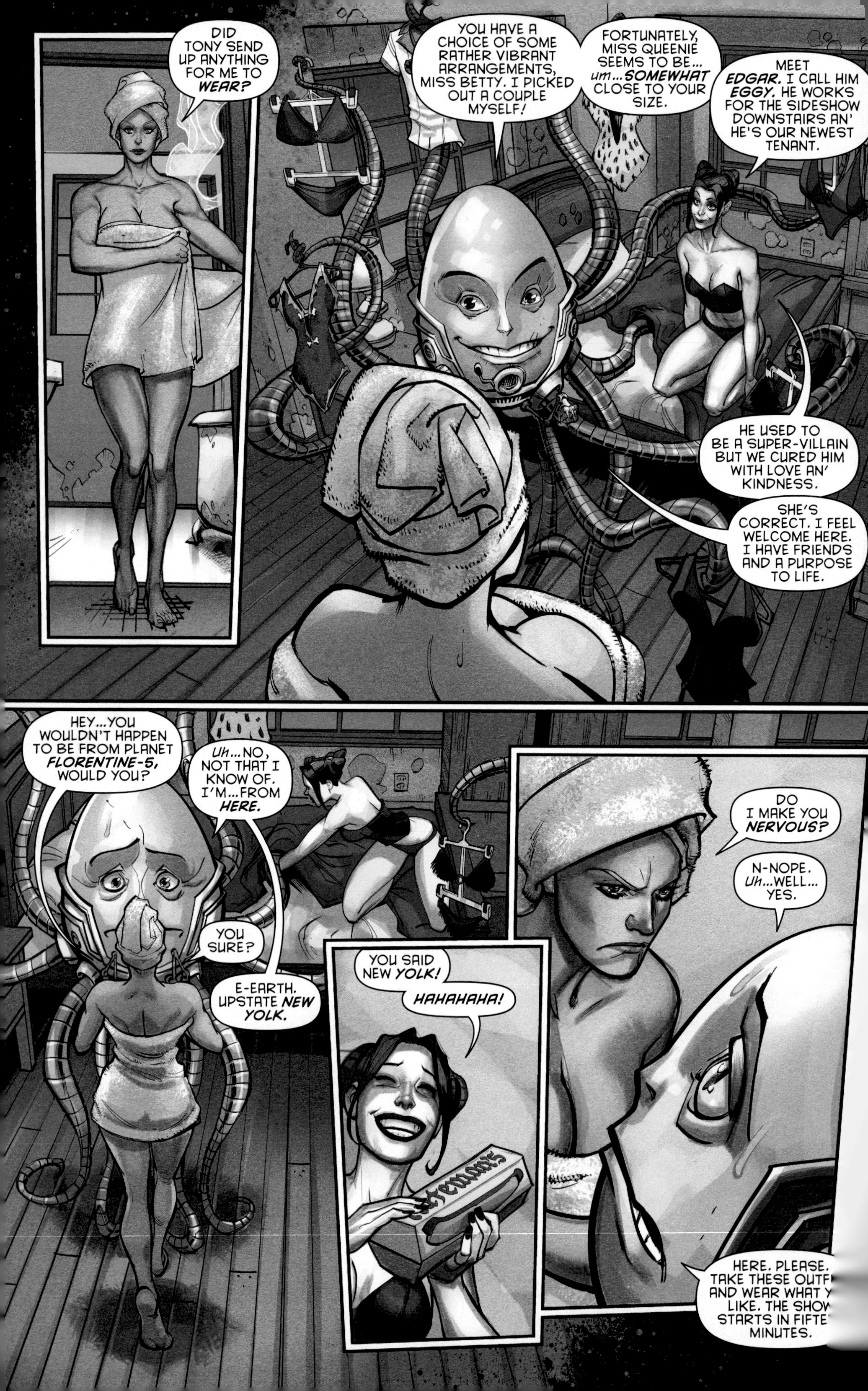
DID TONY SEND UP ANYTHING FOR ME TO *WEAR?*
YOU HAVE A CHOICE OF SOME RATHER VIBRANT ARRANGEMENTS, MISS BETTY. I PICKED OUT A COUPLE MYSELF!
FORTUNATELY, MISS QUEENIE SEEMS TO BE... *UM*...*SOMEWHAT* CLOSE TO YOUR SIZE.
MEET *EDGAR.* I CALL HIM *EGGY.* HE WORKS FOR THE SIDESHOW DOWNSTAIRS AN' HE'S OUR NEWEST TENANT.
HE USED TO BE A SUPER-VILLAIN BUT WE CURED HIM WITH LOVE AN' KINDNESS.
SHE'S CORRECT. I FEEL WELCOME HERE. I HAVE FRIENDS AND A PURPOSE TO LIFE.
HEY...YOU WOULDN'T HAPPEN TO BE FROM PLANET *FLORENTINE-5,* WOULD YOU?
UH...NO, NOT THAT I KNOW OF. I'M...FROM *HERE.*
YOU SURE?
E-EARTH. UPSTATE *NEW YOLK.*
YOU SAID NEW *YOLK!*
HAHAHAHA!
DO I MAKE YOU *NERVOUS?*
N-NOPE. *UH*...WELL... YES.
HERE. PLEASE. TAKE THESE OUTF AND WEAR WHAT Y LIKE. THE SHOW STARTS IN FIFTE MINUTES.

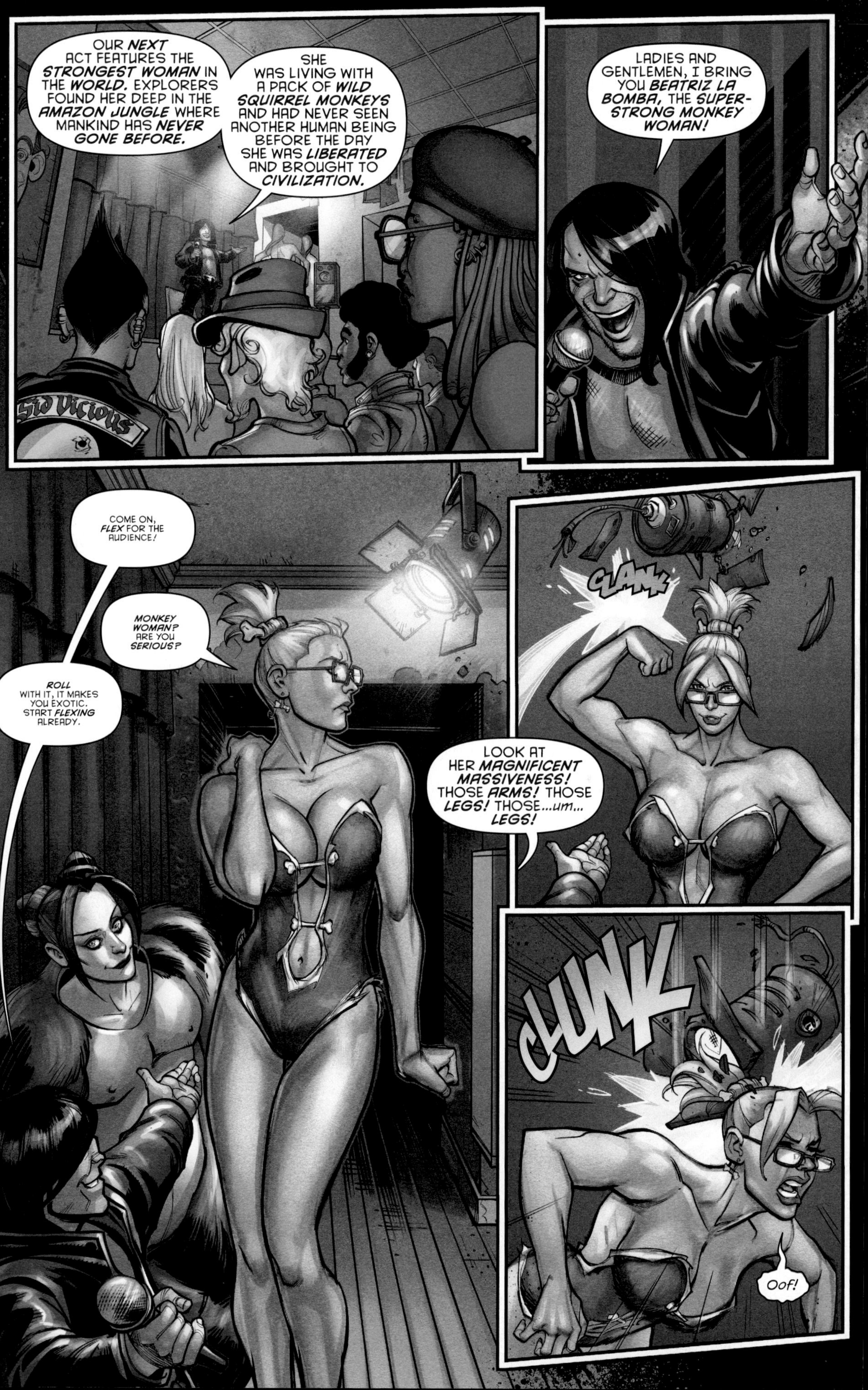
OUR NEXT ACT FEATURES THE STRONGEST WOMAN IN THE WORLD. EXPLORERS FOUND HER DEEP IN THE AMAZON JUNGLE WHERE MANKIND HAS NEVER GONE BEFORE.
SHE WAS LIVING WITH A PACK OF WILD SQUIRREL MONKEYS AND HAD NEVER SEEN ANOTHER HUMAN BEING BEFORE THE DAY SHE WAS LIBERATED AND BROUGHT TO CIVILIZATION.
Sid Vicious
LADIES AND GENTLEMEN, I BRING YOU BEATRIZ LA BOMBA, THE SUPER-STRONG MONKEY WOMAN!
COME ON, FLEX FOR THE AUDIENCE!
MONKEY WOMAN? ARE YOU SERIOUS?
ROLL WITH IT, IT MAKES YOU EXOTIC. START FLEXING ALREADY.
CLANK
LOOK AT HER MAGNIFICENT MASSIVENESS! THOSE ARMS! THOSE LEGS! THOSE...um... LEGS!
CLUNK
Oof!

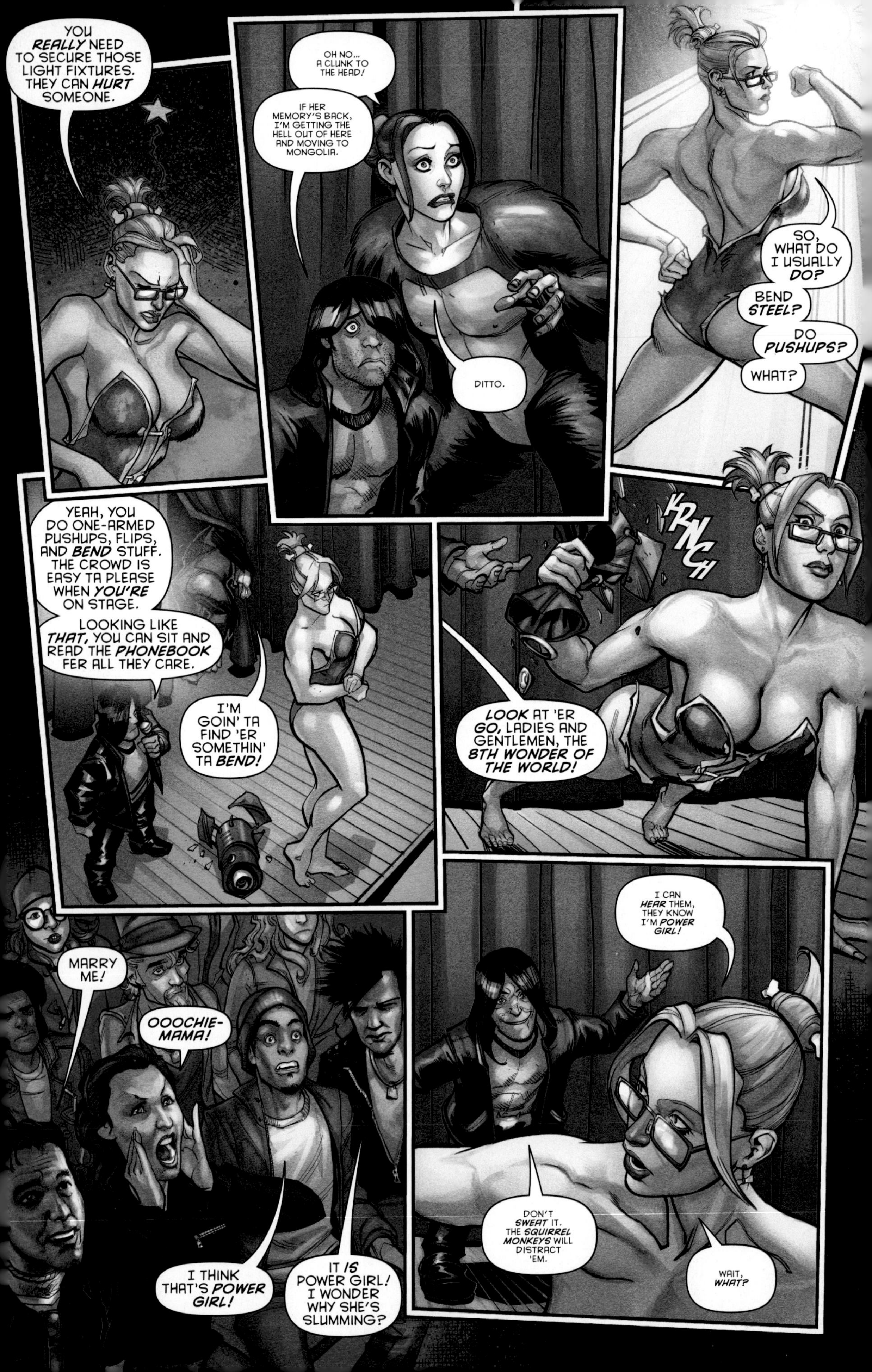
YOU REALLY NEED TO SECURE THOSE LIGHT FIXTURES. THEY CAN HURT SOMEONE.
OH NO... A CLUNK TO THE HEAD!
IF HER MEMORY'S BACK, I'M GETTING THE HELL OUT OF HERE AND MOVING TO MONGOLIA.
DITTO.
SO, WHAT DO I USUALLY DO?
BEND STEEL?
DO PUSHUPS?
WHAT?
YEAH, YOU DO ONE-ARMED PUSHUPS, FLIPS, AND BEND STUFF. THE CROWD IS EASY TA PLEASE WHEN YOU'RE ON STAGE.
LOOKING LIKE THAT, YOU CAN SIT AND READ THE PHONEBOOK FER ALL THEY CARE.
I'M GOIN' TA FIND 'ER SOMETHIN' TA BEND!
KRNCH
LOOK AT 'ER GO, LADIES AND GENTLEMEN, THE 8TH WONDER OF THE WORLD!
MARRY ME!
OOOCHIE-MAMA!
I THINK THAT'S POWER GIRL!
IT IS POWER GIRL! I WONDER WHY SHE'S SLUMMING?
I CAN HEAR THEM, THEY KNOW I'M POWER GIRL!
DON'T SWEAT IT. THE SQUIRREL MONKEYS WILL DISTRACT 'EM.
WAIT, WHAT?

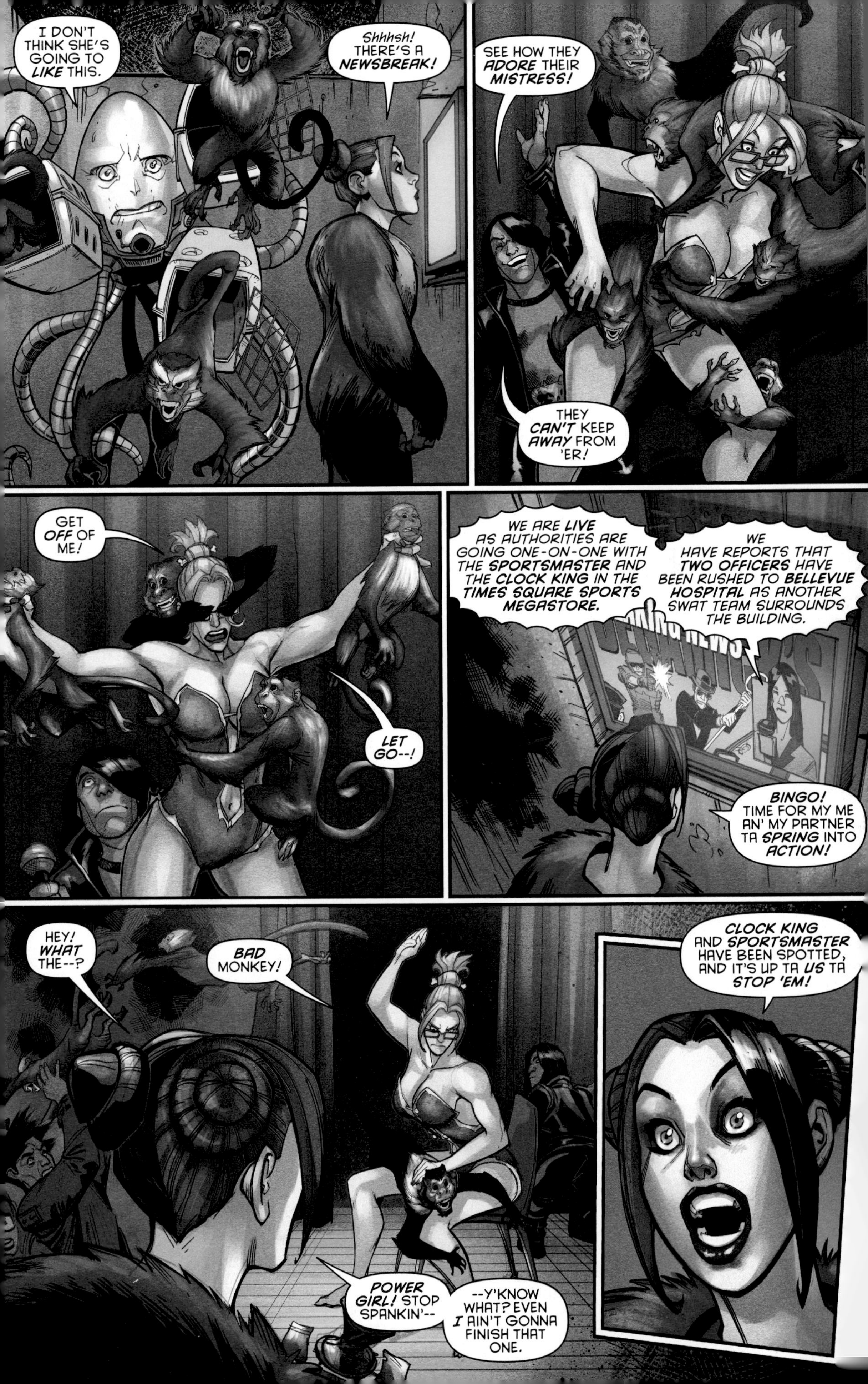

I DON'T THINK SHE'S GOING TO LIKE THIS.
Shhhsh! THERE'S A NEWSBREAK!
SEE HOW THEY ADORE THEIR MISTRESS!
THEY CAN'T KEEP AWAY FROM 'ER!
GET OFF OF ME!
LET GO--!
WE ARE LIVE AS AUTHORITIES ARE GOING ONE-ON-ONE WITH THE SPORTSMASTER AND THE CLOCK KING IN THE TIMES SQUARE SPORTS MEGASTORE.
WE HAVE REPORTS THAT TWO OFFICERS HAVE BEEN RUSHED TO BELLEVUE HOSPITAL AS ANOTHER SWAT TEAM SURROUNDS THE BUILDING.
BINGO! TIME FOR MY ME AN' MY PARTNER TA SPRING INTO ACTION!
HEY! WHAT THE--?
BAD MONKEY!
POWER GIRL! STOP SPANKIN'--
--Y'KNOW WHAT? EVEN I AIN'T GONNA FINISH THAT ONE.
CLOCK KING AND SPORTSMASTER HAVE BEEN SPOTTED, AND IT'S UP TA US TA STOP 'EM!

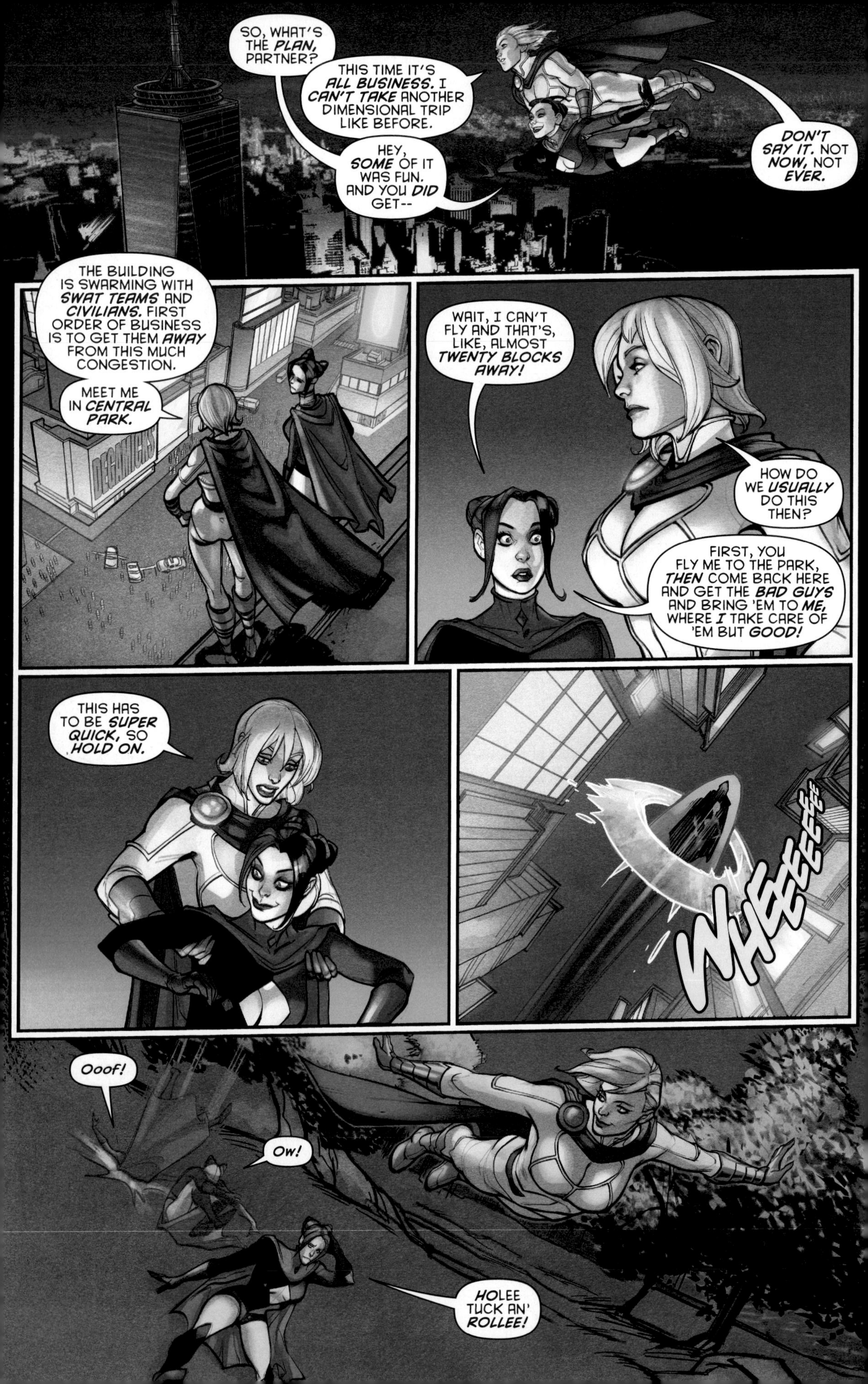
SO, WHAT'S THE PLAN, PARTNER?
THIS TIME IT'S ALL BUSINESS. I CAN'T TAKE ANOTHER DIMENSIONAL TRIP LIKE BEFORE.
HEY, SOME OF IT WAS FUN. AND YOU DID GET--
DON'T SAY IT. NOT NOW, NOT EVER.
THE BUILDING IS SWARMING WITH SWAT TEAMS AND CIVILIANS. FIRST ORDER OF BUSINESS IS TO GET THEM AWAY FROM THIS MUCH CONGESTION.
MEET ME IN CENTRAL PARK.
WAIT, I CAN'T FLY AND THAT'S, LIKE, ALMOST TWENTY BLOCKS AWAY!
HOW DO WE USUALLY DO THIS THEN?
FIRST, YOU FLY ME TO THE PARK, THEN COME BACK HERE AND GET THE BAD GUYS AND BRING 'EM TO ME, WHERE I TAKE CARE OF 'EM BUT GOOD!
THIS HAS TO BE SUPER QUICK, SO HOLD ON.
WHEEEEEEE
Ooof!
Ow!
HOLEE TUCK AN' ROLLEE!

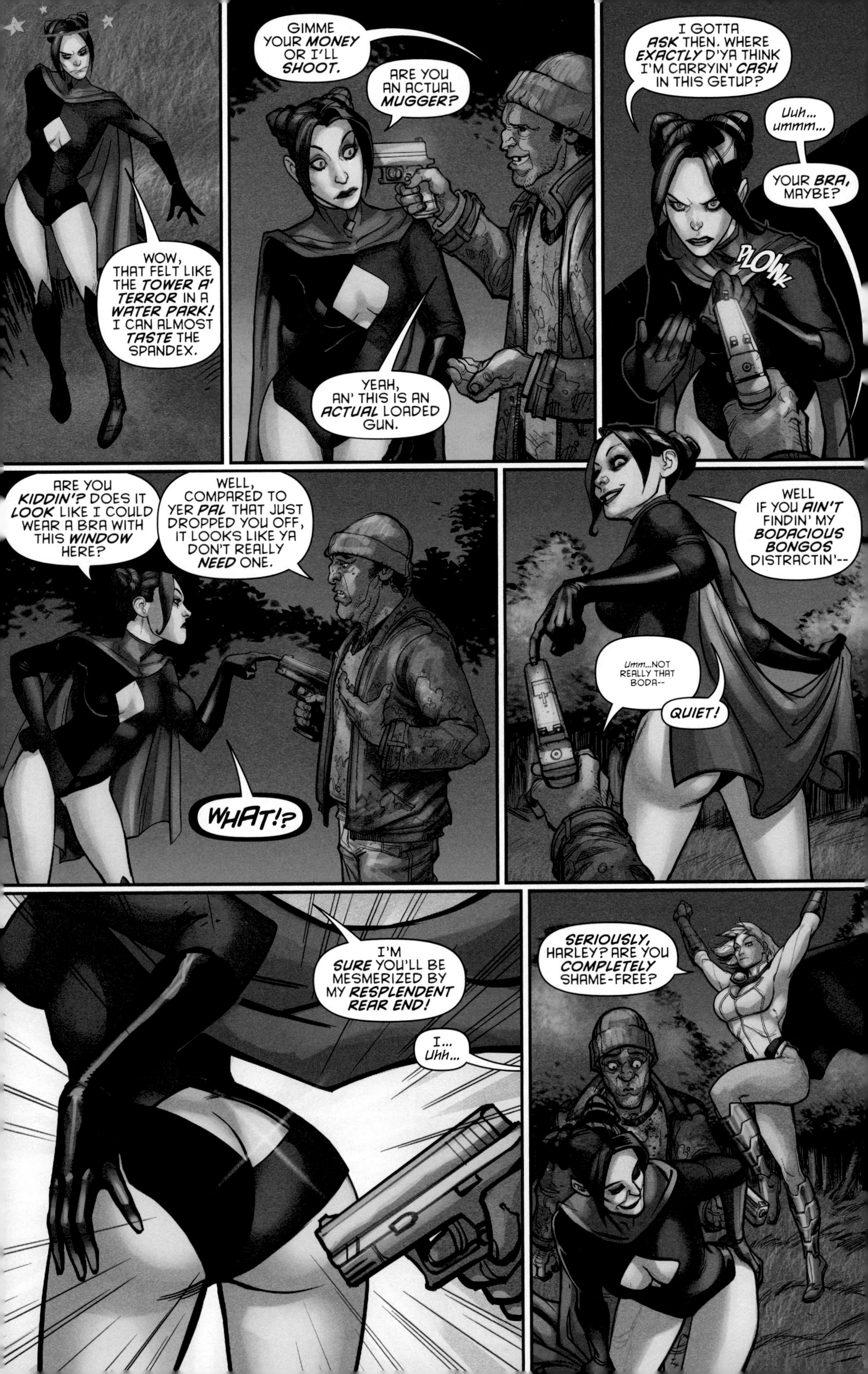
WOW, THAT FELT LIKE THE TOWER A' TERROR IN A WATER PARK! I CAN ALMOST TASTE THE SPANDEX.
GIMME YOUR MONEY OR I'LL SHOOT.
ARE YOU AN ACTUAL MUGGER?
YEAH, AN' THIS IS AN ACTUAL LOADED GUN.
I GOTTA ASK THEN. WHERE EXACTLY D'YA THINK I'M CARRYIN' CASH IN THIS GETUP?
Uuh... ummm...
YOUR BRA, MAYBE?
PLOWK
ARE YOU KIDDIN'? DOES IT LOOK LIKE I COULD WEAR A BRA WITH THIS WINDOW HERE?
WELL, COMPARED TO YER PAL THAT JUST DROPPED YOU OFF, IT LOOKS LIKE YA DON'T REALLY NEED ONE.
WHAT!?
WELL IF YOU AIN'T FINDIN' MY BODACIOUS BONGOS DISTRACTIN'--
Umm...NOT REALLY THAT BODA--
QUIET!
I'M SURE YOU'LL BE MESMERIZED BY MY RESPLENDENT REAR END!
I... Uhh...
SERIOUSLY, HARLEY? ARE YOU COMPLETELY SHAME-FREE?

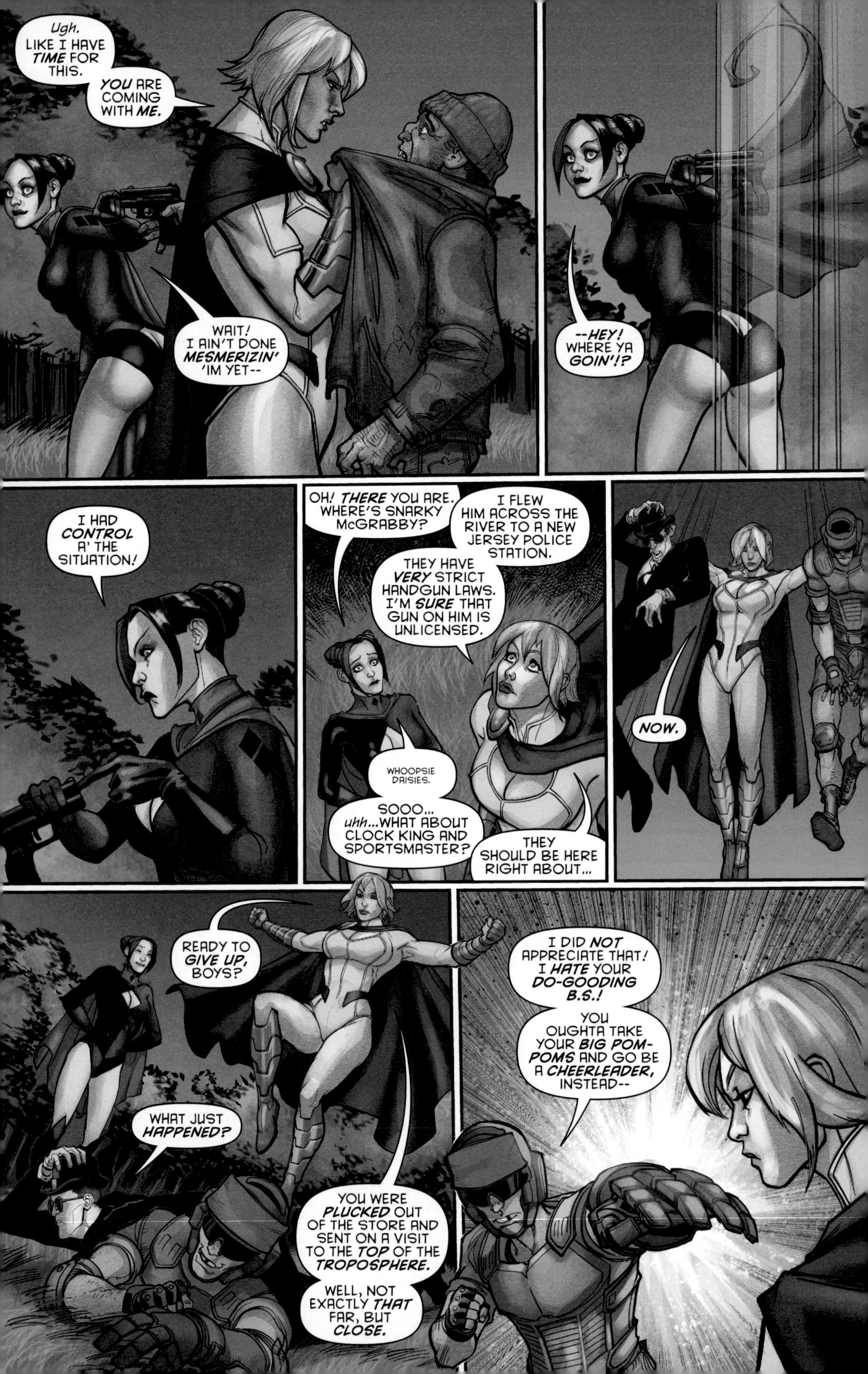

Ugh. LIKE I HAVE TIME FOR THIS.
YOU ARE COMING WITH ME.
WAIT! I AIN'T DONE MESMERIZIN' 'IM YET--
--HEY! WHERE YA GOIN'!?
I HAD CONTROL A' THE SITUATION!
OH! THERE YOU ARE. WHERE'S SNARKY McGRABBY?
I FLEW HIM ACROSS THE RIVER TO A NEW JERSEY POLICE STATION.
THEY HAVE VERY STRICT HANDGUN LAWS. I'M SURE THAT GUN ON HIM IS UNLICENSED.
WHOOPSIE DAISIES.
SOOO... uhh...WHAT ABOUT CLOCK KING AND SPORTSMASTER?
THEY SHOULD BE HERE RIGHT ABOUT...
NOW.
READY TO GIVE UP, BOYS?
WHAT JUST HAPPENED?
YOU WERE PLUCKED OUT OF THE STORE AND SENT ON A VISIT TO THE TOP OF THE TROPOSPHERE.
WELL, NOT EXACTLY THAT FAR, BUT CLOSE.
I DID NOT APPRECIATE THAT! I HATE YOUR DO-GOODING B.S.!
YOU OUGHTA TAKE YOUR BIG POM-POMS AND GO BE A CHEERLEADER, INSTEAD--

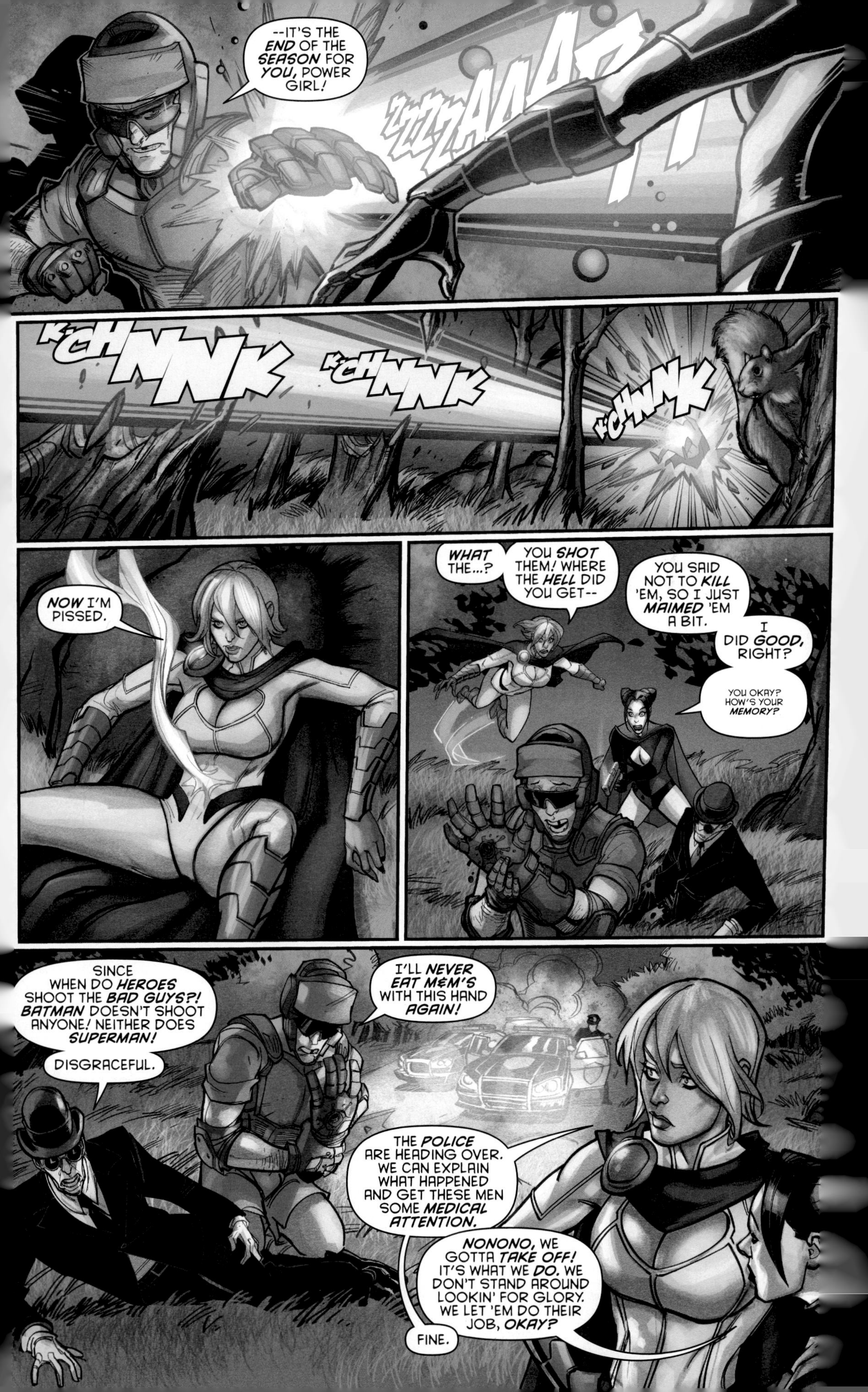
--IT'S THE END OF THE SEASON FOR YOU, POWER GIRL!
ZZZZAAAAP
K'CHNNNK
K'CHNNNK
K'CHNNK
NOW I'M PISSED.
WHAT THE...?
YOU SHOT THEM! WHERE THE HELL DID YOU GET--
YOU SAID NOT TO KILL 'EM, SO I JUST MAIMED 'EM A BIT.
I DID GOOD, RIGHT?
YOU OKAY? HOW'S YOUR MEMORY?
SINCE WHEN DO HEROES SHOOT THE BAD GUYS?! BATMAN DOESN'T SHOOT ANYONE! NEITHER DOES SUPERMAN!
DISGRACEFUL.
I'LL NEVER EAT M&M'S WITH THIS HAND AGAIN!
THE POLICE ARE HEADING OVER. WE CAN EXPLAIN WHAT HAPPENED AND GET THESE MEN SOME MEDICAL ATTENTION.
NONONO, WE GOTTA TAKE OFF! IT'S WHAT WE DO. WE DON'T STAND AROUND LOOKIN' FOR GLORY. WE LET 'EM DO THEIR JOB, OKAY?
FINE.

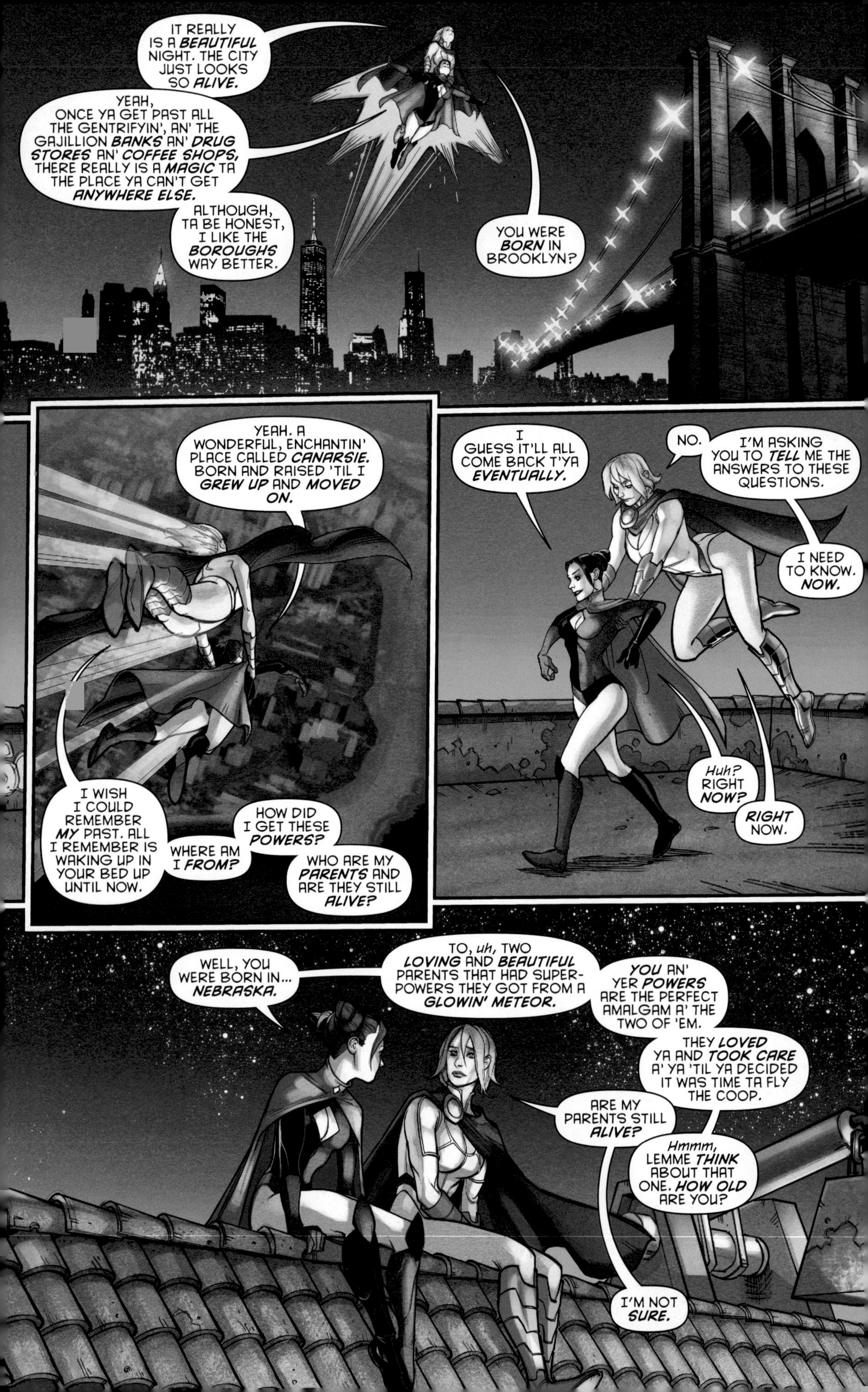

IT REALLY IS A BEAUTIFUL NIGHT. THE CITY JUST LOOKS SO ALIVE.
YEAH, ONCE YA GET PAST ALL THE GENTRIFYIN', AN' THE GAJILLION BANKS AN' DRUG STORES AN' COFFEE SHOPS, THERE REALLY IS A MAGIC TA THE PLACE YA CAN'T GET ANYWHERE ELSE.
ALTHOUGH, TA BE HONEST, I LIKE THE BOROUGHS WAY BETTER.
YOU WERE BORN IN BROOKLYN?
YEAH. A WONDERFUL, ENCHANTIN' PLACE CALLED CANARSIE. BORN AND RAISED 'TIL I GREW UP AND MOVED ON.
I WISH I COULD REMEMBER MY PAST. ALL I REMEMBER IS WAKING UP IN YOUR BED UP UNTIL NOW.
WHERE AM I FROM?
HOW DID I GET THESE POWERS?
WHO ARE MY PARENTS AND ARE THEY STILL ALIVE?
I GUESS IT'LL ALL COME BACK T'YA EVENTUALLY.
NO.
I'M ASKING YOU TO TELL ME THE ANSWERS TO THESE QUESTIONS.
I NEED TO KNOW. NOW.
Huh? RIGHT NOW?
RIGHT NOW.
WELL, YOU WERE BORN IN... NEBRASKA.
TO, uh, TWO LOVING AND BEAUTIFUL PARENTS THAT HAD SUPER-POWERS THEY GOT FROM A GLOWIN' METEOR.
YOU AN' YER POWERS ARE THE PERFECT AMALGAM A' THE TWO OF 'EM.
THEY LOVED YA AND TOOK CARE A' YA 'TIL YA DECIDED IT WAS TIME TA FLY THE COOP.
ARE MY PARENTS STILL ALIVE?
Hmmm, LEMME THINK ABOUT THAT ONE. HOW OLD ARE YOU?
I'M NOT SURE.

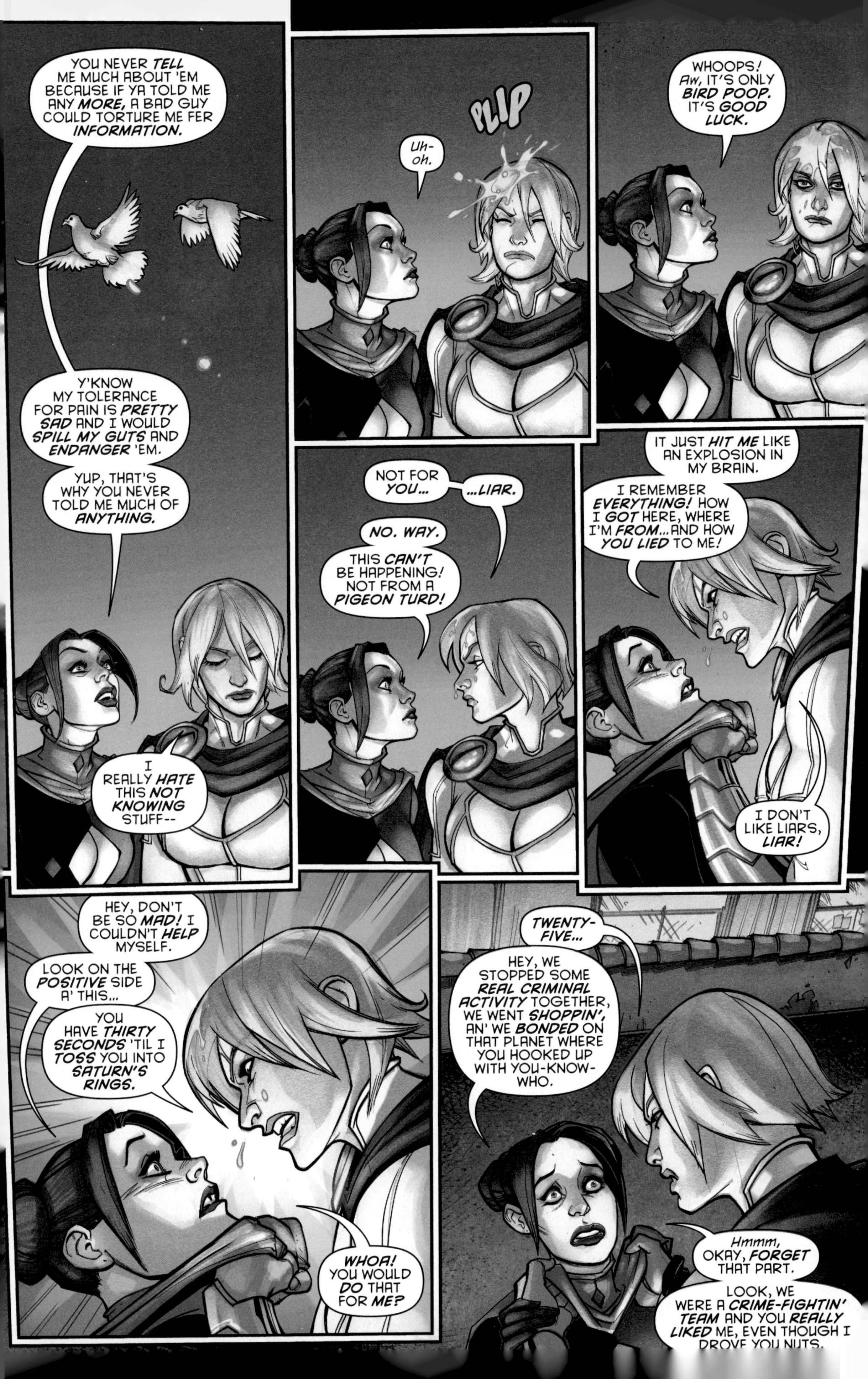
YOU NEVER TELL ME MUCH ABOUT 'EM BECAUSE IF YA TOLD ME ANY MORE, A BAD GUY COULD TORTURE ME FER INFORMATION.
Y'KNOW MY TOLERANCE FOR PAIN IS PRETTY SAD AND I WOULD SPILL MY GUTS AND ENDANGER 'EM.
YUP, THAT'S WHY YOU NEVER TOLD ME MUCH OF ANYTHING.
I REALLY HATE THIS NOT KNOWING STUFF--
PLIP
Uh-oh.
WHOOPS! Aw, IT'S ONLY BIRD POOP. IT'S GOOD LUCK.
NOT FOR YOU...
...LIAR.
NO. WAY.
THIS CAN'T BE HAPPENING! NOT FROM A PIGEON TURD!
IT JUST HIT ME LIKE AN EXPLOSION IN MY BRAIN.
I REMEMBER EVERYTHING! HOW I GOT HERE, WHERE I'M FROM...AND HOW YOU LIED TO ME!
I DON'T LIKE LIARS, LIAR!
HEY, DON'T BE SO MAD! I COULDN'T HELP MYSELF.
LOOK ON THE POSITIVE SIDE A' THIS...
YOU HAVE THIRTY SECONDS 'TIL I TOSS YOU INTO SATURN'S RINGS.
WHOA! YOU WOULD DO THAT FOR ME?
TWENTY-FIVE...
HEY, WE STOPPED SOME REAL CRIMINAL ACTIVITY TOGETHER, WE WENT SHOPPIN', AN' WE BONDED ON THAT PLANET WHERE YOU HOOKED UP WITH YOU-KNOW-WHO.
Hmmm, OKAY, FORGET THAT PART.
LOOK, WE WERE A CRIME-FIGHTIN' TEAM AND YOU REALLY LIKED ME, EVEN THOUGH I DROVE YOU NUTS.

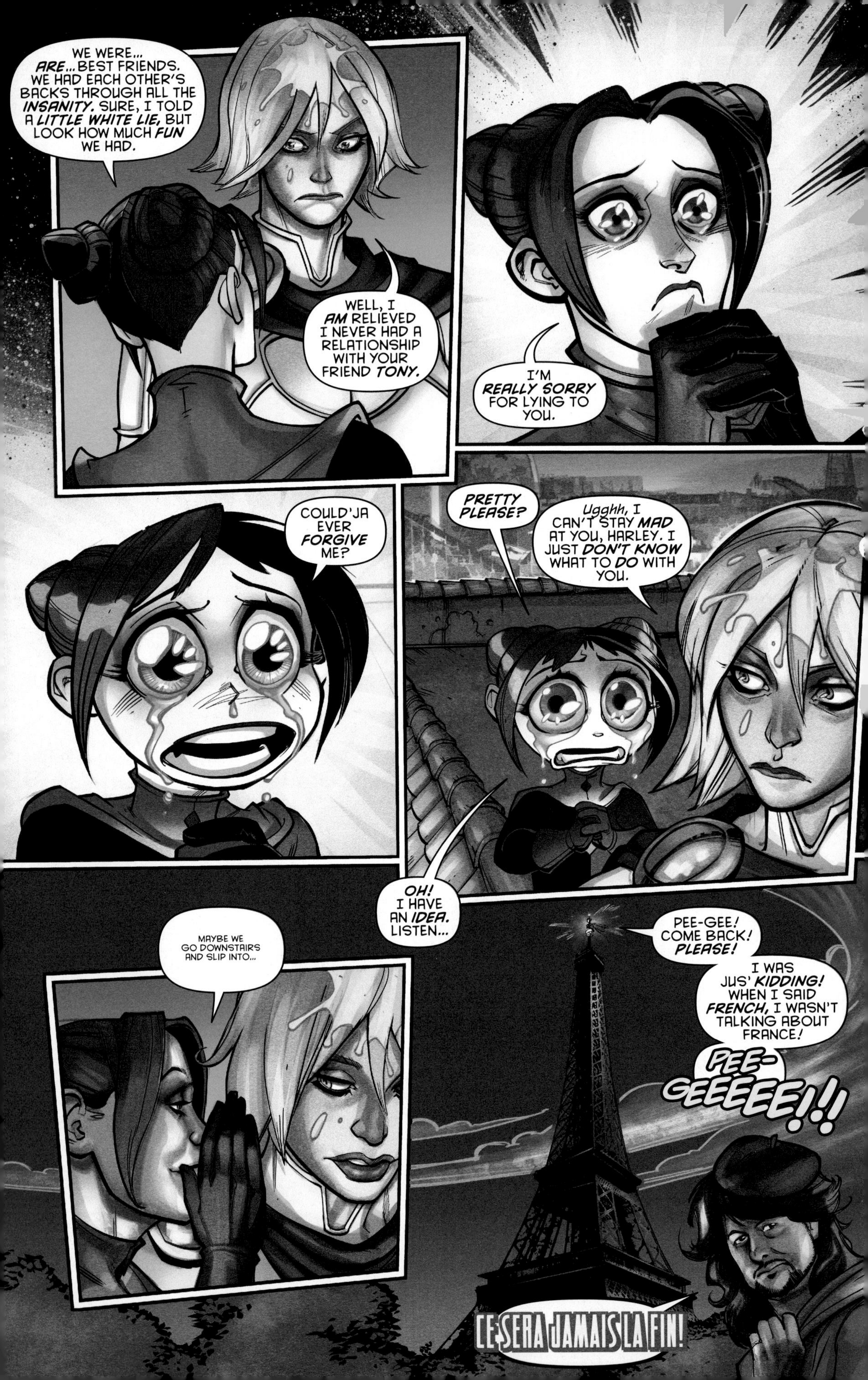
WE WERE... ARE... BEST FRIENDS. WE HAD EACH OTHER'S BACKS THROUGH ALL THE INSANITY. SURE, I TOLD A LITTLE WHITE LIE, BUT LOOK HOW MUCH FUN WE HAD.
WELL, I AM RELIEVED I NEVER HAD A RELATIONSHIP WITH YOUR FRIEND TONY.
I'M REALLY SORRY FOR LYING TO YOU.
COULD'JA EVER FORGIVE ME?
PRETTY PLEASE?
Ugghh, I CAN'T STAY MAD AT YOU, HARLEY. I JUST DON'T KNOW WHAT TO DO WITH YOU.
OH! I HAVE AN IDEA. LISTEN...
MAYBE WE GO DOWNSTAIRS AND SLIP INTO...
PEE-GEE! COME BACK! PLEASE!
I WAS JUS' KIDDING! WHEN I SAID FRENCH, I WASN'T TALKING ABOUT FRANCE!
PEE-GEEEEEE!!!
CE SERA JAMAIS LA FIN!

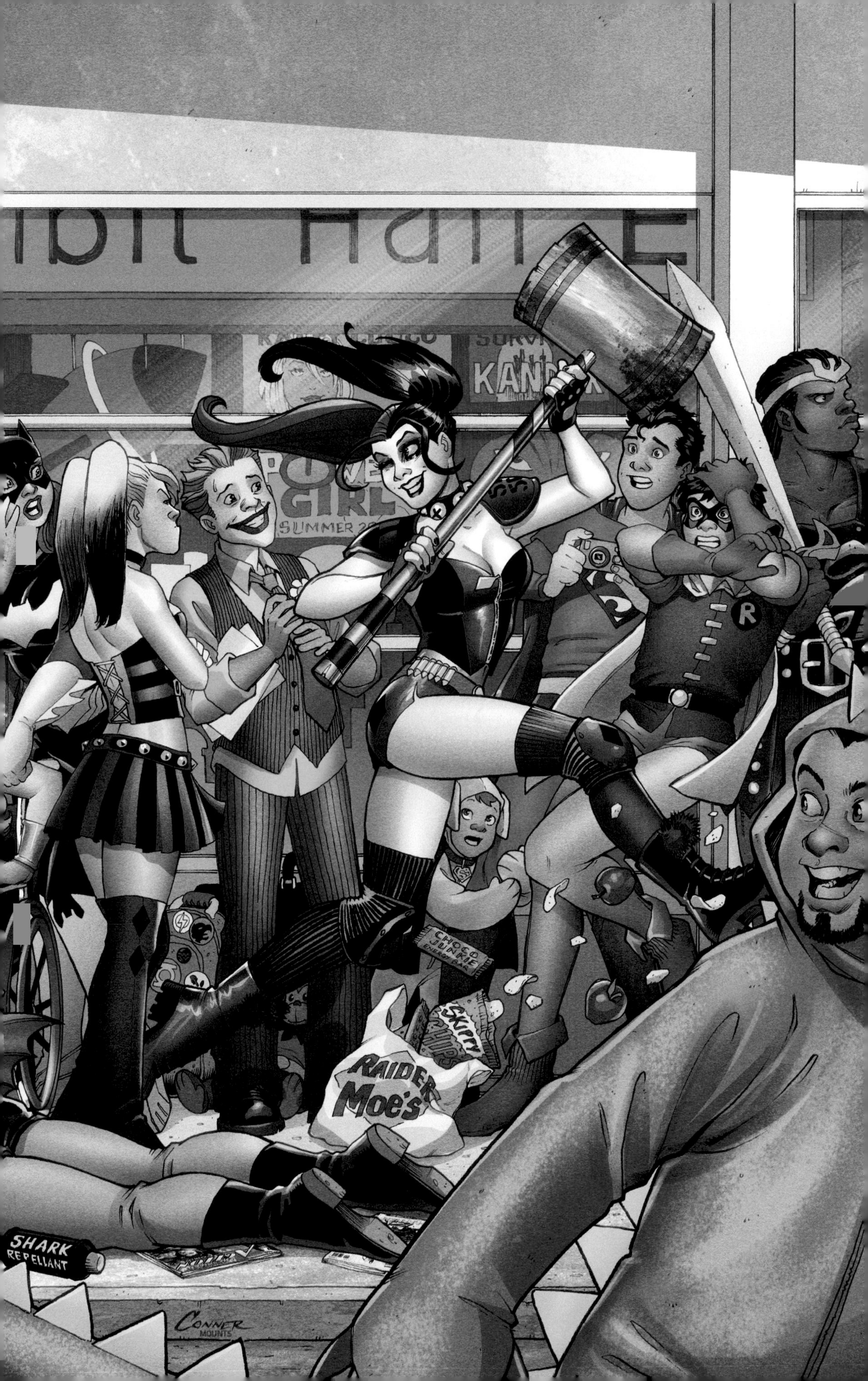

POWER GIRL
SUMMER
KANDOR
CHOCO JUNKIE ENERGY BAR
SKIPPY CHIPS
RAIDER Moe's
SHARK REPELLANT
CONNER
MOUNTS

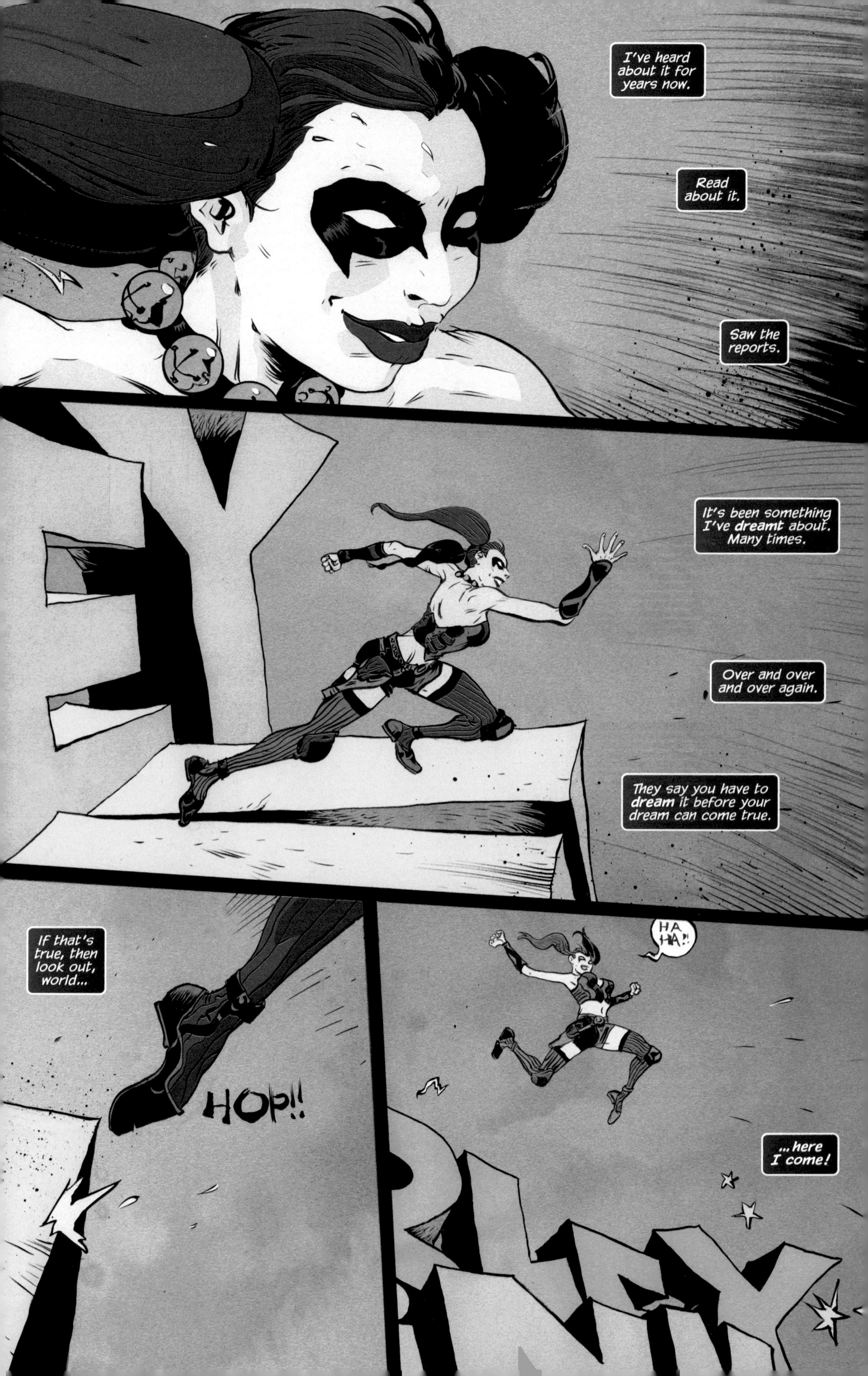
I've heard about it for years now.
Read about it.
Saw the reports.
It's been something I've **dreamt** about. Many times.
Over and over and over again.
They say you have to **dream** it before your dream can come true.
If that's true, then look out, world...
HOP!!
HA HA!!
...here I come!

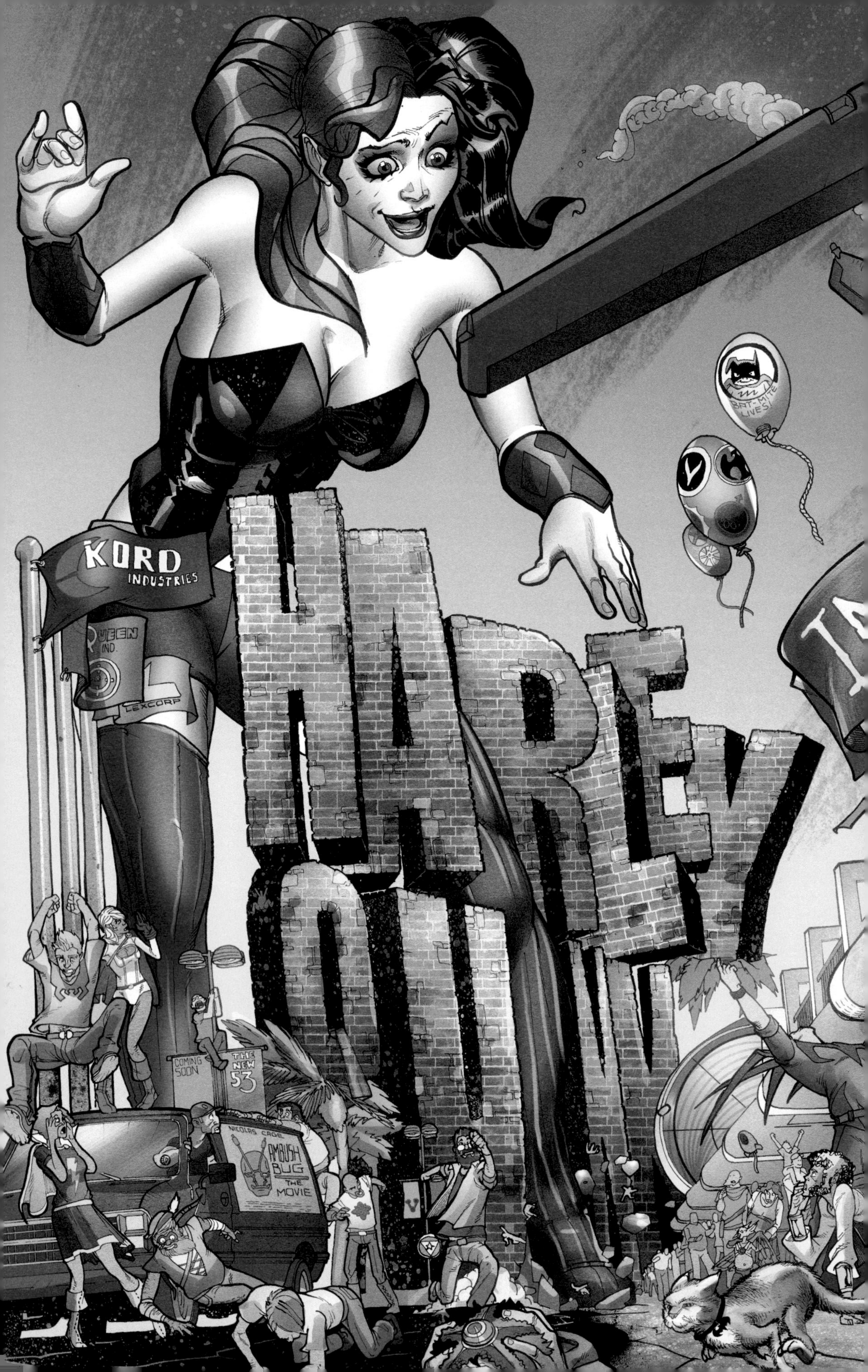
KORD INDUSTRIES
QUEEN IND.
LEXCORP
BAT-MITE LIVES!
COMING SOON
THE NEW 53
NICOLAS CAGE
AMBUSH BUG THE MOVIE

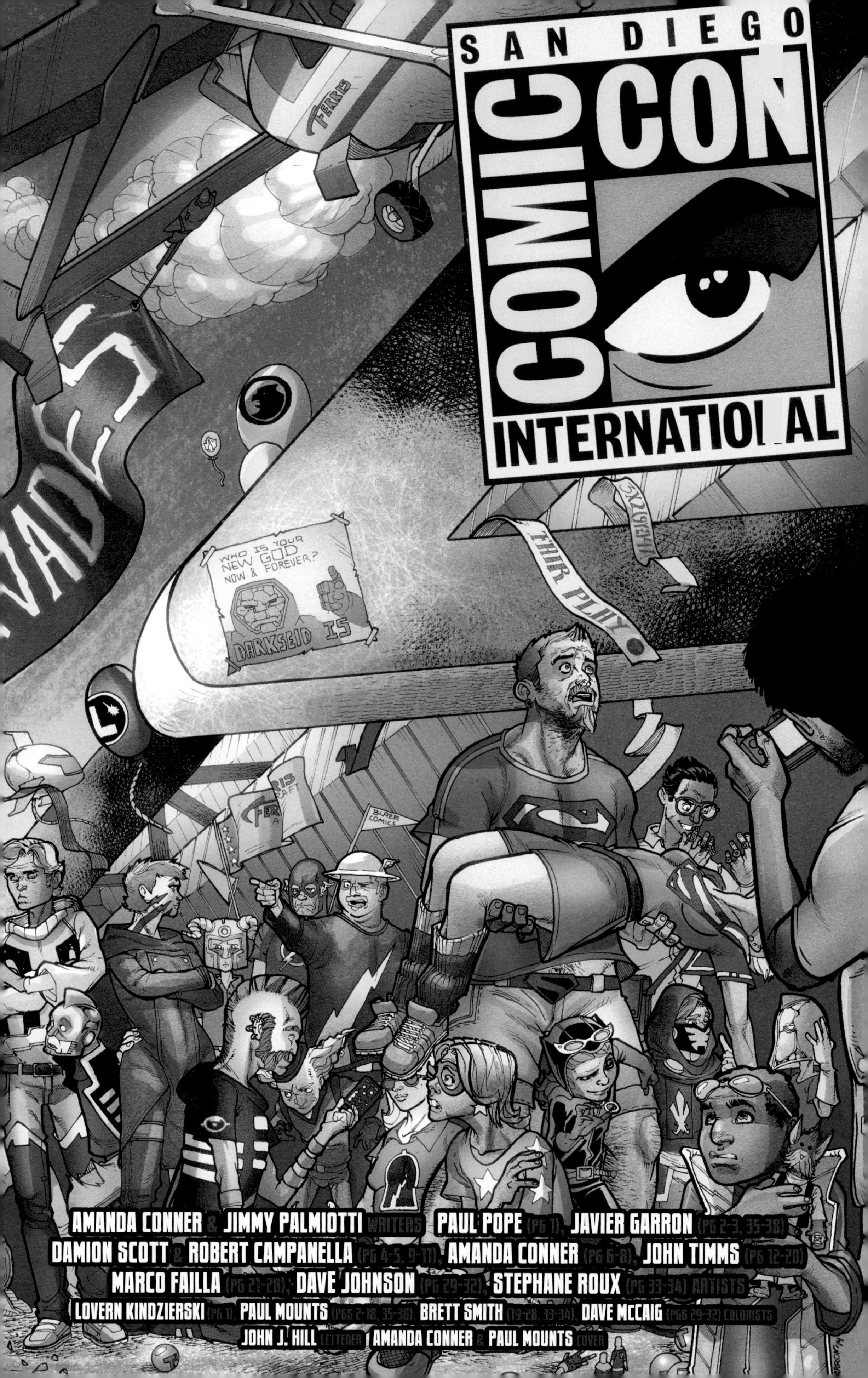
SAN DIEGO
COMIC CON
INTERNATIONAL
WHO IS YOUR NEW GOD NOW & FOREVER?
DARKSEID IS
FAIR PLAY
BLAZE COMICS
AMANDA CONNER & JIMMY PALMIOTTI WRITERS PAUL POPE (PG 1), JAVIER GARRON (PG 2-3, 35-38)
DAMION SCOTT & ROBERT CAMPANELLA (PG 4-5, 9-11), AMANDA CONNER (PG 6-8), JOHN TIMMS (PG 12-20)
MARCO FAILLA (PG 21-28), DAVE JOHNSON (PG 29-32), STEPHANE ROUX (PG 33-34) ARTISTS
LOVERN KINDZIERSKI (PG 1), PAUL MOUNTS (PGS 2-18, 35-38), BRETT SMITH (19-28, 33-34), DAVE McCAIG (PGS 29-32) COLORISTS
JOHN J. HILL LETTERER AMANDA CONNER & PAUL MOUNTS COVER

DAY ONE : TUESDAY.

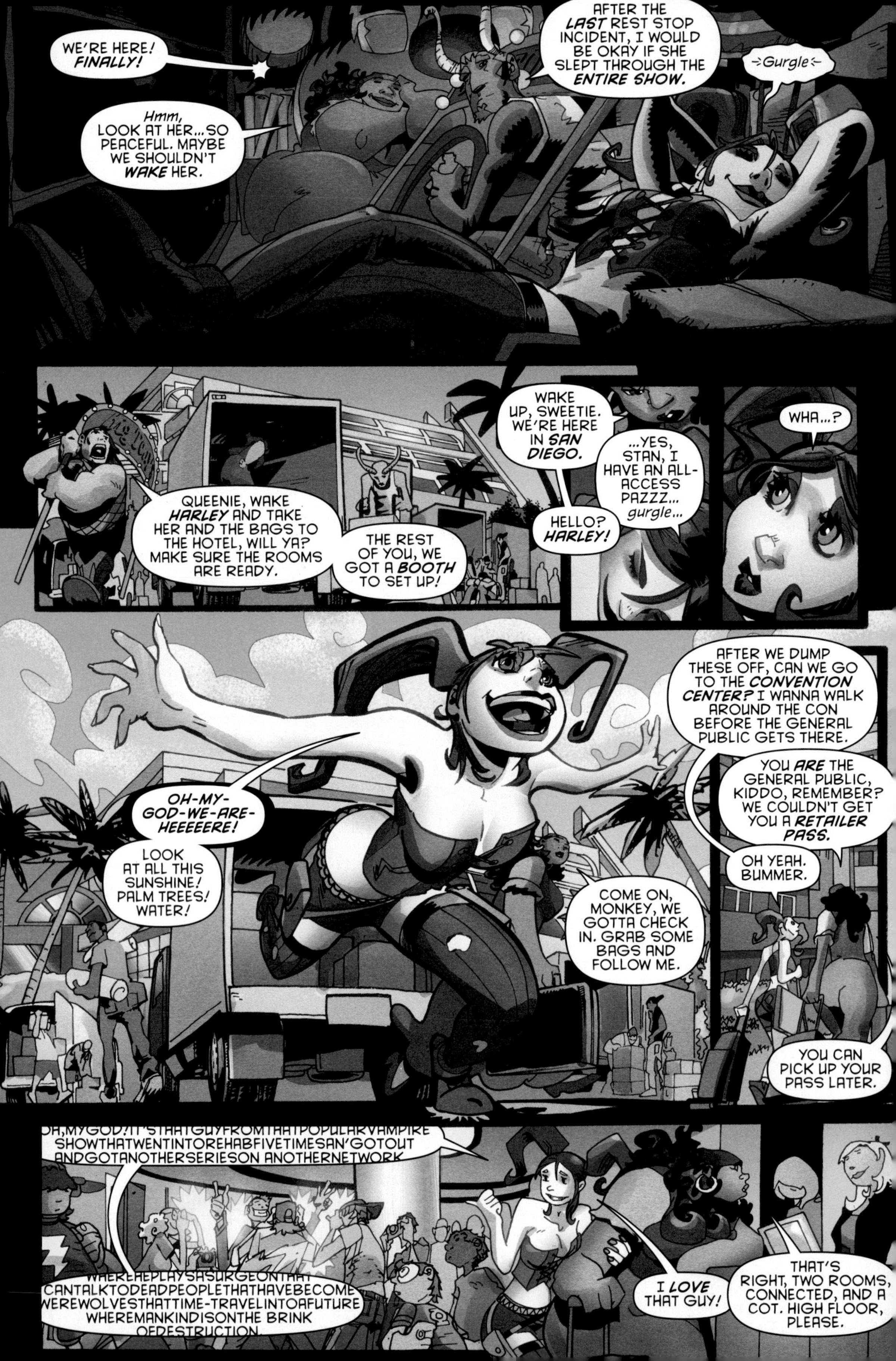

WE'RE HERE! FINALLY!
Hmm, LOOK AT HER... SO PEACEFUL. MAYBE WE SHOULDN'T WAKE HER.
AFTER THE LAST REST STOP INCIDENT, I WOULD BE OKAY IF SHE SLEPT THROUGH THE ENTIRE SHOW.
Gurgle
QUEENIE, WAKE HARLEY AND TAKE HER AND THE BAGS TO THE HOTEL, WILL YA? MAKE SURE THE ROOMS ARE READY.
THE REST OF YOU, WE GOT A BOOTH TO SET UP!
WAKE UP, SWEETIE. WE'RE HERE IN SAN DIEGO.
...YES, STAN, I HAVE AN ALL-ACCESS PAZZZ... gurgle...
HELLO? HARLEY!
WHA...?
OH-MY-GOD-WE-ARE-HEEEEERE!
LOOK AT ALL THIS SUNSHINE! PALM TREES! WATER!
AFTER WE DUMP THESE OFF, CAN WE GO TO THE CONVENTION CENTER? I WANNA WALK AROUND THE CON BEFORE THE GENERAL PUBLIC GETS THERE.
YOU ARE THE GENERAL PUBLIC, KIDDO, REMEMBER? WE COULDN'T GET YOU A RETAILER PASS.
OH YEAH. BUMMER.
COME ON, MONKEY, WE GOTTA CHECK IN. GRAB SOME BAGS AND FOLLOW ME.
YOU CAN PICK UP YOUR PASS LATER.
OH,MYGOD!IT'STHATGUYFROMTHATPOPULARVAMPIRE SHOWTHATWENTINTOREHABFIVETIMESAN'GOTOUT ANDGOTANOTHERSERIESON ANOTHERNETWORK
WHEREHEPLAYSASURGEONTHAT CANTALKTODEADPEOPLETHATHAVEBECOME WEREWOLVESTHATTIME-TRAVELINTOAFUTURE WHEREMANKINDISONTHE BRINK OFDESTRUCTION.
I LOVE THAT GUY!
THAT'S RIGHT, TWO ROOMS, CONNECTED, AND A COT. HIGH FLOOR, PLEASE.

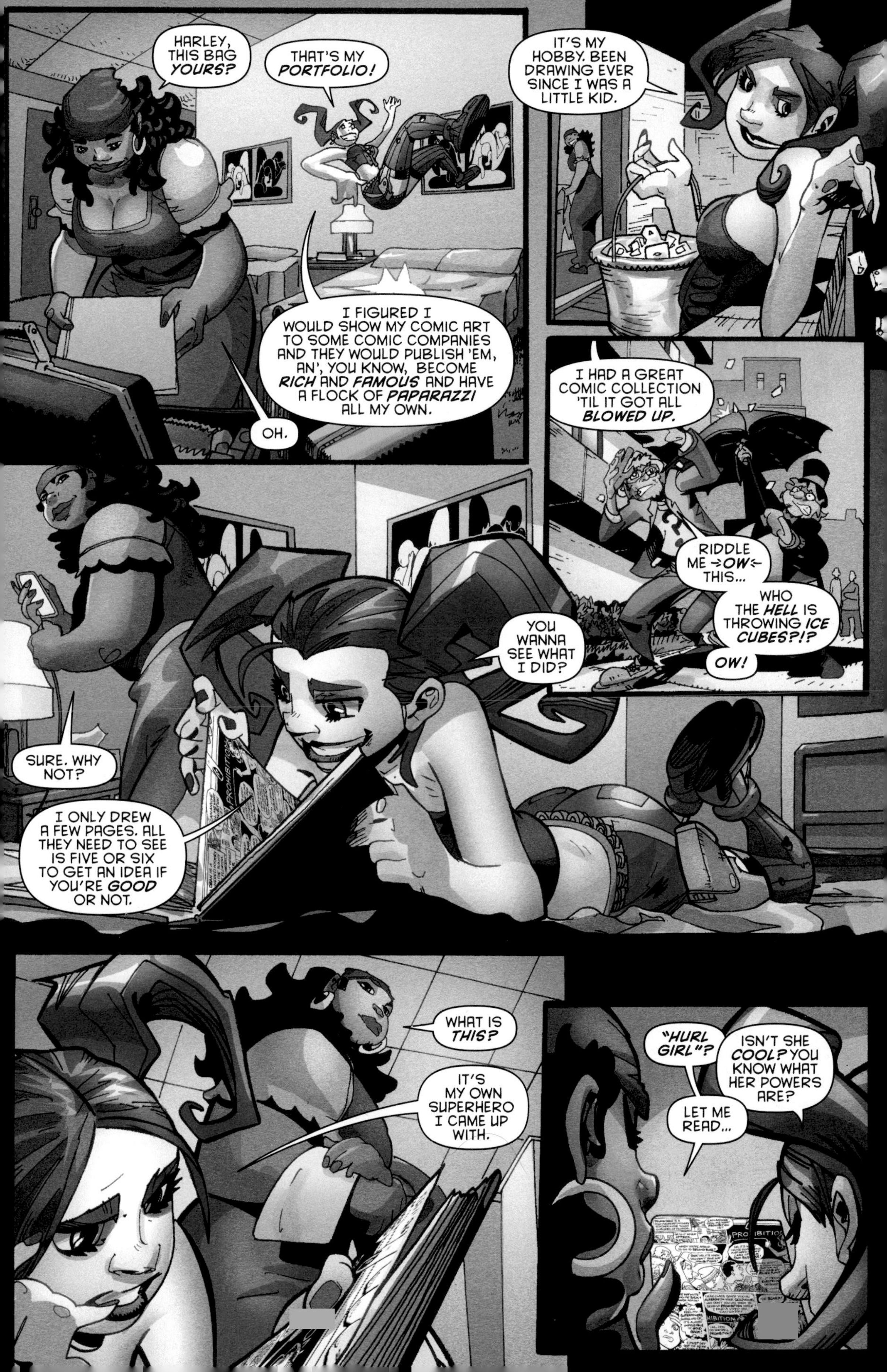
HARLEY, THIS BAG YOURS?
THAT'S MY PORTFOLIO!
I FIGURED I WOULD SHOW MY COMIC ART TO SOME COMIC COMPANIES AND THEY WOULD PUBLISH 'EM, AN', YOU KNOW, BECOME RICH AND FAMOUS AND HAVE A FLOCK OF PAPARAZZI ALL MY OWN.
OH.
IT'S MY HOBBY. BEEN DRAWING EVER SINCE I WAS A LITTLE KID.
I HAD A GREAT COMIC COLLECTION 'TIL IT GOT ALL BLOWED UP.
RIDDLE ME ⇒OW⇐ THIS...
WHO THE HELL IS THROWING ICE CUBES?!?
OW!
YOU WANNA SEE WHAT I DID?
SURE. WHY NOT?
I ONLY DREW A FEW PAGES. ALL THEY NEED TO SEE IS FIVE OR SIX TO GET AN IDEA IF YOU'RE GOOD OR NOT.
WHAT IS THIS?
IT'S MY OWN SUPERHERO I CAME UP WITH.
"HURL GIRL"?
ISN'T SHE COOL? YOU KNOW WHAT HER POWERS ARE?
LET ME READ...

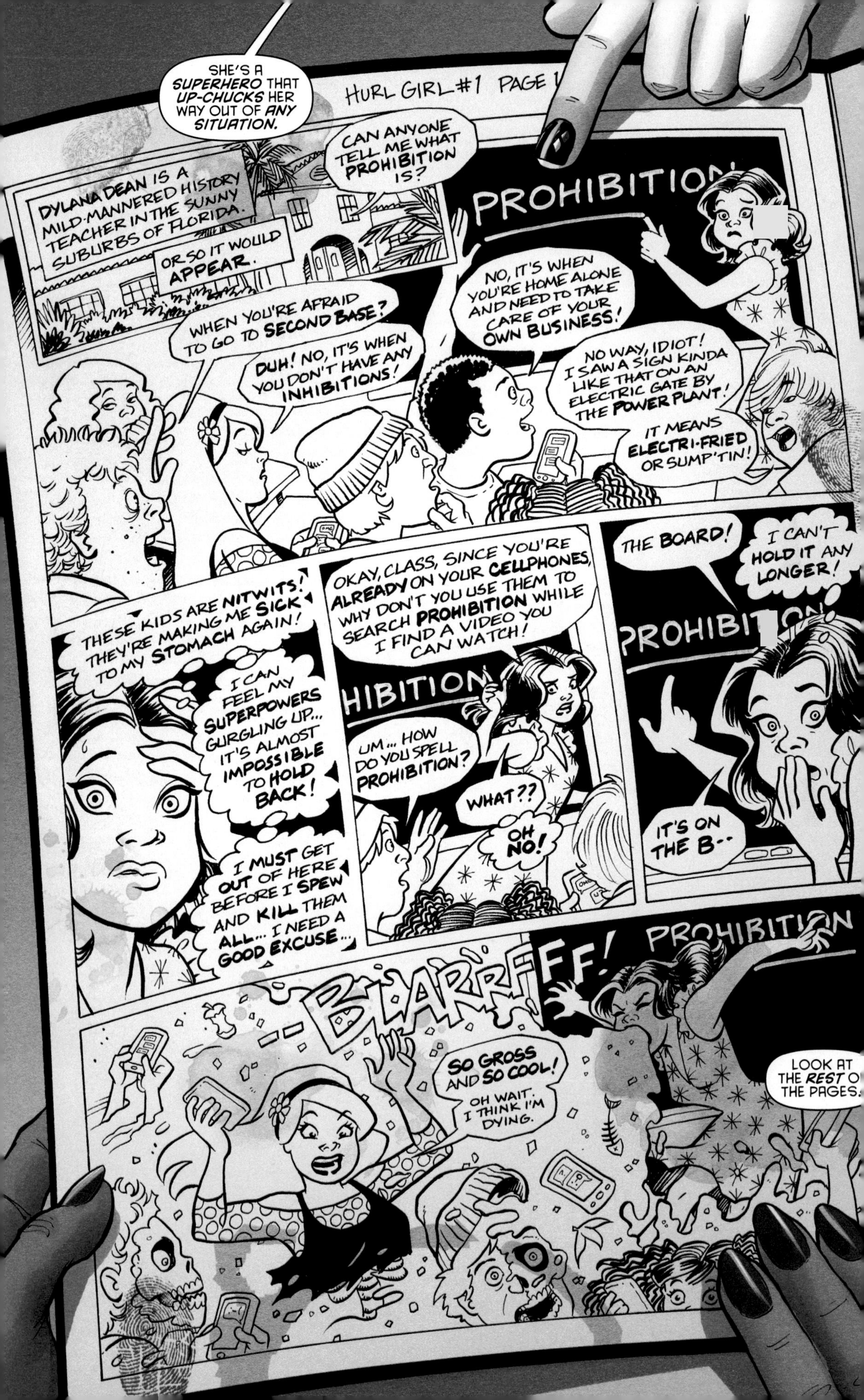

SHE'S A SUPERHERO THAT UP-CHUCKS HER WAY OUT OF ANY SITUATION.
HURL GIRL #1 PAGE
DYLANA DEAN IS A MILD-MANNERED HISTORY TEACHER IN THE SUNNY SUBURBS OF FLORIDA.
OR SO IT WOULD APPEAR.
CAN ANYONE TELL ME WHAT PROHIBITION IS?
PROHIBITION
WHEN YOU'RE AFRAID TO GO TO SECOND BASE?
DUH! NO, IT'S WHEN YOU DON'T HAVE ANY INHIBITIONS!
NO, IT'S WHEN YOU'RE HOME ALONE AND NEED TO TAKE CARE OF YOUR OWN BUSINESS!
NO WAY, IDIOT! I SAW A SIGN KINDA LIKE THAT ON AN ELECTRIC GATE BY THE POWER PLANT!
IT MEANS ELECTRI-FRIED OR SUMP'TIN!
THESE KIDS ARE NITWITS! THEY'RE MAKING ME SICK TO MY STOMACH AGAIN!
I CAN FEEL MY SUPERPOWERS GURGLING UP... IT'S ALMOST IMPOSSIBLE TO HOLD BACK!
I MUST GET OUT OF HERE BEFORE I SPEW AND KILL THEM ALL... I NEED A GOOD EXCUSE...
OKAY, CLASS, SINCE YOU'RE ALREADY ON YOUR CELLPHONES, WHY DON'T YOU USE THEM TO SEARCH PROHIBITION WHILE I FIND A VIDEO YOU CAN WATCH!
HIBITION
UM... HOW DO YOU SPELL PROHIBITION?
WHAT??
OH NO!
THE BOARD!
I CAN'T HOLD IT ANY LONGER!
PROHIBITION
IT'S ON THE B--
--BLARRFFF!
PROHIBITION
SO GROSS AND SO COOL!
OH WAIT. I THINK I'M DYING.
LOOK AT THE REST O THE PAGES.

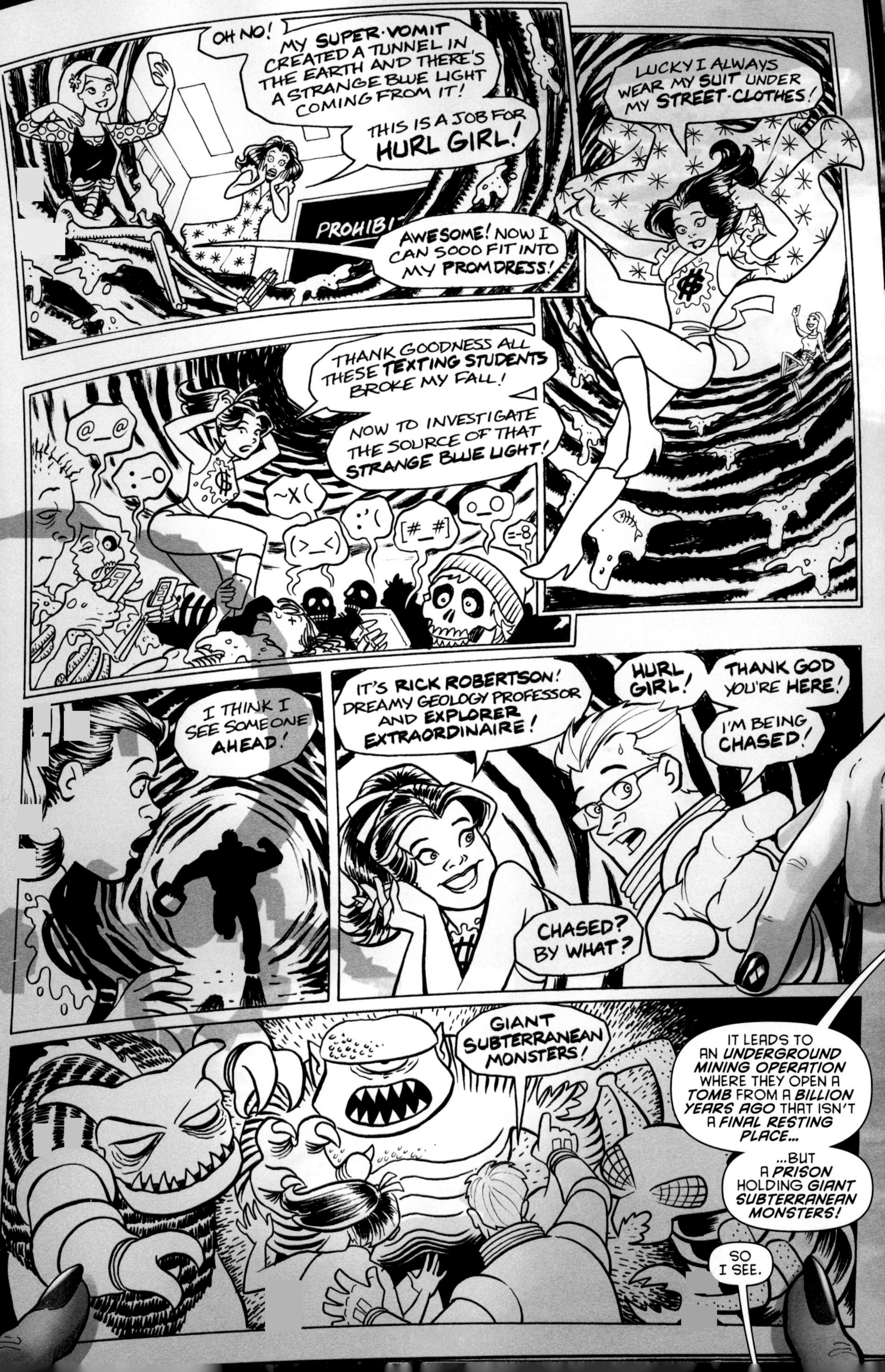
OH NO! MY SUPER-VOMIT CREATED A TUNNEL IN THE EARTH AND THERE'S A STRANGE BLUE LIGHT COMING FROM IT!
THIS IS A JOB FOR HURL GIRL!
PROHIBI
AWESOME! NOW I CAN SOOO FIT INTO MY PROM DRESS!
LUCKY I ALWAYS WEAR MY SUIT UNDER MY STREET-CLOTHES!
THANK GOODNESS ALL THESE TEXTING STUDENTS BROKE MY FALL!
NOW TO INVESTIGATE THE SOURCE OF THAT STRANGE BLUE LIGHT!
@_@
:-O
~X(
(>_<)
:'(
[#_#]
o_O
=-8
I THINK I SEE SOMEONE AHEAD!
IT'S RICK ROBERTSON! DREAMY GEOLOGY PROFESSOR AND EXPLORER EXTRAORDINAIRE!
HURL GIRL!
THANK GOD YOU'RE HERE!
I'M BEING CHASED!
CHASED? BY WHAT?
GIANT SUBTERRANEAN MONSTERS!
IT LEADS TO AN UNDERGROUND MINING OPERATION WHERE THEY OPEN A TOMB FROM A BILLION YEARS AGO THAT ISN'T A FINAL RESTING PLACE...
...BUT A PRISON HOLDING GIANT SUBTERRANEAN MONSTERS!
SO I SEE.

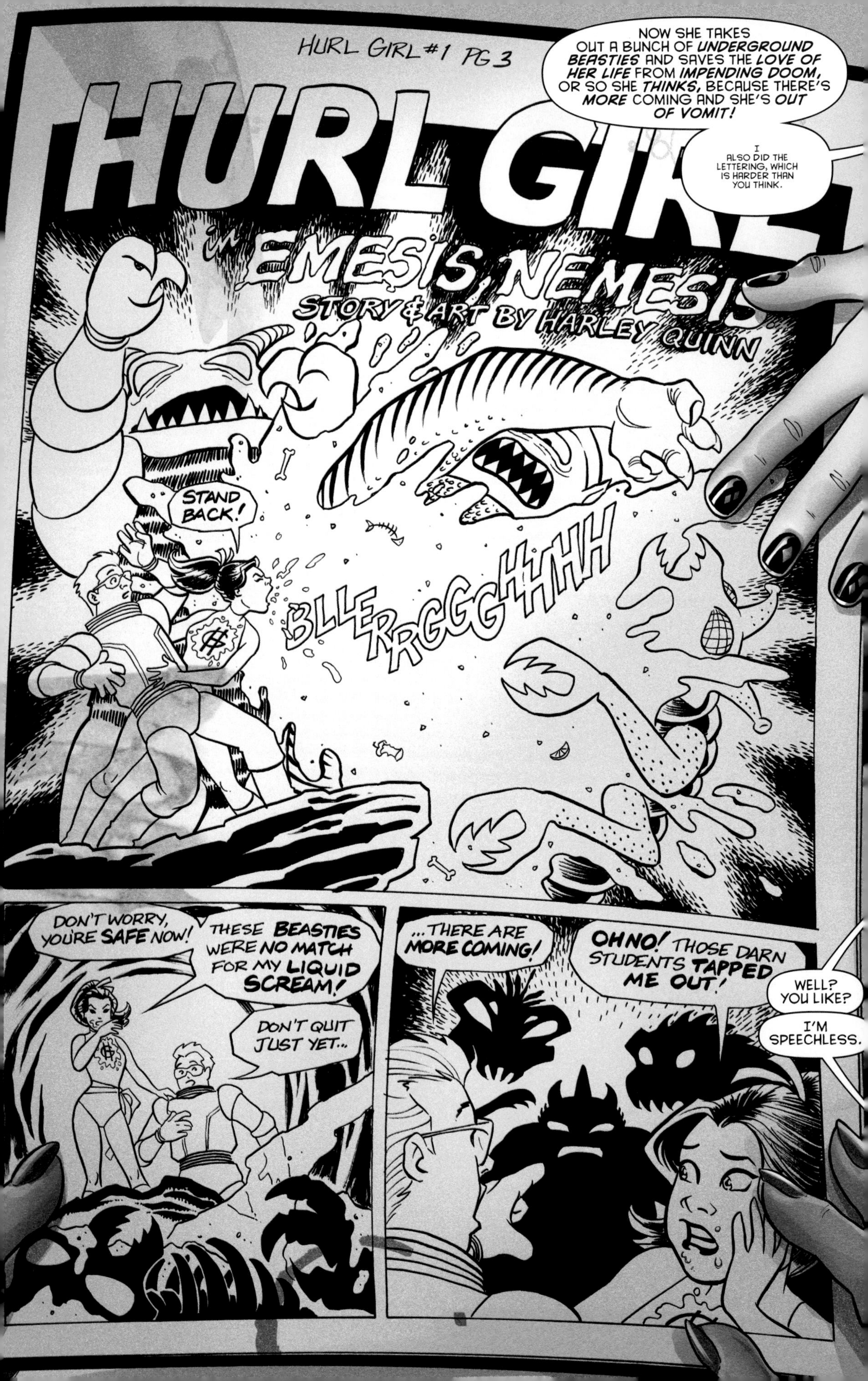
HURL GIRL #1 PG 3
NOW SHE TAKES OUT A BUNCH OF UNDERGROUND BEASTIES AND SAVES THE LOVE OF HER LIFE FROM IMPENDING DOOM, OR SO SHE THINKS, BECAUSE THERE'S MORE COMING AND SHE'S OUT OF VOMIT!
I ALSO DID THE LETTERING, WHICH IS HARDER THAN YOU THINK.
HURL GIRL
in NEMESIS, NEMESIS
STORY & ART BY HARLEY QUINN
STAND BACK!
BLLERRGGGHHHHH
DON'T WORRY, YOU'RE SAFE NOW!
THESE BEASTIES WERE NO MATCH FOR MY LIQUID SCREAM!
DON'T QUIT JUST YET...
...THERE ARE MORE COMING!
OH NO! THOSE DARN STUDENTS TAPPED ME OUT!
WELL? YOU LIKE?
I'M SPEECHLESS.

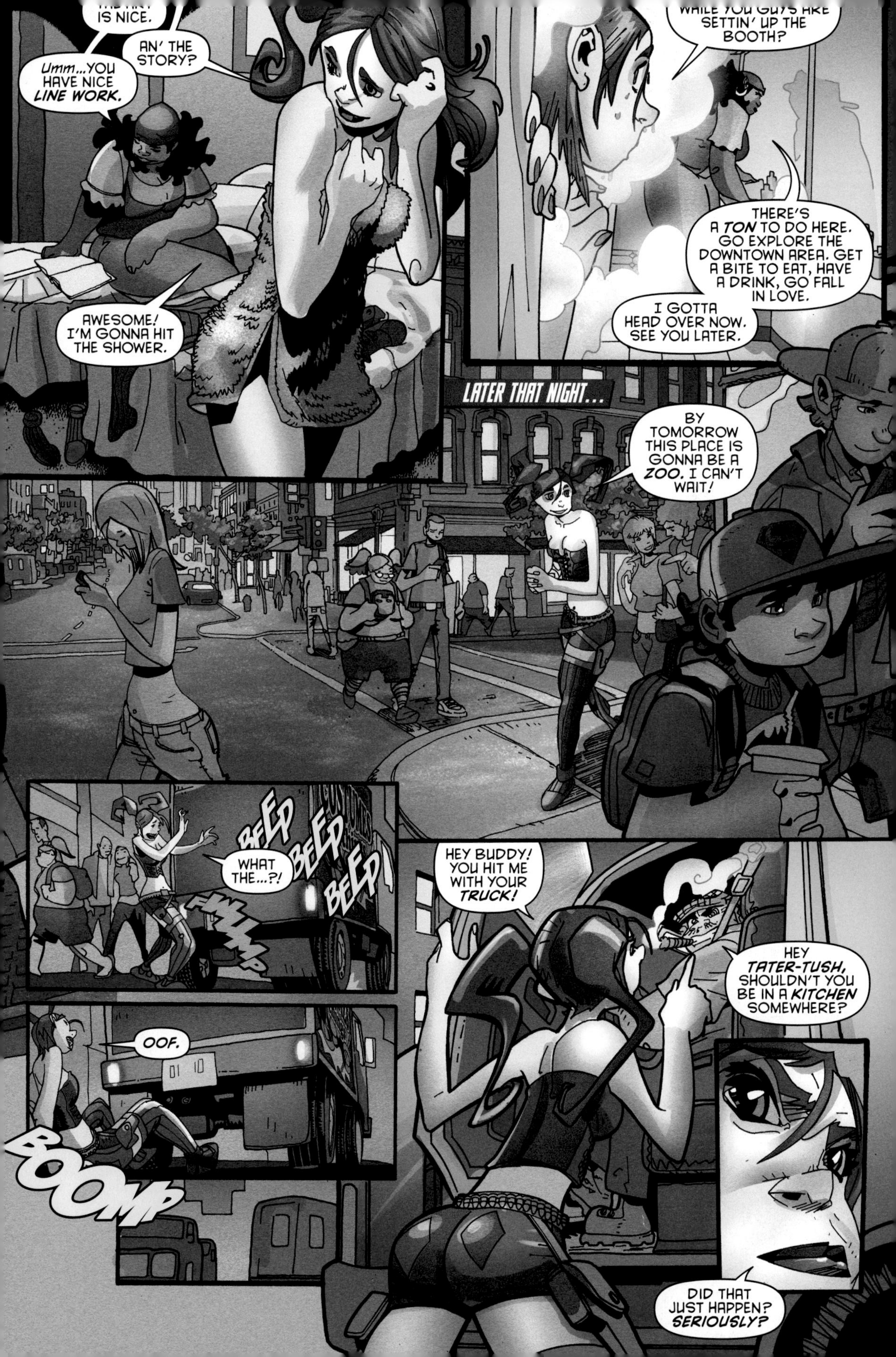

IS NICE.
Umm...YOU HAVE NICE LINE WORK.
AN' THE STORY?
AWESOME! I'M GONNA HIT THE SHOWER.
WHILE YOU GUYS ARE SETTIN' UP THE BOOTH?
THERE'S A TON TO DO HERE. GO EXPLORE THE DOWNTOWN AREA. GET A BITE TO EAT, HAVE A DRINK, GO FALL IN LOVE.
I GOTTA HEAD OVER NOW. SEE YOU LATER.
LATER THAT NIGHT...
BY TOMORROW THIS PLACE IS GONNA BE A ZOO. I CAN'T WAIT!
BEEP BEEP BEEP
WHAT THE...?!
OOF.
BOOMP
HEY BUDDY! YOU HIT ME WITH YOUR TRUCK!
HEY TATER-TUSH, SHOULDN'T YOU BE IN A KITCHEN SOMEWHERE?
DID THAT JUST HAPPEN? SERIOUSLY?

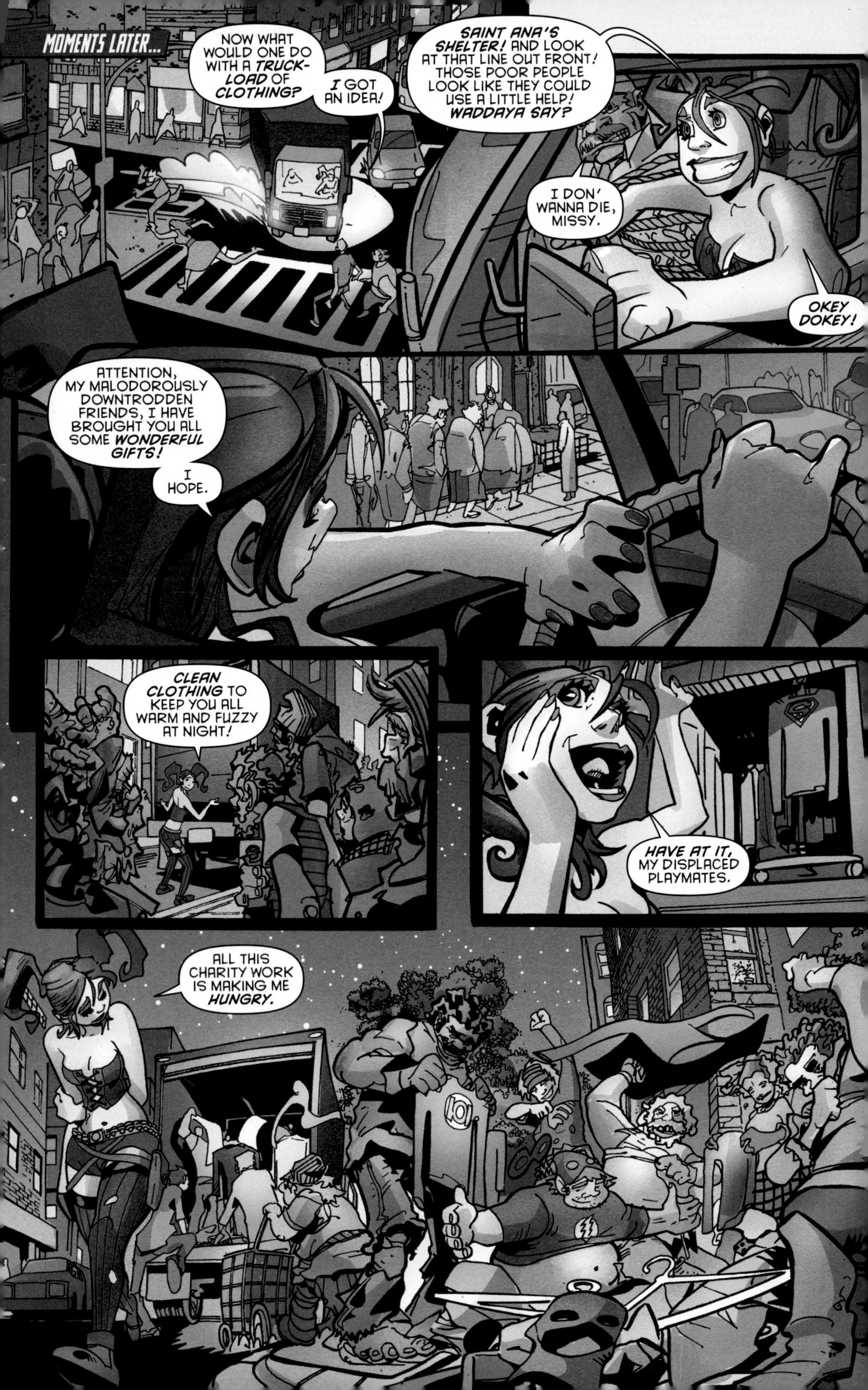
MOMENTS LATER...
NOW WHAT WOULD ONE DO WITH A TRUCK-LOAD OF CLOTHING?
I GOT AN IDEA!
SAINT ANA'S SHELTER! AND LOOK AT THAT LINE OUT FRONT! THOSE POOR PEOPLE LOOK LIKE THEY COULD USE A LITTLE HELP! WADDAYA SAY?
I DON' WANNA DIE, MISSY.
OKEY DOKEY!
ATTENTION, MY MALODOROUSLY DOWNTRODDEN FRIENDS, I HAVE BROUGHT YOU ALL SOME WONDERFUL GIFTS!
I HOPE.
CLEAN CLOTHING TO KEEP YOU ALL WARM AND FUZZY AT NIGHT!
HAVE AT IT, MY DISPLACED PLAYMATES.
ALL THIS CHARITY WORK IS MAKING ME HUNGRY.

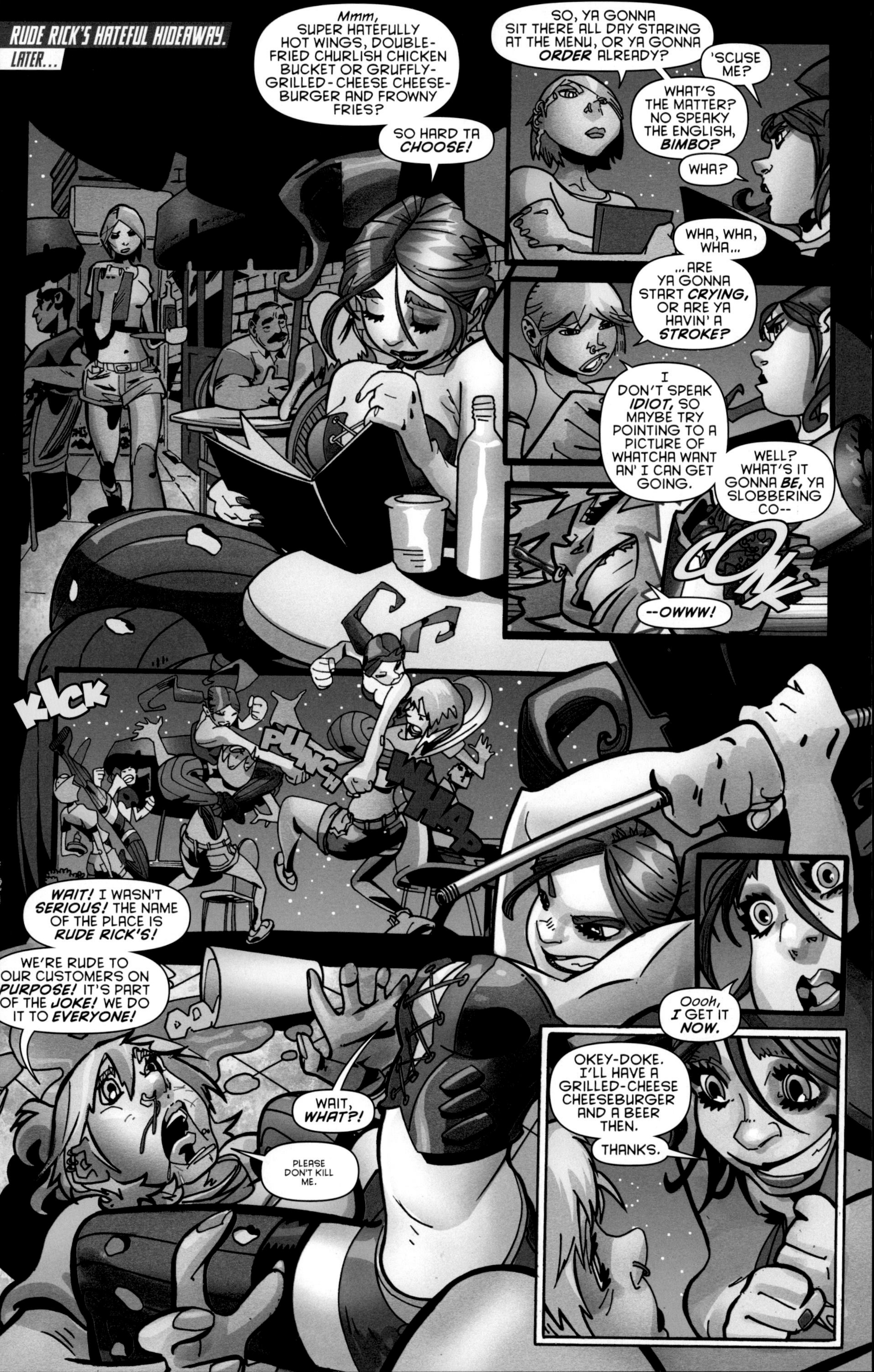
RUDE RICK'S HATEFUL HIDEAWAY.
LATER...
Mmm, SUPER HATEFULLY HOT WINGS, DOUBLE-FRIED CHURLISH CHICKEN BUCKET OR GRUFFLY-GRILLED-CHEESE CHEESE-BURGER AND FROWNY FRIES?
SO HARD TA CHOOSE!
SO, YA GONNA SIT THERE ALL DAY STARING AT THE MENU, OR YA GONNA ORDER ALREADY?
'SCUSE ME?
WHAT'S THE MATTER? NO SPEAKY THE ENGLISH, BIMBO?
WHA?
WHA, WHA, WHA...
...ARE YA GONNA START CRYING, OR ARE YA HAVIN' A STROKE?
I DON'T SPEAK IDIOT, SO MAYBE TRY POINTING TO A PICTURE OF WHATCHA WANT AN' I CAN GET GOING.
WELL? WHAT'S IT GONNA BE, YA SLOBBERING CO--
CONK
--OWWW!
KICK
PUNCH
WHAP
WAIT! I WASN'T SERIOUS! THE NAME OF THE PLACE IS RUDE RICK'S!
WE'RE RUDE TO OUR CUSTOMERS ON PURPOSE! IT'S PART OF THE JOKE! WE DO IT TO EVERYONE!
WAIT, WHAT?!
PLEASE DON'T KILL ME.
Oooh, I GET IT NOW.
OKEY-DOKE. I'LL HAVE A GRILLED-CHEESE CHEESEBURGER AND A BEER THEN.
THANKS.

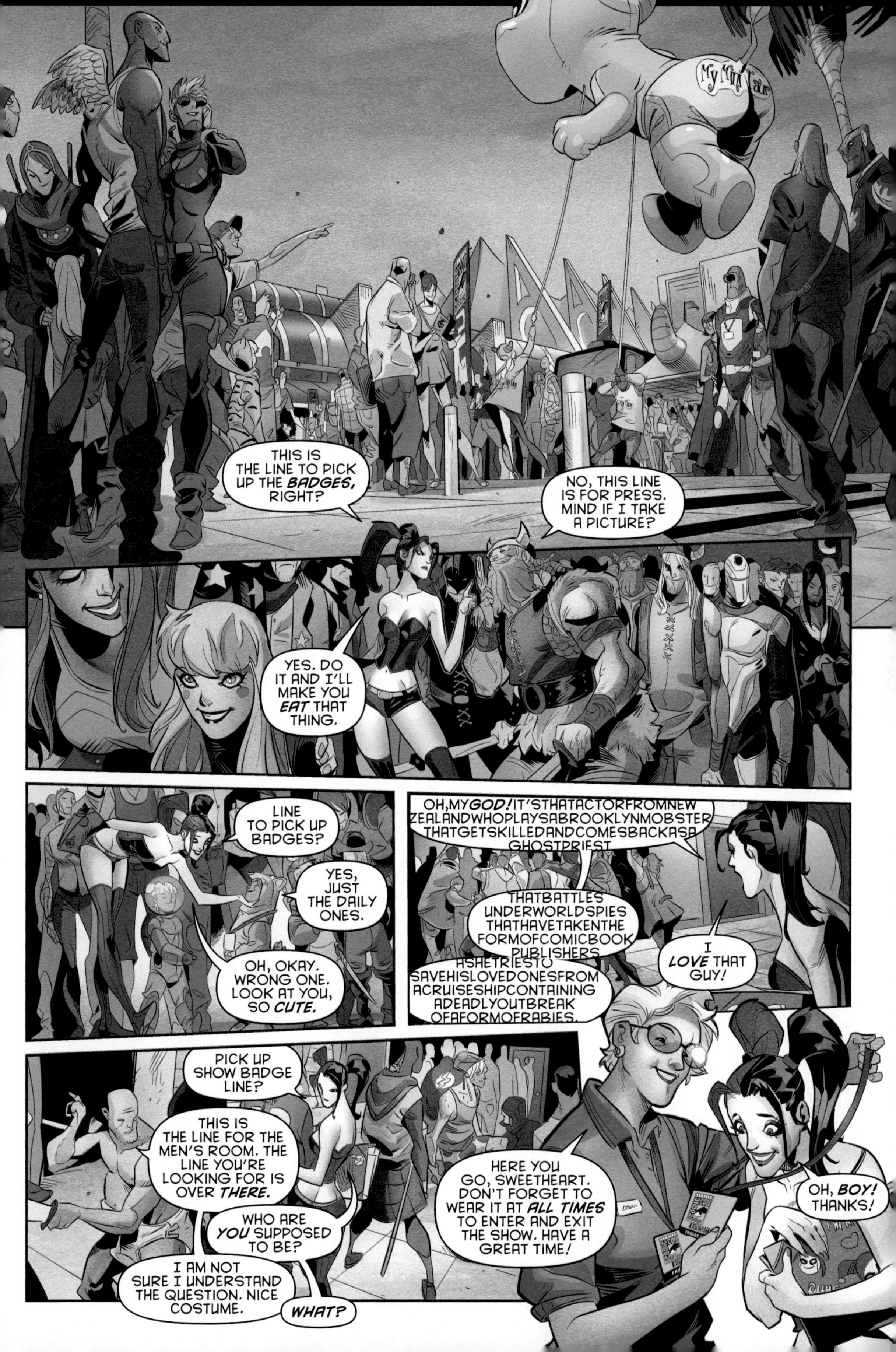
My Mini Taur
THIS IS THE LINE TO PICK UP THE BADGES, RIGHT?
NO, THIS LINE IS FOR PRESS. MIND IF I TAKE A PICTURE?
YES. DO IT AND I'LL MAKE YOU EAT THAT THING.
LINE TO PICK UP BADGES?
YES, JUST THE DAILY ONES.
OH, OKAY. WRONG ONE. LOOK AT YOU, SO CUTE.
OH,MYGOD!IT'STHATACTORFROMNEWZEALANDWHOPLAYSABROOKLYNMOBSTERTHATGETSKILLEDANDCOMESBACKASAGHOSTPRIEST
THATBATTLESUNDERWORLDSPIESTHATHAVETAKENTHEFORMOFCOMICBOOKPUBLISHERS
ASHETRIESTOSAVEHISLOVEDONESFROMACRUISESHIPCONTAININGADEADLYOUTBREAKOFAFORMOFRABIES.
I LOVE THAT GUY!
PICK UP SHOW BADGE LINE?
THIS IS THE LINE FOR THE MEN'S ROOM. THE LINE YOU'RE LOOKING FOR IS OVER THERE.
WHO ARE YOU SUPPOSED TO BE?
I AM NOT SURE I UNDERSTAND THE QUESTION. NICE COSTUME.
WHAT?
HERE YOU GO, SWEETHEART. DON'T FORGET TO WEAR IT AT ALL TIMES TO ENTER AND EXIT THE SHOW. HAVE A GREAT TIME!
OH, BOY! THANKS!

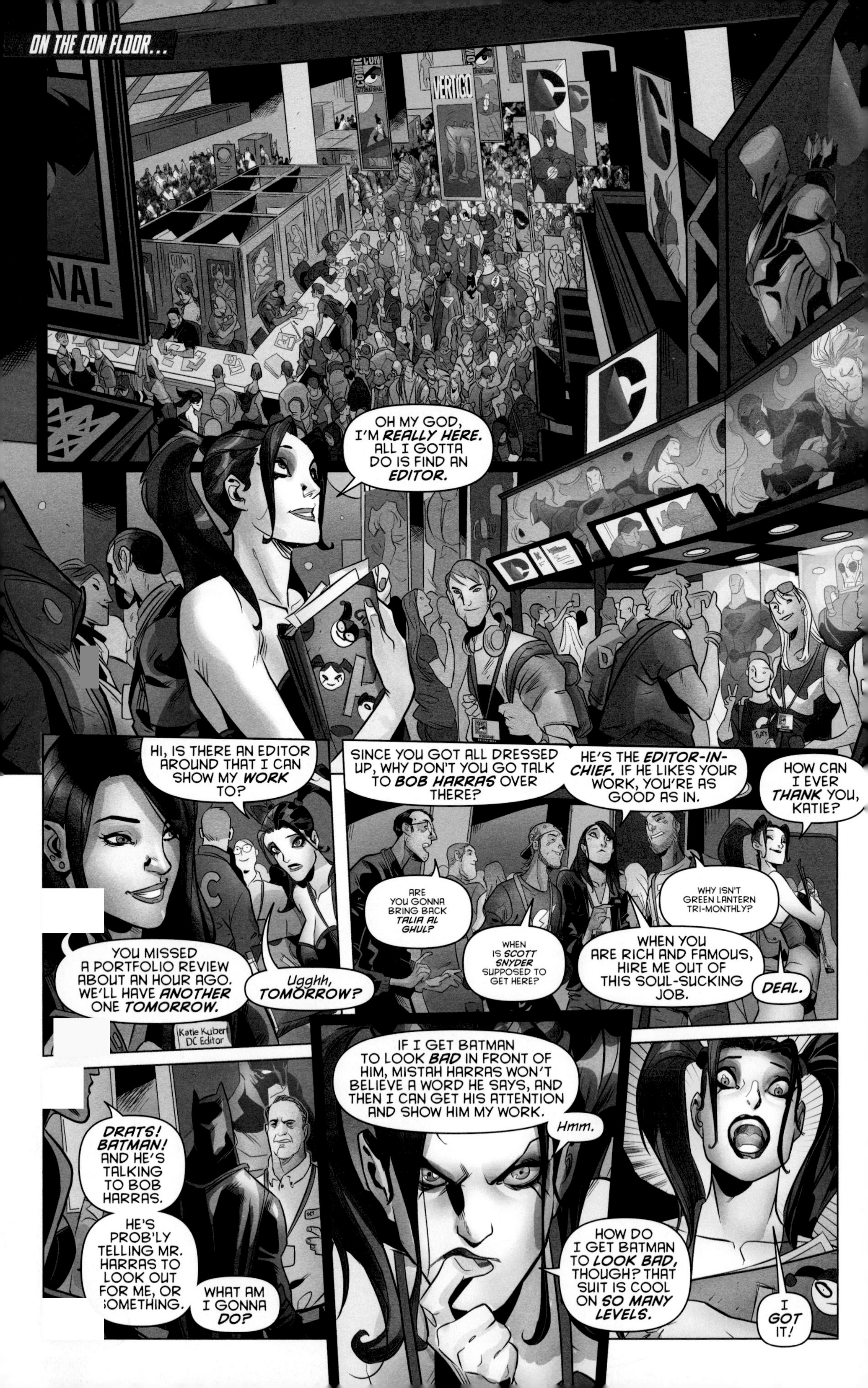
ON THE CON FLOOR...
VERTIGO
OH MY GOD, I'M REALLY HERE. ALL I GOTTA DO IS FIND AN EDITOR.
HI, IS THERE AN EDITOR AROUND THAT I CAN SHOW MY WORK TO?
YOU MISSED A PORTFOLIO REVIEW ABOUT AN HOUR AGO. WE'LL HAVE ANOTHER ONE TOMORROW.
Ugghh, TOMORROW?
Katie Kubert DC Editor
SINCE YOU GOT ALL DRESSED UP, WHY DON'T YOU GO TALK TO BOB HARRAS OVER THERE?
HE'S THE EDITOR-IN-CHIEF. IF HE LIKES YOUR WORK, YOU'RE AS GOOD AS IN.
HOW CAN I EVER THANK YOU, KATIE?
ARE YOU GONNA BRING BACK TALIA AL GHUL?
WHEN IS SCOTT SNYDER SUPPOSED TO GET HERE?
WHY ISN'T GREEN LANTERN TRI-MONTHLY?
WHEN YOU ARE RICH AND FAMOUS, HIRE ME OUT OF THIS SOUL-SUCKING JOB.
DEAL.
DRATS! BATMAN! AND HE'S TALKING TO BOB HARRAS.
HE'S PROB'LY TELLING MR. HARRAS TO LOOK OUT FOR ME, OR SOMETHING.
WHAT AM I GONNA DO?
IF I GET BATMAN TO LOOK BAD IN FRONT OF HIM, MISTAH HARRAS WON'T BELIEVE A WORD HE SAYS, AND THEN I CAN GET HIS ATTENTION AND SHOW HIM MY WORK.
Hmm.
HOW DO I GET BATMAN TO LOOK BAD, THOUGH? THAT SUIT IS COOL ON SO MANY LEVELS.
I GOT IT!

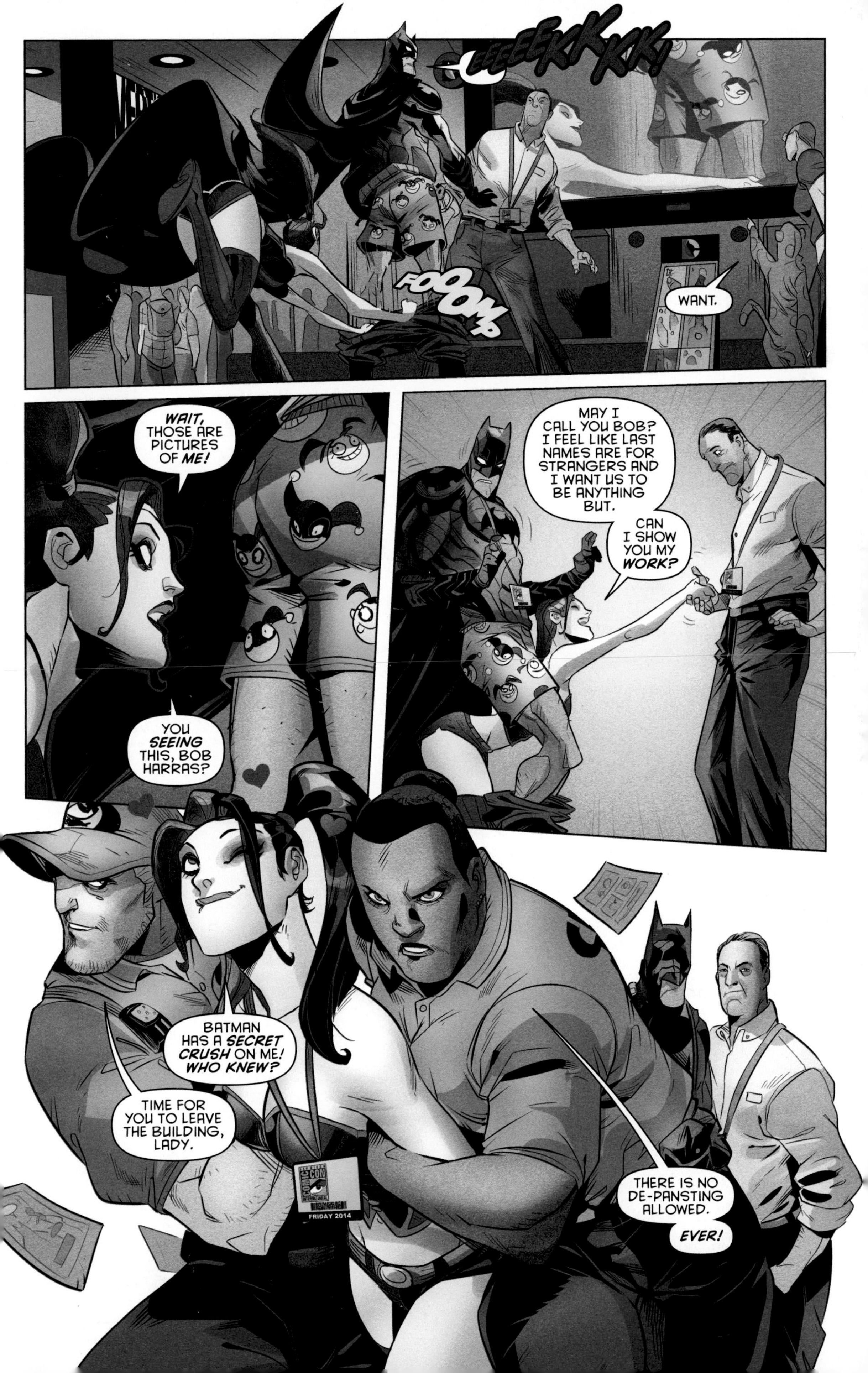
EEEEEKKKK!
FOOOOMP
WANT.
WAIT, THOSE ARE PICTURES OF ME!
YOU SEEING THIS, BOB HARRAS?
MAY I CALL YOU BOB? I FEEL LIKE LAST NAMES ARE FOR STRANGERS AND I WANT US TO BE ANYTHING BUT.
CAN I SHOW YOU MY WORK?
BATMAN HAS A SECRET CRUSH ON ME! WHO KNEW?
TIME FOR YOU TO LEAVE THE BUILDING, LADY.
THERE IS NO DE-PANSTING ALLOWED.
EVER!

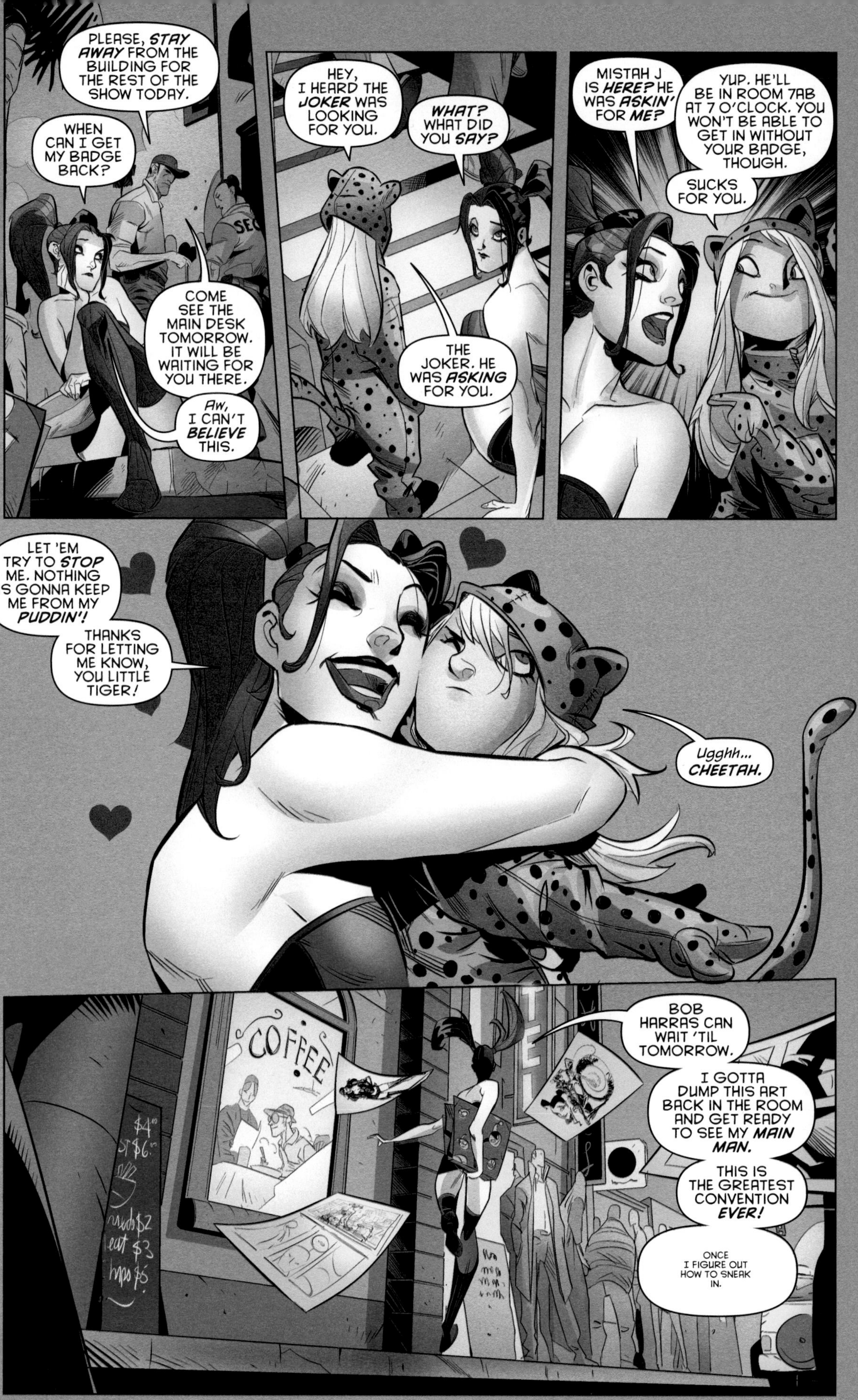
PLEASE, STAY AWAY FROM THE BUILDING FOR THE REST OF THE SHOW TODAY.
WHEN CAN I GET MY BADGE BACK?
COME SEE THE MAIN DESK TOMORROW. IT WILL BE WAITING FOR YOU THERE.
AW, I CAN'T BELIEVE THIS.
HEY, I HEARD THE JOKER WAS LOOKING FOR YOU.
WHAT? WHAT DID YOU SAY?
THE JOKER. HE WAS ASKING FOR YOU.
MISTAH J IS HERE? HE WAS ASKIN' FOR ME?
YUP. HE'LL BE IN ROOM 7AB AT 7 O'CLOCK. YOU WON'T BE ABLE TO GET IN WITHOUT YOUR BADGE, THOUGH.
SUCKS FOR YOU.
LET 'EM TRY TO STOP ME. NOTHING IS GONNA KEEP ME FROM MY PUDDIN'!
THANKS FOR LETTING ME KNOW, YOU LITTLE TIGER!
Ugghh... CHEETAH.
COFFEE
BOB HARRAS CAN WAIT 'TIL TOMORROW.
I GOTTA DUMP THIS ART BACK IN THE ROOM AND GET READY TO SEE MY MAIN MAN.
THIS IS THE GREATEST CONVENTION EVER!
ONCE I FIGURE OUT HOW TO SNEAK IN.

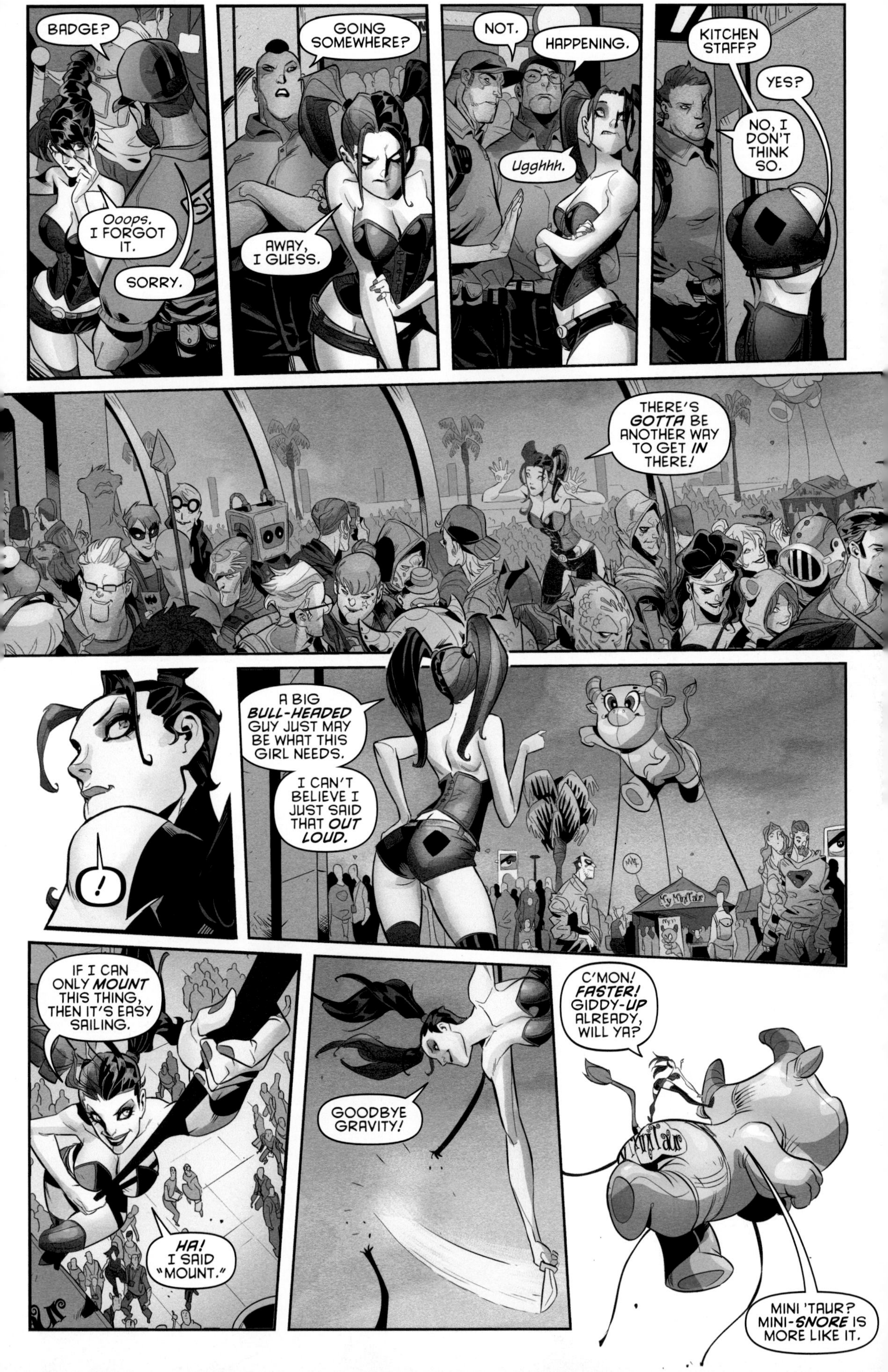
BADGE?
OOOPS. I FORGOT IT.
SORRY.
GOING SOMEWHERE?
AWAY, I GUESS.
NOT.
HAPPENING.
UGGHHH.
KITCHEN STAFF?
YES?
NO, I DON'T THINK SO.
THERE'S GOTTA BE ANOTHER WAY TO GET IN THERE!
!
A BIG BULL-HEADED GUY JUST MAY BE WHAT THIS GIRL NEEDS.
I CAN'T BELIEVE I JUST SAID THAT OUT LOUD.
IF I CAN ONLY MOUNT THIS THING, THEN IT'S EASY SAILING.
HA! I SAID "MOUNT."
GOODBYE GRAVITY!
C'MON! FASTER! GIDDY-UP ALREADY, WILL YA?
MINI 'TAUR? MINI-SNORE IS MORE LIKE IT.

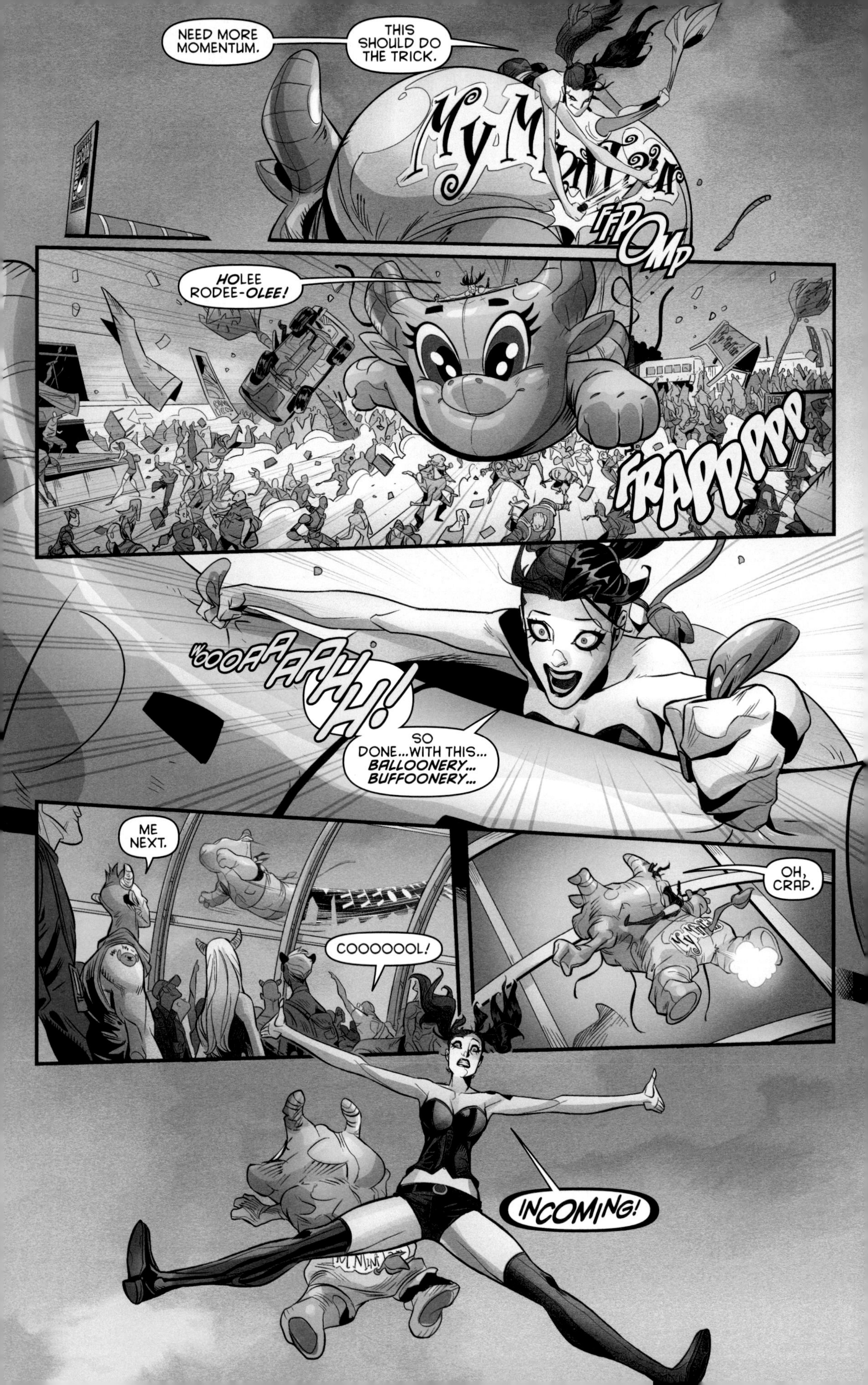
NEED MORE MOMENTUM.
THIS SHOULD DO THE TRICK.
FFPOMP
HOLEE RODEE-OLEE!
FRAPPPPP
WOOOAAAAHH!
SO DONE...WITH THIS... BALLOONERY... BUFFOONERY...
ME NEXT.
COOOOOOL!
OH, CRAP.
INCOMING!

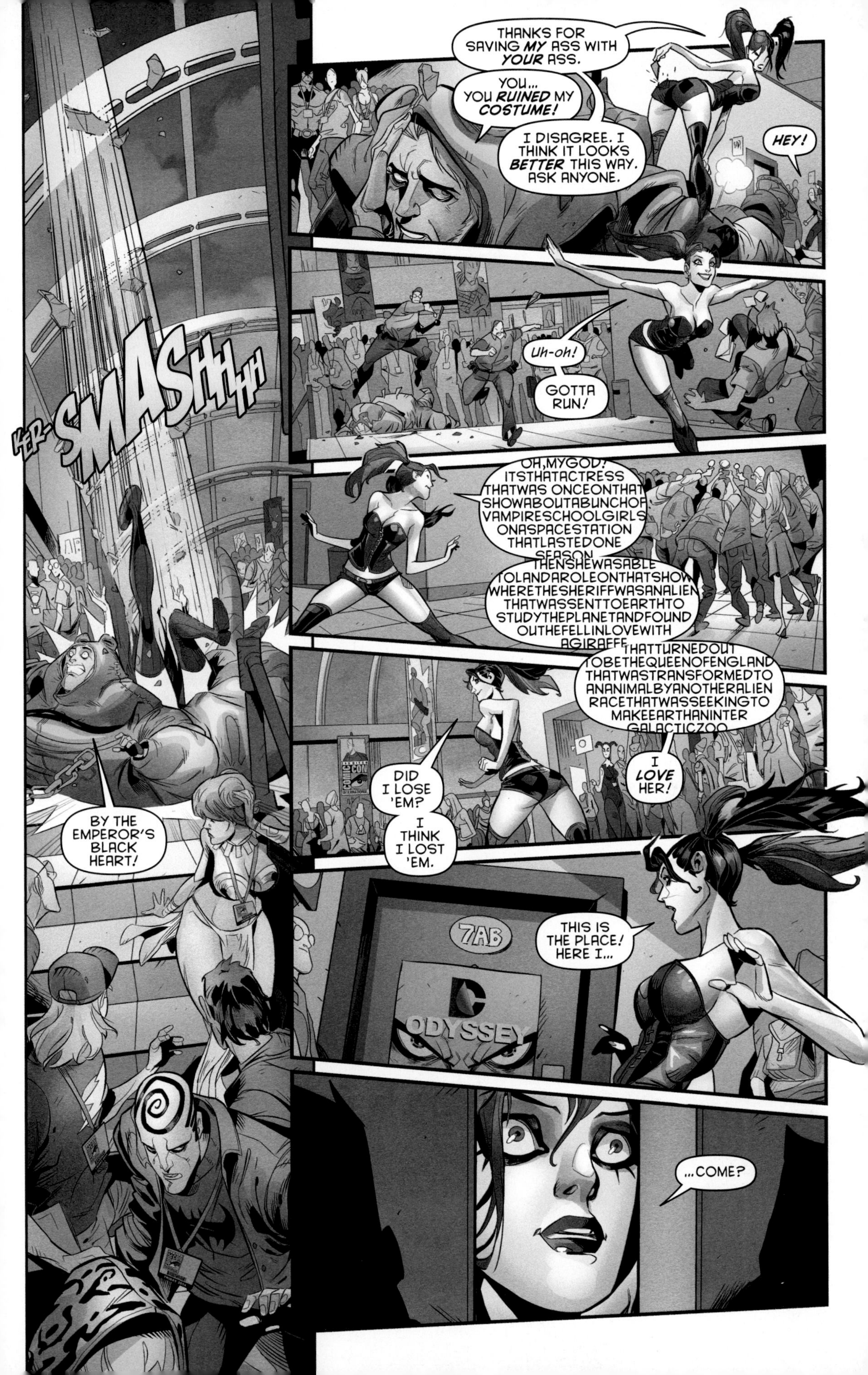
KER-SMASHHHH
BY THE EMPEROR'S BLACK HEART!
THANKS FOR SAVING MY ASS WITH YOUR ASS.
YOU... YOU RUINED MY COSTUME!
I DISAGREE. I THINK IT LOOKS BETTER THIS WAY. ASK ANYONE.
HEY!
Uh-oh!
GOTTA RUN!
OH,MYGOD! ITSTHATACTRESS THATWAS ONCEONTHAT SHOWABOUTABUNCHOF VAMPIRESCHOOLGIRLS ONASPACESTATION THATLASTEDONE SEASON
THENSHEWASABLE TOLANDAROLEONTHATSHOW WHERETHESHERIFFWASANALIEN THATWASSENTTOEARTHTO STUDYTHEPLANETANDFOUND OUTHEFELLINLOVEWITH AGIRAFFE
THATTURNEDOUT TOBETHEQUEENOFENGLAND THATWASTRANSFORMEDTO ANANIMALBYANOTHERALIEN RACETHATWASSEEKINGTO MAKEEARTHANINTER GALACTICZOO
I LOVE HER!
DID I LOSE 'EM?
I THINK I LOST 'EM.
7AB
ODYSSEY
THIS IS THE PLACE! HERE I...
...COME?

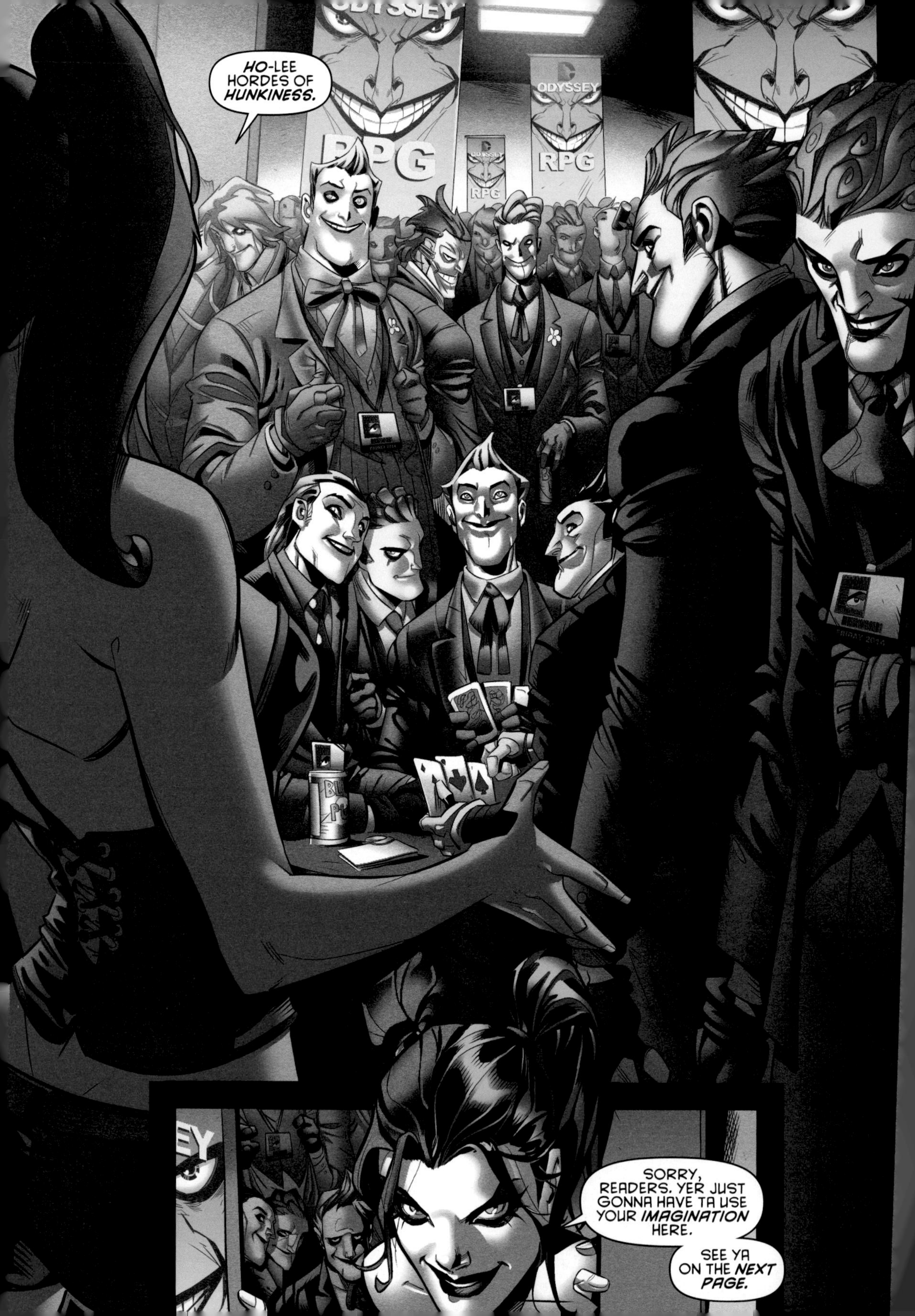
ODYSSEY
RPG
ODYSSEY
RPG
ODYSSEY
RPG
HO-LEE HORDES OF HUNKINESS.
SORRY, READERS. YER JUST GONNA HAVE TA USE YOUR IMAGINATION HERE.
SEE YA ON THE NEXT PAGE.

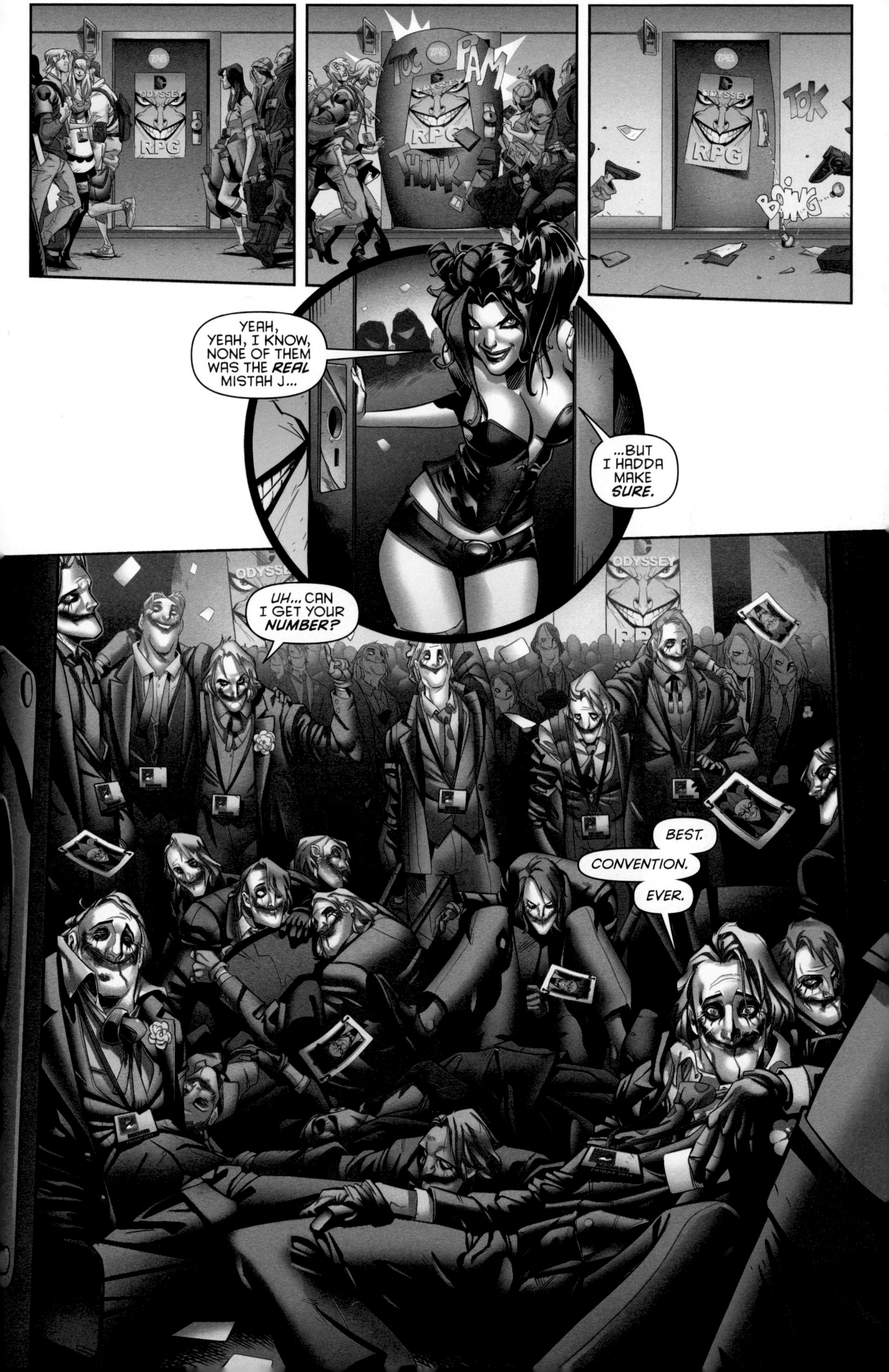
TAB
ODYSSEY
RPG
TOC
PAM
THUNK
TOK
BOING
YEAH, YEAH, I KNOW, NONE OF THEM WAS THE REAL MISTAH J...
...BUT I HADDA MAKE SURE.
UH... CAN I GET YOUR NUMBER?
BEST.
CONVENTION.
EVER.

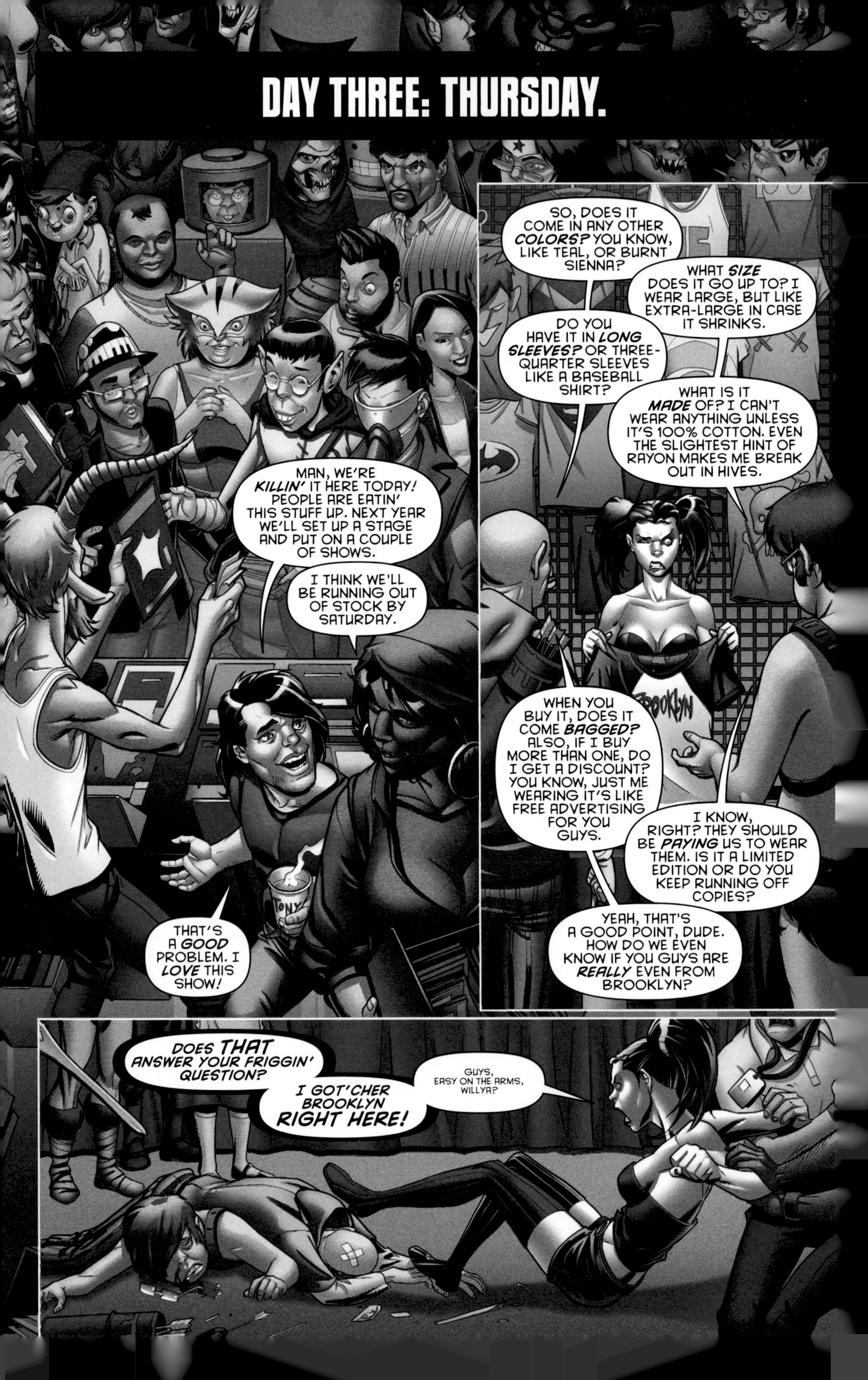
DAY THREE: THURSDAY.
MAN, WE'RE KILLIN' IT HERE TODAY! PEOPLE ARE EATIN' THIS STUFF UP. NEXT YEAR WE'LL SET UP A STAGE AND PUT ON A COUPLE OF SHOWS.
I THINK WE'LL BE RUNNING OUT OF STOCK BY SATURDAY.
THAT'S A GOOD PROBLEM. I LOVE THIS SHOW!
SO, DOES IT COME IN ANY OTHER COLORS? YOU KNOW, LIKE TEAL, OR BURNT SIENNA?
WHAT SIZE DOES IT GO UP TO? I WEAR LARGE, BUT LIKE EXTRA-LARGE IN CASE IT SHRINKS.
DO YOU HAVE IT IN LONG SLEEVES? OR THREE-QUARTER SLEEVES LIKE A BASEBALL SHIRT?
WHAT IS IT MADE OF? I CAN'T WEAR ANYTHING UNLESS IT'S 100% COTTON. EVEN THE SLIGHTEST HINT OF RAYON MAKES ME BREAK OUT IN HIVES.
BROOKLYN
WHEN YOU BUY IT, DOES IT COME BAGGED? ALSO, IF I BUY MORE THAN ONE, DO I GET A DISCOUNT? YOU KNOW, JUST ME WEARING IT'S LIKE FREE ADVERTISING FOR YOU GUYS.
I KNOW, RIGHT? THEY SHOULD BE PAYING US TO WEAR THEM. IS IT A LIMITED EDITION OR DO YOU KEEP RUNNING OFF COPIES?
YEAH, THAT'S A GOOD POINT, DUDE. HOW DO WE EVEN KNOW IF YOU GUYS ARE REALLY EVEN FROM BROOKLYN?
DOES THAT ANSWER YOUR FRIGGIN' QUESTION?
I GOT'CHER BROOKLYN RIGHT HERE!
GUYS, EASY ON THE ARMS, WILLYA?

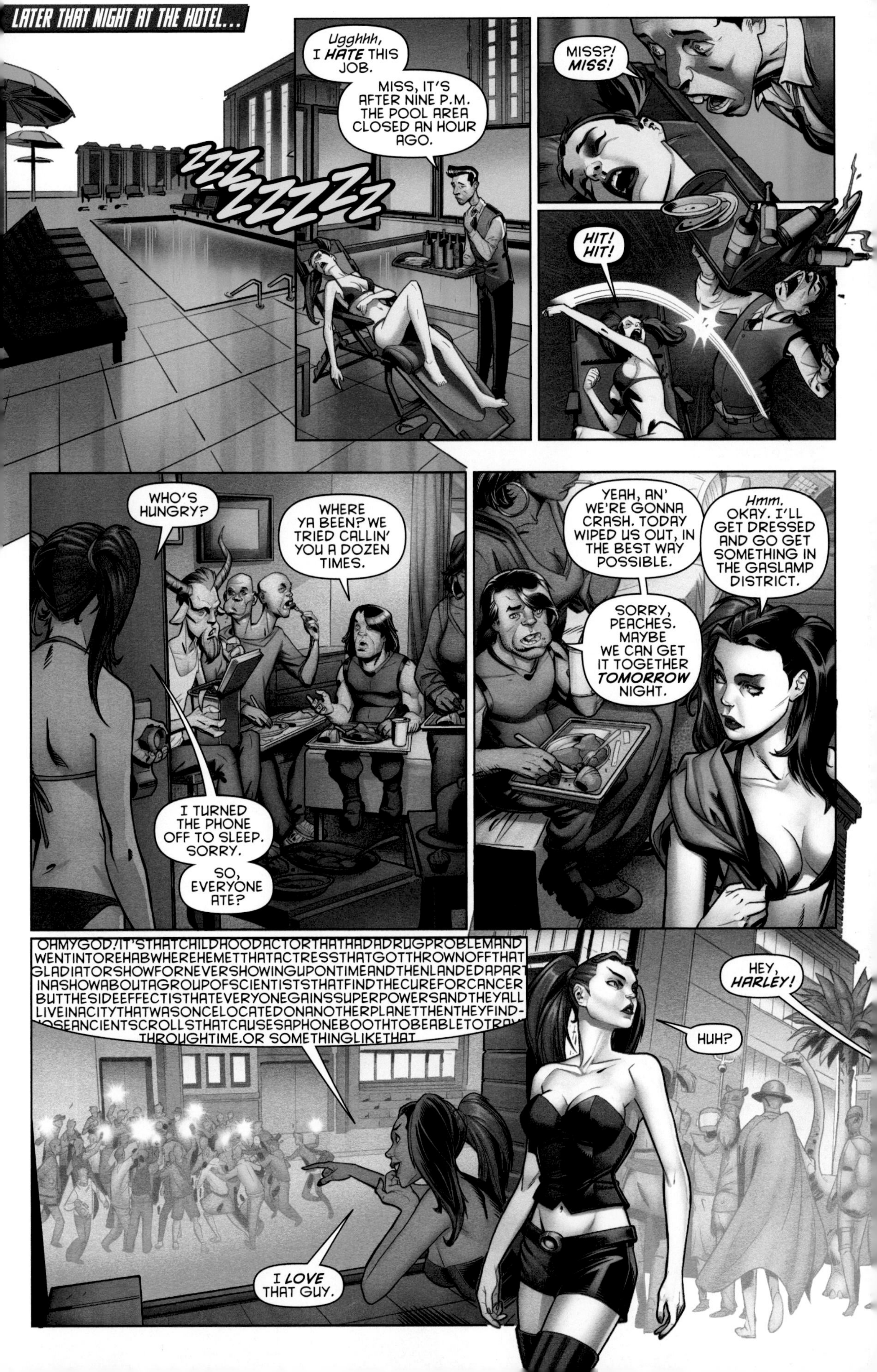
LATER THAT NIGHT AT THE HOTEL...
Ugghhh, I HATE THIS JOB.
MISS, IT'S AFTER NINE P.M. THE POOL AREA CLOSED AN HOUR AGO.
ZZZZZZZZZ
MISS?! MISS!
HIT! HIT!
WHO'S HUNGRY?
WHERE YA BEEN? WE TRIED CALLIN' YOU A DOZEN TIMES.
I TURNED THE PHONE OFF TO SLEEP. SORRY.
SO, EVERYONE ATE?
YEAH, AN' WE'RE GONNA CRASH. TODAY WIPED US OUT, IN THE BEST WAY POSSIBLE.
SORRY, PEACHES. MAYBE WE CAN GET IT TOGETHER TOMORROW NIGHT.
Hmm. OKAY. I'LL GET DRESSED AND GO GET SOMETHING IN THE GASLAMP DISTRICT.
OHMYGOD! IT'STHATCHILDHOODACTORTHATHADADRUGPROBLEMAND WENTINTOREHABWHEREHEMETTHATACTRESSTHATGOTTHROWNOFFTHAT GLADIATORSHOWFORNEVERSHOWINGUPONTIMEANDTHENLANDEDAPART INASHOWABOUTAGROUPOFSCIENTISTSTHATFINDTHECUREFORCANCER BUTTHESIDEEFFECTISTHATEVERYONEGAINSSUPERPOWERSANDTHEYALL LIVEINACITYTHATWASONCELOCATEDONANOTHERPLANETTHENTHEYFIND- OSEANCIENTSCROLLSTHATCAUSESAPHONEBOOTHTOBEABLETOTRA THROUGHTIME.OR SOMETHINGLIKETHAT
HEY, HARLEY!
HUH?
I LOVE THAT GUY.

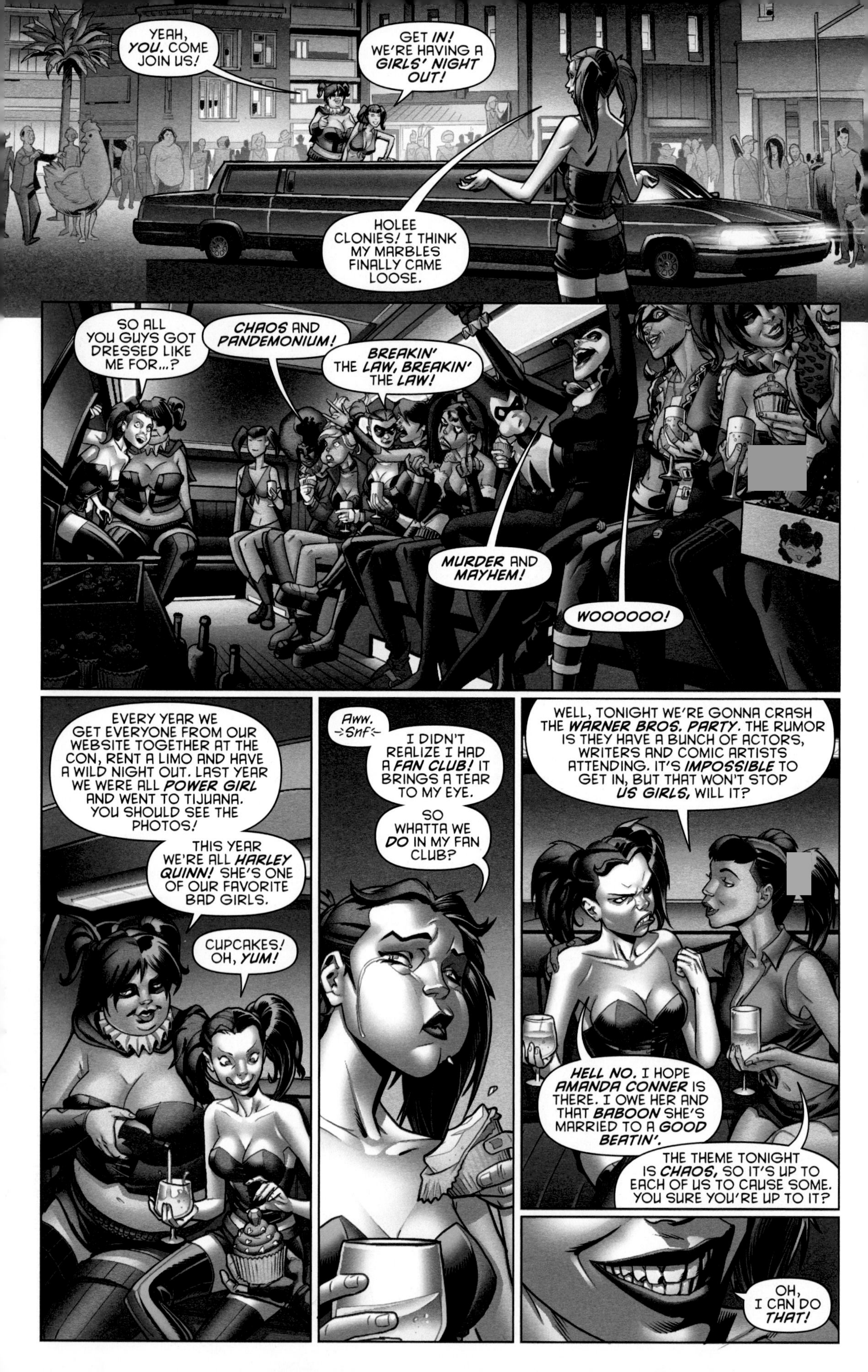
YEAH, YOU. COME JOIN US!
GET IN! WE'RE HAVING A GIRLS' NIGHT OUT!
HOLEE CLONIES! I THINK MY MARBLES FINALLY CAME LOOSE.
SO ALL YOU GUYS GOT DRESSED LIKE ME FOR...?
CHAOS AND PANDEMONIUM!
BREAKIN' THE LAW, BREAKIN' THE LAW!
MURDER AND MAYHEM!
WOOOOOO!
EVERY YEAR WE GET EVERYONE FROM OUR WEBSITE TOGETHER AT THE CON, RENT A LIMO AND HAVE A WILD NIGHT OUT. LAST YEAR WE WERE ALL POWER GIRL AND WENT TO TIJUANA. YOU SHOULD SEE THE PHOTOS!
THIS YEAR WE'RE ALL HARLEY QUINN! SHE'S ONE OF OUR FAVORITE BAD GIRLS.
CUPCAKES! OH, YUM!
Aww. -Snf-
I DIDN'T REALIZE I HAD A FAN CLUB! IT BRINGS A TEAR TO MY EYE.
SO WHATTA WE DO IN MY FAN CLUB?
WELL, TONIGHT WE'RE GONNA CRASH THE WARNER BROS. PARTY. THE RUMOR IS THEY HAVE A BUNCH OF ACTORS, WRITERS AND COMIC ARTISTS ATTENDING. IT'S IMPOSSIBLE TO GET IN, BUT THAT WON'T STOP US GIRLS, WILL IT?
HELL NO. I HOPE AMANDA CONNER IS THERE. I OWE HER AND THAT BABOON SHE'S MARRIED TO A GOOD BEATIN'.
THE THEME TONIGHT IS CHAOS, SO IT'S UP TO EACH OF US TO CAUSE SOME. YOU SURE YOU'RE UP TO IT?
OH, I CAN DO THAT!

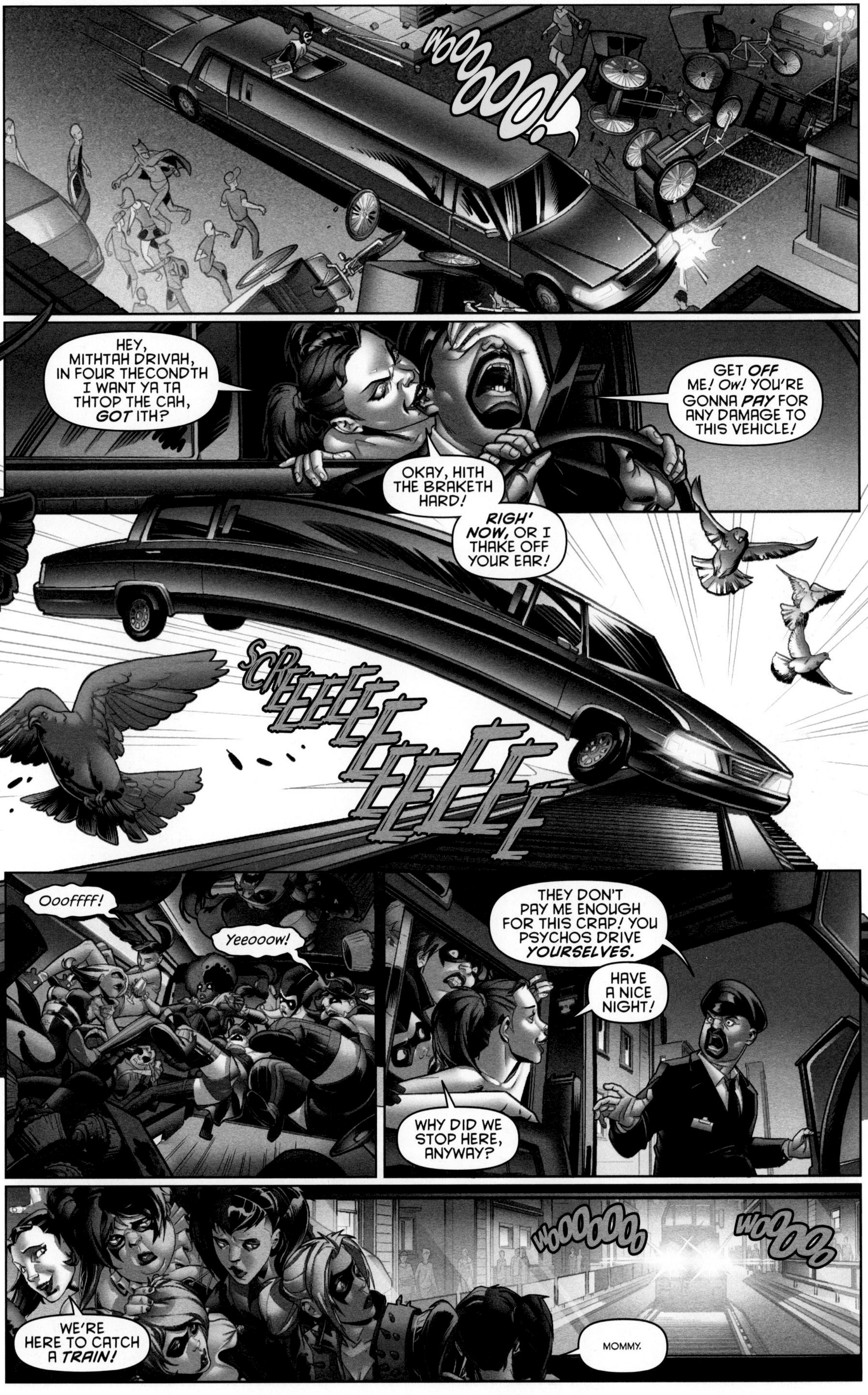

WOOOOOO!
HEY, MITHTAH DRIVAH, IN FOUR THECONDTH I WANT YA TA THTOP THE CAH, GOT ITH?
GET OFF ME! Ow! YOU'RE GONNA PAY FOR ANY DAMAGE TO THIS VEHICLE!
OKAY, HITH THE BRAKETH HARD!
RIGH' NOW, OR I THAKE OFF YOUR EAR!
SCREEEEEEEEEEEEEEEE
Oooffff!
Yeeooow!
THEY DON'T PAY ME ENOUGH FOR THIS CRAP! YOU PSYCHOS DRIVE YOURSELVES.
HAVE A NICE NIGHT!
WHY DID WE STOP HERE, ANYWAY?
WE'RE HERE TO CATCH A TRAIN!
WOOOOOO
WOOOOO
MOMMY.

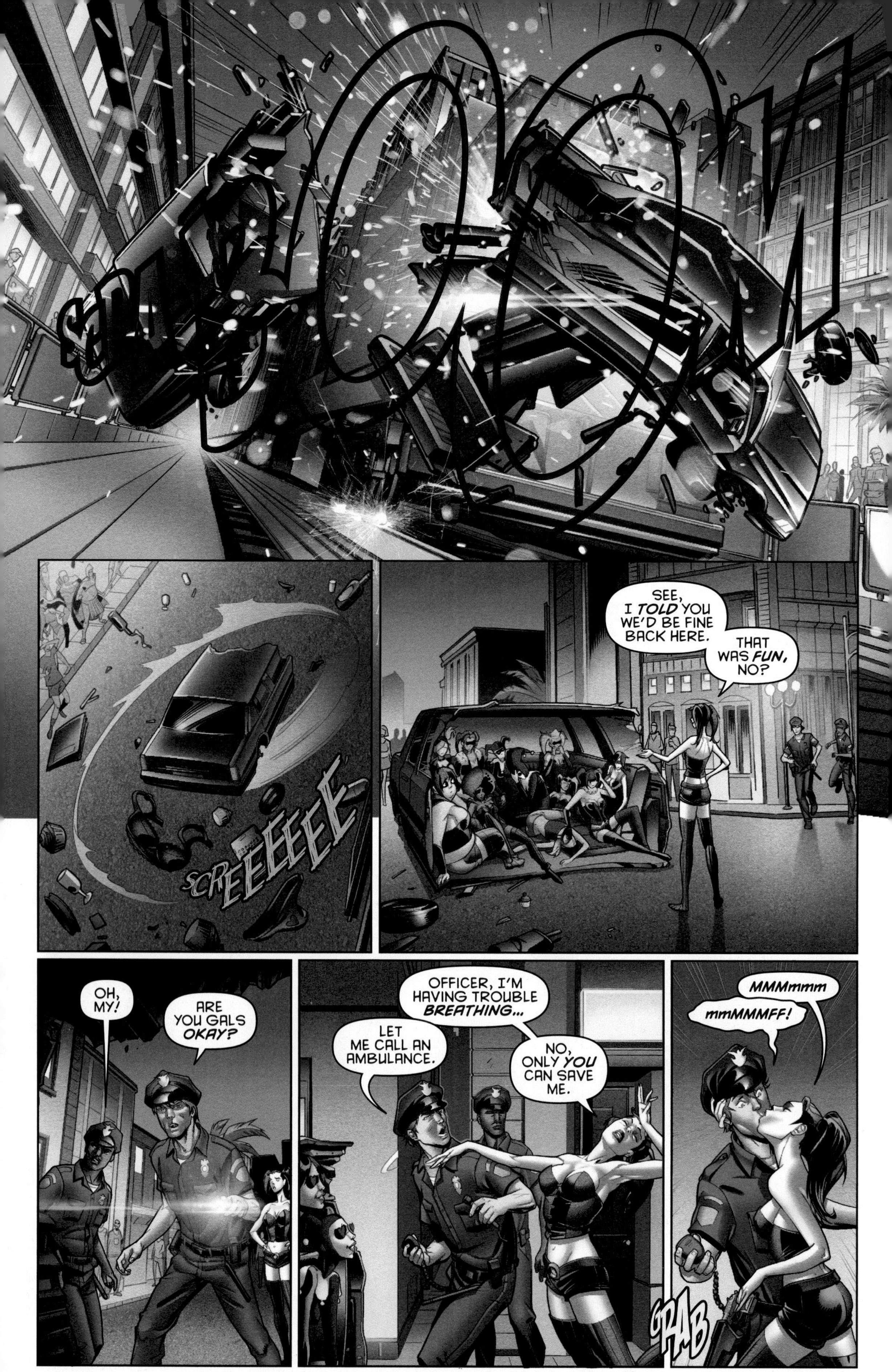

SCREEEEEEE
SEE, I TOLD YOU WE'D BE FINE BACK HERE.
THAT WAS FUN, NO?
OH, MY!
ARE YOU GALS OKAY?
OFFICER, I'M HAVING TROUBLE BREATHING...
LET ME CALL AN AMBULANCE.
NO, ONLY YOU CAN SAVE ME.
GRAB
MMMmmm
mmMMMFF!

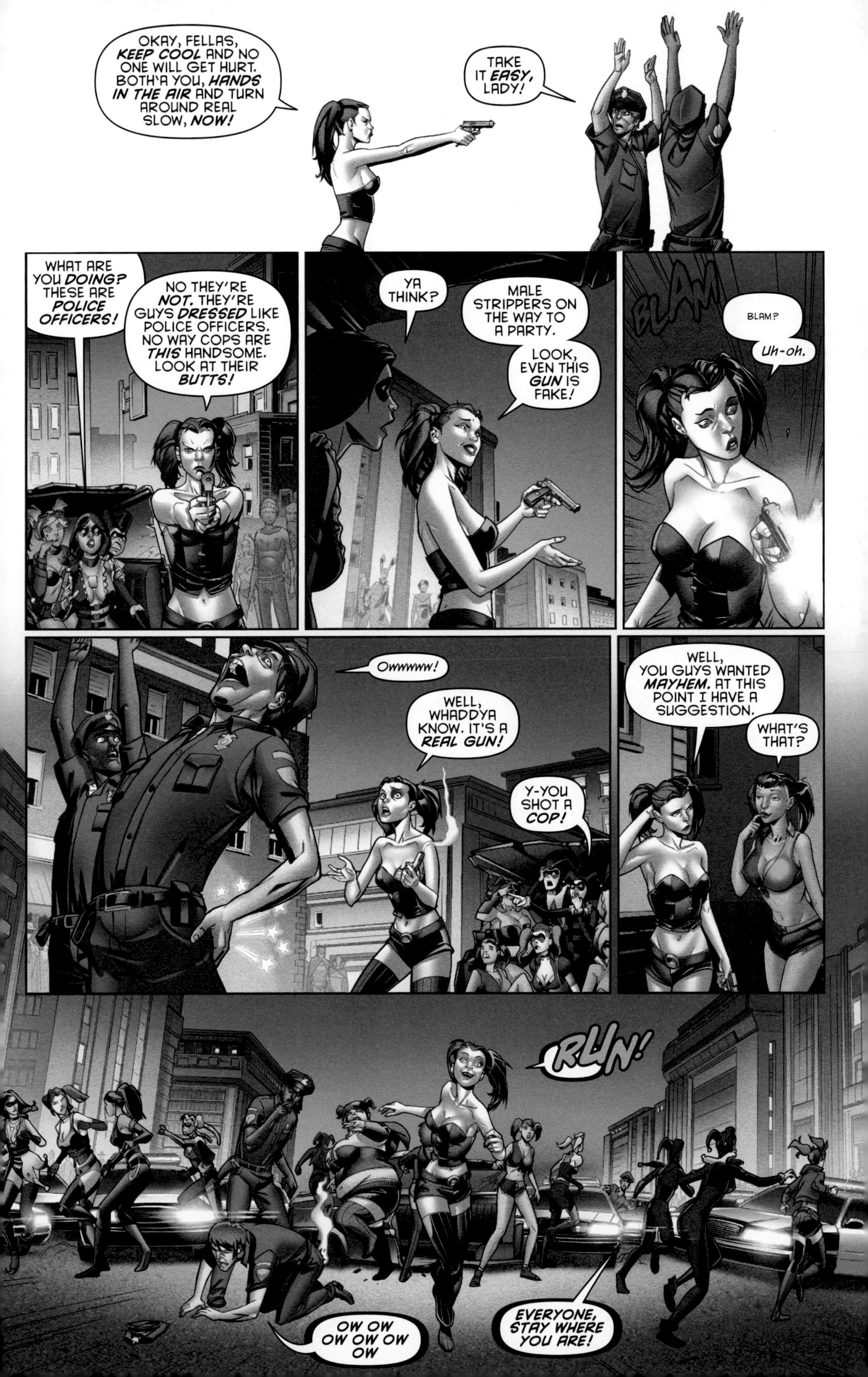
OKAY, FELLAS, KEEP COOL AND NO ONE WILL GET HURT. BOTH'A YOU, HANDS IN THE AIR AND TURN AROUND REAL SLOW, NOW!
TAKE IT EASY, LADY!
WHAT ARE YOU DOING? THESE ARE POLICE OFFICERS!
NO THEY'RE NOT. THEY'RE GUYS DRESSED LIKE POLICE OFFICERS. NO WAY COPS ARE THIS HANDSOME. LOOK AT THEIR BUTTS!
YA THINK?
MALE STRIPPERS ON THE WAY TO A PARTY.
LOOK, EVEN THIS GUN IS FAKE!
BLAM
BLAM?
Uh-oh.
Owwwww!
WELL, WHADDYA KNOW. IT'S A REAL GUN!
Y-YOU SHOT A COP!
WELL, YOU GUYS WANTED MAYHEM. AT THIS POINT I HAVE A SUGGESTION.
WHAT'S THAT?
RUN!
OW OW OW OW OW OW
EVERYONE, STAY WHERE YOU ARE!

DAY FOUR. FRIDAY. 4 A.M.

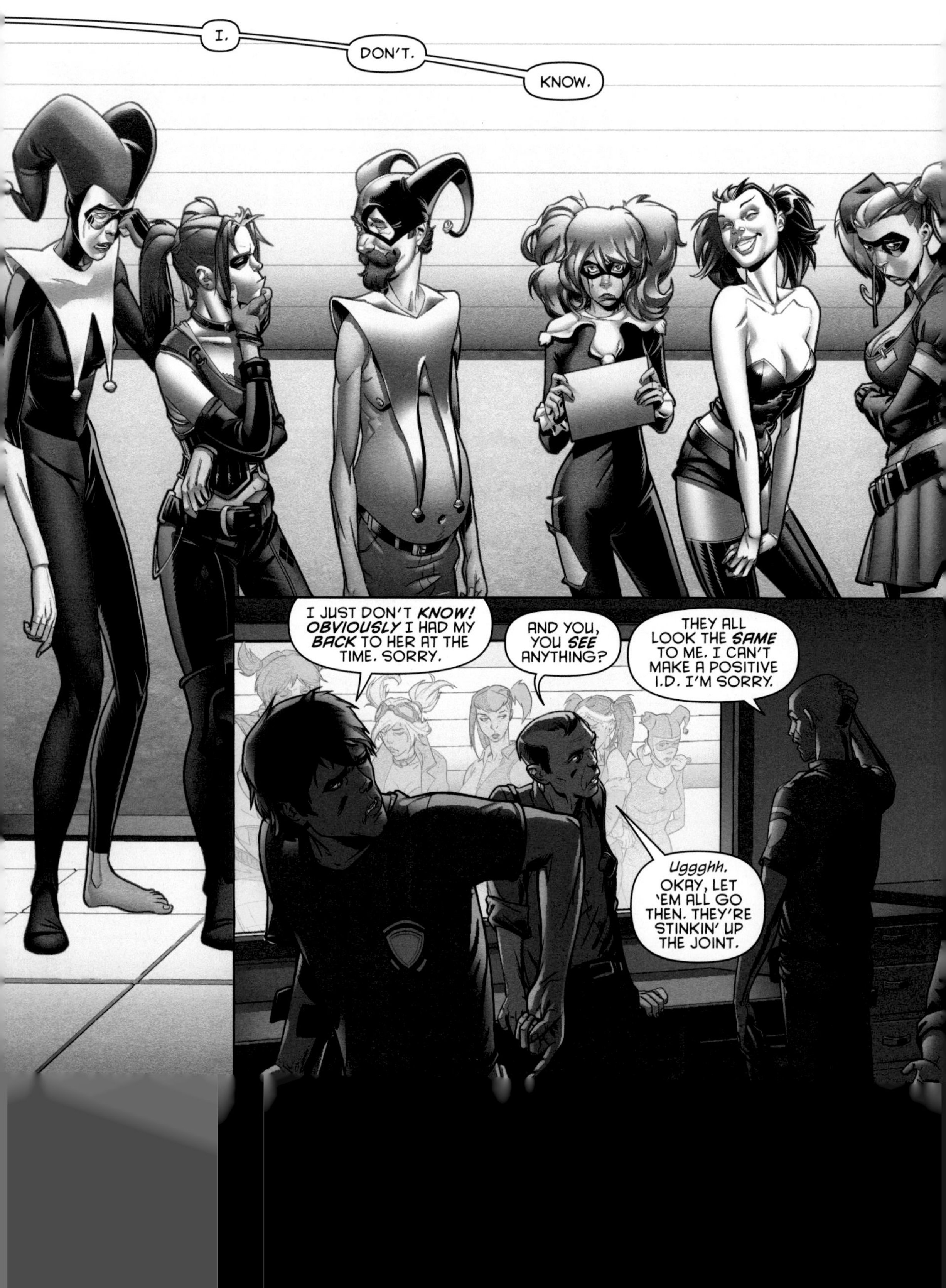
I.
DON'T.
KNOW.
I JUST DON'T KNOW! OBVIOUSLY I HAD MY BACK TO HER AT THE TIME. SORRY.
AND YOU, YOU SEE ANYTHING?
THEY ALL LOOK THE SAME TO ME. I CAN'T MAKE A POSITIVE I.D. I'M SORRY.
Uggghh. OKAY, LET 'EM ALL GO THEN. THEY'RE STINKIN' UP THE JOINT.

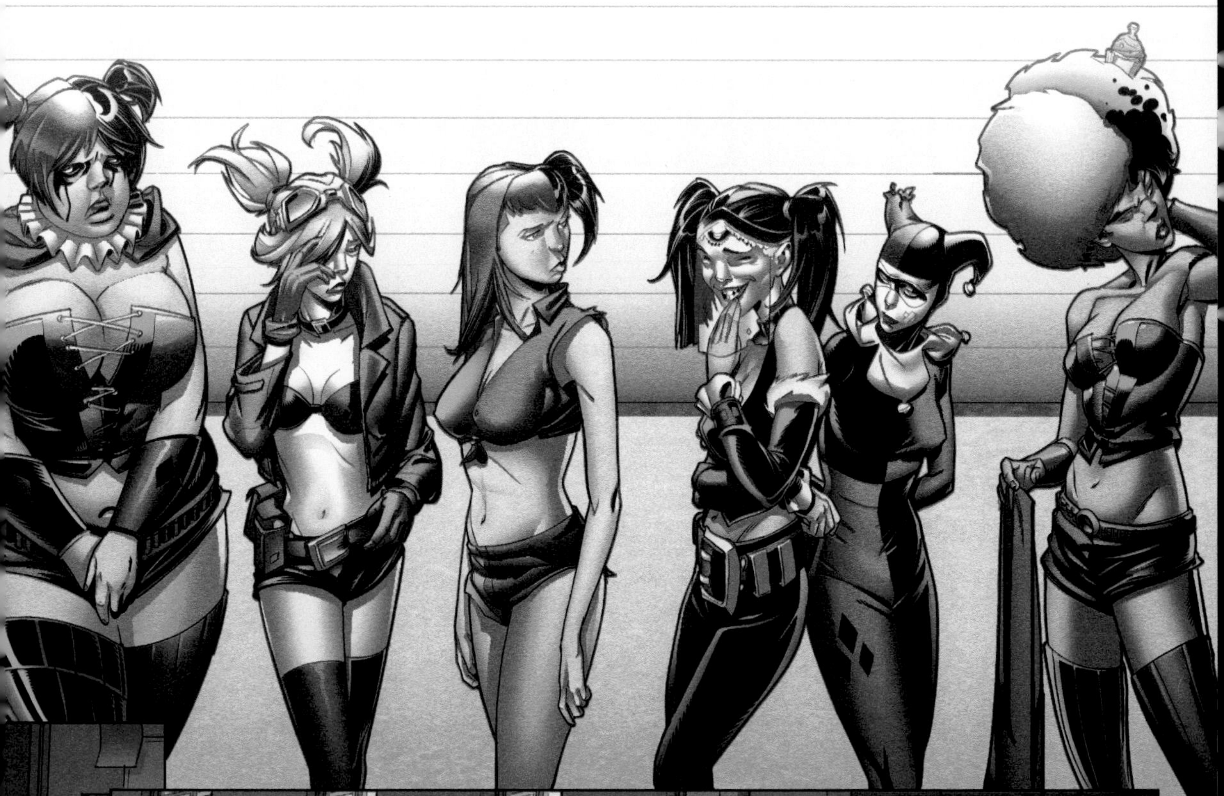

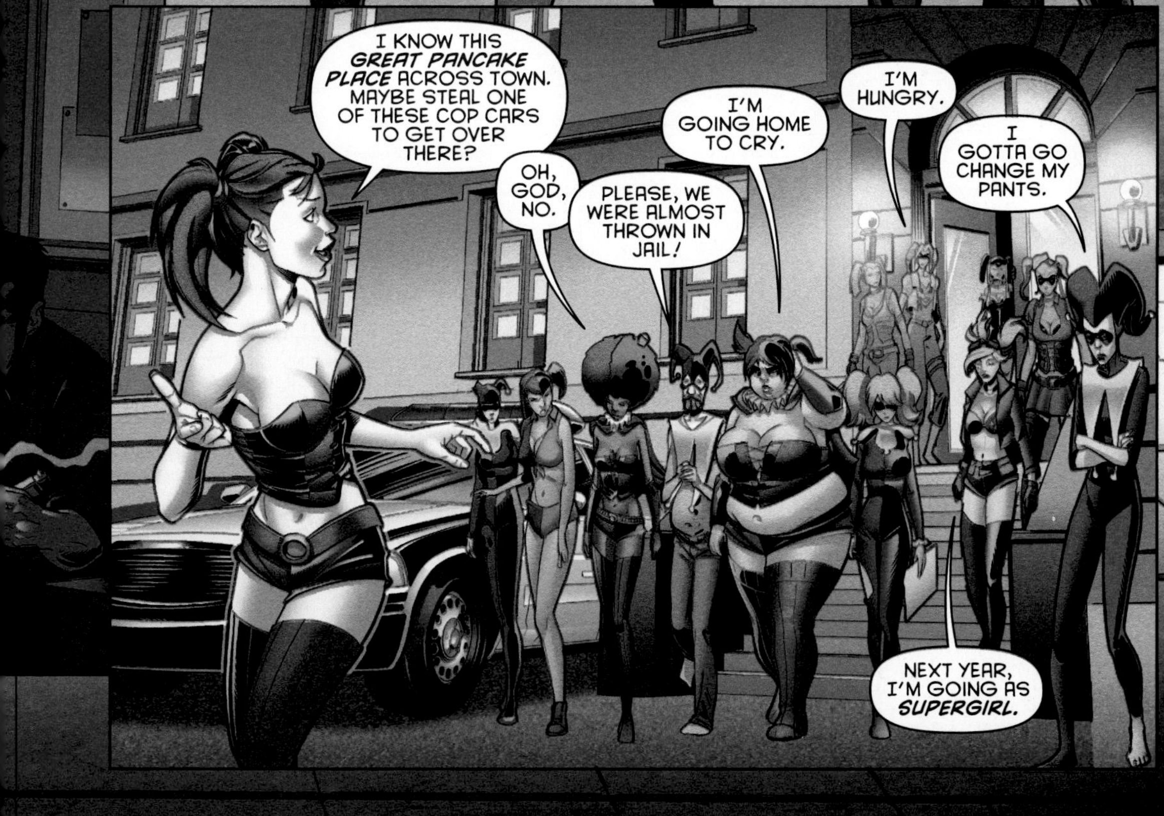
I KNOW THIS GREAT PANCAKE PLACE ACROSS TOWN. MAYBE STEAL ONE OF THESE COP CARS TO GET OVER THERE?
OH, GOD, NO.
PLEASE, WE WERE ALMOST THROWN IN JAIL!
I'M GOING HOME TO CRY.
I'M HUNGRY.
I GOTTA GO CHANGE MY PANTS.
NEXT YEAR, I'M GOING AS SUPERGIRL.

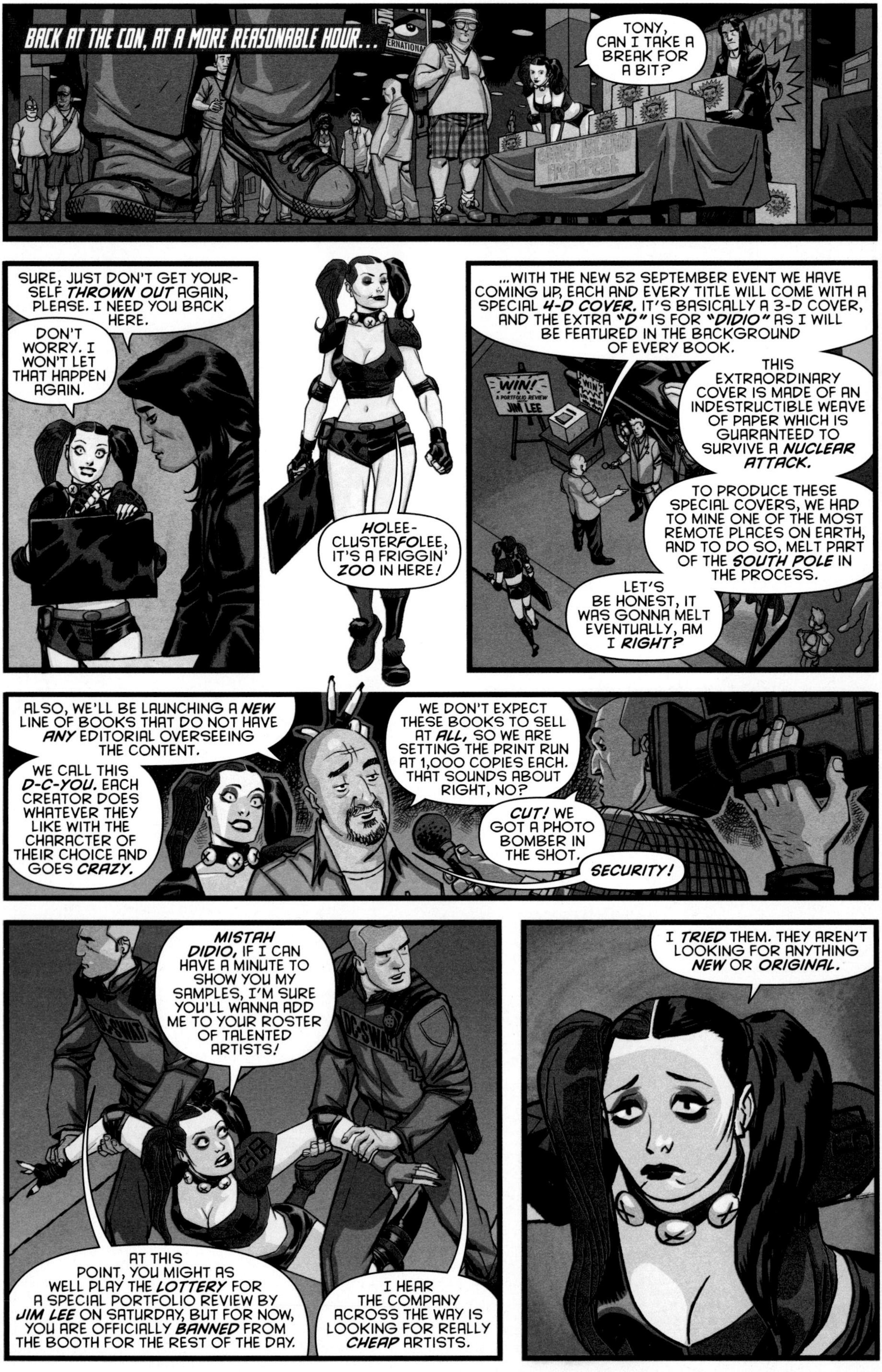
BACK AT THE CON, AT A MORE REASONABLE HOUR...
TONY, CAN I TAKE A BREAK FOR A BIT?
SURE, JUST DON'T GET YOURSELF THROWN OUT AGAIN, PLEASE. I NEED YOU BACK HERE.
DON'T WORRY. I WON'T LET THAT HAPPEN AGAIN.
HOLEE-CLUSTERFOLEE, IT'S A FRIGGIN' ZOO IN HERE!
...WITH THE NEW 52 SEPTEMBER EVENT WE HAVE COMING UP, EACH AND EVERY TITLE WILL COME WITH A SPECIAL 4-D COVER. IT'S BASICALLY A 3-D COVER, AND THE EXTRA "D" IS FOR "DIDIO" AS I WILL BE FEATURED IN THE BACKGROUND OF EVERY BOOK.
WIN!
JIM LEE
THIS EXTRAORDINARY COVER IS MADE OF AN INDESTRUCTIBLE WEAVE OF PAPER WHICH IS GUARANTEED TO SURVIVE A NUCLEAR ATTACK.
TO PRODUCE THESE SPECIAL COVERS, WE HAD TO MINE ONE OF THE MOST REMOTE PLACES ON EARTH, AND TO DO SO, MELT PART OF THE SOUTH POLE IN THE PROCESS.
LET'S BE HONEST, IT WAS GONNA MELT EVENTUALLY, AM I RIGHT?
ALSO, WE'LL BE LAUNCHING A NEW LINE OF BOOKS THAT DO NOT HAVE ANY EDITORIAL OVERSEEING THE CONTENT.
WE CALL THIS D-C-YOU. EACH CREATOR DOES WHATEVER THEY LIKE WITH THE CHARACTER OF THEIR CHOICE AND GOES CRAZY.
WE DON'T EXPECT THESE BOOKS TO SELL AT ALL, SO WE ARE SETTING THE PRINT RUN AT 1,000 COPIES EACH. THAT SOUNDS ABOUT RIGHT, NO?
CUT! WE GOT A PHOTO BOMBER IN THE SHOT.
SECURITY!
MISTAH DIDIO, IF I CAN HAVE A MINUTE TO SHOW YOU MY SAMPLES, I'M SURE YOU'LL WANNA ADD ME TO YOUR ROSTER OF TALENTED ARTISTS!
AT THIS POINT, YOU MIGHT AS WELL PLAY THE LOTTERY FOR A SPECIAL PORTFOLIO REVIEW BY JIM LEE ON SATURDAY, BUT FOR NOW, YOU ARE OFFICIALLY BANNED FROM THE BOOTH FOR THE REST OF THE DAY.
I HEAR THE COMPANY ACROSS THE WAY IS LOOKING FOR REALLY CHEAP ARTISTS.
I TRIED THEM. THEY AREN'T LOOKING FOR ANYTHING NEW OR ORIGINAL.

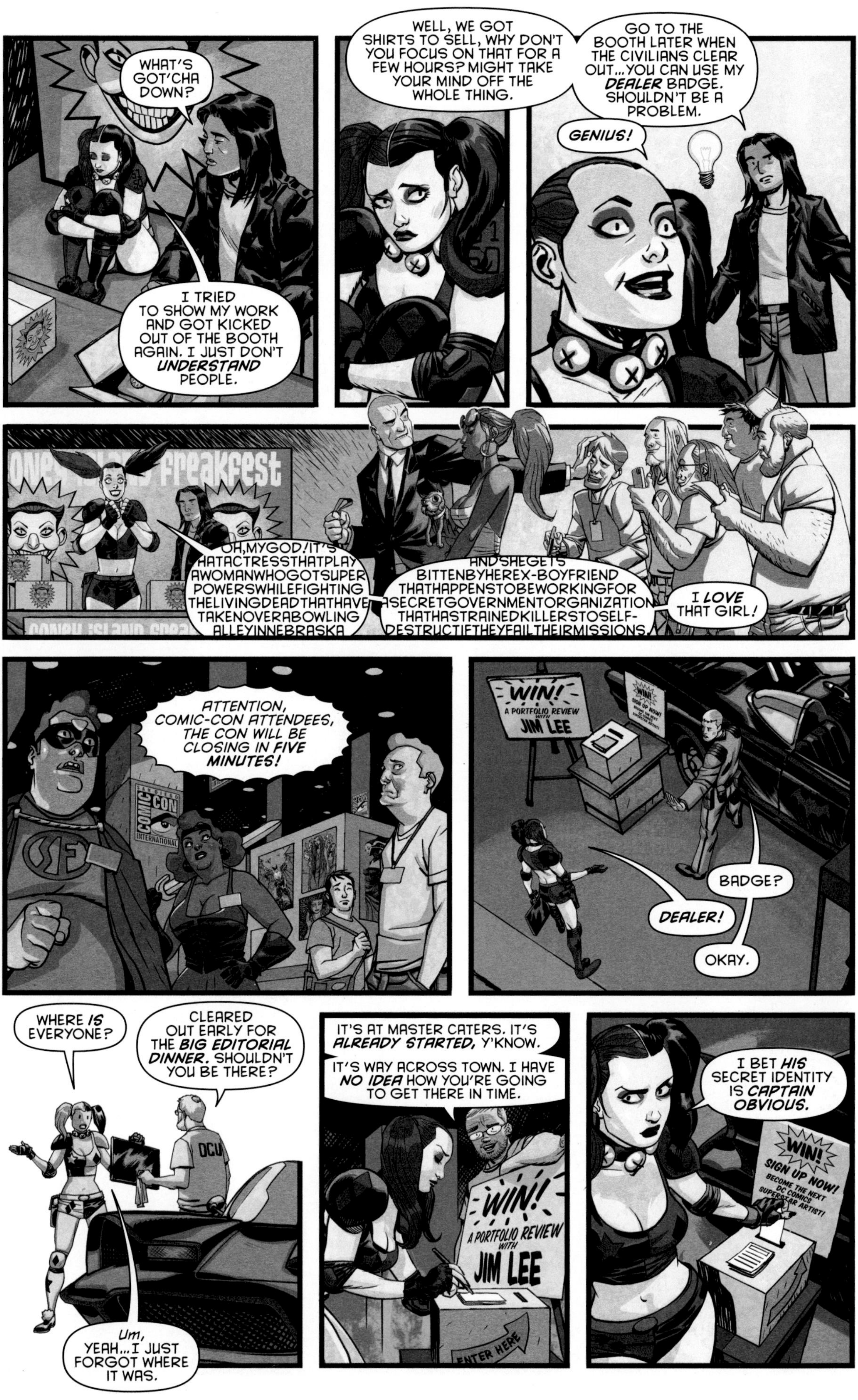
WHAT'S GOT'CHA DOWN?
I TRIED TO SHOW MY WORK AND GOT KICKED OUT OF THE BOOTH AGAIN. I JUST DON'T UNDERSTAND PEOPLE.
WELL, WE GOT SHIRTS TO SELL, WHY DON'T YOU FOCUS ON THAT FOR A FEW HOURS? MIGHT TAKE YOUR MIND OFF THE WHOLE THING.
GO TO THE BOOTH LATER WHEN THE CIVILIANS CLEAR OUT... YOU CAN USE MY DEALER BADGE. SHOULDN'T BE A PROBLEM.
GENIUS!
OH,MYGOD!IT'S HATACTRESSTHATPLAY AWOMANWHOGOTSUPER POWERSWHILEFIGHTING THELIVINGDEADTHATHAVE TAKENOVERABOWLING ALLEYINNEBRASKA
ANDSHEGETS BITTENBYHEREX-BOYFRIEND THATHAPPENSTOBEWORKINGFOR ASECRETGOVERNMENTORGANIZATION THATHASTRAINEDKILLERSTOSELF-DESTRUCTIFTHEYFAILTHEIRMISSIONS.
I LOVE THAT GIRL!
ATTENTION, COMIC-CON ATTENDEES, THE CON WILL BE CLOSING IN FIVE MINUTES!
WIN! A PORTFOLIO REVIEW WITH JIM LEE
BADGE?
DEALER!
OKAY.
WHERE IS EVERYONE?
CLEARED OUT EARLY FOR THE BIG EDITORIAL DINNER. SHOULDN'T YOU BE THERE?
UM, YEAH... I JUST FORGOT WHERE IT WAS.
IT'S AT MASTER CATERS. IT'S ALREADY STARTED, Y'KNOW.
IT'S WAY ACROSS TOWN. I HAVE NO IDEA HOW YOU'RE GOING TO GET THERE IN TIME.
WIN! A PORTFOLIO REVIEW WITH JIM LEE
ENTER HERE
I BET HIS SECRET IDENTITY IS CAPTAIN OBVIOUS.
WIN! SIGN UP NOW! BECOME THE NEXT DC COMICS SUPERSTAR ARTIST!

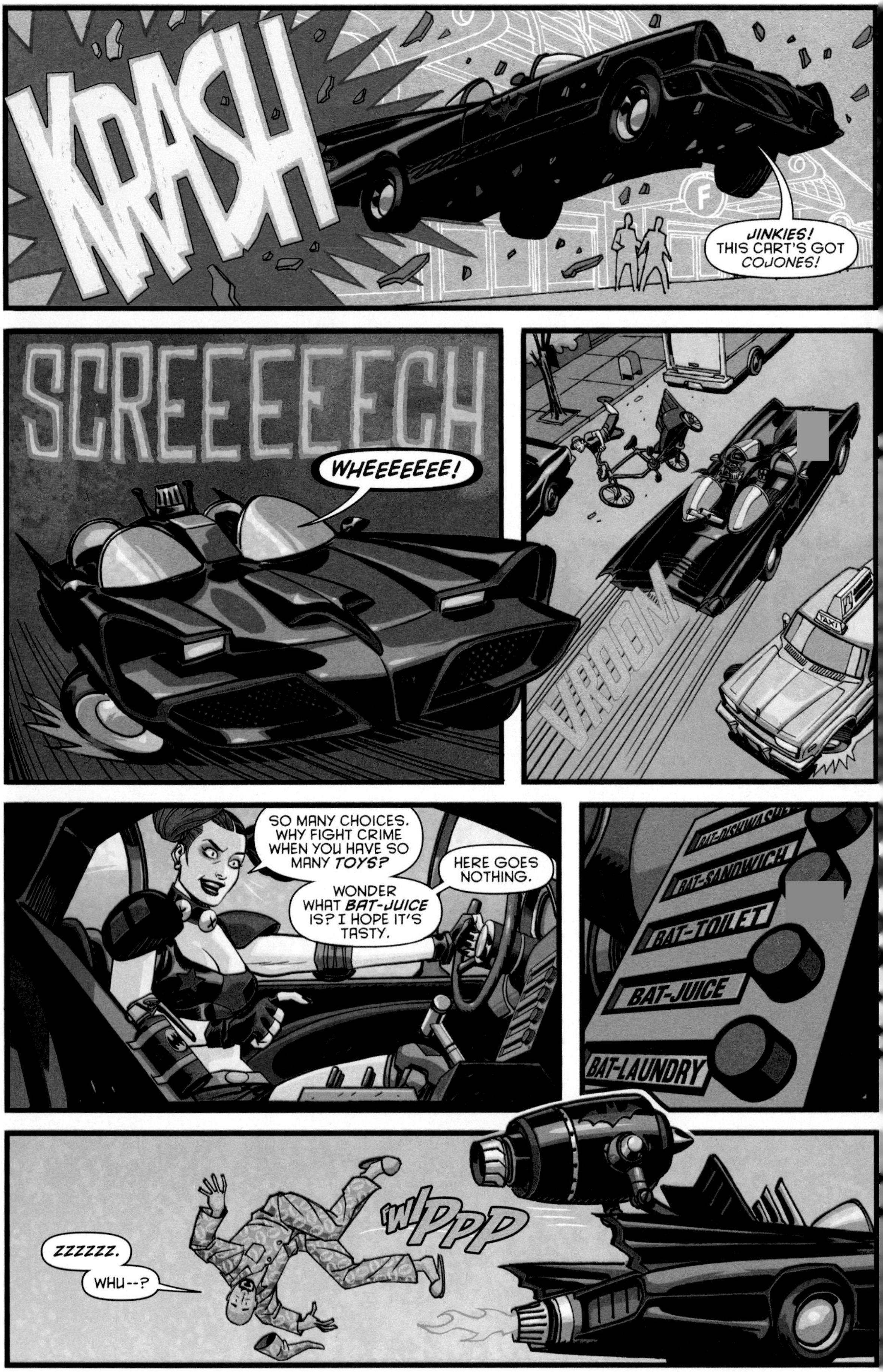
KRASH
JINKIES! THIS CART'S GOT COJONES!
SCREEEEECH
WHEEEEEEE!
VROOM
SO MANY CHOICES. WHY FIGHT CRIME WHEN YOU HAVE SO MANY TOYS?
WONDER WHAT BAT-JUICE IS? I HOPE IT'S TASTY.
HERE GOES NOTHING.
BAT-SANDWICH
BAT-TOILET
BAT-JUICE
BAT-LAUNDRY
'WIPPP
ZZZZZZ.
WHU--?

Ow.

A FIFTEEN-MINUTE NAP.

ALL I WANTED WAS A FREAKIN' FIFTEEN-MINUTE *NAP*.

Ow.

FOOOOOSH

THERE IT IS.

WAIT.

HOW THE HELL DO I *STOP THIS THING?*

BOOM

OOOOHH! COMIC BOOK CHARACTERS! HOW COOL.

ANYONE KNOW WHERE THE *DC EDITORIAL DINNER* IS?

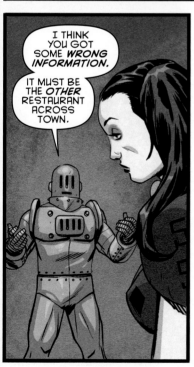

I THINK YOU GOT SOME *WRONG INFORMATION*.

IT MUST BE THE *OTHER* RESTAURANT ACROSS TOWN.

Uggg, I'LL NEVER MAKE IT. THIS SUCKS.

→Whew←

I THINK SHE BOUGHT IT, *FLETCH.*

I SURE HOPE SO, *GEOFF.*

DAY FIVE: SATURDAY.

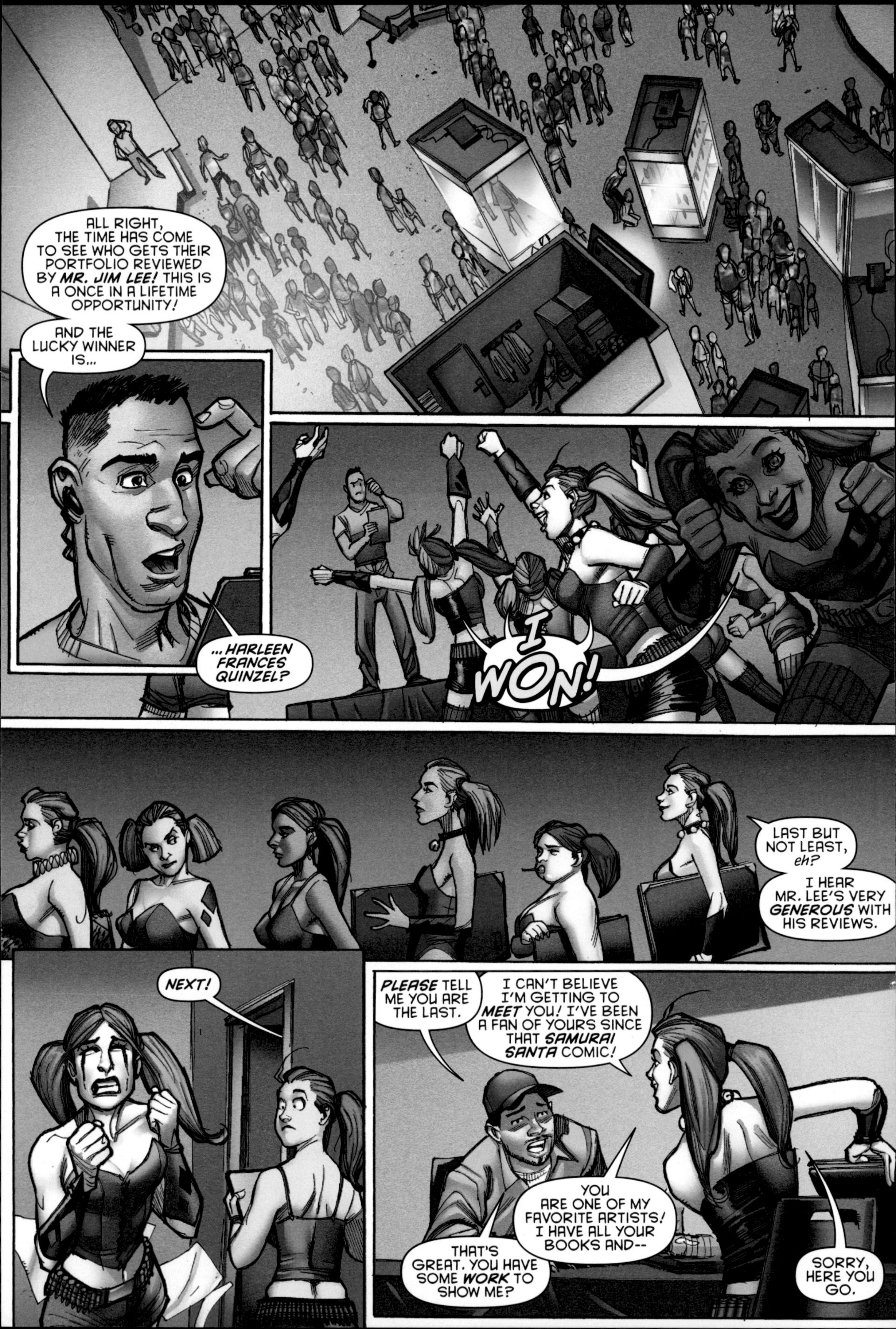

ALL RIGHT, THE TIME HAS COME TO SEE WHO GETS THEIR PORTFOLIO REVIEWED BY MR. JIM LEE! THIS IS A ONCE IN A LIFETIME OPPORTUNITY!
AND THE LUCKY WINNER IS...
...HARLEEN FRANCES QUINZEL?
I WON!
LAST BUT NOT LEAST, eh?
I HEAR MR. LEE'S VERY GENEROUS WITH HIS REVIEWS.
NEXT!
PLEASE TELL ME YOU ARE THE LAST.
I CAN'T BELIEVE I'M GETTING TO MEET YOU! I'VE BEEN A FAN OF YOURS SINCE THAT SAMURAI SANTA COMIC!
YOU ARE ONE OF MY FAVORITE ARTISTS! I HAVE ALL YOUR BOOKS AND--
THAT'S GREAT. YOU HAVE SOME WORK TO SHOW ME?
SORRY, HERE YOU GO.

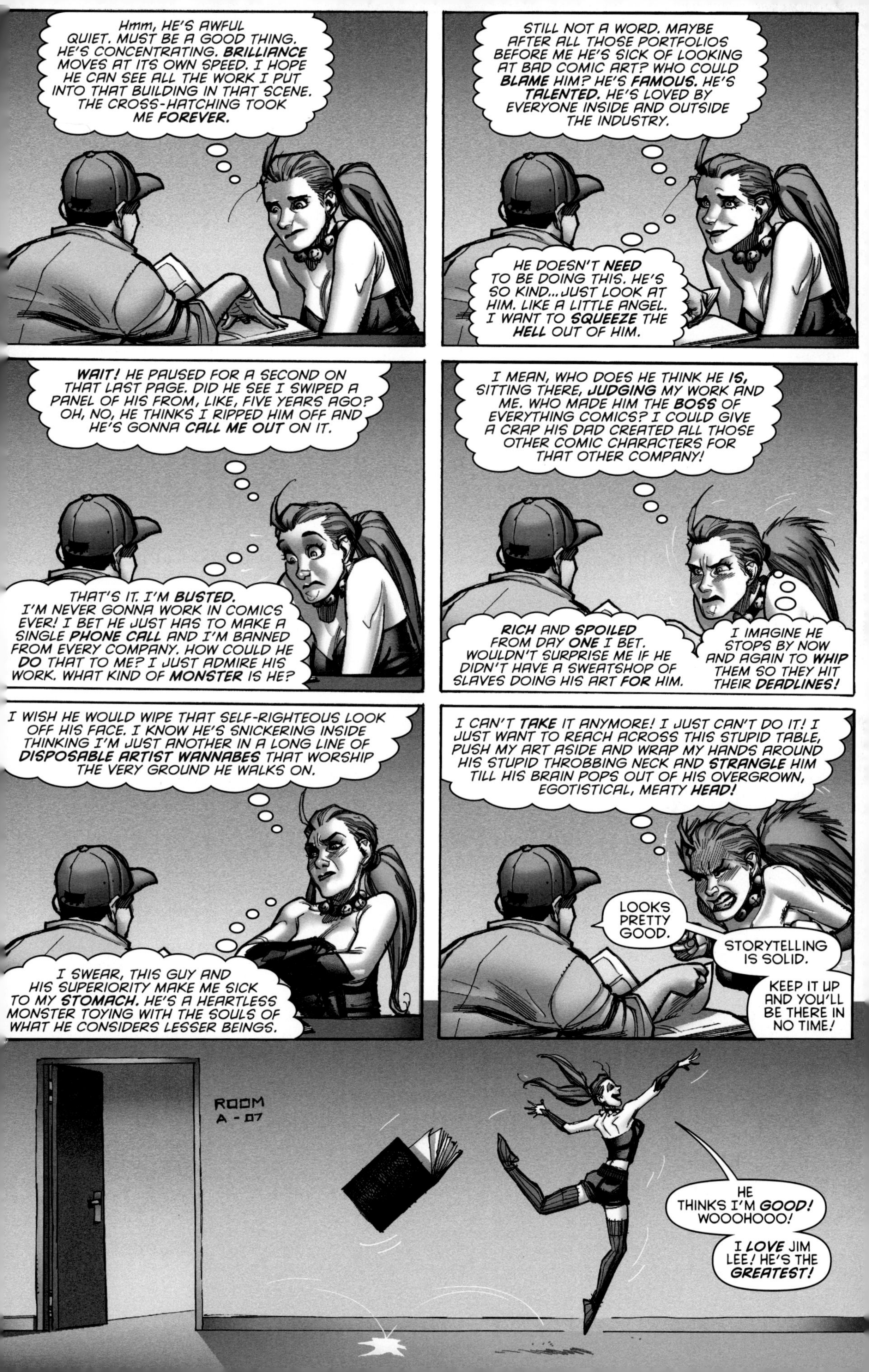
Hmm, HE'S AWFUL QUIET. MUST BE A GOOD THING. HE'S CONCENTRATING. BRILLIANCE MOVES AT ITS OWN SPEED. I HOPE HE CAN SEE ALL THE WORK I PUT INTO THAT BUILDING IN THAT SCENE. THE CROSS-HATCHING TOOK ME FOREVER.
STILL NOT A WORD. MAYBE AFTER ALL THOSE PORTFOLIOS BEFORE ME HE'S SICK OF LOOKING AT BAD COMIC ART? WHO COULD BLAME HIM? HE'S FAMOUS. HE'S TALENTED. HE'S LOVED BY EVERYONE INSIDE AND OUTSIDE THE INDUSTRY.
HE DOESN'T NEED TO BE DOING THIS. HE'S SO KIND... JUST LOOK AT HIM. LIKE A LITTLE ANGEL. I WANT TO SQUEEZE THE HELL OUT OF HIM.
WAIT! HE PAUSED FOR A SECOND ON THAT LAST PAGE. DID HE SEE I SWIPED A PANEL OF HIS FROM, LIKE, FIVE YEARS AGO? OH, NO, HE THINKS I RIPPED HIM OFF AND HE'S GONNA CALL ME OUT ON IT.
THAT'S IT. I'M BUSTED. I'M NEVER GONNA WORK IN COMICS EVER! I BET HE JUST HAS TO MAKE A SINGLE PHONE CALL AND I'M BANNED FROM EVERY COMPANY. HOW COULD HE DO THAT TO ME? I JUST ADMIRE HIS WORK. WHAT KIND OF MONSTER IS HE?
I MEAN, WHO DOES HE THINK HE IS, SITTING THERE, JUDGING MY WORK AND ME. WHO MADE HIM THE BOSS OF EVERYTHING COMICS? I COULD GIVE A CRAP HIS DAD CREATED ALL THOSE OTHER COMIC CHARACTERS FOR THAT OTHER COMPANY!
RICH AND SPOILED FROM DAY ONE I BET. WOULDN'T SURPRISE ME IF HE DIDN'T HAVE A SWEATSHOP OF SLAVES DOING HIS ART FOR HIM.
I IMAGINE HE STOPS BY NOW AND AGAIN TO WHIP THEM SO THEY HIT THEIR DEADLINES!
I WISH HE WOULD WIPE THAT SELF-RIGHTEOUS LOOK OFF HIS FACE. I KNOW HE'S SNICKERING INSIDE THINKING I'M JUST ANOTHER IN A LONG LINE OF DISPOSABLE ARTIST WANNABES THAT WORSHIP THE VERY GROUND HE WALKS ON.
I SWEAR, THIS GUY AND HIS SUPERIORITY MAKE ME SICK TO MY STOMACH. HE'S A HEARTLESS MONSTER TOYING WITH THE SOULS OF WHAT HE CONSIDERS LESSER BEINGS.
I CAN'T TAKE IT ANYMORE! I JUST CAN'T DO IT! I JUST WANT TO REACH ACROSS THIS STUPID TABLE, PUSH MY ART ASIDE AND WRAP MY HANDS AROUND HIS STUPID THROBBING NECK AND STRANGLE HIM TILL HIS BRAIN POPS OUT OF HIS OVERGROWN, EGOTISTICAL, MEATY HEAD!
LOOKS PRETTY GOOD.
STORYTELLING IS SOLID.
KEEP IT UP AND YOU'LL BE THERE IN NO TIME!
ROOM A - 07
HE THINKS I'M GOOD! WOOOHOOO!
I LOVE JIM LEE! HE'S THE GREATEST!

DAY SIX: SUNDAY.

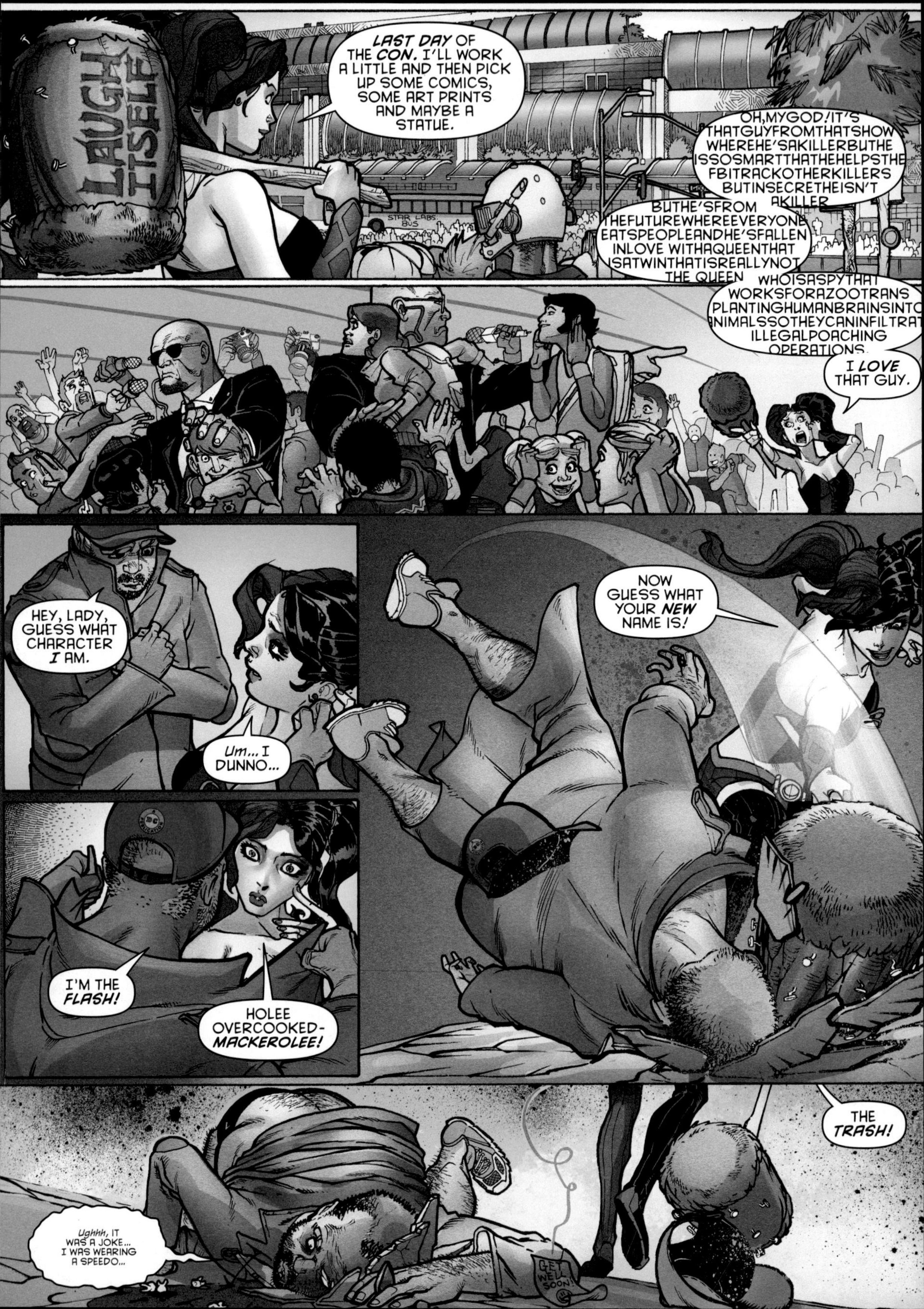

LAUGH ITSELF
LAST DAY OF THE CON. I'LL WORK A LITTLE AND THEN PICK UP SOME COMICS, SOME ART PRINTS AND MAYBE A STATUE.
STAR LABS BUS
OH,MYGOD!IT'S THATGUYFROMTHATSHOW WHEREHE'SAKILLERBUTHE ISSOSMARTTHATHEHELPSTHE FBITRACKOTHERKILLERS BUTINSECRETHEISN'T AKILLER
BUTHE'SFROM THEFUTUREWHEREEVERYONE EATSPEOPLEANDHE'SFALLEN INLOVE WITHAQUEENTHAT ISATWINTHATISREALLYNOT THE QUEEN
WHOISASPYTHAT WORKSFORAZOOTRANS PLANTINGHUMANBRAINSINTO ANIMALSSOTHEYCANINFILTRATE ILLEGALPOACHING OPERATIONS.
I LOVE THAT GUY.
HEY, LADY, GUESS WHAT CHARACTER I AM.
Um... I DUNNO...
I'M THE FLASH!
HOLEE OVERCOOKED-MACKEROLEE!
NOW GUESS WHAT YOUR NEW NAME IS!
THE TRASH!
Ughhh, IT WAS A JOKE... I WAS WEARING A SPEEDO...
GET WELL SOON!

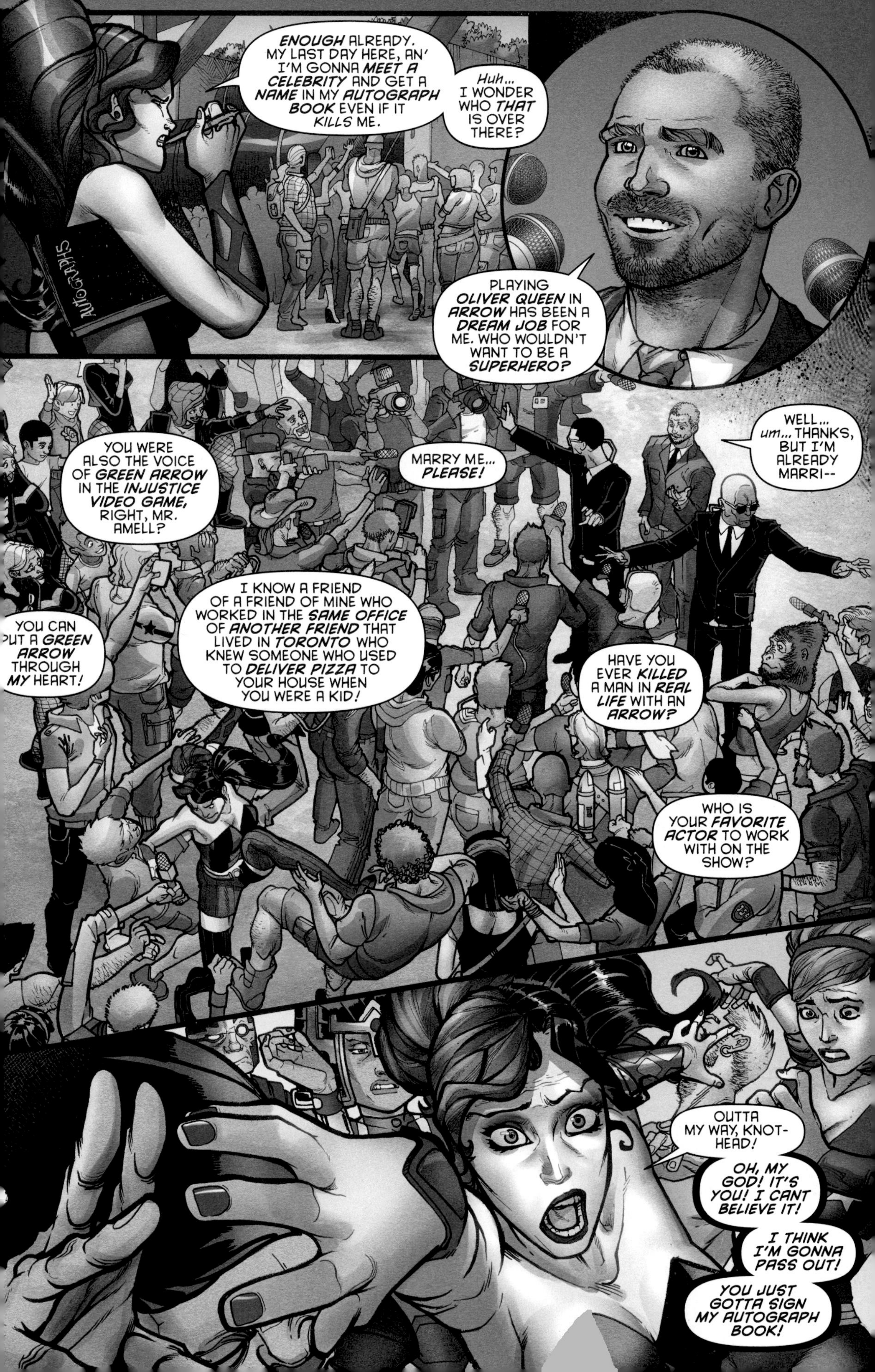
ENOUGH ALREADY. MY LAST DAY HERE, AN' I'M GONNA MEET A CELEBRITY AND GET A NAME IN MY AUTOGRAPH BOOK EVEN IF IT KILLS ME.
AUTOGRAPHS
Huh... I WONDER WHO THAT IS OVER THERE?
PLAYING OLIVER QUEEN IN ARROW HAS BEEN A DREAM JOB FOR ME. WHO WOULDN'T WANT TO BE A SUPERHERO?
YOU WERE ALSO THE VOICE OF GREEN ARROW IN THE INJUSTICE VIDEO GAME, RIGHT, MR. AMELL?
MARRY ME... PLEASE!
WELL... um... THANKS, BUT I'M ALREADY MARRI--
YOU CAN PUT A GREEN ARROW THROUGH MY HEART!
I KNOW A FRIEND OF A FRIEND OF MINE WHO WORKED IN THE SAME OFFICE OF ANOTHER FRIEND THAT LIVED IN TORONTO WHO KNEW SOMEONE WHO USED TO DELIVER PIZZA TO YOUR HOUSE WHEN YOU WERE A KID!
HAVE YOU EVER KILLED A MAN IN REAL LIFE WITH AN ARROW?
WHO IS YOUR FAVORITE ACTOR TO WORK WITH ON THE SHOW?
OUTTA MY WAY, KNOT-HEAD!
OH, MY GOD! IT'S YOU! I CANT BELIEVE IT!
I THINK I'M GONNA PASS OUT!
YOU JUST GOTTA SIGN MY AUTOGRAPH BOOK!

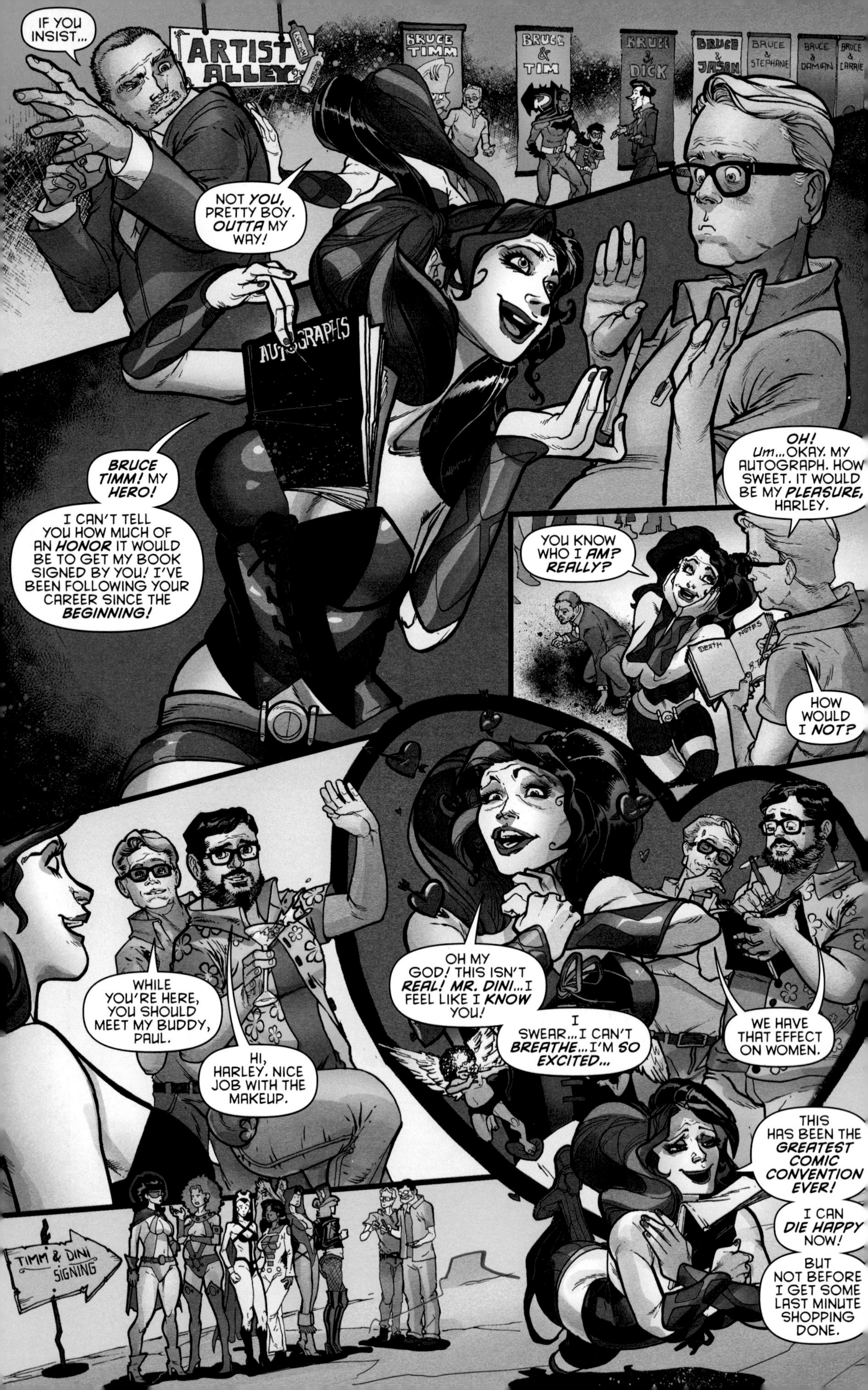
IF YOU INSIST...
ARTIST ALLEY
BRUCE TIMM
BRUCE & TIM
BRUCE & DICK
BRUCE & JASON
BRUCE & STEPHANIE
BRUCE & DAMIAN
BRUCE & CARRIE
NOT YOU, PRETTY BOY. OUTTA MY WAY!
AUTOGRAPHS
BRUCE TIMM! MY HERO!
I CAN'T TELL YOU HOW MUCH OF AN HONOR IT WOULD BE TO GET MY BOOK SIGNED BY YOU! I'VE BEEN FOLLOWING YOUR CAREER SINCE THE BEGINNING!
OH! Um...OKAY. MY AUTOGRAPH. HOW SWEET. IT WOULD BE MY PLEASURE, HARLEY.
YOU KNOW WHO I AM? REALLY?
DEATH NOTES
HOW WOULD I NOT?
WHILE YOU'RE HERE, YOU SHOULD MEET MY BUDDY, PAUL.
HI, HARLEY. NICE JOB WITH THE MAKEUP.
OH MY GOD! THIS ISN'T REAL! MR. DINI...I FEEL LIKE I KNOW YOU!
I SWEAR...I CAN'T BREATHE...I'M SO EXCITED...
WE HAVE THAT EFFECT ON WOMEN.
TIMM & DINI SIGNING
THIS HAS BEEN THE GREATEST COMIC CONVENTION EVER!
I CAN DIE HAPPY NOW!
BUT NOT BEFORE I GET SOME LAST MINUTE SHOPPING DONE.

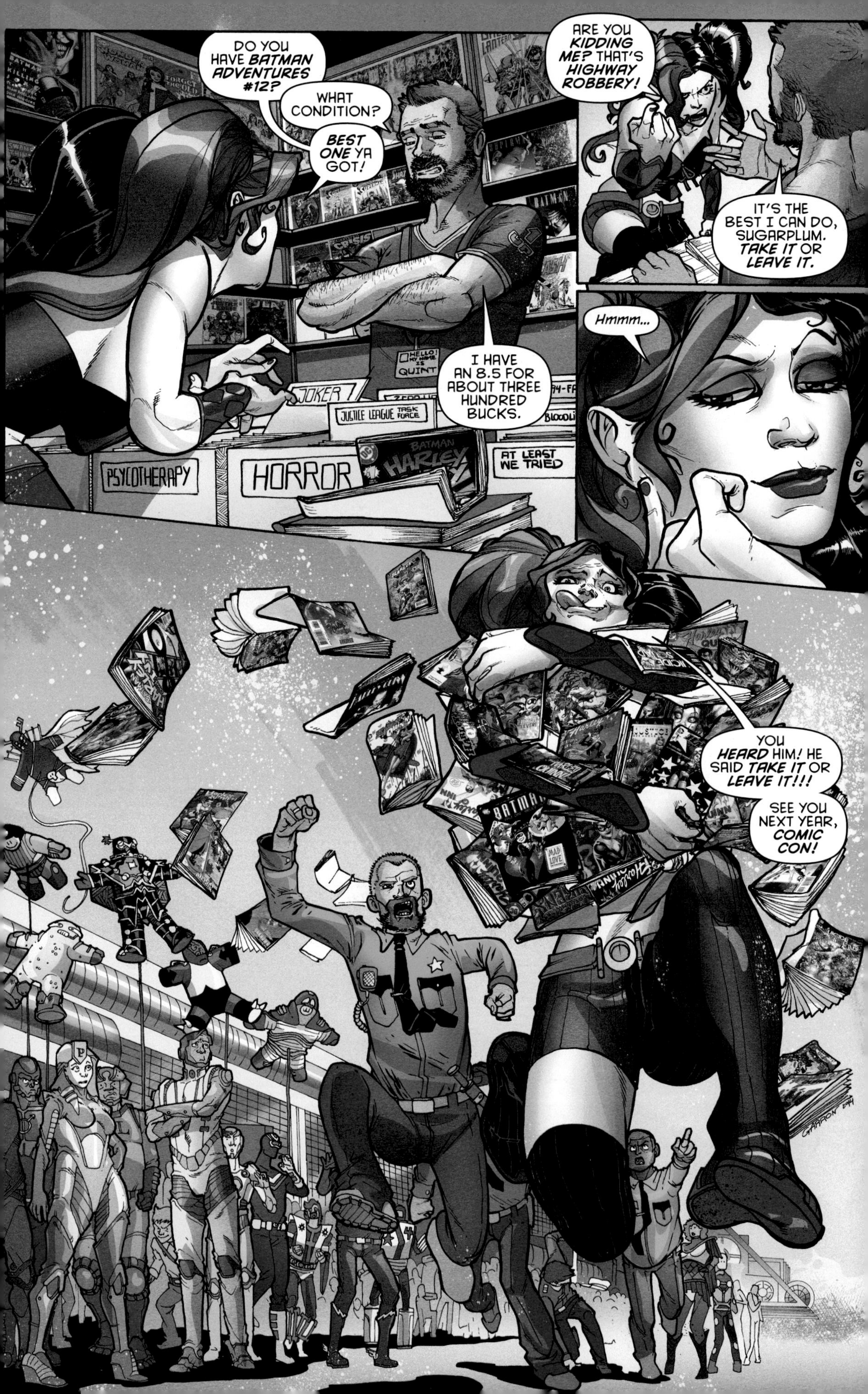
DO YOU HAVE BATMAN ADVENTURES #12?
WHAT CONDITION?
BEST ONE YA GOT!
I HAVE AN 8.5 FOR ABOUT THREE HUNDRED BUCKS.
HELLO! MY NAME IS QUINT
JOKER
JUSTICE LEAGUE TASK FORCE
PSYCOTHERAPY
HORROR
AT LEAST WE TRIED
ARE YOU KIDDING ME? THAT'S HIGHWAY ROBBERY!
IT'S THE BEST I CAN DO, SUGARPLUM. TAKE IT OR LEAVE IT.
Hmmm...
YOU HEARD HIM! HE SAID TAKE IT OR LEAVE IT!!!
SEE YOU NEXT YEAR, COMIC CON!

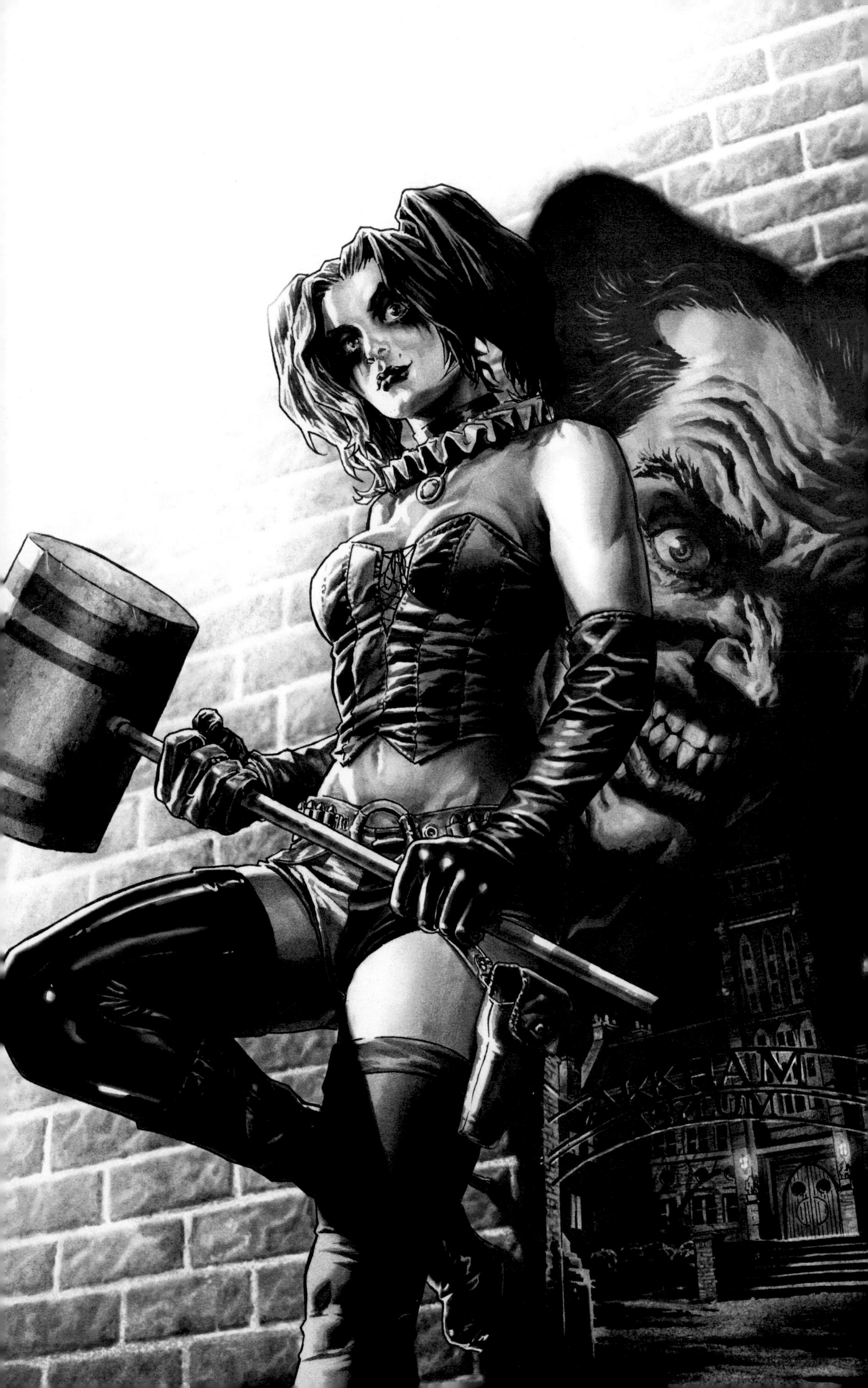

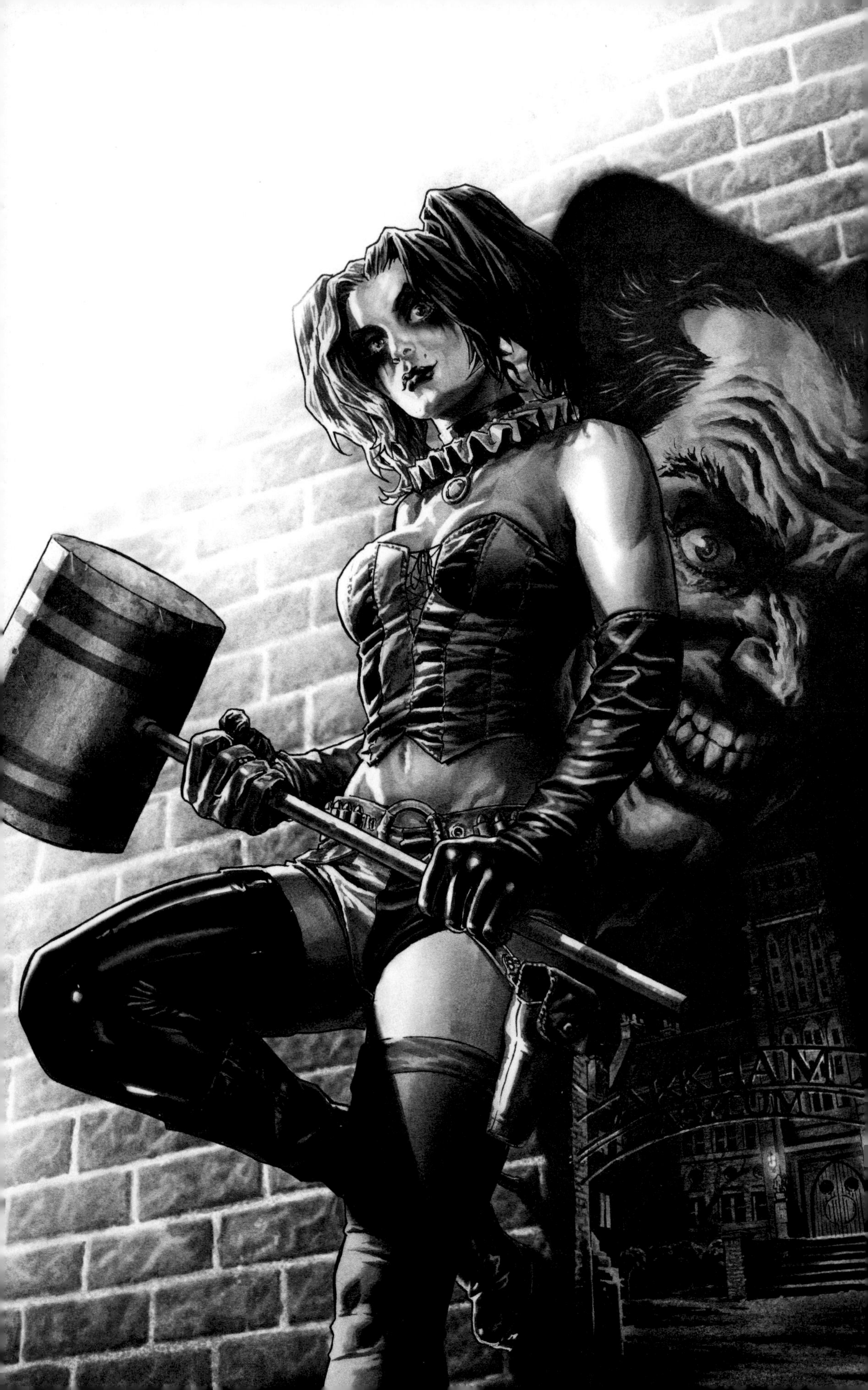

I'M *TELLIN'* YOU THIS STORY BECAUSE I KNOW I CAN TRUST YOU ALL TA *NEVER REPEAT* IT.
HOW DID I BECOME THE *WONDERFUL PERSON* YOU SEE BEFORE YOU?
A COUPL'A WAYS, ACTUALLY, BUT THE FUNNY THING IS, EACH TIME I *TELL* THIS STORY, IT'S A *BIT DIFFERENT.*
THAT HAPPENS, Y'KNOW. AS TIME GOES ON, THE DETAILS CHANGE, BUT THE PLAYERS... THE *PLAYERS* STAY THE *SAME.*
TRUST ME, THIS IS A STORY THAT WILL *BRING DOWN* THE *HOUSE!*
ORIGINS
HARLEY QUINN
Amanda Conner &
Jimmy Palmiotti writers
Stephane Roux artist
Brett Smith colors
John J. Hill letters
Lee Bermejo cover

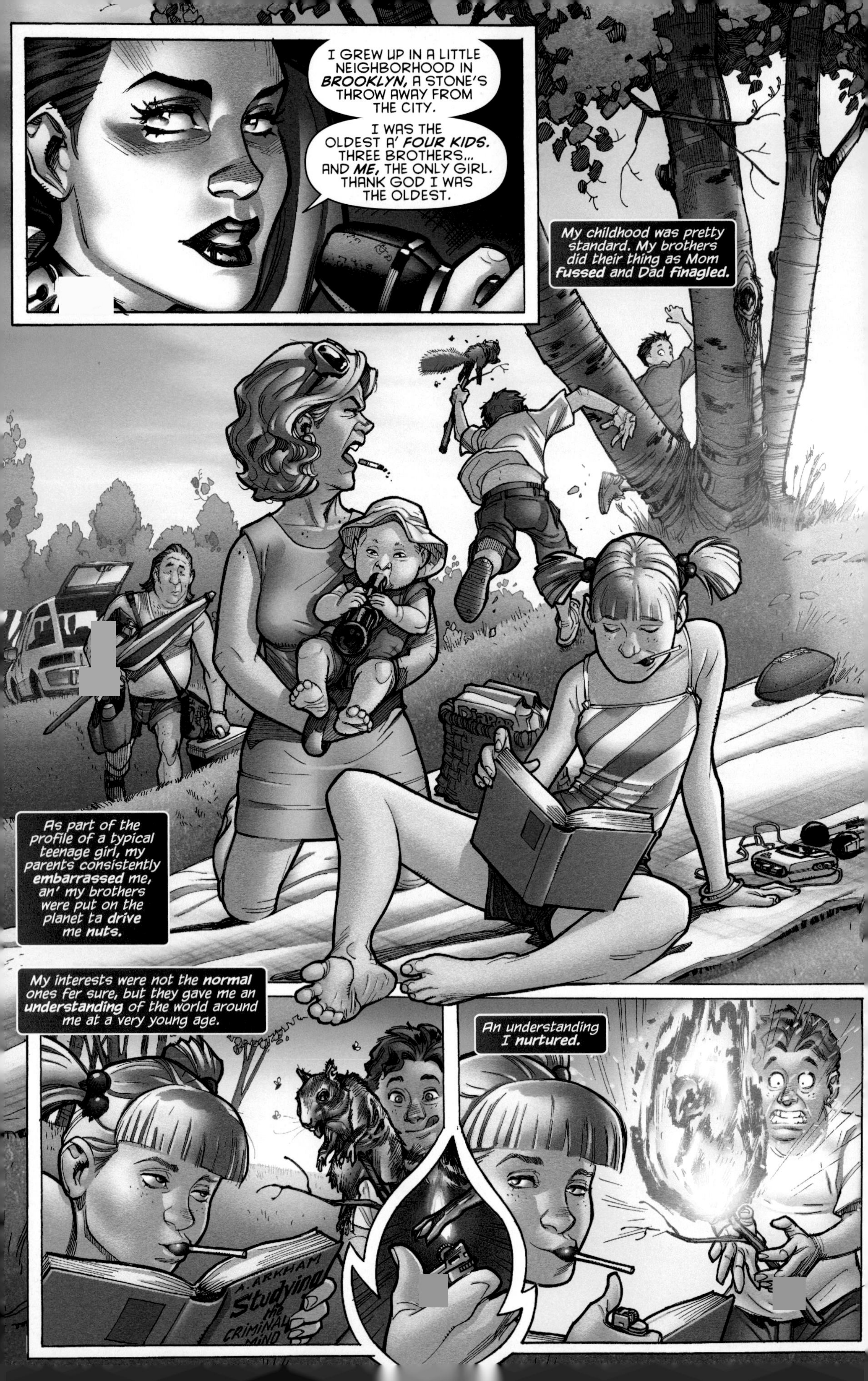
I GREW UP IN A LITTLE NEIGHBORHOOD IN BROOKLYN, A STONE'S THROW AWAY FROM THE CITY.
I WAS THE OLDEST A' FOUR KIDS. THREE BROTHERS... AND ME, THE ONLY GIRL. THANK GOD I WAS THE OLDEST.
My childhood was pretty standard. My brothers did their thing as Mom fussed and Dad finagled.
As part of the profile of a typical teenage girl, my parents consistently embarrassed me, an' my brothers were put on the planet ta drive me nuts.
My interests were not the normal ones fer sure, but they gave me an understanding of the world around me at a very young age.
A. ARKHAM
An understanding I nurtured.

Unlike my classmates, I knew early on what I wanted ta do with my life. It was a while before I met a single person that understood me.

His name was *Bernie Bash.*

Y'EVER SEE A REAL *DEAD* PERSON?

NO. *YOU?*

YES.

REALLY?

YEAH, I SAW A GUY DROWN THIS LADY AT *ROCKLAND LAKE* ONE NIGHT. I WAS IN THE BUSHES WATCHING.

DIDN'CHA TRY TA *STOP IT?* DID HE *SEE* YOU?

NAW, I WAS TOO *SCARED.* WHEN HE WAS DONE HE JUST *LEFT* HER THERE AND *WENT AWAY.*

DIDJA GO OVER TA *SEE* HER?

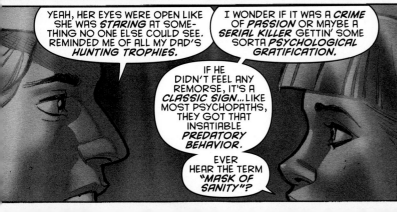

YEAH, HER EYES WERE OPEN LIKE SHE WAS *STARING* AT SOMETHING NO ONE ELSE COULD SEE. REMINDED ME OF ALL MY DAD'S *HUNTING TROPHIES.*

I WONDER IF IT WAS A *CRIME OF PASSION* OR MAYBE A *SERIAL KILLER* GETTIN' SOME SORTA *PSYCHOLOGICAL GRATIFICATION.*

IF HE DIDN'T FEEL ANY *REMORSE,* IT'S A *CLASSIC SIGN...* LIKE MOST *PSYCHOPATHS,* THEY GOT THAT INSATIABLE *PREDATORY BEHAVIOR.*

EVER HEAR THE TERM *"MASK OF SANITY"?*

NO.

HEY, IF YOU COULD KILL *ONE PERSON* IN THIS ROOM, WHO WOULD IT *BE?*

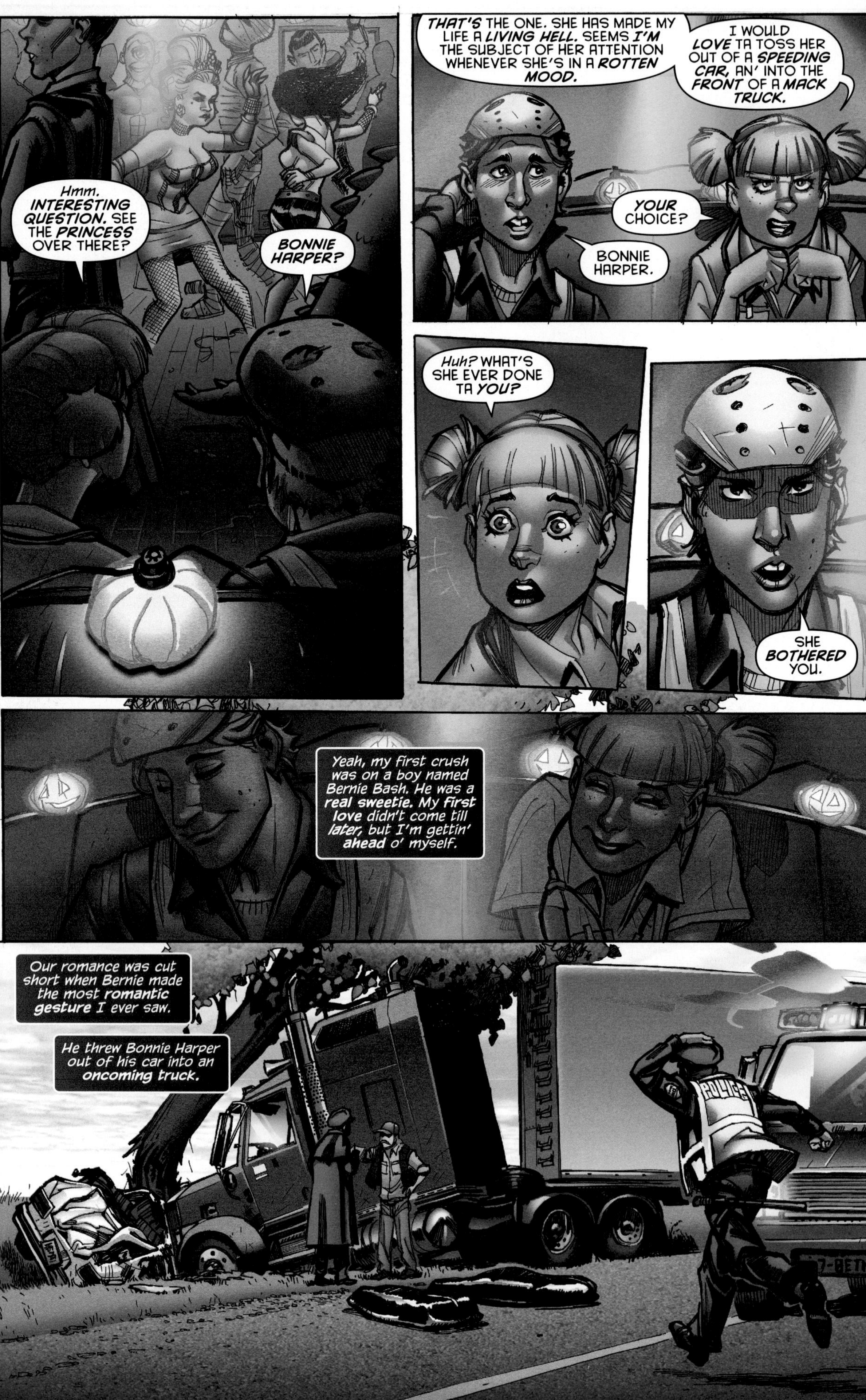
Hmm. INTERESTING QUESTION. SEE THE PRINCESS OVER THERE?
BONNIE HARPER?
THAT'S THE ONE. SHE HAS MADE MY LIFE A LIVING HELL. SEEMS I'M THE SUBJECT OF HER ATTENTION WHENEVER SHE'S IN A ROTTEN MOOD.
I WOULD LOVE TA TOSS HER OUT OF A SPEEDING CAR, AN' INTO THE FRONT OF A MACK TRUCK.
YOUR CHOICE?
BONNIE HARPER.
Huh? WHAT'S SHE EVER DONE TA YOU?
SHE BOTHERED YOU.
Yeah, my first crush was on a boy named Bernie Bash. He was a real sweetie. My first love didn't come till later, but I'm gettin' ahead o' myself.
Our romance was cut short when Bernie made the most romantic gesture I ever saw.
He threw Bonnie Harper out of his car into an oncoming truck.
POLICE

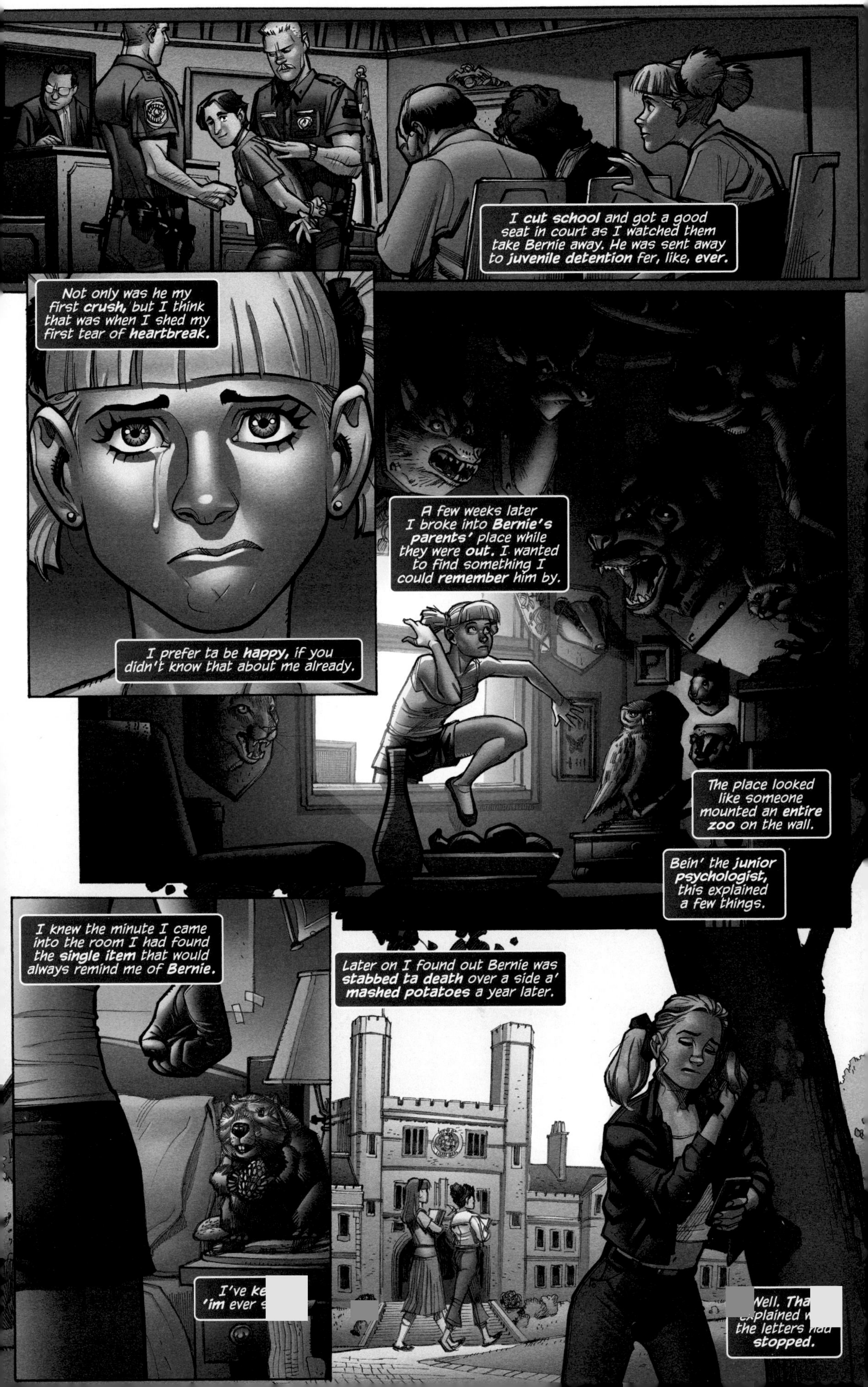
I cut school and got a good seat in court as I watched them take Bernie away. He was sent away to juvenile detention fer, like, ever.
Not only was he my first crush, but I think that was when I shed my first tear of heartbreak.
I prefer ta be happy, if you didn't know that about me already.
A few weeks later I broke into Bernie's parents' place while they were out. I wanted to find something I could remember him by.
The place looked like someone mounted an entire zoo on the wall.
Bein' the junior psychologist, this explained a few things.
I knew the minute I came into the room I had found the single item that would always remind me of Bernie.
I've ke
'im ever
Later on I found out Bernie was stabbed ta death over a side a' mashed potatoes a year later.
Well. Tha
explained
the letters had stopped.

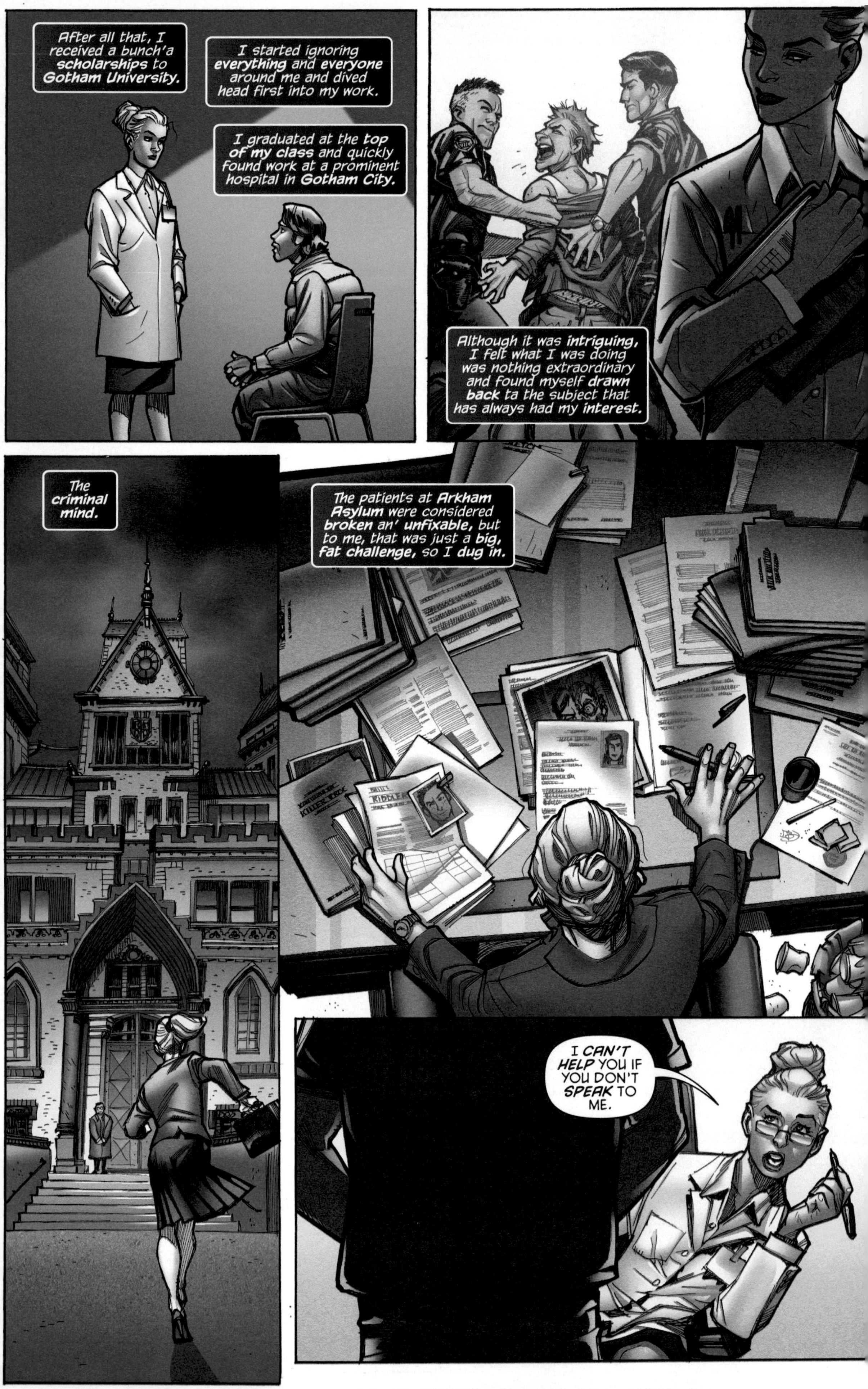
After all that, I received a bunch'a scholarships to Gotham University.
I started ignoring everything and everyone around me and dived head first into my work.
I graduated at the top of my class and quickly found work at a prominent hospital in Gotham City.
Although it was intriguing, I felt what I was doing was nothing extraordinary and found myself drawn back ta the subject that has always had my interest.
The criminal mind.
The patients at Arkham Asylum were considered broken an' unfixable, but to me, that was just a big, fat challenge, so I dug in.
I CAN'T HELP YOU IF YOU DON'T SPEAK TO ME.

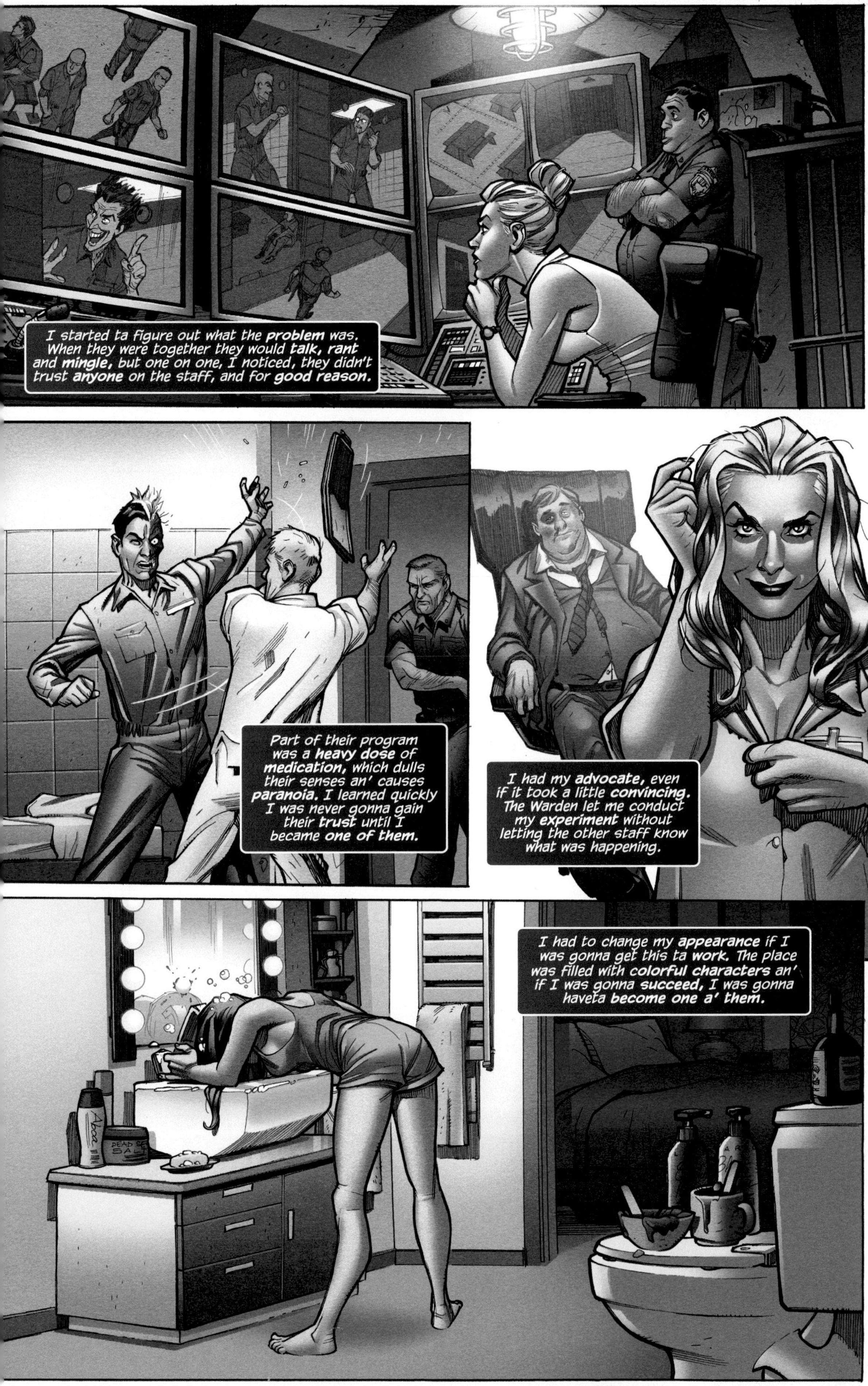
I started ta figure out what the problem was. When they were together they would talk, rant and mingle, but one on one, I noticed, they didn't trust anyone on the staff, and for good reason.
Part of their program was a heavy dose of medication, which dulls their senses an' causes paranoia. I learned quickly I was never gonna gain their trust until I became one of them.
I had my advocate, even if it took a little convincing. The Warden let me conduct my experiment without letting the other staff know what was happening.
I had to change my appearance if I was gonna get this ta work. The place was filled with colorful characters an' if I was gonna succeed, I was gonna haveta become one a' them.

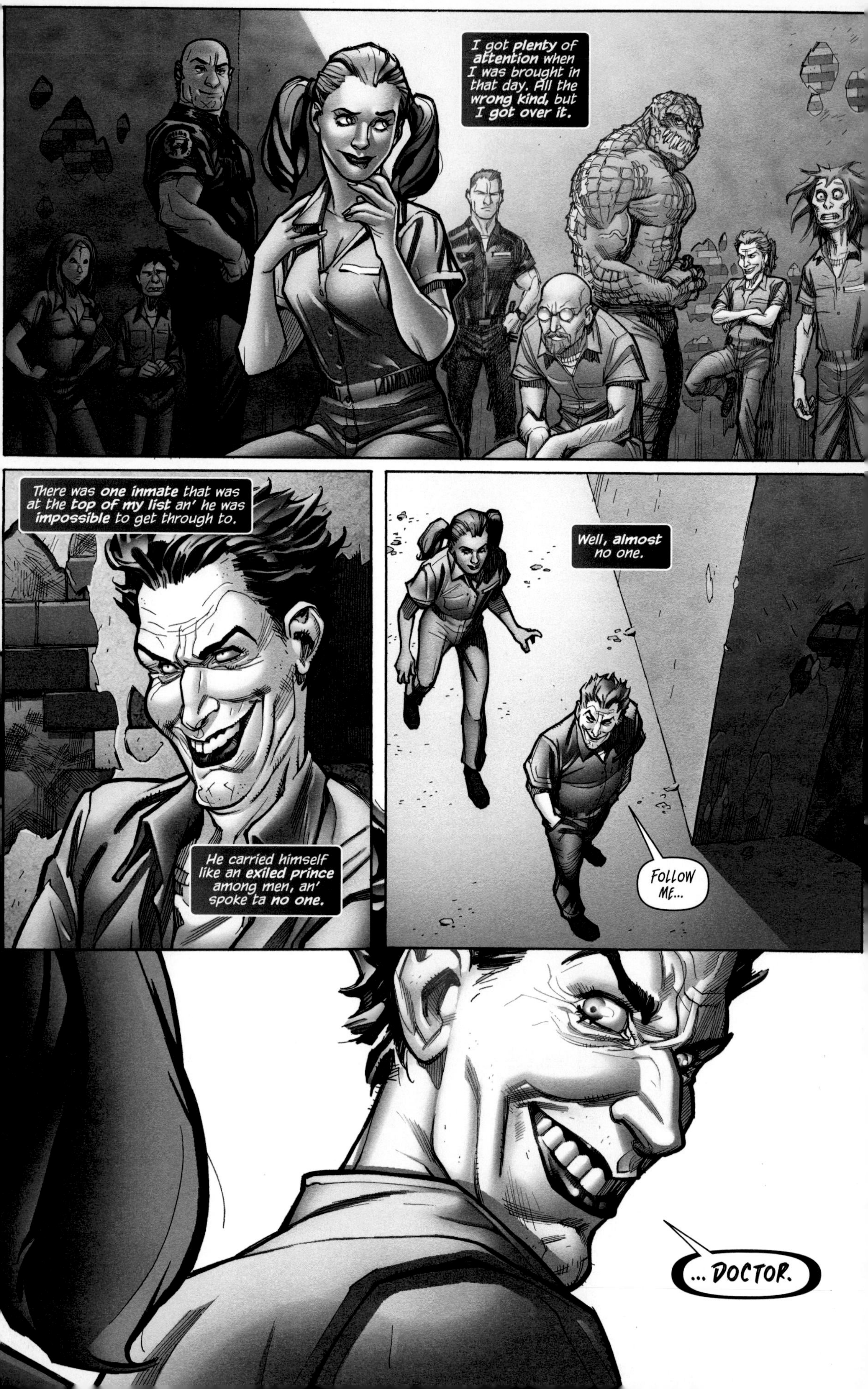
I got plenty of attention when I was brought in that day. All the wrong kind, but I got over it.
There was one inmate that was at the top of my list an' he was impossible to get through to.
He carried himself like an exiled prince among men, an' spoke ta no one.
Well, almost no one.
FOLLOW ME...
...DOCTOR.

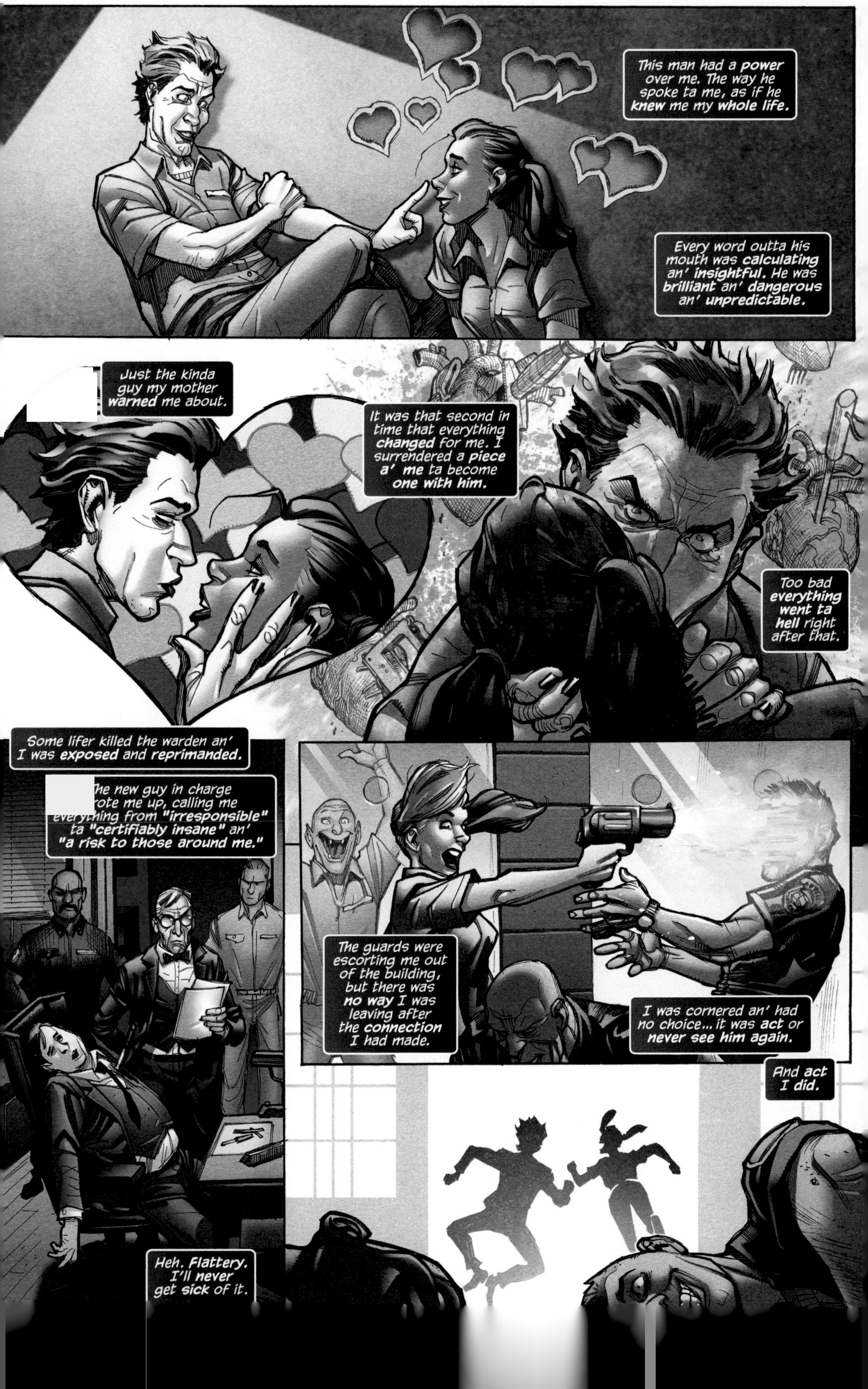
This man had a power over me. The way he spoke ta me, as if he knew me my whole life.
Every word outta his mouth was calculating an' insightful. He was brilliant an' dangerous an' unpredictable.
Just the kinda guy my mother warned me about.
It was that second in time that everything changed for me. I surrendered a piece a' me ta become one with him.
Too bad everything went ta hell right after that.
Some lifer killed the warden an' I was exposed and reprimanded.
he new guy in charge rote me up, calling me everything from "irresponsible" ta "certifiably insane" an' "a risk to those around me."
Heh. Flattery. I'll never get sick of it.
The guards were escorting me out of the building, but there was no way I was leaving after the connection I had made.
I was cornered an' had no choice... it was act or never see him again.
And act I did.

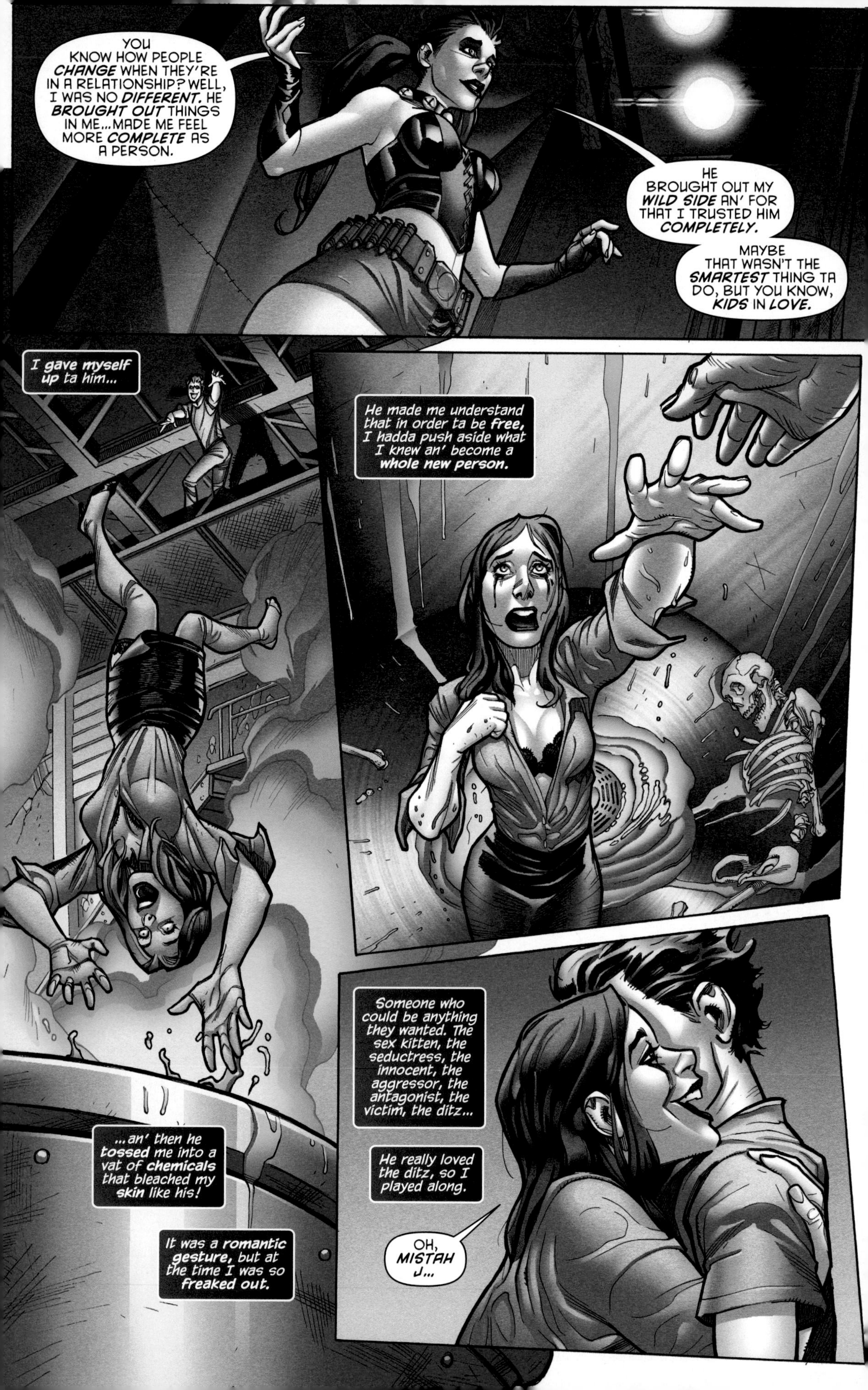

YOU KNOW HOW PEOPLE CHANGE WHEN THEY'RE IN A RELATIONSHIP? WELL, I WAS NO DIFFERENT. HE BROUGHT OUT THINGS IN ME...MADE ME FEEL MORE COMPLETE AS A PERSON.
HE BROUGHT OUT MY WILD SIDE AN' FOR THAT I TRUSTED HIM COMPLETELY.
MAYBE THAT WASN'T THE SMARTEST THING TA DO, BUT YOU KNOW, KIDS IN LOVE.
I gave myself up ta him...
He made me understand that in order ta be free, I hadda push aside what I knew an' become a whole new person.
...an' then he tossed me into a vat of chemicals that bleached my skin like his!
It was a romantic gesture, but at the time I was so freaked out.
Someone who could be anything they wanted. The sex kitten, the seductress, the innocent, the aggressor, the antagonist, the victim, the ditz...
He really loved the ditz, so I played along.
OH, MISTAH J...

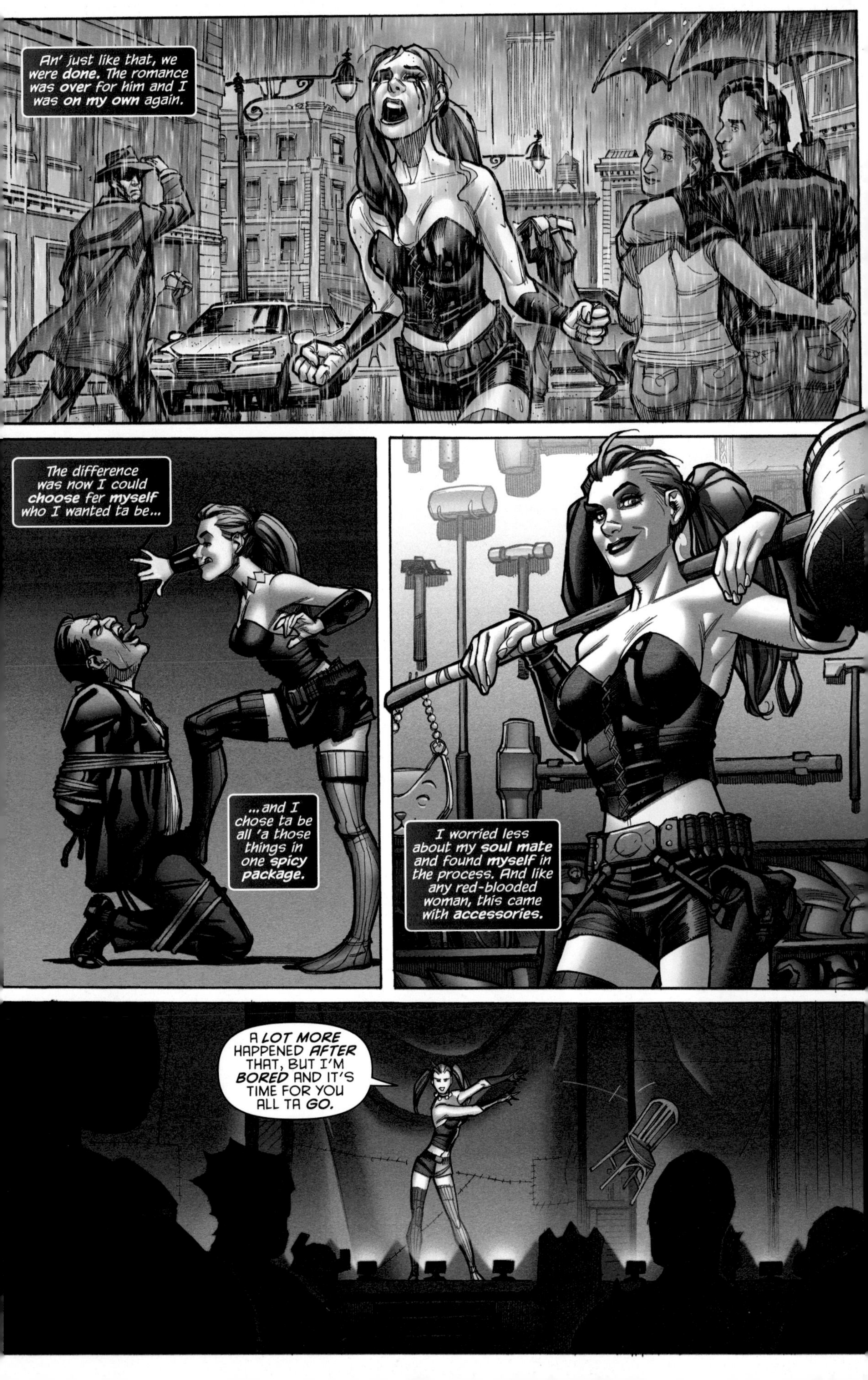
An' just like that, we were done. The romance was over for him and I was on my own again.
The difference was now I could choose fer myself who I wanted ta be...
...and I chose ta be all 'a those things in one spicy package.
I worried less about my soul mate and found myself in the process. And like any red-blooded woman, this came with accessories.
A LOT MORE HAPPENED AFTER THAT, BUT I'M BORED AND IT'S TIME FOR YOU ALL TA GO.

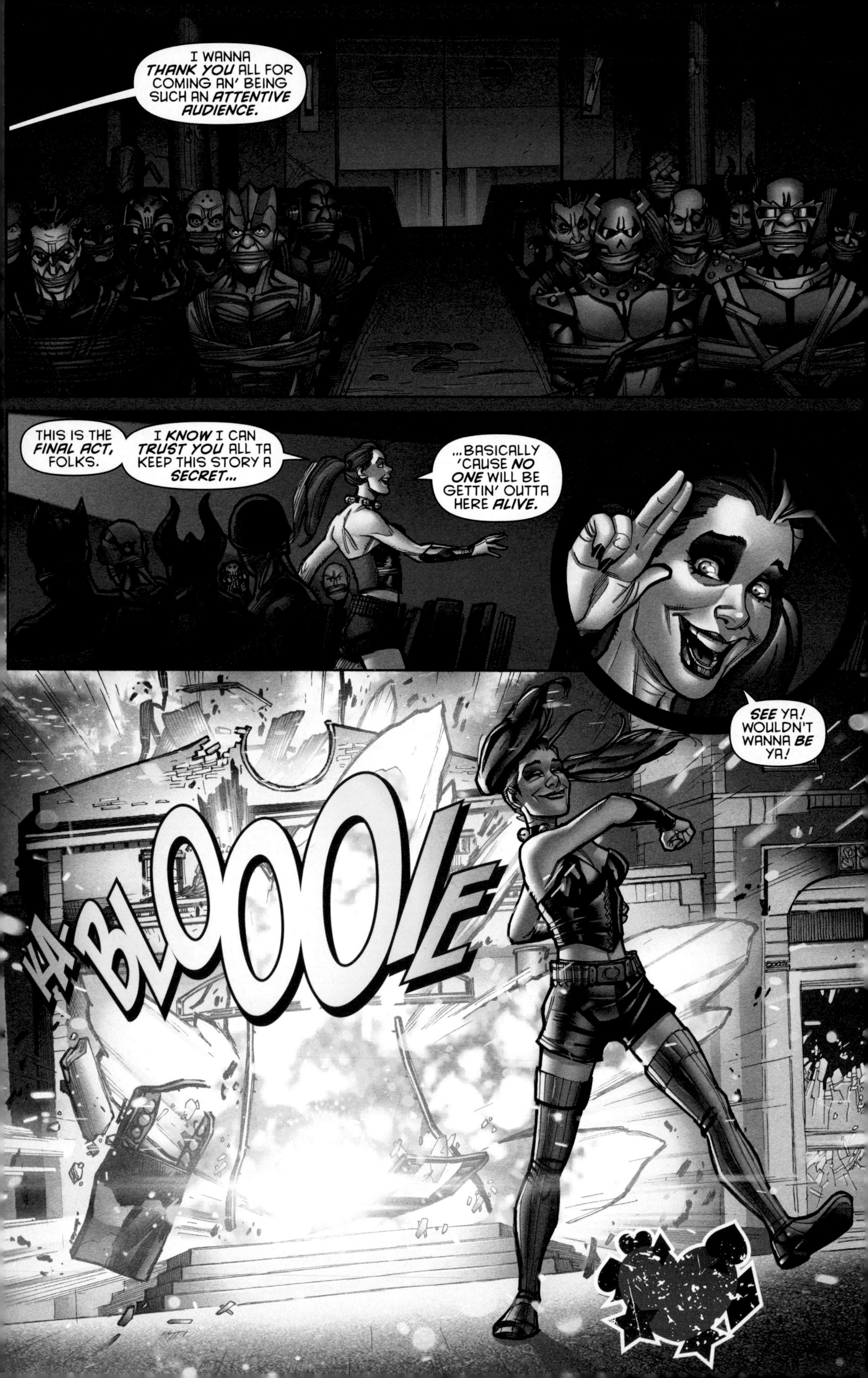

I WANNA THANK YOU ALL FOR COMING AN' BEING SUCH AN ATTENTIVE AUDIENCE.
THIS IS THE FINAL ACT, FOLKS.
I KNOW I CAN TRUST YOU ALL TA KEEP THIS STORY A SECRET...
...BASICALLY 'CAUSE NO ONE WILL BE GETTIN' OUTTA HERE ALIVE.
SEE YA! WOULDN'T WANNA BE YA!
KA-BLOOOIE

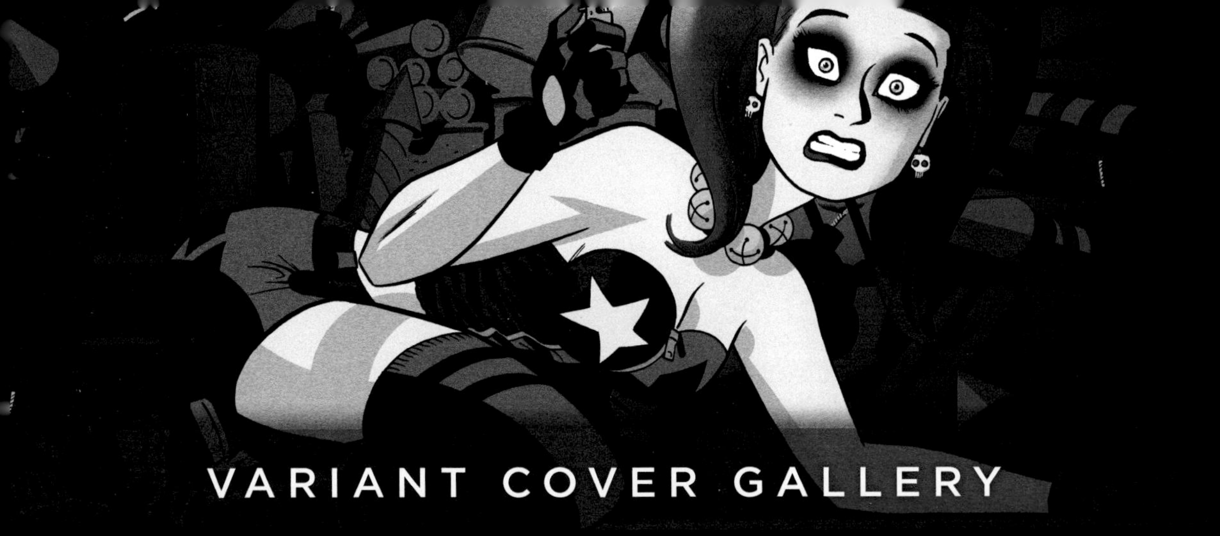

VARIANT COVER GALLERY

HARLEY QUINN #9
Selfie variant cover by Amanda Conner and Paul Mounts

HARLEY QUINN #10
Variant cover by Amanda Conner and Paul Mounts

HARLEY QUINN #11
Variant cover by Amanda Conner and Paul Mounts

HARLEY QUINN #11
Monster variant cover by Yanick Paquette and Nathan Fairbairn

HARLEY QUINN #12
Variant cover by Amanda Conner and Paul Mounts

HARLEY QUINN #12
LEGO variant cover

HARLEY QUINN #13
Variant cover by Amanda Conner and Alex Sinclair

HARLEY QUINN #13
Variant cover by Darwyn Cooke

HARLEY QUINN INVADES COMIC-CON INTERNATIONAL SAN DIEGO #1
Full wraparound cover by Amanda Conner and Paul Mounts

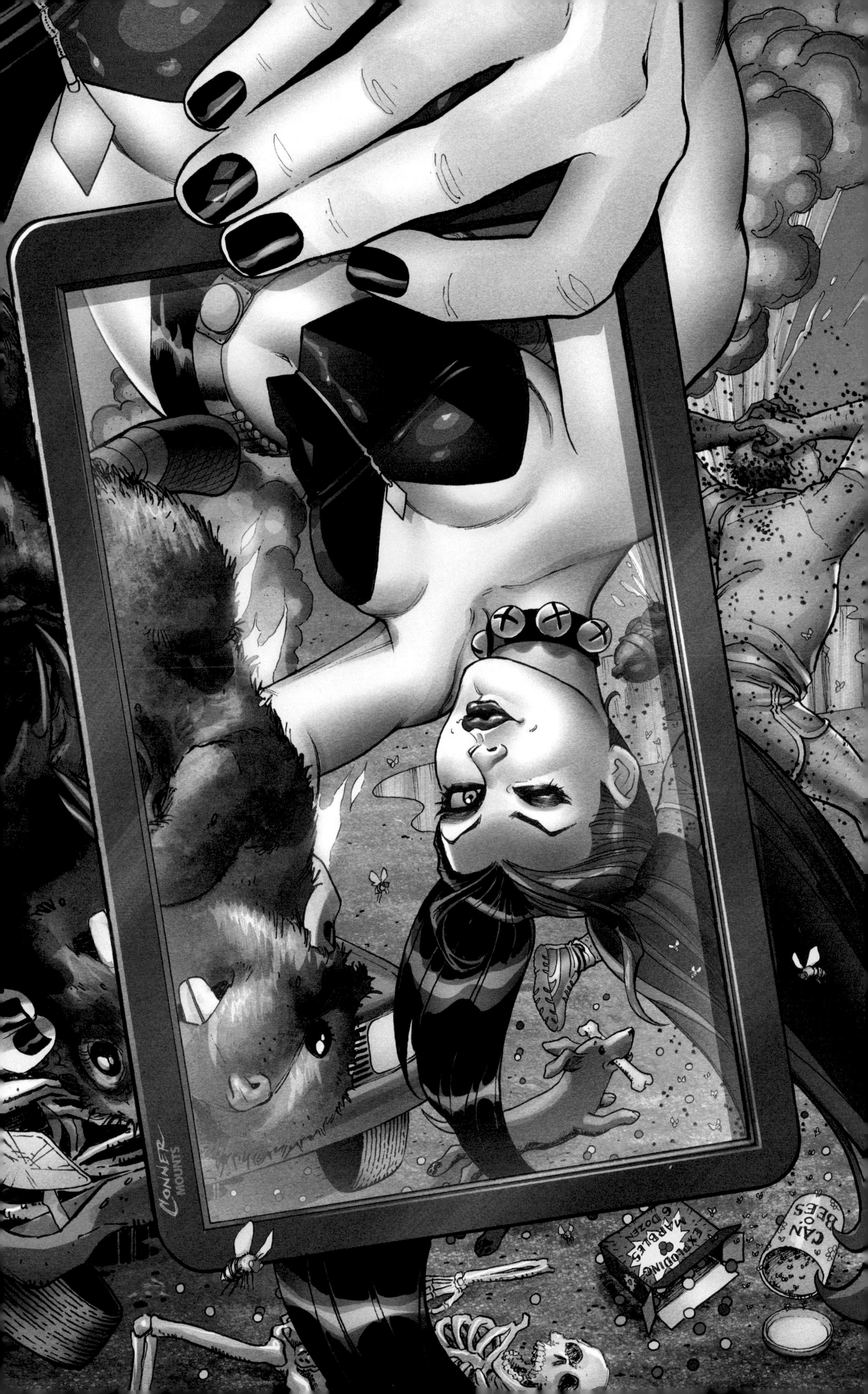
CONNER
MOUNTS
EXPLODING MARBLES
6 DOZEN
CAN O BEES

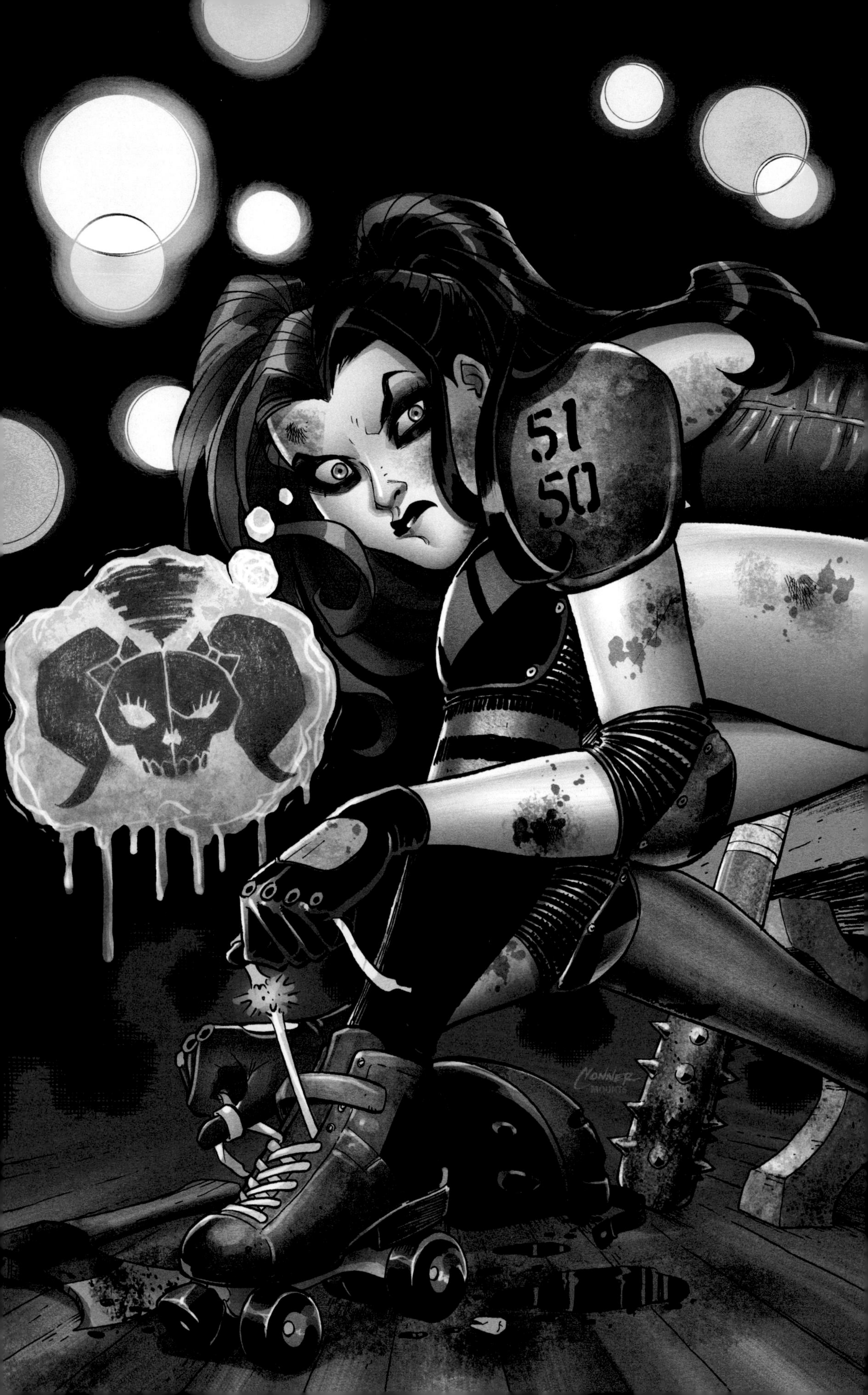
51
50

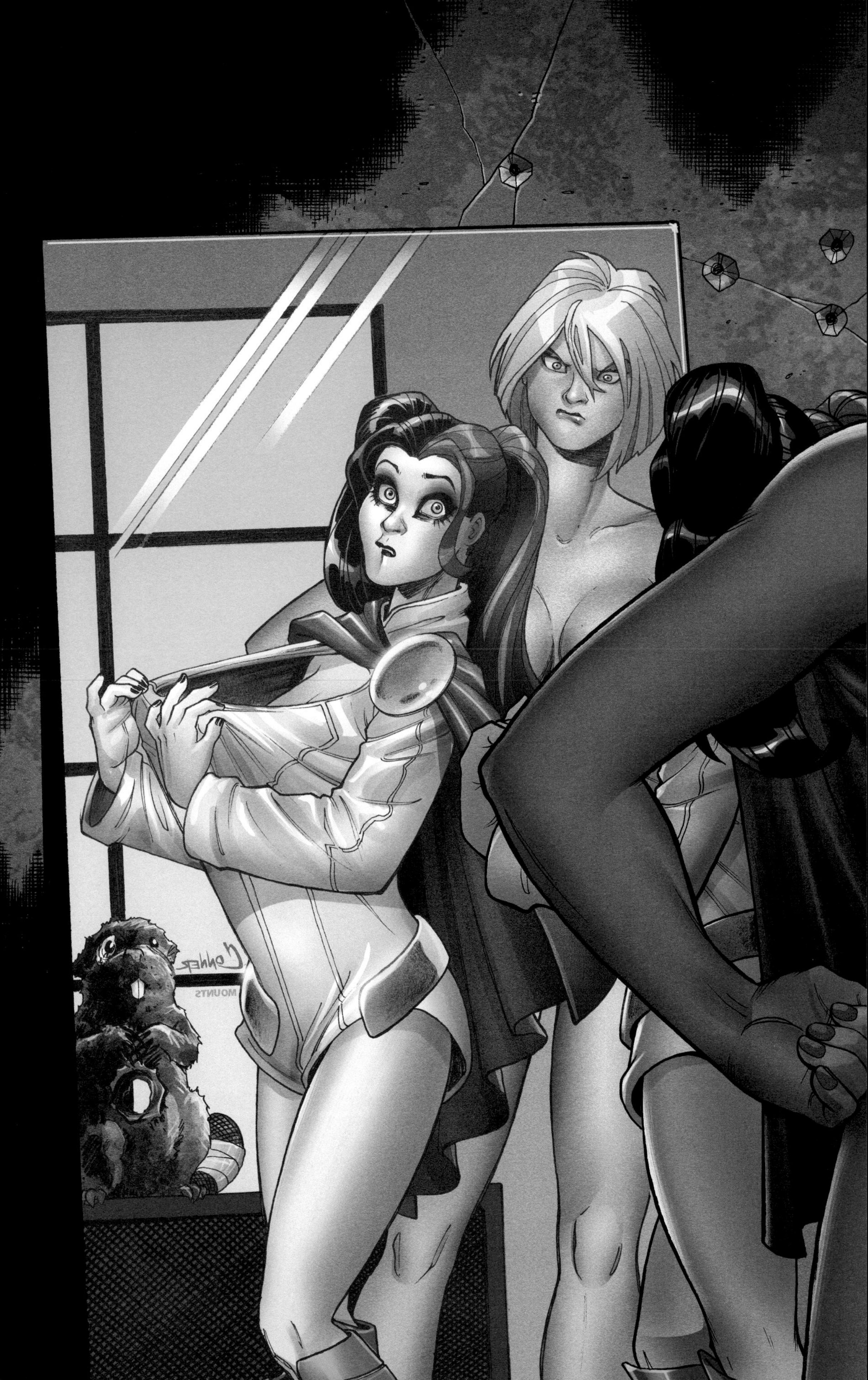

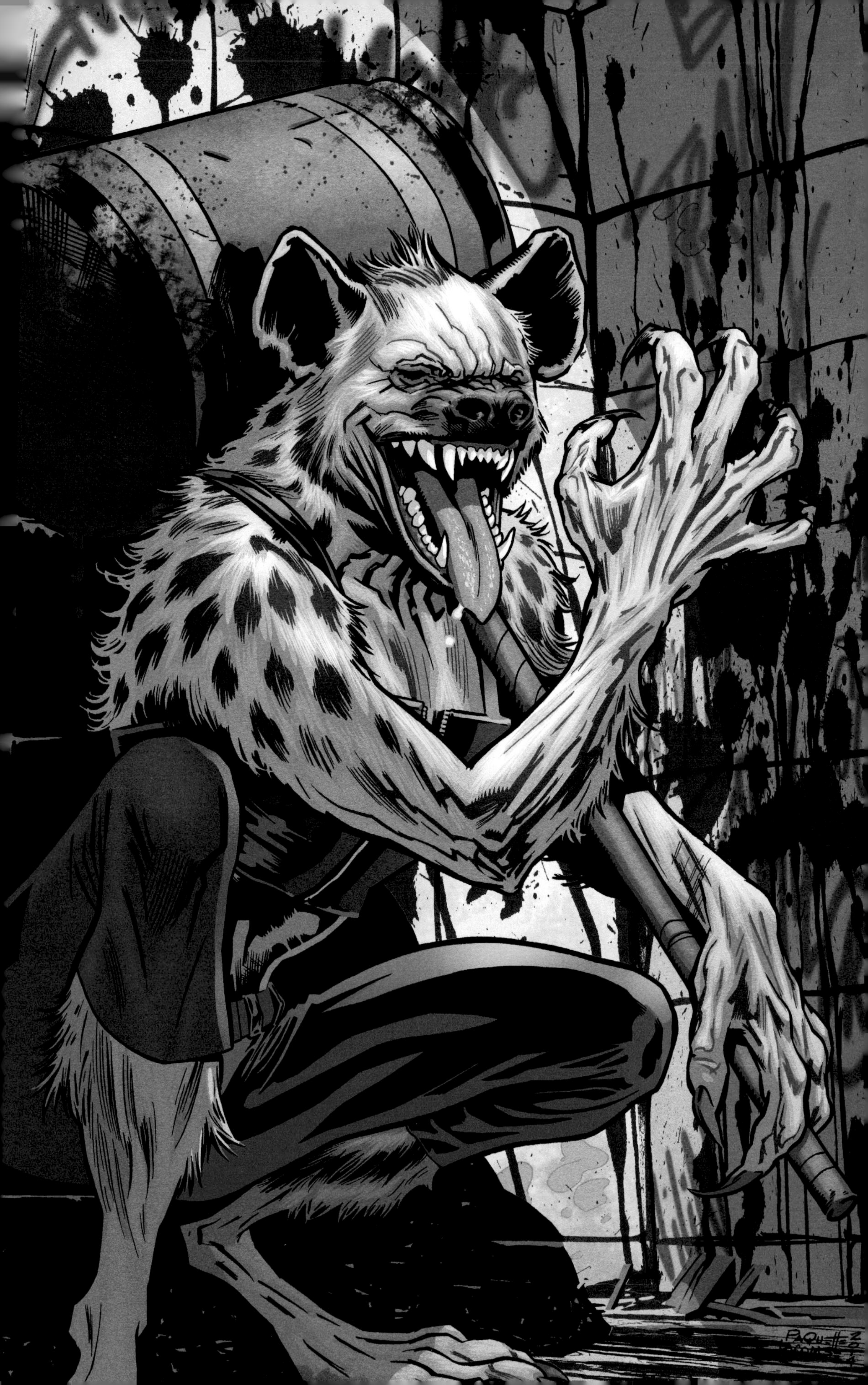

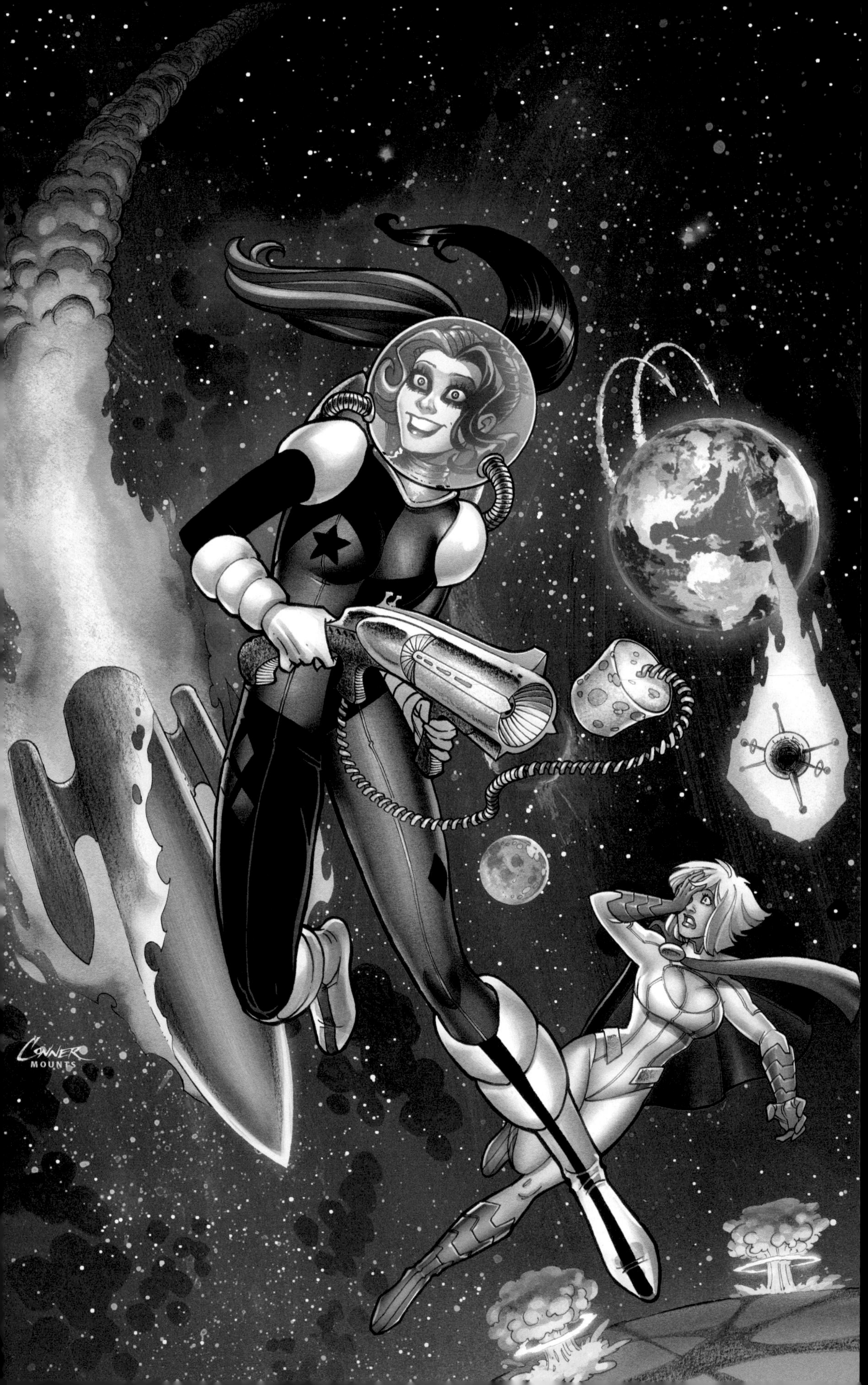
CONNER
MOUNTS

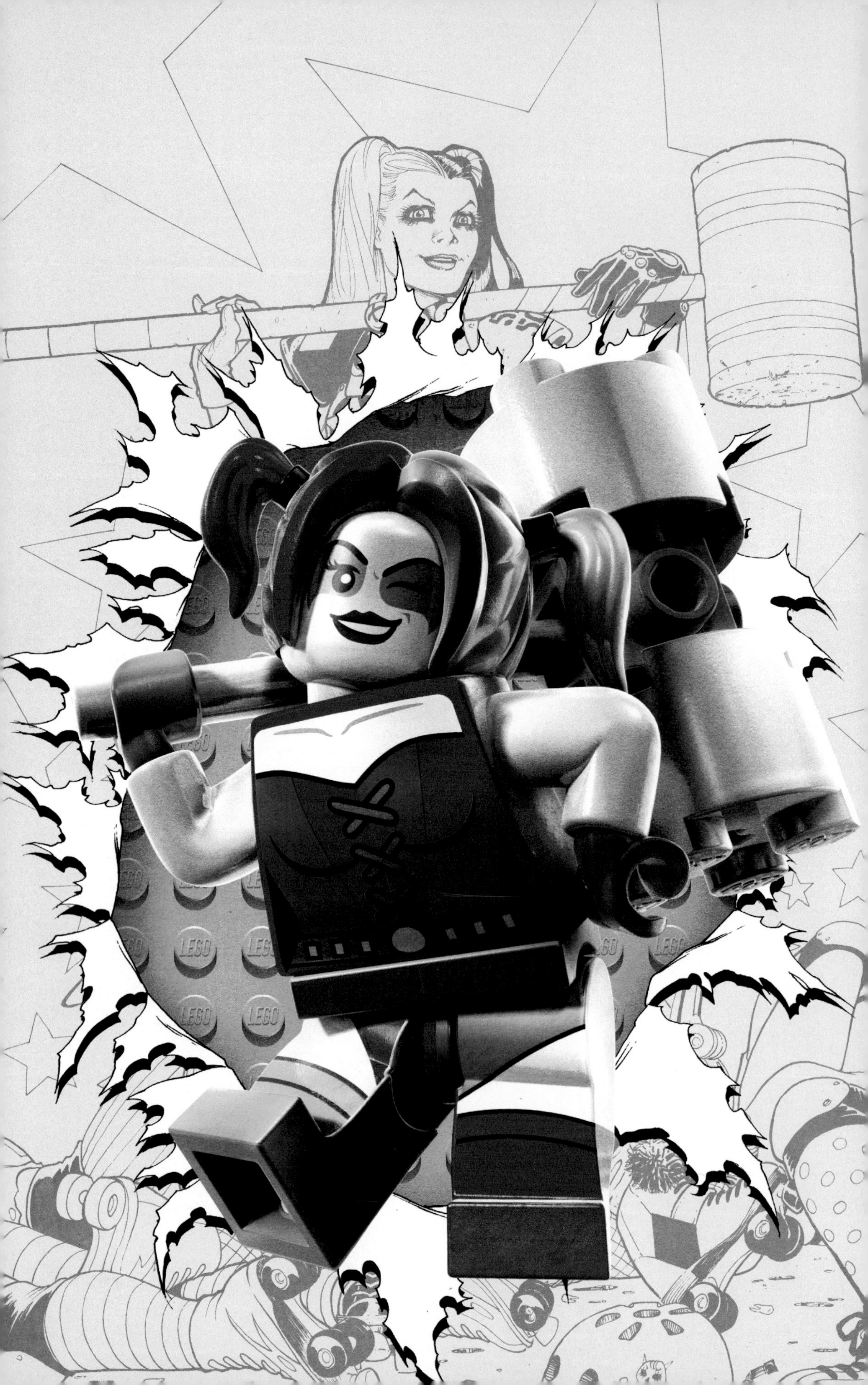

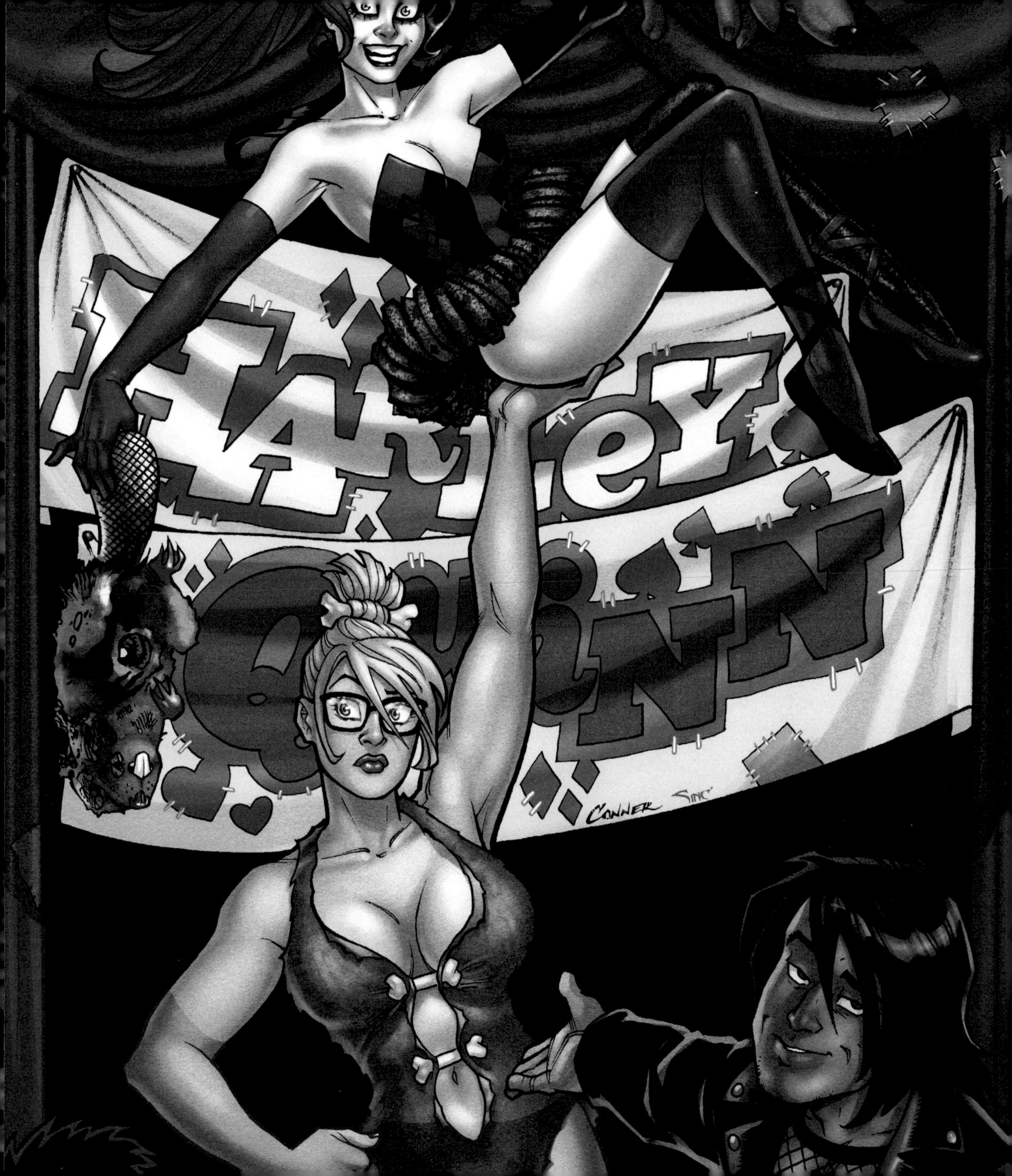
CONNER SINC'

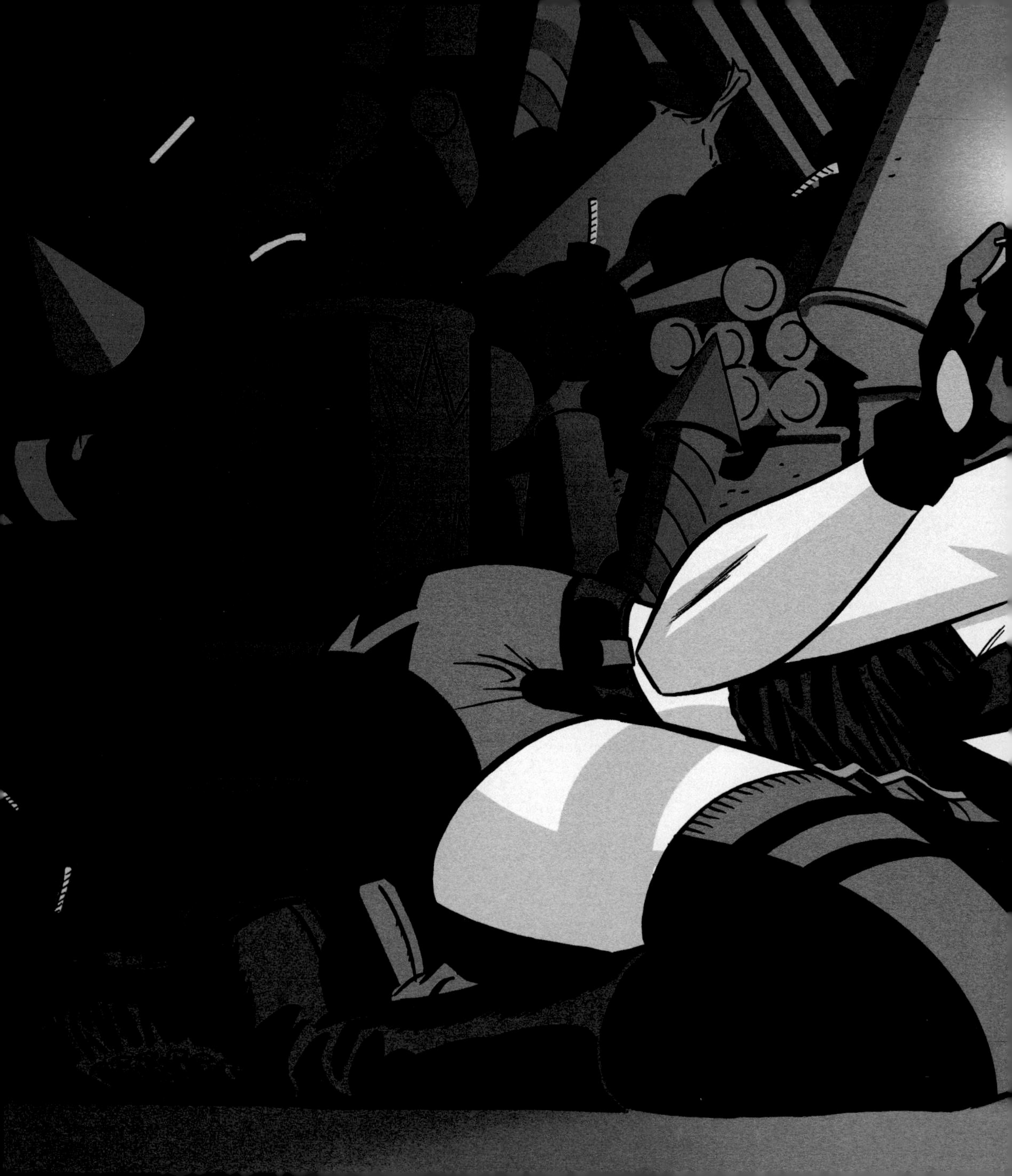

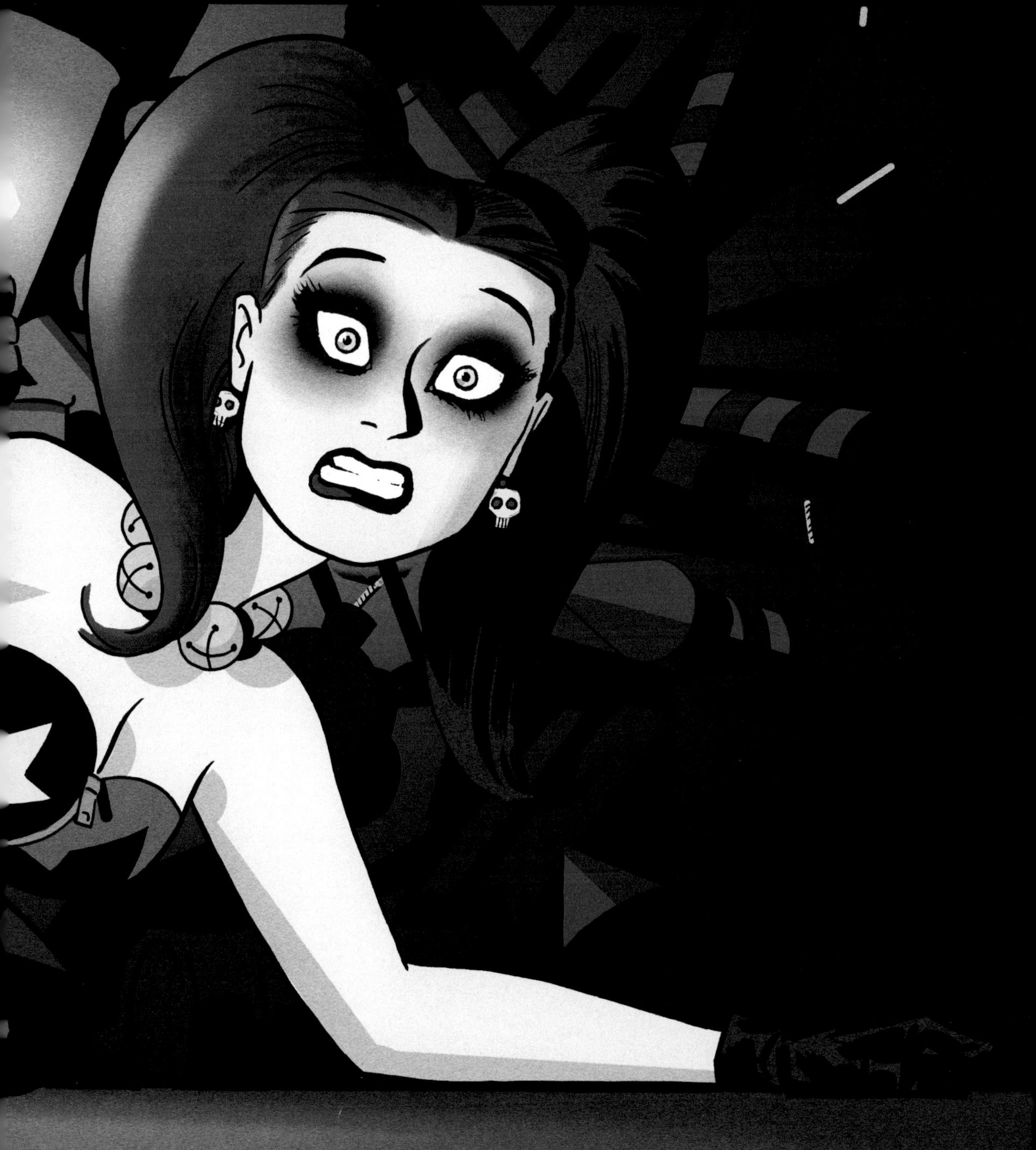

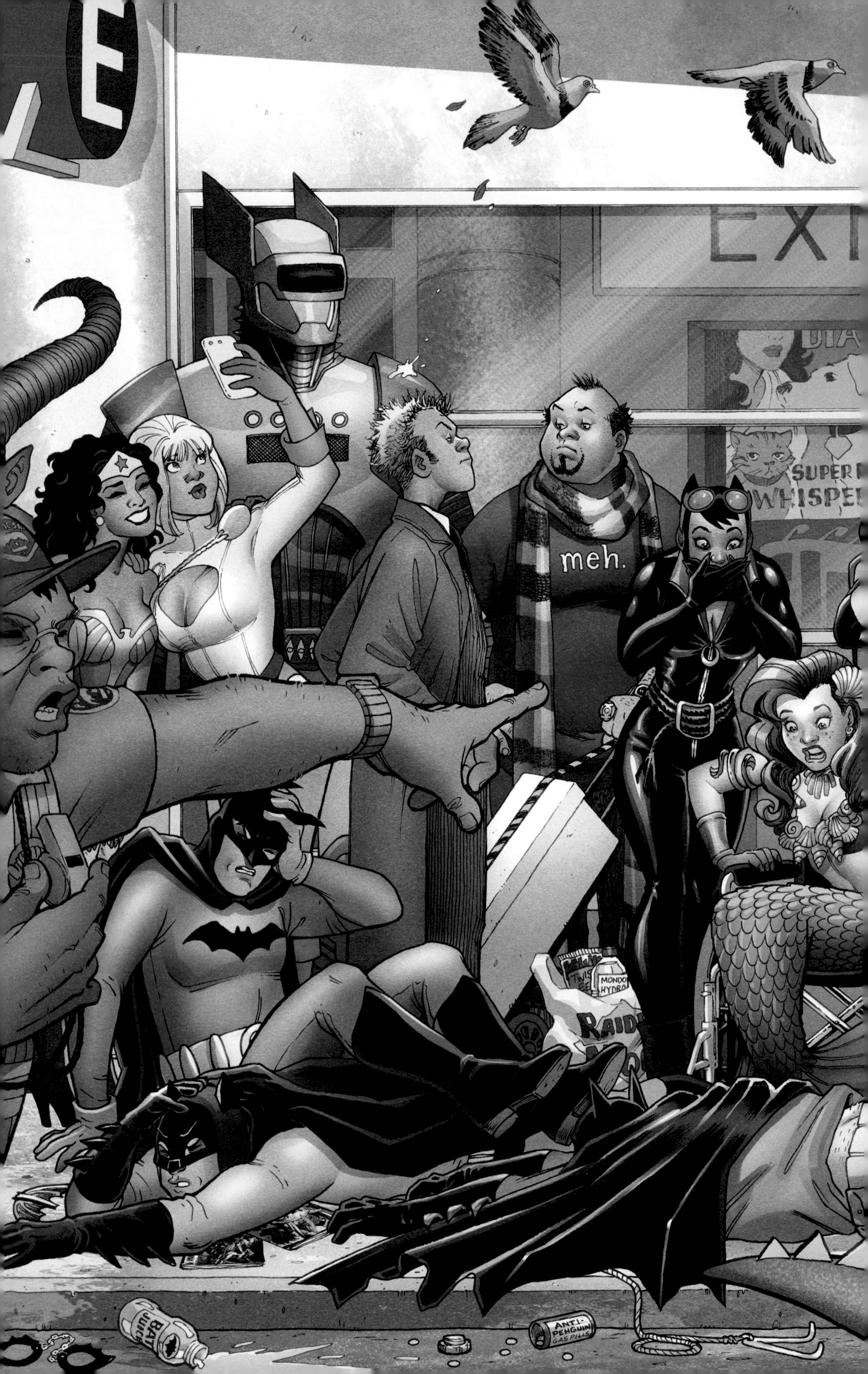
meh.
ANTI-PENGUIN
GAS PILLS

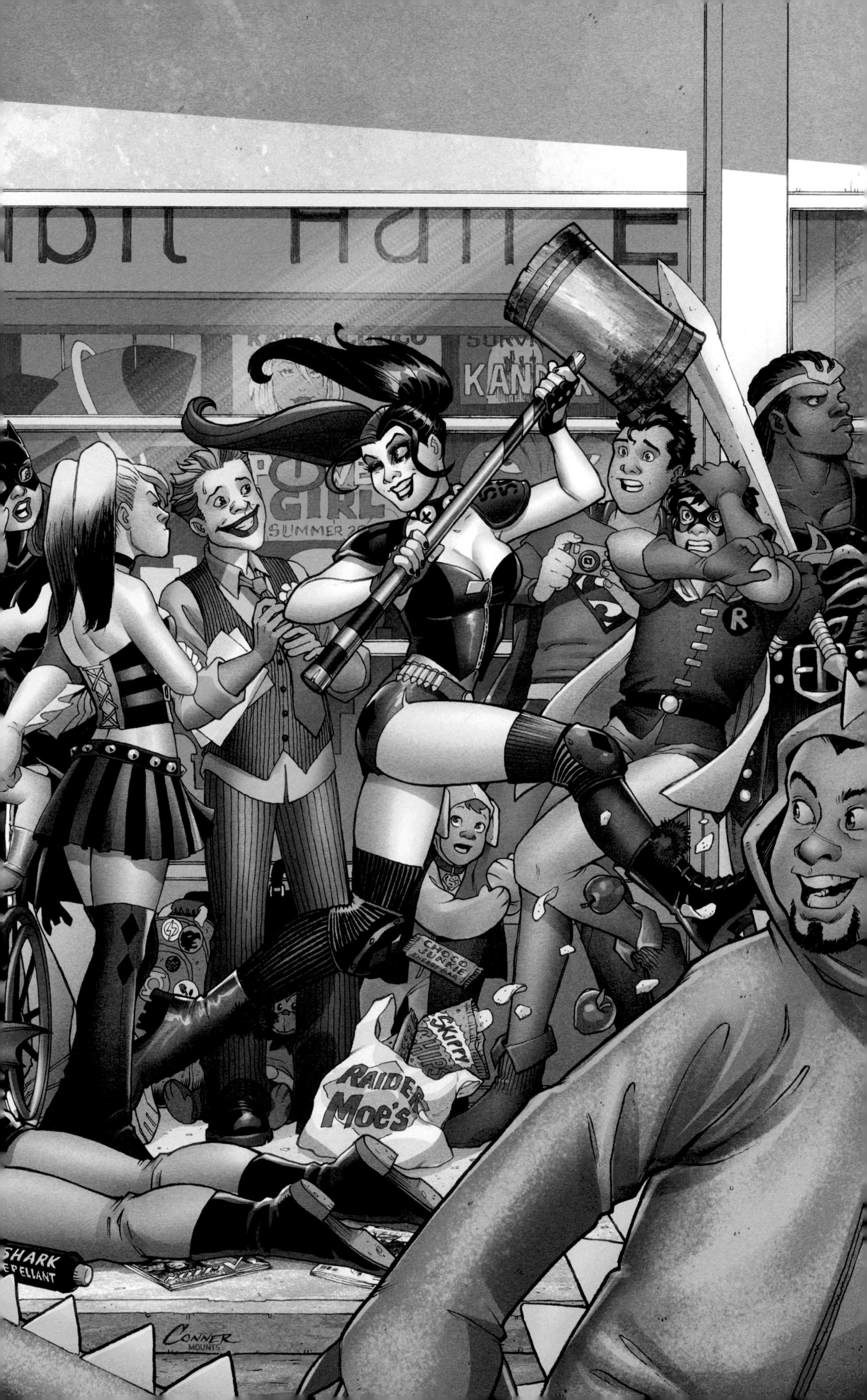
GIRL
SUMMER 20
CHOCO JUNKIE
SKIPPY CHIPS
RAIDER Moe's
SHARK
EPELLANT
CONNER
MOUNTS

Cover sketches by Amanda Conner

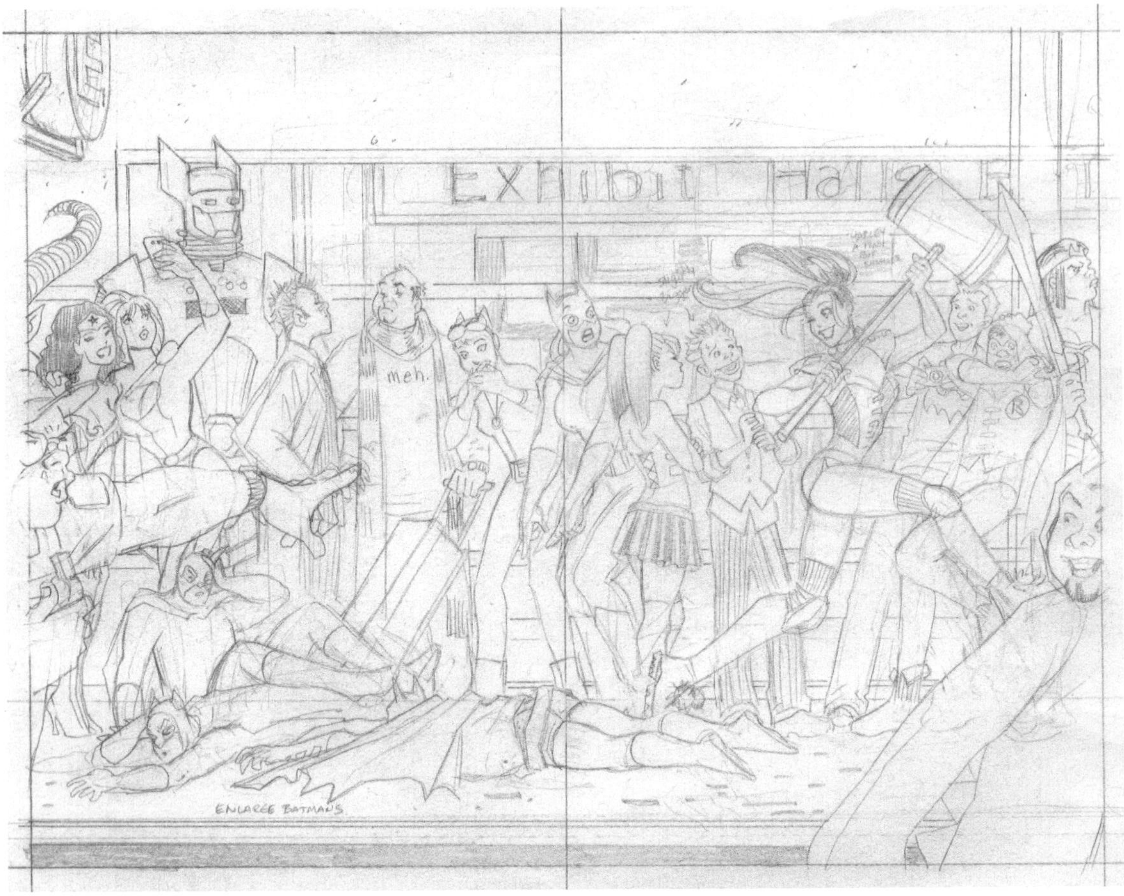
Exhibit Hall
meh.
ENLARGE BATMANS

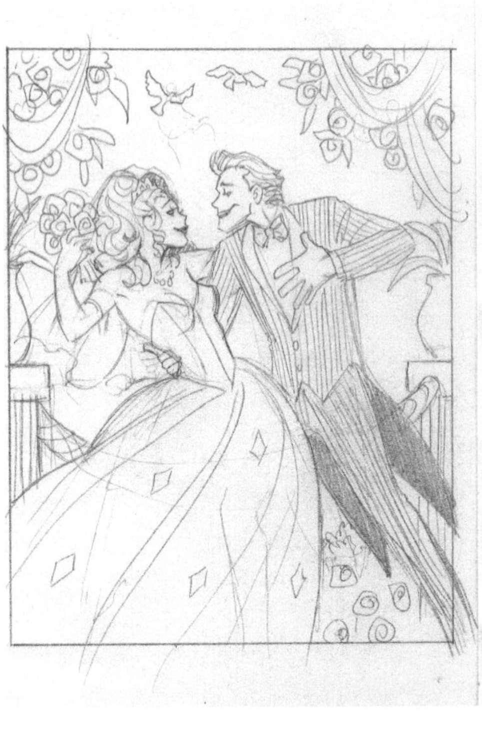

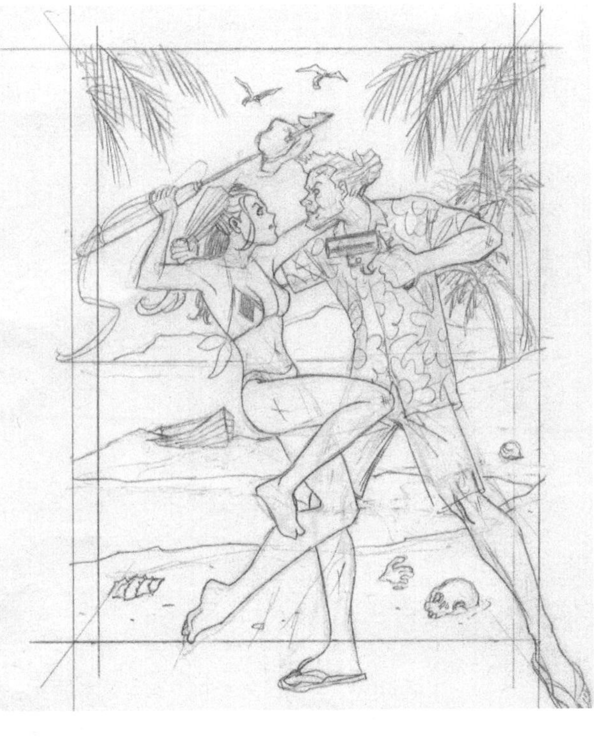

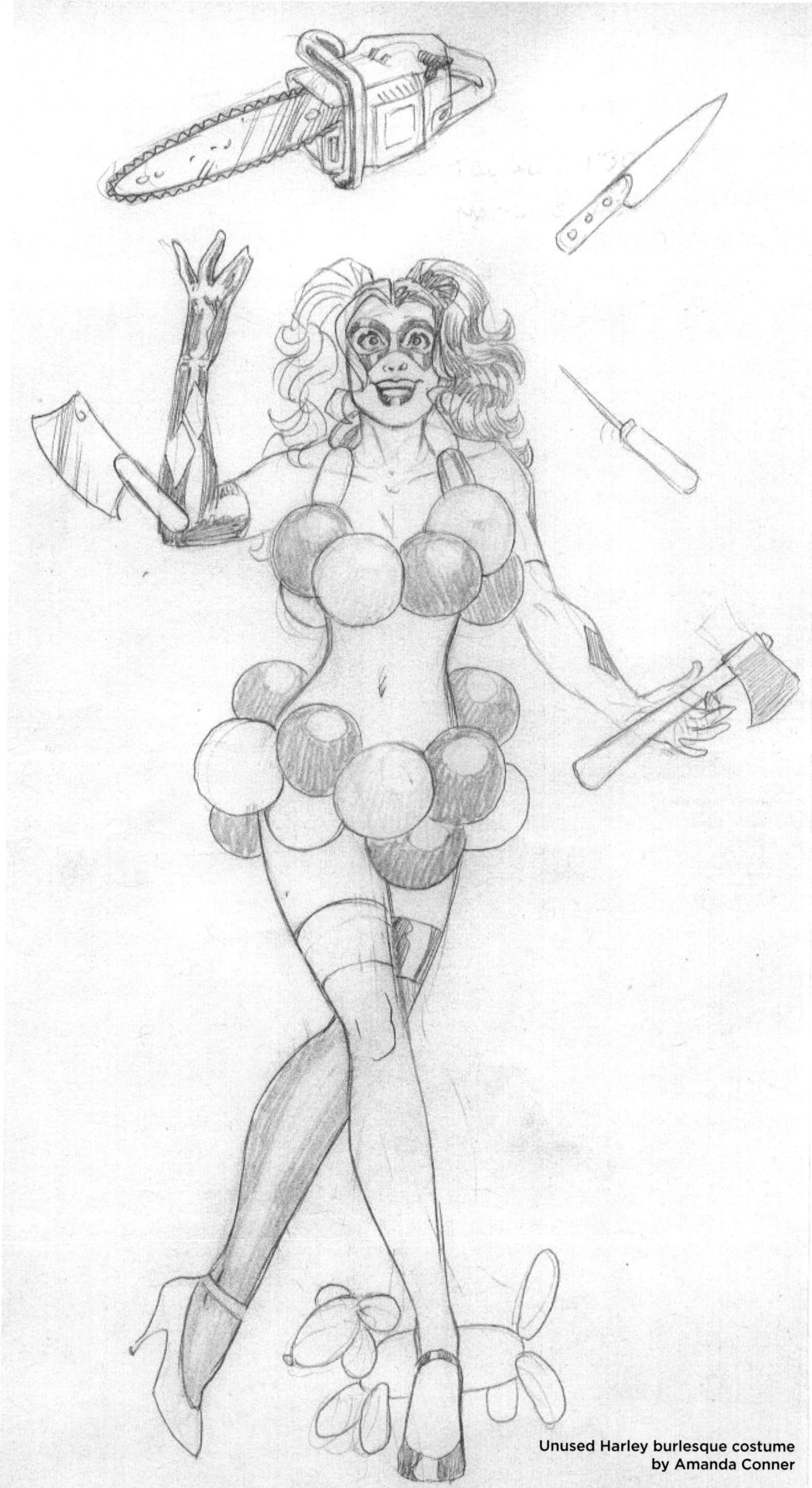

Unused Harley burlesque costume
by Amanda Conner

"Chaotic and unabashedly fun."—IGN

"I'm enjoying HARLEY QUINN a great deal;
it's silly, it's funny, it's irreverent."
—COMIC BOOK RESOURCES

HARLEY QUINN
VOLUME 1: HOT IN THE CITY

**SUICIDE SQUAD VOL. 1:
KICKED IN THE TEETH**

with ADAM GLASS and
FEDERICO DALLOCCHIO

**HARLEY QUINN:
PRELUDES AND
KNOCK-KNOCK JOKES**

with KARL KESEL and
TERRY DODSON

**BATMAN: MAD LOVE
AND OTHER STORIES**

with PAUL DINI
and BRUCE TIMM

AMANDA **CONNER** JIMMY **PALMIOTTI** CHAD **HARDIN**
STEPHANE **ROUX** ALEX **SINCLAIR** PAUL **MOUNTS**